Taking the Gospel to the Japanese,
1901 to 2001

Studies in Latter-day Saint History

An imprint of BYU Studies and the
Joseph Fielding Smith Institute for Latter-day Saint History

Brigham Young University
Provo, Utah
United States of America

Taking the Gospel to the Japanese, 1901 to 2001

Edited by
Reid L. Neilson and Van C. Gessel

Brigham Young University Press
Provo, Utah

This volume is part of the Joseph Fielding Smith Institute and BYU Studies series
Studies in Latter-day Saint History

Also included in this series:

Nearly Everything Imaginable: The Everyday Life of Utah's Mormon Pioneers

Voyages of Faith: Exploration in Mormon Pacific History

Trail Furnace: Southern Utah's Iron Mission

Mormon Missionaries Enter Eastern Europe

Walking in the Sand: A History of The Church of Jesus Christ of Latter-day Saints in Ghana

© 2006 Brigham Young University. All rights reserved.

Cover and jacket design by Kimberly Chen Pace; Japanese calligraphy by Michio Zushi

Opinions expressed in this publication are the opinions of the authors and their views should not necessarily be attributed to The Church of Jesus Christ of Latter-day Saints, Brigham Young University, BYU Studies, or the Joseph Fielding Smith Institute for Latter-day Saint History.

No part of this book may be reprinted or reproduced or utilized in any form or by any electronic, digital, mechanical or other means, now known or hereafter invented, including photocopying and recording or in an information storage or retrieval system, without permission in writing from the publisher. To contact BYU Studies, write to 403 CB, Brigham Young University, PO Box 24098, Provo, Utah 84602, or visit http://byustudies.byu.edu.

Library of Congress Cataloging-in-Publication Data

Taking the gospel to the Japanese, 1901–2001 / edited by Reid L. Neilson and Van C. Gessel.
    p. cm. — (Studies in Latter-day Saint history)
Includes bibliographical references and index.
ISBN 0-8425-2595-5 (pbk. : alk. paper)
    1. Church of Jesus Christ of Latter-day Saints—Missions—Japan—History—20th century. 2. Japan—Church history—20th century. I. Neilson, Reid Larkin. II. Gessel, Van C. III. Title. IV. Series.

BX8617.J3T35 2005
266'.9352—dc22

2005023722

Printed in the United States of America
10 9 8 7 6 5 4 3 2 1

Contents

Preface   ix

Acknowledgments   xvii

Prologue

1 Historical and Cultural Challenges to Successful Missionary Work in Japan   1
   R. Lanier Britsch

Setting the Stage for the Church in Japan

2 The Japan Mission: First Efforts   31
   Reid L. Neilson

3 The Iwakura Mission and Its Stay in Salt Lake City   57
   Wendy Butler

4 Tomizo and Tokujiro: The First Japanese Mormons   83
   Shinji Takagi

5 Translator or Translated? The Portrayal of The Church of Jesus Christ of Latter-day Saints in Print in Meiji Japan   127
   Sarah Cox Smith

The First Japan Mission

  6 Strangers in a Strange Land:
Heber J. Grant and the Opening of the Japan Mission   147
Ronald W. Walker

  7 Mormons in the Press:
Reactions to the 1901 Opening of the Japan Mission   179
Shinji Takagi

  8 Two Meiji Scholars Introduce the Mormons to Japan   221
Frederick R. Brady

  9 Languages of the Lord:
The Japanese Translations of the Book of Mormon   233
Van C. Gessel

10 The Closing of the Early Japan Mission   263
R. Lanier Britsch

11 Members without a Church:
Latter-day Saints in Japan from 1924 to 1945   285
Chris Conkling

The Church and the Japanese

12 The Reopening and Foundation Years   307
R. Lanier Britsch

13 Memoirs of the Relief Society in Japan, 1951–1991   333
Yanagida Toshiko
Translated by Numano Jiro

14 The Church in Japan Comes of Age, 1968–1980   345
Terry G. Nelson

15 The Genealogical Society of Utah and Japan:
A Personal Perspective   363
Greg Gubler

16 A Geographical Study of the Acceptance of
    The Church of Jesus Christ of Latter-day Saints
    in Japanese Provincial Cities   381
    Takemura Kazuo

17 Japanese Members of the LDS Church:
    A Qualitative View   401
    John P. Hoffmann and Charlie V. Morgan

18 Japanese and American Mormons in Utah:
    Bridging Cultures   421
    Jessie L. Embry

19 Mormonism and the Japanese:
    A Guide to the Sources   435
    Reid L. Neilson

Contributors   445
Index   447

Preface

One century after Elder Heber J. Grant and his companions arrived in Japan to introduce the gospel there, a centennial conference was held on October 13, 2001, at Brigham Young University in Provo, Utah. The celebration was sponsored by the Joseph Fielding Smith Institute for Latter-day Saint History at BYU. Elder L. Edward Brown of the Second Quorum of the Seventy of The Church of Jesus Christ of Latter-day Saints, and R. Lanier Britsch offered the opening addresses on the state of the Church and missionary work in Japan. Nearly two dozen fresh topics were researched and presented; furthermore, previous scholarship was updated and again made accessible. A reception followed for all Japan mission presidents, missionaries, and members; the celebration concluded that evening with a centennial banquet. Over five hundred friends of the Church in Japan enjoyed a Japanese dinner, Japanese koto playing, musical entertainment, and the concluding keynote address by Elder Yoshihiko Kikuchi of the First Quorum of the Seventy.

Since the centennial celebration, the conference organizing committee has received numerous requests for printed conference proceedings or a book chronicling the history of the Church in Japan—and for good reason. Though many articles and book chapters have been devoted to the topic, not one book in English has been written on the subject. We decided to edit a compilation of some of the essays written on the Latter-day Saints and the Japanese that would give an overview of Mormon history in Japan. Of this volume's nineteen essays, about half are appearing for the first time; the remainder have previously appeared in various academic publications. We have taken a fresh look at each essay and done some minor editing to bring consistency to the volume. In keeping with Japanese tradition, family names precede given names throughout the book except in the notes and bibliography, where authors have followed the Western naming convention; the only exception to this occurs in Shinji Takagi's chapters, where names follow Western standards throughout. Due to space and other limitations, we were unable to include all the centennial celebration papers, but with each presenter's consent we have placed many of the unedited conference papers in an archive file, "A Centennial Celebration: The Church of Jesus Christ of Latter-day Saints in Japan, 1901–2001," selected conference papers, at the L. Tom Perry Special Collections, Harold B. Lee Library, Brigham Young University, Provo, Utah. Celebrating this centennial was even more significant because the Japan Mission was one of only a few missions to ever be closed and then reopened; since its reopening, the mission has become an anchor of the Church in that area of the world.

This compilation of essays on the Church in Japan is just one of many books that highlights international Church history. *Taking the Gospel to the Japanese, 1901 to 2001* is part of the Studies in LDS History series, put out by BYU Studies and the Joseph Fielding Smith Institute for Latter-day Saint History, which also includes volumes on the Church in West Africa, Eastern Europe, and the Pacific Islands.

We have divided the essays in this volume into four chronological and topical sections: Prologue, Setting the Stage for the Church in Japan, The Early Japan Mission, and The Church and the Japanese. R. Lanier Britsch's opening conference address, "Historical and Cultural Challenges to Successful Missionary Work in Japan," works well as our prologue. Having written more on the history of the Church in Japan and Asia than any other scholar, Britsch is well suited to discuss the "problems and pitfalls" of missionary work in Japan. He helps us better understand the challenges to Latter-day Saint proselytizing and ecclesiastical stability in Japan.

The second section of the book provides an overview of events and personalities instrumental in setting the stage for the Church in Japan. This section begins with an edited version of Reid L. Neilson's centennial celebration paper, "The Japan Mission: First Efforts," in which he identifies several important contacts made between the Latter-day Saints and the Japanese beginning in the late 1850s and culminating in the creation of the Japan Mission in February 1901. Few realize that Church authorities tried twice before 1901 to formally initiate missionary work in Japan: first in 1860 through Walter Murray Gibson and again in 1895 through Elder Abraham H. Cannon. These and other early efforts can now be seen as important stepping stones to the First Presidency's calling of Elder Heber J. Grant to take the gospel to Japan.

Next is Wendy Butler's essay, "The Iwakura Mission and its Stay in Salt Lake City." Butler relates the story of the 1872 Iwakura Mission, a delegation of high-ranking Japanese government officials, and its nineteen-day unscheduled stay in Salt Lake City due to a massive snowstorm. She describes the interaction and impressions made between these Japanese dignitaries and their impromptu Mormon hosts. Almost thirty years later, President Lorenzo Snow indicated that the Iwakura Mission's stopover in Salt Lake City was an important factor in his decision to open the Japan Mission in 1901.

Although most Church members assume Latter-day Saint mission overtures to the Japanese began with the opening of the Japan Mission in 1901, Shinji Takagi chronicles the lives and conversions of two Japanese residents of Hawaii—Tomizo Katsunuma and Tokujiro Sato—each of whom might be considered the original Japanese Latter-day Saint. Takagi contextualizes both of these Japanese "path breakers" as they struggled "to reconcile the tenets of Mormonism with the demands of Japanese culture, the same struggle that has continued to this day among their fellow Mormons of Japanese ancestry."

The final paper of this preparatory section, "Translator or Translated? The Portrayal of The Church of Jesus Christ of Latter-day Saints in Print in Meiji Japan," was presented at the conference by Sarah Cox Smith. After reviewing various late nineteenth- and early twentieth-century Japanese periodicals, she offers new research on how the Church was represented in print during the Meiji period before Elder Grant and his companions arrived in 1901. Most articles were written by anti-Mormon Protestants, warning their readers of polygamy. She concludes by chronicling the efforts of early Latter-day Saint missionaries in Japan to favorably retranslate the Church's message.

The third section of the book is comprised of essays detailing the early Japan Mission, the years between the 1901 dedication of Japan by Elder Grant, and the reestablishment of the Church in Japan following World War II. "Strangers in a Strange Land: Heber J. Grant and the Opening of the Japan Mission," is Ronald W. Walker's insightful study of Elder Grant's missionary experiences in Japan. Walker's essay traces Grant's call to open and lead the Japan Mission in February 1901 until his release in September 1903. Relying on Grant's personal journals and correspondence, Walker describes the young Apostle's unique missionary challenges with the Japanese language and life in a foreign culture.

Shinji Takagi's second essay in this volume is titled "Mormons in the Press: Reactions to the 1901 Opening of the Japan Mission." Takagi reviews and analyzes the press coverage of the newly arrived Mormon missionaries in August and September 1901 by influential newspapers in Tokyo, Osaka, and other regional Japanese presses as well as national magazines. In doing so, he helps us understand the "historical and social context within which Mormon missionary work began in Japan."

In "Two Meiji Scholars Introduce the Mormons to Japan," Frederick R. Brady compares how Takahashi Gorō, author of *Morumonkyō to Morumon Kyōto* (Mormons and Mormonism), and Uchida Yū, author of *Morumon shū* (The Mormon Sect), helped introduce the Church to the Japanese through their writings. Both authors provide useful overviews of the Church and evaluate Joseph Smith's prophetic claims and his followers' practice of polygamy. Brady concludes that Takahashi's Church-sanctioned book did not do as much good as hoped, and Uchida's less favorable publication probably did not do the young mission much harm.

A noted translator himself, Van C. Gessel discusses the Book of Mormon translations of Alma O. Taylor, Satō Tatsui, and a Church translation committee, in "Language of the Lord: The Japanese Translations of the Book of Mormon," originally presented at the centennial conference. He claims the three translators and their translations offer observers of the Church a "microcosmic view of the progress of the Church in Japan, replicating the shift from foreign to native administration of Church affairs."

In his second essay in this volume, "The Closing of the Early Japan Mission," R. Lanier Britsch describes the 1924 closing of the Japan Mission by President Heber J. Grant, the Apostle who had opened the mission in 1901. Britsch reviews the mission's internal problems such as the missionaries' struggle with the Japanese language and culture, their long tenure of service, and their unproductive missionary approach, which led to "almost negligible results." He also sees President Grant's decision to close the mission as a product of external stresses such as political and military conditions in Japan, growing anti-American sentiment, the passage of Japanese exclusion laws in the United States, the Church's failure to acquire much property, and the great Tokyo earthquake of 1923. All these factors, together with inspiration on the part of the First Presidency, combined to shutter the early Japan Mission.

Chris Conkling, in "Members without a Church: Mormons in Japan from 1924 to 1945," starts where Britsch left off with the closing of the Japan Mission. Conkling analyzes how the abandoned Japanese Saints coped with the closing and the resulting ecclesiastical isolation for over two decades. He looks at the reactions of the two dozen or so active Latter-day Saints living in Kōfu, Tokyo, Osaka, and Sapporo, and discusses the leadership efforts of Brothers Nara Fujiya and Fujiwara Takeo. He concludes with an overview of the Hawaiian era, 1936–50, during which time the Church focused its efforts on the Japanese in Hawaii.

The final section of this book, the Church and the Japanese, chronicles the reestablishment of the Church in Japan following World War II until the close of the twentieth century. In R. Lanier Britsch's third essay, "The Reopening and Foundation Years," he examines the Japanese surrender in August 1945 and the reestablishment of religious freedom in Japan. Two decades after closing the early Japan Mission, Church leaders were again able to share the gospel through the efforts of servicemen and previously converted Church members like Nara Fujiya. Britsch also sketches the mission presidencies of Edward L. Clissold, Vinal G. Mauss, Hilton A. Robertson, Paul Andrus, and Dwayne N. Andersen.

Japanese Church member Yanagida Toshiko's autobiographical account, "Memoirs of the Relief Society in Japan, 1951–1991," tells the story of the women's auxiliary movement in Japan after World War II.

Initially called as president of the entire Relief Society of Japan, she is uniquely suited to chronicle the rise of Mormonism in her country from a much needed woman's perspective. She shares the challenges and successes of her organization as it attempted to fulfill its role within the larger church in East Asia.

"The Church in Japan Comes of Age: 1968–1980," by Terry G. Nelson, details the explosive growth in the Church in Japan from the end of the 1960s until the dedication of the Tokyo Temple in 1980. He discusses the numerous divisions of the original Northern Far East Mission, the Mormon Pavilion at Expo '70, the creation of the Japanese Language Training Mission, the creation of the first Asian stake, and the construction and dedication of the Tokyo Temple—all signs of the Church's maturity.

Working as an East Asia researcher within the Church's genealogical department for many years, Greg Gubler "came to understand and participate in the Church's efforts to acquire and preserve Japanese records and promote family history work in Japan." In this article he tells the story of the early genealogical efforts in Japan in "The Genealogical Society of Utah and Japan: A Personal Perspective," presented at the conference. Having conducted research on both sides of the Pacific, he is able to offer an insider's perspective on this important Church mission.

Japanese scholar Takemura Kazuo presented the paper, "A Geographical Study of the Acceptance of The Church of Jesus Christ of Latter-day Saints in Japanese Provincial Cities," reprinted herein, at "A Symposium Commemorating the 100th Year of the Japan Mission," held in Shinagawa Hoken Center, Tokyo, Japan, 2001. This essay is an investigation of regional differences in acceptance and member retention in the Church in provincial cities of Japan, with the Yamagata and Toyama areas as examples.

John P. Hoffman and Charlie V. Morgan offer another view of the contemporary Church in Japan in "Japanese Members of the LDS Church: A Qualitative View," presented at the conference. In 1998 the senior author served as a visiting faculty member at Hokkaidō University and determined to investigate what "social and cultural factors might attract or dissuade the potential Japanese member" and "what types of family, behavioral, and cultural conflicts" active Latter-day Saints in Japan faced. By conducting interviews and administering questionnaires in a local Church congregation, the authors were able to better understand how members "negotiated and reconciled membership in the Church with their Japanese identities."

Jessie L. Embry's paper, "Japanese and American Mormons in Utah: Bridging Cultures," provides a fascinating glimpse into the minds and hearts of Japanese members living in Utah. Her findings are the outgrowth of the Latter-day Saint Asian American Oral History Project conducted by the Charles Redd Center for Western Studies at Brigham Young University. Drawing from the experiences of twenty-three Japanese Latter-day Saint immigrants living in Utah, Embry describes how these Japanese Saints have assimilated into American and Mormon culture.

Lastly, "Mormonism and the Japanese: A Guide to the Sources," is Reid L. Neilson's attempt to provide researchers inside and outside the Church with a much-needed bibliography of the most important sources for studying the intersection of the Church and Japan on both shores of the Pacific Rim.

Photographs for this book were difficult to obtain. Perhaps because the book deals with fairly recent history, many relevant pictures have yet to find their way from private possession into archives. We hope that owners of these photographs will be able to donate copies of their important pictures to easily accessible repositories in the coming years.

Although a single volume cannot begin to cover all the important events and aspects of the century-long Latter-day Saint missionary effort in Japan, it is our hope that these essays will provide an introduction as well as an impetus to further study and contemplation of what it means to take the restored gospel of Jesus Christ to nations such as Japan.

Reid L. Neilson
Van C. Gessel

Acknowledgments

The Joseph Fielding Smith Institute for Latter-day Saint History at Brigham Young University is to be thanked for the success of our Centennial Celebration and for the publication of this book. From the beginning, Ronald W. Walker, professor of history and a senior researcher at the institute, championed both endeavors and was responsible for obtaining the sponsorship of his research institute. After the institute agreed to sponsor our proposed conference, the department's executive committee named Ronald W. Walker and Reid L. Neilson conference co-chairs, and Van C. Gessel, R. Lanier Britsch, Masakazu Watabe, Russell Hancock, and Dean W. Collinwood as committee members. Together we organized the academic conference, "A Centennial Celebration: The Church of Jesus Christ of Latter-day Saints in Japan, 1901–2001." Our hope was to generate new scholarship and highlight existing research on the Church in Japan. We also wanted to join in the centennial celebrations planned in Japan to honor its members and missionaries.

We are grateful for all the Church leaders and scholars who presented papers at our conference. Elder L. Edward Brown, Second Quorum of the Seventy, spoke on "The Church in Japan Today" and R. Lanier Britsch shared "Historical and Cultural Challenges to Successful Missionary Work in Japan," in the opening plenary session. The first of four concurrent sessions included presentations by Dean W. Collinwood, "The First Samurais in Zion," Reid L. Neilson, "The Japan Mission: First Efforts, 1854–1900," Ronald W. Walker, "Strangers in a

Strange Land: Heber J. Grant and the Opening of the Japanese Mission," Gordon Madsen, "Heber J. Grant in Japan: A Personal Account," Van C. Gessel, "The Languages of the Lord: Japanese Translations of the Book of Mormon," Sarah Cox Smith, "Translator or Translated? The Portrayal of The Church of Jesus Christ of Latter-day Saints in Print in Meiji Japan," Eric Walz, "Japanese Immigrants and the Mormons," and Wendy Butler, "Eyes Only for the Orient: Early Twentieth-Century Neglect of Salt Lake City Japanese."

During the plenary session luncheon, Russell Hancock moderated a panel discussion, "The State of the Work in Japan," featuring the personalities and insights of several former Japan mission presidents. The two afternoon concurrent sessions included papers by Paul V. Hyer, "The Establishment of a Mission in Postwar Japan: Paul Hyer's 'Mini-MTC' in Honolulu," Greg Gubler, "The Genealogical Society of Utah and Japan," Cyril I. A. Figuerres, "The Ammon Strategy: Achieving Real Growth and Establishing the First-Generation Church in Japan," John P. Hoffman and Charlie V. Morgan, "Japanese Members' Experiences in the Church: A Qualitative View," Michael Sudlow, "Years of Anticipation, Years of Growth: 1967–1971," Paul L. Anderson, "The 1970 Mormon Expo in Japan," Roger R. Keller, "Non-attachment in Buddhism and Mormonism," Masakazu Watabe, "Human Behavior, Language, and Culture," Honam Rhee, "The History of the Church in Korea," Malan R. Jackson, "One Hundred Fifty Years on the Periphery: A Short History of the Church in China," Ian Anderson, "Brother and Sister Koshiba: Pioneers in Japan," and Jessie Embry, "Japanese-American Mormons in Utah." Lastly we thank the musicians who played the koto and who performed LDS songs in Japanese; Marilyn Parks, who helped everything run smoothly; and Elder Yoshihiko Kikuchi, First Quorum of the Seventy, who presented the concluding keynote address, "Our Children Be Restored."

We want to thank the BYU Studies staff, expecially John W. Welch, Heather M. Seferovich, Caitlin E. Shirts, Marny K. Parkin, and Kimberly Chen Pace for producing this volume. Finally, we extend special appreciation to our anonymous Japanese donors who helped defray publication costs of this volume.

Historical and Cultural Challenges to Successful Missionary Work in Japan

R. Lanier Britsch

Long before I served my own mission in Hawaii in 1959 and 1960, I became aware that doing missionary work in Japan was more difficult than in most places. One of my uncles had spent three years in Japan, and I had no interest in spending so much of my youth in a similar way. There is a certain irony in my own teaching and writing career because I ended up worrying about Japan as a mission field—a field in which I had hoped I would not have to serve. However, worry about Japan I have, and I must report that after almost forty years of trying to figure out the problems and pitfalls of doing missionary work in Japan, I have learned much more about what the challenges are than what the solutions are to those challenges.

To say that Japan offers many missionary challenges is not to say that we do not love and admire much of that which is Japanese. Among the world cultures, Japan is clearly one of the great nations—economically, technologically, artistically, governmentally, religiously, and so on. But that very greatness has presented many challenges to successful Christian missionary work, including Latter-day Saint proselytizing.

Few people who are acquainted with the Church in Japan would deny that serious problems exist. In his informative article of 1996, Numano Jiro asked: "Since Japan as a nation has made such remarkable economic and technological progress, why is the church in Japan not also making comparable progress, but in fact is stagnant?" He goes on to say, "For some years now such a question has arisen among LDS members in the U.S. and particularly among church leaders."[1] To paraphrase the question in my own words: Why, despite religious liberty, economic prosperity, national security, and the ability of missionaries to move about freely and visit citizens without restraint, are the Japanese such a challenging missionary target?

Because of space restraints I can only make a few statements regarding the problems that contribute to the situation. I have chosen to divide my subject into two general parts—history and culture—but the two knowledge realms are so intertwined that in many instances it is not possible to distinguish between the two.

Christian History in a Non-Christian Land

The history of Christianity in Japan extends back to 1549 when the great Jesuit missionary Francis Xavier arrived in Japan from India. The work he commenced bore considerable fruit. Estimates vary, but at its peak the Japanese mission could claim between 300,000 and 500,000 converts. This was at a time when Japan had under 25 million people. For a complex set of reasons, Christianity was later discouraged in the 1590s and finally banned by an anti-*Kirishitan* (Christian) edict in 1614. Over the next several decades, thousands of brutal martyrdoms followed before the budding Kirishitan movement was almost annihilated in 1638 by the Tokugawa government.

The Tokugawa government saw Christianity as a serious threat to Japan's sovereignty. Considering what had already happened in the Philippines under the Spanish Christians, their fears were not entirely unfounded. There was also an issue of social control involved. The Tokugawa disdain for Christianity was not a matter of religious truth. Around 1640 the government closed its doors to foreign relations with all but the Dutch from Europe (they were anti-Romanist Protestants who had trading, not missionary, interests) and the Chinese and Koreans from Asia. *Sakoku* (closed country) remained the official policy until 1854, when Commodore Matthew C. Perry and his fleet of American naval vessels forced the Tokugawa government to enter into more normal diplomatic and trade relations.[2]

During the Tokugawa, or Edo, period (1603–1867) the Japanese government was steadfast in its determination to keep the Christian movement down. Anti-Christian edicts adorned public signboards in every village, town, and city in Japan. But even before the Tokugawa regime destroyed Christianity, serious questions had been raised regarding the religious tradition's viability in Japan. Endō Shūsaku, Christian author of the great novel *Silence,* clearly portrayed the conflict Christians had during the early period. He questioned whether the Japanese have a concept of God and even wonders whether Japan is a swamp in which Christianity could not and cannot take root.[3]

Soon after the Harris Treaty of 1858 allowed Americans to live in Japan, Protestant ministers and Catholic priests entered the country. But they were unwelcome as missionaries and mostly limited their activities to the role of chaplain or minister to the foreign community. The welcome mat was not put out until 1873, five years after the establishment of the new Meiji government (1868–1912), and then the anti-Christian policy was modified only because of foreign pressure.

Much changed regarding Japanese views of Christianity during the next decade or so, but there was a tremendous foundation of anti-Christian history and policy that was never eliminated from the minds of Meiji policy makers. The Meiji government did not want to open Japan to foreign religions and thought. There is no evidence that high-ranking government officials or industrial magnates had any interest in Christianity; they were the people who enforced the traditions and customs of Japan. Ironically, even though Latter-day Saint leaders were impressed with the intelligence and forward-looking attitudes of the Japanese who were part of the Iwakura diplomatic mission that visited Salt Lake City in 1872, those Japanese representatives were officially and emotionally anti-Christian. And they remained so.

From 1870 until 1884, Meiji leaders carefully established a new system that extolled the place and the role of the emperor. Robert Lee, a long-time Protestant missionary in Japan, summarized these actions as follows:

> In their establishment of State Shinto as the national cult of the emperor, the new religious leaders built upon the theology of *kokugaku* [national learning] scholars and defined the divinity of the emperor in terms of the eternal, unbroken lineage of the imperial household. Hence, the emperor as the direct lineal descendent of the founding sun-goddess, Amaterasu, was seen as "coeval with eternity" (Imperial Rescript on Education), the divine link between time immemorial and the present. As *kami* [something worthy of

awe], the emperor was eternal, pure, "inviolable and sacred" (Meiji Constitution), the divine channel for blessing and nurture from the ancestral gods to their descendants.[4]

The Meiji government used an old symbol, the Imperial Household, to unify the country. In contrast to many Western nations that had generally separated the state from religion, the Meiji leaders avoided this issue by declaring State Shintō a national cult—not a religion.[5]

Although Christianity was welcomed as part of the package of Western ideas and ways by a few Japanese intellectuals during the 1870s and 1880s, most Japanese opinions were being shaped by an increasingly sophisticated propaganda machine in Tokyo. During the Tokugawa era, the government had operated on the belief that the *gumin* (the ignorant masses that made up approximately 90 percent of the populace) were incapable of contributing anything to the government of the nation. During the Meiji period, however, the new political elite "began to demand the active spiritual participation of the common people in the realization of national objectives."[6] This included the destruction of many local shrines and the abolition of folk traditions (such as phallicism and *misogi harai,* or purification rites using a waterfall) and forced participation in a growing national system of rites, symbols, customs, beliefs, and practices. In 1875 and following, Buddhism was de-emphasized while Shintō was exalted.[7] The government constructed numerous *jinja* (Shintō shrines) to extol the virtues of past national heroes. Fujitani called this the process of homogenizing an "official culture fostered by the state."[8]

Almost surprisingly, through the 1880s a number of Christian organizations had some success, but the promise of further significant growth was curtailed in 1889 when the emperor issued what is known as the Meiji Constitution and, in 1890, the Rescript on Education. The Constitution was a gift from the emperor, the father of the nation. No blood was spilled to gain its blessings. Technically, Christianity was not legal until freedom of religion was included in the Constitution,[9] so Protestant and Catholic missionaries had a moment of hope for more freedom of activity and greater success. But the Rescript on Education turned hope into increasing discouragement. The Rescript was worded so as to shape the moral character of the Japanese people and to create loyalty to the emperor system.[10] National policy required that the

Rescript be read in all schools on a regular basis and on occasions of national holidays and celebrations. Students were to stand bowed before a picture of the emperor while the school principal read the Rescript. The object of education was to serve the purposes of the state, not the individual. The result of the Rescript was heightened nationalism and anti-foreignism. In coming decades the influence of such words sank deeply into the hearts and minds of the Japanese people. George B. Sansom observed that the Rescript "proclaims a return to native tradition and implicitly gives notice to the people that they are not to be led astray by Western ideas in moral and political philosophy."[11] As a result, wrote Joseph Kitagawa, "Christianity came under severe attack as an unpatriotic religion."[12] This was particularly true during the first part of the 1890s.

Fortunately, several developments had a softening effect on the anti-Christian movement. The Sino-Japanese War of 1894–95 could have brought anti-Christian crusades along with burgeoning nationalism, but it did not. The war was an Asian war and thus had no relation to Christianity. A number of Christian Japanese fought side by side with their fellow countrymen, showing that claims that they were unpatriotic were unfounded. A second boon to the Christian image came following charitable acts performed by Christians at times of natural disasters, such as providing relief and food for earthquake victims. A third help to the Christian image was the changing economic situation that created a larger pool of investigators. Industrialization and urbanization created a class of white-collar workers who were fairly well educated and separated from their more conservative compatriots in the countryside. Japan's increasing success in international diplomacy also helped the Christian situation. By the early 1900s, Japan had eliminated several unequal treaties and entered into others on an equal footing. Being part of the international family of nations made friendships with Christians and membership in a Christian church more acceptable for Japanese.

Just after the end of this difficult but gradually improving decade, leaders of The Church of Jesus Christ of Latter-day Saints decided to send missionaries to Japan. Ten years earlier, opening Japan to Latter-day Saint missionary work would have been legal but impractical for the reasons already mentioned. Unfortunately, the Church did not thrive during this twenty-three year mission.[13] The period covered by the first Japan Mission, from 1901 to 1924, was a time of peace at home for the Japanese. But during that time the Japanese participated in two major foreign wars—the Russo-Japanese War of 1904–5 and World War I. Japan was affected economically, socially, psychologically, and politically in its international relations by both wars. Ultra-nationalism gradually gained strength during this period. Other Christian churches added modest but greater numbers than the Latter-day Saints during the first quarter of the twentieth century; however, these Christian denominations fielded hundreds more missionaries to accomplish their work. Christian missionary work and other Christian activities continued to grow without much hindrance from the government or other forces until the 1930s. But from the Japanese invasion of Manchuria in 1931 and the so-called state of emergency that lasted until the end of World War II, government and military control of all religious activities again became steadily greater. State Shintō, in conjunction with the emperor system, required obeisance from all Japanese citizens. In 1939, under the infamous Religious Organizations Law, most Protestant churches were forced to combine into one large organization called the Church of Christ in Japan (*Nihon Kirisuto Kyōdan*—usually referred to as the *Kyōdan*); only the Roman Catholics were allowed to remain separate.[14] The years of World War II that followed the passage of this law were extremely difficult for Japanese Christians. Japanese Latter-day Saints referred to this era (1924–45) as the "dark ages."[15]

The more than half-century since the end of World War II has brought tremendous changes in religion. Perhaps most important was the series of actions taken by the Occupation government under General Douglas MacArthur, Supreme Commander Allied Powers (SCAP), that created religious liberty in Japan. Between October 4, 1945—with MacArthur's Basic Directive that "ordered the Japanese government to remove all restrictions on political, civil, and religious liberties"—and May 3, 1947, SCAP imposed several measures, including enforcement of the new Constitution, to ensure religious liberty for all Japanese, to disestablish State Shintō, and to repudiate the divinity of the emperor.[16] Among the results of these actions was the re-entry of Latter-day Saint missionaries. Another result was a tremendous surge of religious interest and growth. Within a few years, hundreds of new religions (*Shinkō*

Shūkyō) arose, and many relatively new religions flourished. The years of the Occupation (1945–52) have been called the "Christian boom," but because almost all religions prospered, the time might better be called the "religion boom."

It is fortunate that the Church was able to take advantage of part of this boom time. Edward L. Clissold, who had served in the Occupation forces, returned to Tokyo as mission president in March 1948 and was joined in June by five young missionaries. Although additional missionaries were added in coming months, the small band of Latter-day Saint missionaries was never large enough to take full advantage of the moment. The Korean War in 1950 and following years further curtailed the missionary effort. The Churchwide number of missionary callings topped at 3,015 in 1950 but dropped to 1,801 and 872 in the next two years.[17] The year 1952 brought the end of the Occupation and almost simultaneously the end of the Christian boom. Most of the years since then have been best characterized as a time of impressive economic growth and materialistic success. Since 1952 the Church has had generally steady but unexciting growth in Japan—the only statistical exception being the years from 1978 to 1982, when the growth was enormous. The last two decades of the twentieth century were quite disappointing if convert baptisms are the measurement of success. The current period of retreat and contraction—combining of missions and reduction of missionary numbers—manifests recognition that matters are not expected to change soon.[18]

Recent Historical Challenges to Missionary Work

Two events stand out as challenges to Latter-day Saint missionary work in Japan since 1988. The first was the death of Emperor Hirohito, known since his death on January 7, 1989, as Emperor Shōwa. The second was the March 20, 1995, Tokyo subway attack with poisonous sarin gas by members of a new Japanese religion known as *Aum Shinrikyō*.

First, new challenges of the *tennōsei* (the emperor system) encouraged many Japanese to consider the role of State Shintō in their lives. The period immediately following World War II saw the re-creation of the emperor's image from semidivine warlord to benign scholar and gentle father of the Japanese nation. Many non-Japanese historians of Japan have sustained this pleasant image of Japan's symbolic head of state. But events surrounding the death of the emperor and the enthronement of his son Akihito—who took the reign name of Emperor Heisei—have raised new questions about the meaning of the emperor within Japanese history and culture. Rituals surrounding the emperor's death, particularly the long months of *jishuku* (self-restraint) before his death and then the elaborate series of ceremonies following it, presented evidence of the actual place of the emperor in the psyche of the Japanese people and especially among influential government leaders. Particularly discomforting to some observers were the *takamikura* and *daijosai* rituals that followed over a year after Hirohito's death. Robert Lee described these ceremonies this way:

> Although historically both ceremonies have had religious significance, the government carried out the first as a simple public ceremony and then elaborately staged the *daijosai* as a national ceremony, using public funds.
>
> Traditionally, both ceremonies have had to do with the deification of the emperor. On November 10 [1990] the emperor ascended the imperial throne (*takamikura,* literally the high seat of the emperor) in a ceremony now largely secular. Earlier, under Buddhist influence, in this ritual the emperor, while chanting a magic sutra, became the reincarnation of *dainichi nyorai,* the great Sun Buddha; but under current Shintō influence, the older ritual, *daijosai,* the great thanksgiving festival, had become the more important ceremony.
>
> The *daijosai,* which began the evening of November 14 at eight o'clock and continued until the dawn of the next day, ritually recapitulated the ancient myth of the descent of Prince Ninigi, the first emperor of Japan and the grandson of the sun-goddess, Amaterasu. In this ritual, originally a fertility rite in the agricultural cycle, the new emperor becomes Prince Ninigi, who communes with the mother sun-goddess and unites with her, and thus is transformed into a female who is impregnated by the gods and then is reborn as a deified ancestor, a living god *(ara hito gami).*[19]

In 1995, Christian Professor Chiyozaki Hideo, in reaction to the aforementioned rituals, labeled the rise of greater interest in the emperor system as "the inescapable missiological issue." He wrote:

> Before the war . . . all discussion of the emperor system was suppressed . . . we knew little about its important factors. . . . However,

after the war many thought that the problem of the emperor system had disappeared and there was no urgent need to examine it. In light of recent events [the passing of Emperor Shōwa and the enthronement of Emperor Heisei in 1989], Christians are waking up to the painful understanding that such neglect was indeed a mistake.[20]

Chiyozaki's concern is not new. While not speaking directly to the missionary issue, in 1968 historian John Whitney Hall observed:

> Few Asian nations entered the modern world by strengthening a monarchical system rather than destroying it. . . . Reborn out of the ashes of military defeat and wartime disillusionment, the Showa emperor by virtue of retaining the same body under a new constitutional system, has again become the symbol of continuity despite drastic change.[21]

Hendrik Kraemer, well-known missiologist, concluded that even though much had changed after World War II, much had remained the same. He wrote in 1960:

> Yet it will be wise to reckon with the fact that Japan's spiritual core has not changed, that her adjustment to the symbiosis with Western civilization is a process unknown and this is a tale written not on a clean slate (as the "democratization" of Japan under American leadership seemed to assume) but on a palimpsest, remarkable for its age and its specific, ineffaceable configuration. Shinto will continue to enshrine the real soul of Japan.[22]

There is an irony in this statement. State Shintō, to which he alludes, was not always the "real soul" of Japan, but it has become so through the efforts of the Meiji leaders and those who followed them—Shintō has been regenerated for the most part during the past two decades. Old practices such as mountain climbing for worship, pilgrimages to *jinja* (Shintō shrines), and *misogi harai* (purification rituals) have become more popular.

Following the war, shrines dropped in number from 176,000 to between 70,000 and 80,000, but by the 1980s the number of shrines had grown to about 110,000.[23] The missionary implications of the resurgence of such foundational beliefs and practices are obvious. Although most Japanese do not spend much time in Shintō ritual practice, especially outside the home, Japan's real soul is founded on these national symbols, rites, and beliefs. Changing religions is tantamount to becoming non-Japanese, something few Japanese are willing to do.

The second event of the late twentieth century that affected missionary work was the sarin gas attack by members of *Aum Shinrikyō* (literally "teaching the universal or supreme truth") and its aftermath. Ishii Kenji succinctly described the attack in these words:

> On March 20, 1995, the deadly nerve gas sarin was planted in five subway cars on three lines in the Tokyo subway system, killing [twelve and] injuring more than five thousand people. Rumors linked the attack to Aum Shinrikyō. Two days later, police searched Aum Shinrikyō's offices at twenty-five locations across Japan on suspicion of the sect's involvement in the abduction and illegal confinement of a notary public. On April 14, 120 Aum Shinrikyō facilities throughout Japan were raided simultaneously. On May 16, in connection with the sarin gas attack, Aum Shinrikyō's founder, Asahara Shōkō, was arrested on suspicion of murder.
>
> That a religious organization would use nerve gas for mass slaughter and paralyze an entire city has profoundly shaken Japanese society.[24]

The attack had an immediate and continuing impact on Japanese society. It also caused changes to the Religious Corporation Law, imposing more central government supervision, greater financial oversight, and the right of the government to investigate religious leaders more easily than previously. But the most important reaction has been antipathy toward religious groups, Japanese and others, that proselytize new members or that do not represent a mainstream, purely Japanese image to the public. Following the sarin attack, rumors as well as truth spread throughout Japan, causing fear of and resentment toward any group that was considered a cult or a deviance. I conclude this section with the question and comments of a Japanese student at Brigham Young University who is not a member of the Church:

> So how does one differentiate the Aum [Shinrikyō] from other religions? Parents tell their children to stay away from strangers, so how does one differentiate a stranger from a friend? The door to door proselytizing and the street corner proselytizing are often associated with Christian missionaries. And when one becomes affiliated with the church, fear strikes those that are close, such as their families

and friends, all because of mysterious standards set forth by cult groups.... It is saddening to see that the mainstream of Japan continues to be distant from religion altogether, as it almost seems that staying away from religions is becoming a religion itself.... Religious cults have scared many Japanese away, and society is still defensive about the LDS culture.[25]

Japanese Culture as a Challenge to Successful Missionary Work

The word *culture* is one of the most common and most frequently maligned pieces of jargon used by social scientists. Among the numerous definitions of *culture*, the thoughts of Clifford Geertz are useful. He defined *culture* as "an historically transmitted pattern of meanings embodied in symbols, a system of inherited conceptions expressed in symbolic forms by means of which men communicate, perpetuate, and develop their knowledge about and attitudes toward life." Geertz goes on to explain the importance of sacred symbols to the creation of meaning:

> Sacred symbols function to synthesize a people's ethos—the tone, character, and quality of their life, its moral and aesthetic style and mood—and their world-view—the picture they have of the way things in sheer reality are, their most comprehensive ideas of order. In religious belief and practice a group's ethos is rendered intellectually reasonable by being shown to represent a way of life ideally adapted to the actual state of affairs the world-view describes, while the world-view is rendered emotionally convincing by being presented as an image of an actual state of affairs peculiarly well arranged to accommodate such a way of life.[26]

Latter-day Saint missionary efforts in Japan and elsewhere in Asia, as measured by convert baptisms, have been about as successful as proselytizing performed by other Christian denominations. The same historical, cultural, economic, and international issues and changes have affected the work of all Christian missionaries. The similarity of response by Asian peoples to various Christian missionary groups is a manifestation of the general difficulty of transmitting religious messages and meanings from one culture to another. Communication is largely based on foundations of shared meaning and understanding. As a general rule, the foundational beliefs of Asian peoples are not similar to those of Christian European or American background. Universalists frequently express belief that religions are all alike at their core. The notion that "all roads lead to the top of Mt. Fuji" or "to Rome" prevails among many of this persuasion. Others assert that just as the goose flying from north to south is called by different names by different people, so God is at root the same regardless of name. I am not denying that truth exists in most religions. But I am saying that the universalist approach is naive in its failure to recognize that religious truth is not held to be the same thing in different cultures.

I remember Professor John Sorenson lecturing an anthropology class at BYU and discussing cultural differences. His message was that even though some observers would have us believe that "under the skin we're all alike," the truth is that our greatest similarities are biological and our greatest differences are cultural. All people do not "feel" the same about shared events. We do not all find the same things funny or clever. Believing that a warm smile will always evoke the same response among various cultures is not necessarily true. There does seem to be a universal feeling regarding basic matters of right and wrong, but even in the moral and ethical realm there is great diversity of response regarding what people should and should not do. Different peoples are in fact culturally different.

Acknowledgment of real differences is an important step toward effective missionary work. Every teacher knows that learning is based first on common understandings and shared knowledge. Successful teachers do not start a lecture in the middle of the lesson plan. At the beginning of the semester, university teachers usually establish early what the subject of the course is and what prerequisites are needed to continue on from earlier knowledge bases. A probable next step is a statement that builds a foundation required for understanding what is coming in the course. Pedagogically, Christian missionaries in general—including Latter-day Saints—have been burdened with a very difficult task, specifically, building a shared-knowledge base or creating common ground. The responsibility is ours to establish common ground, not that of the Japanese or other Asian peoples.

My reason for discussing foundational knowledge is that I strongly believe that without conscious planning on our part as the sending organization, our representatives will wander somewhat blindly through their mission experiences, never fully connecting with the target people. I am not denying the power of the Holy Spirit to carry our message to the hearts of the Japanese people. I am merely suggesting that more knowledge on our part would increase the possibility of getting to the point where the Spirit can play an important role.

Cultural differences result in a variety of challenges. I will deal with the subtopics of religiosity, morality and ethics, the role of the individual in society, and the Japanese language barrier.

Religiosity

Edwin O. Reischauer's view on the matter of religiosity is insightful to this discussion. In his book *The Japanese*, he commenced chapter 21, "Religion," with this explanation:

> If this book dealt with a South Asian or Middle Eastern people, it might well have started with a consideration of religion. Even for most Western nations, religion would have required earlier and fuller treatment. But religion occupies a more peripheral position in Japan.... [B]ut the trend toward secularism that has recently become marked in the West dates back at least three centuries in Japan.[27]

Social scientists and religionists have long struggled with the question of where to place the Japanese people on international scales of religiosity. When asked questions about belief in God, the importance of religious beliefs, and belief in life after death, the Japanese rank below India, the United States, the United Kingdom, Scandinavia, and Western Europe, in that order.[28] But defenders of Japanese-style religiosity offer the explanation that Japanese religions do not evoke the same high rates of public participation and outward manifestation of belief that Christianity, Judaism, Islam, and some other religions do. Congregational meetings have traditionally not been part of Japanese worship. Further, some experts suggest, and probably rightly so, that Japanese reticence to express strong views and opinions to strangers limits levels of response to surveyors. It would be highly unusual for most Japanese, especially Japanese men, to express strong commitments regarding matters of religion even if they have such beliefs. Winston Davis concluded that "Japan has become a *relatively* secular culture." And although Shintō and Buddhist festivals are "celebrated with gusto . . . by and large the old religions have failed to provide the Japanese with a philosophy adequate for life and death in the modern (or 'postmodern') world."[29]

But personal observation, statistics, and even scholarly studies lead to few clear conclusions. Many Japanese will assert that Japanese religiosity is simply different from such practices in other parts of the world and then point to Ministry of Education figures to justify their position. In a country of 126 million people, the survey listed 219,838,670 claims of religious affiliation.[30] This confusing figure represents the total number of adherents claimed by all religious organizations. Clearly, many people were listed as adherents by more than one organization. Belonging to two or three religions, particularly Buddhism (89,828,502 adherents) and Shintō (117,378,185 adherents), is common. Nevertheless, does not such a figure of more than two hundred million prove that the Japanese are religious? It certainly indicates a strong interest in affiliation if not deep inner commitment. Additionally, as Jack Seward noted, there is the

> contrary theory that the Japanese are so profoundly religious that everything connected with simply being Japanese and living in Japan—from the smallest act of common courtesy and the obligations of *giri* (duty) to the leaves of the forests and the stones in the river beds—are sacred; that whereas the Christian may leave his religiosity at the door of the church, the Japanese carries his with him, deeply imbedded at subconscious levels.[31]

Because of these complex religious attitudes, many investigators misunderstand the level of commitment required by the Latter-day Saint missionaries.

Morality and Ethics

Another difference between Western and Japanese religious cultures is their respective definitions of ethics and morality. In 1968, Dr. Joseph J. Spae, a Jesuit scholar, published *Christianity Encounters Japan,* a useful sociological study of the place of Christianity among the religions of Japan. He cited at length a study done by Kōmoto Tsugumi, a schoolteacher, that revealed many religious tendencies among Japanese both young and old. Kōmoto questioned sixty-seven religious workers and found interesting answers under the heading of morality and ethics. He asked, "As a religionist, what do you think of [as] the role of religion?" His findings appear in table 1.[32]

Although surveys seldom reveal more than trends, the strong preference for *anshinritsumei* (religion providing spiritual peace or peace of mind) among religionists of Japanese churches in contrast to morality, more typical of Christian responses, including Latter-day Saint responses, provides a useful contrast. In a way, the Shintō use of the word *morality* is most misleading if a Christian is seeking similar meaning. Shintō is noted for its lack of clear moral teaching as related to sexual morality, honesty, and the like. That is not to say that Shintō encourages immoral action. It simply does not deal well with such issues.

In his book *The Japanese*, Edwin O. Reischauer devotes a chapter to "Relativism." He suggests that, "In a society in which people see themselves primarily as members of groups, specific intragroup and also intergroup relationships may reasonably take precedence over universal principles. In other words, ethics may be more relativistic or situational than universal."[33] And Van Gessel concurs that Japan is "a

Table 1: Religious Tendencies among Japanese

Role of Religion	Anshinritsumei*	A panacea	Morality†	Revolution	Formalism	Other‡
Tenriko	100%					
Buddhism	95	5				
Soka Gakkai	82			12		
Shintō	40		46†		7	7
Christianity	6		35			59‡

*Anshinritsumei, lit. "spiritual peace," "peace of mind," or "resignation."
† Implying Shintō-style morality, that is, loyalty to country, emperor, etc.
‡ Answers given included "Religion proclaims God's will towards men" or "Religion means worship, gratitude," etc.

society of relativistic morality. . . . In such a society, the supreme virtue becomes the preservation of social harmony and the absolution of all crimes that either do not disturb that harmony or that are committed in the name of preserving social tranquility."[34] Morality in a more definite Western sense is largely lacking from much of Japanese religious culture. Again, quoting Reischauer:

> Some observers have characterized Japan as having a shame culture rather than a guilt culture like that of the West, that is, shame before the judgment of society is a stronger conditioning force than guilt over sin in the eyes of God. . . . Despite the didacticism of their education, the Japanese certainly have less sense of sin than Westerners or of a clear and inflexible line of demarcation between right and wrong. There are no obviously sinful areas of life. Most things seem permissible in themselves, so long as they do not do some damage in other ways.[35]

Gessel also says many Japanese live their lives with a deficient sense of sin and its consequences. God is not a large part of their lives. In explaining this problem, Gessel quotes from *Yellow Men,* one of Endō's novels:

> Kimiko, the Japanese woman who lives with the outcast [Catholic] priest, can't understand the tragic drama he creates within his own mind [through his immorality and apostasy from the church]: "Why can't you . . . forget about God?," she asks him. "It would be better for you if you could forget. You gave up the Church, didn't you? Then why is it the only thing that constantly weighs on your mind? Buddha, who would forgive you if you'd just utter his name, would be so much better for you."
>
> Hearing these words, [the priest] Durand mutters to himself, "Today for the first time I understood the happiness of the stranger— of those, that is, who are strangers to God. I can't actually declare whether they are happy or not. But I feel at least that I have understood the secret of those narrow, murky eyes peculiar to the yellow race. . . . They are eyes apathetic to God and to sin, eyes unmoved by death." Durand becomes almost envious of the Japanese ability to remain numb to the hellish torments of sin, declaring just before he kills himself, "While I have rejected God, I cannot deny His existence. . . . And yet . . . the Japanese are able to handle everything without God. They are able to live with their ambiguity, showing no

feeling for or interest in the Church, in the torments of sin, in the yearning for salvation—in all the things we white men have thought to be the fundamental requirements to live as a human being. How can this be? How can this be?"[36]

Perhaps Durand's conclusion that the Japanese are "able to handle everything without God" is a bit extreme, but at its heart Buddhism is atheistic. When the historic Buddha attained his para-nirvana he was annihilated; his composite self ceased to be. Mahayana schools of Buddhism have provided personal Buddhas and Bodhisattvas (Buddhas becoming) such as Amida, Vairocana, Miroku, and Kannon in whom believers may place their faith, but even Amida's Pure Land or Western Paradise is ultimately *upaya* (a crutch) to salve the souls of weak sentient mortals. And Amida, the Buddha in whom most Japanese place their faith, does not hear and answer prayers or provide inspiration to his followers. However, Buddhism does provide some solace and comfort to suffering mankind. It teaches more about the moral life than most of its followers ever learn. The Buddha set the example of compassion, and many of his followers seek to follow that way. But most Japanese do not know much about the religion that the majority of the population claims to follow.

As said previously, Shintō, as it is understood and followed by most Japanese, has little to say about morality in the sense of rules for proper conduct. There has been an attempt on the part of some scholars since World War II to create Shintō ethics, but most Japanese know little about such formal, obscure efforts. Shintō provides an affirmative view of nature and of various *kami* that bring a feeling of reverence or awe—for example, heroes, animals, the sun, waterfalls, trees. But Shintō does not provide guidelines for the righteous life or explain how to deal ethically with one's neighbor.

A third religious tradition that affects Japanese culture is Confucianism. This system of thought was introduced into Japan during the sixth century. Although most Japanese do not consider themselves Confucianists, they live their lives according to the teachings of the sage. The underlying rules for ethical behavior—social stratification, filial piety, respect for age, moderation, decorum, humaneness, duty, honesty, and so forth, at home, at school, and in the workplace—are Confucian. Missionaries are met by the challenge to present their view of ethics and morality in a way that will be understood by people of this varied religious heritage.

Role of the Individual in Society

Confucian ethics, which aim for smooth interpersonal relations, exemplify some Japanese cultural values. There is much literature that defines these values in terms of Japanese society. The Japanese themselves speak of their identity crisis and wonder who they are. Among the numerous explanations of Japanese personality, I will list several theories that have received the widest attention. The philosopher Watsuji Tetsurō suggested the importance of *ie* (the house). He wrote that the

> house [meaning household] as a whole is always of greater importance than the individual, so, as a fourth feature, the latter threw away his life with the utmost selflessness. The most striking feature of Japanese history is this readiness to stake one's life for the sake of a parent or child, or to cast away life for the house. . . . The concept of house in Japan takes on a unique and important significance of, if you like, the community of all communities. This is the real essence of the Japanese way of life and the Japanese family system, built on this foundation, has roots more deeply laid than any ideology.[37]

Sociologist Nakane Chie emphasized the importance of the "constant consciousness of distinctions based on rank," on hierarchy, and on the vertical nature of all relations in society.[38]

Doi Takeo, a Christian psychologist, forwarded the idea of the influence of *amae* (dependency on or presumption of someone else's benevolence). Doi explained:

> Perhaps it is better to define it as the principle of mutuality that must be present to guarantee smooth transaction. All interpersonal communications in Japanese society have an emotional undertone of *amae*. It is not surprising, then, that Japanese tend to have many short breaks in their conversation. During those breaks they try to feel out one another and assess the situation, because what is most important for them is to reassure themselves on every occasion of a mutuality based upon *amae*. One could say that for the Japanese, verbal communication is something that accompanies nonverbal communication and not the other way round. In other words,

they are very sensitive to the atmosphere that pervades human relationships.[39]

Reischauer emphasized "group-ism" as the organizing principle of Japanese society. In his view, "no difference is more significant between Japanese and Americans, or Westerners in general, than the greater Japanese tendency to emphasize the group, somewhat at the expense of the individual." Going on Reischauer wrote:

> The group emphasis has affected the whole style of interpersonal relations in Japan. A group is obviously appreciated more than a solo star and team spirit more than individual ambition.... As the old Japanese saying goes, the nail that sticks up gets banged down.... Cooperativeness, reasonableness, and understanding of others are the virtues most admired, not personal drive, forcefulness and individual self-assertion.

The key Japanese value is harmony.[40]

More recently, Hamaguchi Esyun has created a meta-theory that contrasts Western "individual actors" with Japanese "relational actors." He suggests:

> Each culture formulates its own "outlook on man," namely, a definition of the nature of human beings. This intrinsic notion of each society provides a self-evident standard for understanding human nature, allowing members of a particular society to know in what sense people have social existence. In some cultures, for example, there is a firm belief that the fundamental form of human existence consists of separate and independent actors [Western man in Western society], while in other cultures it is taken as the natural state of "people" to mutually depend on others as long as they live in a collectivity [Japan].[41]

In Hamaguchi's Japanese relational scheme, the collectivity eschews individual ego and seeks the sense of the group. Almost like a flock of geese flying in formation or a school of fish darting and turning in unison, the Japanese tend to feel or to sense where the group is moving or what it is thinking. The penchant for conformity, harmony, and smooth interpersonal relations is explained by each of the foregoing views.

Many Americans were discomforted a few years ago with the publication of a book titled *The Japan That Can Say "No."*[42] It contained the thoughts of Morita Akio and Ishihara Shintarō regarding doing business with the United States. Morita was the chairman of Sony, obviously a voice to be reckoned with. The title of the book was most disturbing, sounding like an assault of some kind. However, it dealt with one of Japan's most cherished values—avoiding confrontation. In his chapter titled "Let's Become a Japan That Can Say No," Morita gives his own people a lesson on using the negative:

> It is the rule in the West to say "no" whenever one's position is clearly negative. We are in a business environment where "well" or "probably" have no place in normal business conduct. . . .
>
> My purpose in advocating saying "no" is to promote that awareness. "No" is not the beginning of a disagreement or a serious argument. On the contrary, "no" is the beginning of a new collaboration. If Japan truly says "no" when it means "no" it will serve as a means of improving the US–Japan relationship. . . .
>
> Living in a homogeneous society since childhood, we Japanese have grown up without practical experience in quarreling and fighting in a heterocultural environment. Many of us feel that eventually other people will understand our true feelings on an issue without verbalizing them. . . . Japanese . . . even if they feel that they are not properly understood, remain hopeful that they will eventually be understood or that the truth will reveal itself sooner or later. They do the same with foreigners in foreign countries. They feel that sincerity and effort should automatically be reciprocated. In my mind, this can happen only in Japan, but never in foreign countries. Wordless communication and telepathy will just not happen.[43]

Morita is speaking of business, but his counsel applies as well to all other interpersonal relationships. It is difficult for the Japanese who do not want a *tairitsu* (confrontation) in any setting to communicate with people from more confrontational cultures.

Japanese individuals are psychologically and socially quite different from Americans. Harmony and cooperation far outweigh individual effort and aggressiveness as social virtues. Speaking one's mind is seen as inappropriate behavior. Important life decisions in Japan are seldom made alone. Most Japanese feel a powerful sense of responsibility and loyalty to households, country, religious traditions, ancestors, companies, work groups, school classes, clubs, or teams. To decide to leave established groups and create new relationships is far more difficult for Japanese than for Americans and most Westerners. In his book *City Life in Japan,* Ronald Dore explained how difficult conversion to Christianity can be. He wrote:

> [A] woman who had been to a Catholic Mission School, told how she had been on the verge of conversion at the persuasion of one of the nuns. . . . If the whole family had been converted all would have been well, but for her alone to take the step would have been "selfish". She eventually decided against it. The fact that adherence to the Christian faith to a certain extent isolates the individual from his family by making it impossible for him to participate in the rituals which have the deepest meaning for the family group, is probably the biggest obstacle to conversion.[44]

One area of thought that has received attention in the Japanese press for many years is *Nihonjinron.* The word, which could be translated as "Japanness" or "Japanology," refers to the theory or argument that the Japanese people are unique in literature, language, management, the arts, and, of course, religion. Much of what I have written in this essay fits into this broad genre (or the theory fits this essay). Winston Davis has provided a critical assessment of the characteristics and history of Japan theory in his book *Japanese Religion and Society.* Much of what he says is somewhat condemnatory of some of the theories or studies mentioned previously, particularly their lack of true comparative grounding.[45] For our purposes, however, the fact that the Japanese spend so much effort debating the Nihonjinron issue is an indication of their focus on their own character and the meaning of their lives individually and collectively. The tendency of such discussion to focus the Japanese on their unity makes missionary work difficult among them individually. Nevertheless, faith in Jesus Christ's redemption and the Atonement is an individual decision. Repentance of sins is an individual matter. Becoming a member of the Church is an extremely courageous—and disruptive—act for Japanese, far more so than making the same decision in most other cultures.

The Language Barrier

The most basic cultural challenge that missionaries in Japan face is the language barrier. Francis Xavier purportedly concluded that

Japanese "had been devised by Satan."[46] Centuries have passed and not many have disputed his observation. I am not going to discuss the tedious problem of memorizing thousands of *kanji* (Chinese-style characters), the difficulties of knowing which reading or pronunciation to use for a character in a given context, or how to remember which levels of speech require and fail to require honorifics. Nor do I intend to go into the history of why the same character can be read in different ways depending on the period of time during which its meaning was borrowed from the Chinese. More linguistic exegesis on the perils of Japanese is not needed, but a paper on the difficulties of doing missionary work in Japan would not be complete without a few observations in this area.

Language teachers have established that the common European languages—French, German, Spanish, and Italian—require one-fourth to one-third the amount of formal study that is required to learn Japanese, Chinese, Korean, and Arabic. Catholics and Protestants have assumed the need for many more years of language learning, historical and cultural studies, and extended residence in the country to develop the basic skills necessary to create even a shallow foundation of shared understanding. Latter-day Saints believe that missionaries receive the "gift of tongues," and this fact is readily apparent, especially in those serving in Japan.

From his many years as a Protestant missionary in Japan, Robert Lee believes "language constitutes a barrier to faith." He says:

> One has to understand the Japanese mode of communication, which Westerners might think devious or circuitous, but which actually is subtle, symbolic, and sensitive to feelings. It is pictorial and often hints at meanings rather than expresses them directly. It is not so much a task of logically defining and seeking direct dialogue on the basis of a given definition. Rather it seeks to elicit identity and evoke approval, to assess the other person's feelings. Therefore, a conversation involves not so much being outwitted as outfelt![47]

From a Latter-day Saint perspective, one must question whether even a small number of our elders and sisters attain such a sensitive language level. But without such language skill, how can missionaries have much success? Lee continues:

Even in language there is a heavy aesthetic note. The Japanese language is full of "linguistic rituals". Just as nature instead of revealing can conceal. . . . Not only is there a complex elaboration of honorifics, but special pronouns or verbal inflections are required for superiors, equals, inferiors, intimates, and strangers. The language is so dictated by custom that different phrases and nuances of expressions are used appropriately, depending on the person being addressed, that is, according to his age, status, sex, social standing, degree of friendship established, etc. Entirely different words may be used, or the same phrase varied slightly may be employed, or identical words but a different intonation given, depending upon who is being spoken to. In the Japanese language there are no fewer than twenty expressions alone for the word "I".[48]

Of all the struggles and difficulties placed before our missionaries in Japan, the language may be the greatest single problem.

Conclusion

Latter-day Saint missionaries in Japan have never faced conflicts with the government or with religious liberty, but there has been a subtle foundation of anti-Christian feeling ever since the 1590s. This problem was greater prior to World War II, but it showed itself even at the beginning of the twenty-first century in the feelings of many Japanese who believe that affiliating with a Christian religion would be an act of disloyalty to family, society, and state.

Culturally, the Japanese are the most homogeneous nation in the world. Their appearance, language, cuisine, architecture, social customs, willingness to endure high population density, refusal to accept foreigners into their society, and so on are the most uniform in the world. Fortunately, many of their cultural traits are much in conformity with the gospel of Jesus Christ. Their love of and loyalty to family, group, and nation is admirable if it does not stand in the way of righteous individual choices. The high value they place on harmony and non-confrontation is a quality most Americans could use more of. Appropriate respect for ancestors is beneficial and is compatible with the restored gospel. The general graciousness of Japanese aesthetics and appreciation for nature offers much that any people in the world could appreciate and include in their lives.

The problem is how non-Japanese missionaries can best weave through the various historical and cultural barriers and become part of the network of beliefs and practices that make the Japanese, Japanese. Latter-day Saint missionary success in Japan will have to be founded on an understanding of and appreciation for Japanese culture. Without honest appreciation for the Japanese and their ways of interacting, speaking, and avoiding confrontation, our missionary work will be stymied. Every missionary who wishes to succeed needs a good understanding of how the Japanese think and interact. Language study must be at the heart of any success. The Japanese people have no obligation to learn why the missionaries are there, why they act the way they do, or what they have to say. The burden of appreciation and action is entirely upon the shoulders of the elders and sisters. Until they can understand how Japanese think about religion, missionaries' success will be limited. The Latter-day Saint message is very intrusive and discomforting, and it is likely to bring domestic explosions and major difficulty for those who accept it. It must be delivered in a way that brings trust and comfort.

This leads to one last thought. My heart and admiration go out to the Japanese people who have had the strength and courage to become Latter-day Saints. They deserve all the love and support we can give them. An effort needs to be made to help Japanese Saints re-create their natural social groups as part of their Church affiliation. Everything possible should be done to create cohesive wards and branches and smaller units within these organizations. Branch and ward boundaries should be left intact as long as possible to encourage friendships, group affiliation, and consciousness. In short, I believe the Church must become a safe refuge and a comfortable *ie* for all who would be brave enough to venture into it.

This paper was presented at "A Centennial Celebration: The LDS Church in Japan, 1901–2001," October 13, 2001, Brigham Young University, Provo, Utah.

Notes

1. Jiro Numano, "Mormonism in Modern Japan," *Dialogue: A Journal of Mormon Thought* 29 (Spring 1996): 223.

2. Standard references include C. R. Boxer, *The Christian Century in Japan: 1549-1650* (Berkeley: University of California Press, 1951); George Elison [Jurgis Elisonas], *Deus Destroyed: The Image of Christianity in Early Modern Japan* (Cambridge, Mass.: Harvard University Press, 1993); Richard H. Drummond, *A History of Christianity in Japan* (Grand Rapids, Mich.: William B. Eerdmans, 1971); Endō Shōsaku, *The Final Martyrs* [Stories of early Japanese Christianity], trans. Van C. Gessel (Tokyo: Charles E. Tuttle, 1993); Neil S. Fujita, *Japan's Encounter with Christianity: The Catholic Mission in Pre-Modern Japan* (New York: Paulist Press, 1991); Johannes Laures, *The Catholic Church in Japan* (Rutland, Vt.: Charles E. Tuttle, 1954); and Joseph E. Spae, *Catholicism in Japan: A Sociological Study* (Tokyo: I S R Press, 1964).

3. Van Gessel has identified the most informative passage as follows:

> The Japanese have never had a concept of God, and they never will. . . . [They] do not have the capacity to imagine a god completely divorced from man; the Japanese do not have the ability to conceive of an existence that transcends the human. . . . [They] call any idealized or exalted man a god. . . . In the churches we built throughout this country the Japanese were not praying to the Christian God. They twisted God to their own way of thinking in a way we can never imagine. . . . It is like a butterfly caught in a spider's web. At first it is certainly a butterfly, but the next day only the externals, the wings and the trunk, are those of a butterfly; it has lost its true reality and has become a skeleton. In Japan our God is just like that butterfly caught in the spider's web: only the exterior form of God remains, but it has already become a skeleton with no essence. (Endō Shōsaku, *Silence*, trans. William Johnston [London: Peter Owen, 1976], 240-41)

4. Robert Lee, *The Clash of Civilizations: An Intrusive Gospel in Japanese Civilization* (Harrisburg, Pa.: Trinity Press International, 1999), 27.

5. See Helen Hardacre, "Creating State Shintō: The Great Promulgation Campaign and the New Religions," *The Journal of Japanese Studies* 12 (Winter 1986): 29-63. See also D. C. Holtom, *The National Faith of Japan: A Study in Modern Shinto* (London: Kegan Paul, Trench, Trubner & Co., 1938); and Holtom, *Modern Japan and Shinto Nationalism: A Study of Present-Day Trends in Japanese Religions*, 1943, reprint edition (New York: Praeger Book Reprint Corp., 1963). The best study so far is Hardacre, *Shinto and the State, 1868-1888* (Princeton: Princeton University Press, 1989).

6. T. Fujitani, *Splendid Monarchy: Power and Pageantry in Modern Japan* (Berkeley: University of California Press, 1996), 19.

7. Some of Japan's greatest minds, among them Fukuzawa Yukichi, did not believe Shintō had "an established doctrine" and saw it as "the puppet of Buddhism." The disestablishment of Buddhism was confusing to many Japanese, but in time Shintō ideas were substituted in the minds of most Japanese. See Kuroda Toshio, James C. Dobbins, and Suzanne Gay, "Shinto in the History of Japanese Religion," *Journal of Japanese Studies* 7 (Winter 1981): 1–21; and Hardacre, "Creating State Shintō," 29. For additional information about governmentally sponsored changes to folk Shintō practices, see Winston Davis, *Japanese Religion and Society: Paradigms of Structure and Change* (New York: State University of New York Press, 1992), 237–38.

8. Fujitani, *Splendid Monarchy,* 20.

9. The government's policy toward Christianity began after the Iwakura Mission visited the U.S., and the group sent home word that Western religions should be quietly allowed to practice.

10. The full text of the Rescript is as follows:

> Know ye, Our Subjects:
>
> Our Imperial Ancestors have founded our Empire on a basis broad and everlasting, and have deeply and firmly implanted virtue; Our subjects ever united in loyalty and filial piety have from generation to generation illustrated the beauty thereof. This is the glory of the fundamental character of Our Empire, and herein also lies the source of Our Education. Ye, Our Subjects, be filial to your parents, affectionate to your brothers and sisters; as husbands and wives be harmonious, as friends true; bear yourselves in modesty and moderation; extend your benevolence to all; pursue learning and cultivate arts, and thereby develop intellectual faculties and perfect moral powers; furthermore, advance public good and promote common interests; always respect the Constitution and observe the laws; should emergency arise, offer yourselves courageously to the State; and thus guard and maintain the prosperity of Our Imperial Throne coeval with heaven and earth. So shall ye not only be Our good and faithful subjects, but render illustrious the best traditions of your forefathers.
>
> The Way here set forth is indeed the teaching bequeathed by Our Imperial Ancestors, to be observed alike by Their Descendants and the subjects, infallible for all ages and true in all places. It is Our wish to lay it to heart in all reverence, in common with you, Our subjects, that we may all attain to the same virtue.

The 30th day of the 10th month of the 23rd year of Meiji. (G. B. Sansom, *The Western World and Japan: A Study in the Interaction of European and Asiatic Cultures* [New York: Alfred A. Knopf, 1951], 464)

11. Sansom, *The Western World and Japan*, 465.

12. Joseph M. Kitagawa, *Religion in Japanese History* (New York: Columbia University Press, 1966), 243. See also Tetsunao Yamamori, *Church Growth in Japan: A Study in the Development of Eight Denominations, 1859–1939* (South Pasedena, Calif.: William Carey Library, 1974), 75–76.

13. See R. Lanier Britsch, "Japan: 1901–1924: The Early Japanese Mission," in *From the East: The History of the Latter-day Saints in Asia, 1851–1996* (Salt Lake City: Deseret Book, 1998), 43–70; see also R. Lanier Britsch, "The Closing of the Early Japan Mission," *BYU Studies* 15 (Winter 1975): 171–90, reprinted herein.

14. Kitagawa, *Religion in Japanese History*, 247.

15. J. Christopher Conkling, "Members without a Church: Japanese Mormons in Japan From 1924 to 1948," *BYU Studies* 15 (Winter 1975): 207–9, reprinted herein.

16. Kitagawa, *Religion in Japanese History*, 271–73.

17. The worldwide demand for missionaries was great. Almost all young missionaries had been withdrawn from the mission fields of the world during the war. New opportunities in new lands taxed the Church's ability to exploit the opportunity. Only 400 missionaries were set apart in 1945; 2,297 in 1946; 2,132 in 1947; 2,161 in 1948; 2,363 in 1949; and 3,015 in 1950. See *Deseret News 1999–2000 Church Almanac* (Salt Lake City: Deseret News, 1998), 554.

18. See Numano, "Mormonism in Modern Japan," 223–26.

19. For a detailed recounting of the "Passing of An Emperor", see Lee, *Clash of Civilizations*, 18–20.

20. Chiyozaki Hideo, "The Japanese Emperor System: The Missiological Issue," [English trans. of chap. 1 of *Tennōsei no kenshō: Nihon senkyō ni okeru fukaki no kadai*] (Tokyo: Tokyo Mission Research Institute, 1995), 1.

21. Quoted in Lee, *Clash of Civilizations*, 20–21. See also John Whitney Hall, "A Monarch for Modern Japan," in *Political Development in Modern Japan*, ed. Robert E. Ward (Princeton: Princeton University Press, 1968), 11–64.

22. Quoted in Lee, *Clash of Civilizations*, 22.

23. Stuart D. B. Picken, *Japanese Religion and the 21st Century: Problems and Prospects* (Tokyo: Japan Foundation, 1987), 7.

24. Ishii Kenji, "Aum Shinrikyō," in *Religion in Japanese Culture: Where Living Traditions Meet a Changing World*, ed. Noriyoshi Tamaru and David Reid (Tokyo: Kodansha International, 1996), 209.

25. Seiga Ohmine, "Japan at the End of the World: Why are Religions Often Incompatible with Japanese Society?" student paper, Brigham Young University, April 2000, copy in possession of author.

26. Clifford Geertz, "Religion as a Cultural System," in *Anthropological Approaches to the Study of Religion*, ed. Michael Banton (New York: Frederick A. Praeger, 1966), 3.

27. Edwin O. Reischauer, *The Japanese* (Cambridge, Mass.: Belknap Press of Harvard University Press, 1978), 213.

28. Davis has a useful discussion of this issue in his chapter titled "The Secularization of Japanese Religion," in Davis, *Japanese Religion and Society*, 229–51.

29. Davis, *Japanese Religion and Society*, 253.

30. *1995 Shūkyō nenkan* (Religions yearbook), Ministry of Education, Agency for Cultural Affairs, 30–31, 46–49, in Tamaru and Reid, eds., *Religion in Japanese Culture*, 222–23.

31. Jack Seward, *The Japanese: The Often Misunderstood, Sometimes Surprising, and Always Fascinating Culture and Lifestyles of Japan* (Lincolnwood, Ill.: Passport Books, 1992), 186.

32. Joseph J. Spae, *Christianity Encounters Japan* (Tokyo: Oriens Institute for Religious Research, 1968), 45–46.

33. Reischauer, *The Japanese*, 138.

34. Van Gessel, "For Whom No Bell Tolls: Endō Shōsaku, A Christian Writer in Japan," 15, paper presented at P. A. Christensen Humanities Lecture, Brigham Young University, Provo, Utah, February 8, 1995.

35. Reischauer, *The Japanese*, 139, 141–42. Shame is resolved or done away with through the established ways or mores of a people. It is a social matter, one that can be resolved according to social rules. Sin, on the other hand, is a matter between the individual and God. Clearing up sins is a more complicated matter with less clear resolution.

36. Gessel, "For Whom No Bell Tolls," 13–14.

37. Watsuji Tetsurō, *Climate and Culture*, trans. Geoffrey Bownas, (Tokyō: Mombushō, 1961; reprint, New York: Greenwood Press, 1988), 143–44.

38. Chie Nakane, *Japanese Society* (London: Weidenfeld and Nicolson, 1970), 25–40.

39. Doi Takeo, "Dependency in Human Relationships," in Daniel I. Okimoto and Thomas P. Rohlen, eds., *Inside the Japanese System: Readings on Contemporary Society and Political Economy* (Stanford: Stanford University Press, 1988), 21; see Doi Takeo, *The Anatomy of Dependence*, trans. John Bester (Tokyo: Kodansha International, Ltd., 1973).

40. Reischauer, "The Group," in *The Japanese*, 127–35.

41. Hamaguchi Esyun, Kumon Shumpei, and Mildren R. Creighton, "A Contextual Model of the Japanese: Toward a Methodological Innovation in Japan Studies," *Journal of Japanese Studies* 11 (Summer 1985): 297. Another scholar whose work in this area has been appreciated is S. N. Eisenstadt. See S. N. Eisenstadt, *Japanese Civilization: A Comparative View* (Chicago: University of Chicago Press, 1996).

42. It should be noted here that this well-known title is a literal rendition of the title of the book originally published in Japan by Morita and Ishihara: *"No" to ieru Nihonjin*. It was widely circulated in the United States in a hastily completed, unauthorized translation; several years later Ishihara had a book published in English, also under the title *The Japan That Can Say "No,"* but it contains only Ishihara's writings, which are not identical to his portion of the book published in Japan.

43. Akio Morita and Shintaro Ishihara, *The Japan That Can Say "No"* (Washington, D.C.: The Jefferson Educational Foundation, 1990), 71, 73–74. This is the unauthorized translation mentioned in the previous note.

44. R. P. Dore, *City Life in Japan: A Study of a Tokyo Ward* (Berkeley: University of California Press, 1958), 361.

45. See "Japan Theory and Civil Religion," in Davis, *Japanese Religion and Society*, 253–70.

46. Jack Seward, *The Japanese* (Lincolnwood, Ill.: Passport Books, 1992), 163.

47. Robert Lee, *Stranger in the Land: A Study of the Church in Japan* (London: Lutterworth Press, 1967), 165.

48. Lee, *Stranger in the Land*, 265.

2

The Japan Mission: First Efforts

Reid L. Neilson

Missionary work has been the lifeblood of The Church of Jesus Christ of Latter-day Saints since its organization in 1830. "From its founding Mormonism was designed to be a world faith. Its religious message was intended not for the few, but for the many," observed Latter-day Saint historian Leonard Arrington.[1] The Church's first prophet, Joseph Smith, sent missionaries to spread the gospel throughout the United States and Canada and to parts of Europe. In 1852, his successor, Brigham Young, "motivated by a conviction that the Millennium was imminent," called 108 elders to proselytize throughout the world.[2] These elders traveled to Europe, Gibraltar, South Africa, the West Indies, British Guiana, Siam (Thailand), Hindustan (India), Australia, China, and parts of the United States.

It was not remarkable that Japan was overlooked, because it was closed to the commercial, diplomatic, and religious overtures of the West until 1854.[3] However, from the late 1850s until the turn of the century, there was a series of positive contacts between Japan and the West. Church leaders attempted to send the gospel to Japan, first in 1861 with Walter Murray Gibson and second in 1895 under the direction of Elder Abraham H. Cannon. Both attempts ended in failure—Gibson was excommunicated en route to Japan, and Elder Cannon's efforts ended when he passed away. Finally, in 1901, the First Presidency announced the opening of the Japan Mission and called Elder Heber J. Grant, a member of the Quorum of the Twelve Apostles, to perform the task. Between Gibson's failed mission and Grant's successful opening of the mission, both the Church and Japan became better positioned to commence spreading the gospel. The Church overcame political difficulties at home and became more able to expand. Meanwhile, Japan was developing into a modern nation-state, more receptive to receiving the Church's missionaries.

Japan Opens Its Door to Western Nations

Two hundred years before the Restoration of the gospel in 1830, Japan had closed itself to the broader world. Beginning in 1639, the Tokugawa government introduced a policy of national seclusion, which limited its trade relations solely to China, Korea, and the Netherlands—the Tokugawa government wanted to gain absolute control over its foreign relations and establish the government's internal and external authority. By the early 1800s, this policy of *sakoku* (closed country) had deepened to the point that foreign trade and cultures were essentially closed to the Japanese populace.

Around the end of the eighteenth century, the Dutch were being challenged for supremacy in the Far East as other Western nations began to act on their own colonial ambitions. Russia began sending its ships and men to Hokkaidō in the 1790s, trying to engage in trade with the Japanese. Britain continued to expand its colonial influence into India, Malaysia, and China. These and other outside threats to the isolationist Japanese government seemingly encouraged it to further tighten the control on its borders. In 1825 the Tokugawa government issued its Expulsion Edict, which mandated that foreign ships coming close to its shores would be fired upon.

By the middle of the nineteenth century, the United States also turned its attention to the Far East. In 1852, President Millard Fillmore sent Commodore Matthew C. Perry to Japan with the goal of opening diplomatic and commercial relations. In July 1853, Perry and his fleet initiated the U.S.'s first direct contact with Japan by sailing into Edo Bay, now Tokyo Bay. His visit and demands for treaty relations were received with mixed reactions from various political factions festering in the closed country. The following February, Perry returned with a larger naval fleet to coerce the Tokugawa government to sign a treaty to normalize relations. Made official March 31, 1854, at Kanagawa, the treaty required Japan to open two of its ports—Shimoda and

Hakodate—to American ships and trade and to allow an American consular agent to live in Shimoda. In following years, Japanese officials entered into similar agreements with several European nations. Japan's era of national seclusion had ended.[4]

For the U.S. government and its navy, Perry's success in Japan was but another confirmation of America's growing power. To the Latter-day Saints, however, the diplomatic opening of Japan suggested something very different. In September 1854 the *Millennial Star,* the Church's British periodical, featured an article entitled "Opening of Japan." Part of it read:

> To us, as Latter-day Saints, this treaty with Japan has more important interests connected with it than the mere interest of trade, or the temporary policy of nations. It takes hold of futurity, and has an important bearing on the salvation of the inhabitants of that country.

Many believed the Lord was "at work in His own way, breaking down the barriers" between nations, "pleading with them by His judgments" and "preparing the way for His servants to go forth to declare the glad tidings of salvation."[5]

On March 22, 1857, Brigham Young announced that Japan would soon be opened to Latter-day Saint missionaries. "We have got to send men to the Islands to liberate those who are there," Young was reported to have said. "We would gather the saints from there but the Japanese laws are against it."[6]

Within a year, President Young's statement about the opening of Japan began to be realized. In 1858, American Consul Townsend Harris negotiated and expanded upon the provisions of the earlier Kanagawa Treaty. Known as the Harris Treaty, it stipulated the opening of Edo, Kobe, Nagasaki, Niigata, and Yokohama to foreign trade, placed Japanese tariffs under international control, fixed import duties at low levels, and established extraterritoriality for foreign residents living in Japan. Most importantly for the Church, the treaty allowed the reintroduction of Christianity into Japan, though initially only for the benefit of foreign nationals living in Japan. Soon, other Western powers demanded similar treaties. These unequal treaties, called the Ansei commercial treaties, plagued the Tokugawa's domestic and international power by demoting Japan into a "semi-colonial status."[7]

Elder Wilford Woodruff saw gospel opportunities in these new treaties with Japan. In his journal he wrote, "Europe & America have made liberal treaties with China & Jappan which have opened their ports to the trade, Commerce & intercourse with the whole world which have been heretofore entirely Closed up for thousands of Generations."[8] Elder Woodruff realized that proselytizing possibilities might follow diplomatic and commercial agreements.

The first recorded contact between the Latter-day Saints and the Japanese occurred in 1858 when William Wood, a twenty-one-year-old member of the British Navy, sailed from Hong Kong to Japan. His ship, HMS *Retribution,* had been ordered to escort a "beautiful yacht" that the British had specially built as a gift for the emperor of Japan to encourage better relations between the two nations. Arriving at Yokohama, the British presented their maritime gift, and Wood had the opportunity to walk among the Japanese. "I discerned a remarkable spirit of reform in them; more so than in any people I had met," he said. "I felt a desire to preach the Gospel to them."[9]

Wood went back to Britain, never to return to Japan. Subsequently, he immigrated to Utah, served colonizing missions to Arizona and Canada, and later served a proselytizing mission to his native England. Yet despite these events and the passage of time, Japan still held a special place in Wood's heart. He recorded, "I have thought it possible that I was the first Mormon to visit Japan, and this increased my desire to present the Gospel to them." Wood continued:

> Years after, when I had gathered to Zion and had been ordained a Seventy, this feeling increased in my mind so much that in my prayers I often mentioned it. However, it was some years before the door for the Gospel was opened by Apostle Grant to the Japanese people, and I had become an old man.[10]

Although William Wood was likely the first Church member to come in contact with the Japanese, others soon followed—some with similar proselytizing ambitions and one with more personal ambitions.

Walter Murray Gibson in Asia and the South Pacific

Perhaps the Church's most colorful and bizarre attempt to contact the Japanese began in 1860 when Walter Murray Gibson (illus. 2-1) met with religious leaders in Salt Lake City. As a boy, Gibson had heard enchanting tales of the Far East. "The spirit of adventure, to see strange people and far-off countries, sprang up in me. . . . I felt a longing to go to sea." Growing into manhood, he "looked forth toward the Pacific, and thought of early plans of fortune and renown as [he] looked on the pathway to the East." A doer as well as a dreamer, Gibson traveled to the island of Sumatra in the Dutch-controlled East Indian Archipelago in 1852 and impetuously offered to help its inhabitants overthrow their colonial masters. Dutch officials discovered his plan and charged him with treason.[11]

Escaping incarceration, Gibson fled to the safety of the United States and filed a claim against the Dutch government. While his legal petition was languishing in the halls of the U.S. Congress, Gibson met John M. Bernhisel, a Church member representing the Territory of Utah in its claim for statehood. When Bernhisel spoke passionately about the persecutions of the Saints and their recent conflict with the U.S. government—the so-called Utah War—Gibson devised a new self-serving South Seas plan: perhaps he could help the Mormons find peace by relocating them to the islands of New Guinea. His enthusiasm renewed, Gibson traveled to Salt Lake City to meet Brigham Young. While rejecting Gibson's entreaty, President Young did encourage him to begin an investigation of the Church. Gibson was baptized January 15, 1860, by Heber C.

Courtesy Church Archives, The Church of Jesus Christ of Latter-day Saints

Illus. 2-1. Walter Murray Gibson. In 1861, Gibson left Salt Lake City with the intent of founding a Japanese mission; he made it only as far as the Sandwich Islands (Hawaii).

Kimball. Three months later, Church authorities called him on a mission to the eastern United States.[12]

While serving his new church on the East Coast, Gibson met several Japanese officials.[13] Gibson falsely reported to Church leaders that he was able to converse in the Japanese tongue, and he was invited to visit Japan as a missionary. In a letter dated July 1, 1860, he shared his newly created vision of Church expansion in Japan and Oceania with President Young. "Japan with her 30 millions of souls opens a great field for the missionary labor of the Saints," he wrote. "I have faith that a wonderful work will be accomplished there, but I doubt not that the Spirit of God will enlighten you as to the right time, when it shall be commenced. . . . Dear brother, I long to be engaged in this work; but I will be obedient unto your dictation."[14]

In November 1860, Gibson returned to Utah and again sought permission to carry the gospel to Japan, China, the East Indies (India), and the Malay Islands.[15] Later that month, he and President Young shared the Old Tabernacle pulpit in Salt Lake City. Gibson expressed his excitement of going "forth with a message of life and salvation to the dark and benighted people of the Eastern hemisphere." In turn, President Young announced that he had given Gibson authority "to negotiate with all the nations of the world who would obey the gospel of Christ."[16] Afterward, Young and his counselors in the First Presidency issued Gibson an official missionary certificate to be presented as credentials to the "Illustrious and Renowned Potentate His Imperial Majesty the Tycoon of Niphon," the Emperor of Japan.[17] The document may be viewed as the first official act toward the creation of the Church's Japan Mission.

Armed with his ecclesiastical commission and filled with personal ambition, Gibson left Salt Lake City for California, where he boarded a ship bound for the Sandwich (Hawaiian) Islands. He arrived in the islands June 30, 1861. Seeing the advantages offered in Hawaii, Gibson aborted his wider ecclesiastical commission for life in the mid-Pacific. A series of Gibson's intrigues and misrepresentations convinced the untutored Hawaiian Saints—bereft of Church leadership due to the recalling of missionaries to Salt Lake City during the recent Utah War—to look to him as their spiritual shepherd. He girded himself in a white robe, forced the natives to enter his presence on hands and knees, and declared the island of Lanai the true Zion and the future site of a great temple. In 1864 elders from Utah returned to the Sandwich Islands to excommunicate Gibson. Clearly Gibson was not the anticipated messenger of "life and salvation" to the Japanese or to the other "dark and benighted people of the Eastern hemisphere."[18] Thus, the first attempt to preach the gospel in Japan died abruptly.

Japan Encounters the American West and the Mormons

Four years after Gibson was excommunicated, political changes in Japan further relaxed its relationship with the West. Having been pressured to sign the unequal treaties with the United States and other foreign powers, the Tokugawa government had dramatically weakened its already tenuous authority in Japan and abroad. In time the revolutionary Choshu and Satsuma samurai domains grew in power and ultimately joined forces to overthrow the Tokugawa government in January 1868. They replaced the Tokugawa government with the fifteen-year-old emperor Mutsuhito, later known as the Meiji Emperor. After two and a half centuries, the Tokugawa regime was supplanted.[19]

This "Meiji Restoration," as it was called, increased Japan's openness to the West. One of the bright stars of the new imperial government was a Choshu samurai, Itō Hirobumi. In 1863 members of his faction sent him to England to study. His experiences there exposed him to the force of economic industrialization and to the technological superiority of the West and converted him to a policy of Westernization. Upon returning to Japan, Itō, a junior councilor in the Meiji government, was initially responsible for foreign affairs.

In 1870, Itō was sent to the United States to study American currency, politics, and business practices.[20] Traveling on the transcontinental railroad from San Francisco to Washington, Itō changed trains in Ogden, Utah. Angus M. Cannon, business manager of the *Deseret News* who was also President of the Salt Lake Stake and brother of Elder George Q. Cannon, happened to board the same train. A train conductor introduced the curious newspaperman to Itō.

Soon the two men were engaged in "interesting conversation, each interviewing and being interviewed." Years later, Cannon described Itō as a "bright, earnest and interesting character who absorbed information as a sponge does water." Cannon also noted that Itō seemed proud of his fellow countrymen and their recent advancements as a modern nation. According to Itō, the Japanese were the "equals if not the superiors" of the Chinese as a society. When the conversation turned to religion, Itō "exhibited a lively interest" in the history of the Church. Before they separated in Omaha, Nebraska, Itō asked his Latter-day Saint companion for more information about his religion.[21] This chance meeting of Cannon and Itō would prove important in the formation of the Church leader's impression of Japan and vice versa.

Back in Japan, Itō was selected to accompany another Meiji government delegation, this one to tour the United States, Europe, and Russia, as well as Malaya, Indochina, and Hong Kong. This Iwakura Mission—with forty-nine official members and nearly sixty attendants—was the largest and most important Japanese delegation ever to leave Japan, and Itō was one of its most important members.[22] Through these efforts, the Meiji government hoped to display its power so it would be positioned to renegotiate the earlier Ansei commercial treaties. Moreover, the Meiji government wanted to know how to organize its military and its educational system. As one historian summarized the concerns of the Iwakura Mission: "Did Japan need to alter its culture and its class system, or did these need to be discarded altogether in its quest for modernization?"[23]

The Iwakura Mission embarked from Yokohama on December 23, 1871. Arriving in San Francisco, members of the mission boarded a train for Washington, D.C. However, near Ogden, Utah, snowstorms temporarily blocked the mountain railway passes and the delegation could not proceed. While stranded in Utah, the Japanese were given tours of Salt Lake City and were exposed to the Latter-day Saints and their culture. The embassy entered the newly completed Mormon Tabernacle, toured a local museum, and viewed the foundation of the Salt Lake Temple. They visited with members of the Utah Territorial Legislature, the Utah Supreme Court, and Church President Brigham Young. Moreover, the Japanese observed the territorial military, assessed the local educational system, and attended numerous receptions and banquets prepared by their Utah hosts. Several delegates even attended Latter-day Saint religious services.[24]

Nineteen days after the delegation's arrival to Utah, the snows melted sufficiently to allow the travelers to continue their journey. Over the next two years the delegates visited the principal cities of America's eastern coast and traveled throughout the nations of Europe. The group was exposed to the world's most advanced nations and determined to Westernize Japan. While traveling, they also became aware of how their anti-Christian policies might thwart their entrance into the modern political world, and they thereby sent messages back to Japan recommending the removal of anti-Christian edicts. Thus, by February 1873, Christians and Christian missionaries were at least nominally accepted in Japan.[25]

Upon the delegation's return, government officials read the massive report and implemented more of its suggestions. The Japanese began adopting new technology and institutions by hiring over three thousand foreign advisors throughout the Meiji Period. All things Western, including Christianity, became objects of curious investigation by the Japanese. Thus, the years between 1873 and 1889 were the golden era of Christian progress in modern Japan. Unfortunately for the Church and its missionary program, Latter-day Saint expansion into Japan during these years was subordinate to the pioneer settlement of the Great Basin, federal prosecution of polygamy, and Utah territory's quest for statehood.

The Church Becomes Friendly with Japan

Of particular importance to the eventual opening of the Japan Mission were the opinions about the Iwakura Mission formed by Elders Lorenzo Snow and Angus M. Cannon and President George Q. Cannon (illus. 2-2). Snow, then president of the Utah territorial legislature and later President of the Church, was particularly impressed by the Japanese delegation. Nearly three decades later he acknowledged that the Iwakura Mission had made a lasting impression and was a catalyst for sending elders to Japan. "This is how the thought [of the Japan Mission] originated with me," Snow recalled:

> When I was president of the Legislative council . . . a party of distinguished officials of the Japanese government [Iwakura Mission] visited Salt Lake enroute to Washington from their own country. . . . They expressed a great deal of interest in Utah and the manner in which it has been settled by the Mormons. Our talk was altogether very pleasant and they expressed considerable wonderment as to

why we had not sent missionaries to Japan. That, together with the knowledge that they are a progressive people has remained with me until the present time, and while it may not be the actuating motive in attempting to open a mission there now, it probably had something to do with it.[26]

The visit of the Iwakura Mission gave Angus M. Cannon the opportunity to renew his friendship with Itō.[27] "I recognized him at once and his recognition of me was just as prompt," Cannon recalled. Members of Itō's party "marveled at the familiarity that Itō showed concerning our faith and people, adding that his knowledge seemed much more extensive in this particular than that of most Americans."[28] George Q. Cannon—editor of the *Juvenile Instructor* and later a member of the First Presidency—also formed a positive opinion of the Japanese. Cannon believed that the Iwakura Mission's visit to Utah was providential:

Illus. 2-2. George Q. Cannon. During the last three decades of the nineteenth century, Elder George Q. Cannon was an advocate for opening a mission in Japan.

Courtesy Church Archives, The Church of Jesus Christ of Latter-day Saints

> However great the importance that others may attach to this movement, it possesses a deep significance to the members of the [Church] than it possibly can to any other class, for in it they are preparing the way for the accomplishment of His purposes and the spread of His gospel. . . . It is perhaps not hazarding too much to say that the visit of the Japanese Embassy to Salt Lake . . . is the fore-runner of measures which may, at some future day, be the cause of some of the youth who read this article being sent as missionaries to Japan.[29]

The Iwakura Mission delegates were not the only Asian visitors in Salt Lake City. Utahns watched Japanese visitors' activities with fascination. For example, one year earlier, in 1870, Utahns had their first glimpse of Japanese popular culture when the Royal Satsuma Japanese Troupe performed acrobatics in Salt Lake City—the same year as Itō's first visit.[30]

Over the next three decades, George Q. Cannon became a strong advocate for the establishment of a Japan Mission. His *Juvenile Instructor* magazine played a major role in preparing the way. For example, during the 1870s alone, Cannon's publication printed nine articles on Japan,[31] and when describing Japan, Cannon often included encouraging words about the country being a possible missionary labor. "It is not too much to expect that Western customs and the Christian religion will in a few years gain such a foothold in Japan that the folly of idol worship will be entirely unknown amongst its highly intelligent people," said one article.[32] Similarly, another article, "A Country Scene in Japan," had these words:

> It is probable that the next few years will effect a still greater improvement in that country, as quite a number of young men from Japan are being educated in the United States, who, of course, will carry home with them American ideals of living. . . . It is possible they will modify their laws so as to admit of the gospel being preached there, as it will certainly be at some future time.[33]

During the 1880s, the *Juvenile Instructor* featured an additional eleven articles on the subject.[34] Convinced of the fruits of the gospel, Cannon wrote, "We firmly believe that Japan will yet be successfully visited by the Elders of our Church, and that from that race thousands of obedient souls will yet be gathered to swell the multitudes of those who shall be called to Zion."[35]

Contemporary events in Japan seemed to bolster Cannon's sentiments and warrant further comment. By the mid-1880s, the Asian balance of power was shifting. "Of all the Asiatic nations perhaps Japan is making the greatest strides at the present time in the way of education and an adoption of the inventions and discoveries of modern times," the *Juvenile Instructor* printed. "The people of this empire are unquestionably more progressive than their neighbors the Chinese, and the interest that is now being taken in that people by civilized nations is very great."[36]

While Japan continued to Westernize, Church leaders determined to rekindle missionary work in another Far Eastern country, India, where the work had been abandoned in the 1850s.[37] In 1884, William Willes, George Booth, Henry F. McCune, and Milson Pratt traveled from Salt Lake City to San Francisco, where they boarded the *City of New York* bound for India via Japan. While onboard, Willes broke up an argument between a drunken crewmember and Ishiye K., an English-speaking Japanese Christian. Grateful to Willes, Ishiye manifested kind feelings to the four Latter-day Saints. In response, Willes and his companions preached to Ishiye during their voyage. They read to him Joseph Smith's history, shared with him passages from John Jaques's *Book of References*, and presented him with a copy of the works of Orson Pratt. Willes recorded his hopes for Ishiye: "He is very much at home with us. Very much the gentlemen and speaks fluently in educated English: his complexion is quite fair, and has an Israelitish appearance." Willes continued, "I pray my Eternal Father that he will yield obedience to His commandments, and be the opening power for converting millions of his countrymen."[38]

Ishiye seemed receptive and offered to introduce the elders to the Japanese people if they were ever to return to Yokohama.[39] He also taught the elders about Japan and informed them about proselytizing prospects, disclosing that all religious teachers were under the protection of the Japanese government. Furthermore, Ishiye promised to "obtain light from heaven" regarding his own baptism. Once convinced of the truthfulness of the gospel, he promised he would "not hesitate a moment" to join. He also offered to have "a favorable mention made" of the Church in Japanese newspapers,[40] and he invited the elders to return to Japan as his guests the following year.[41]

When the *City of New York* arrived in Yokohama, the elders disembarked and visited with several expatriate Americans. They learned that while Japan was open to Christianity, it was still "very much hampered with restrictions that are galling to free Americans." For example, while Westerners were free to move about the coastal foreign settlement ports, they were forced to travel with Japanese guides throughout the interior of Japan. Undaunted, Willes penned a letter to George Q. Cannon and described his recent experiences and impressions of Japan: "All with whom I have conversed are agreed that the

Japanese are a superior race to the Chinese, which fills me with hope that some day the Lord will call many of them to be Saints."[42] After posting his letter, Willes and his companions continued their voyage to India, never to return to Japan. Willes's journals are silent on whether Ishiye did later "obtain light from heaven."

Elder Abraham H. Cannon's Role in the Japan Mission

As historian Kenneth B. Pyle has argued, "For the quarter of a century preceding 1890 Japan had passed through a time of unprecedented ferment, a time of experimentation and groping, as it sought to reorient its institutions to the realities of the international order into which it was so suddenly thrust."[43] Many Japanese intellectuals and leaders felt that Japan had gone too far in adopting Western ways at the expense of Japanese culture and tradition. The Meiji government sensed this growing discontent and sought to unify their nation with an imperial ideology.

To gain support for their modern Japanese state, government officials "resorted to the traditional language of loyalty and obligation and drew on a mythical past to yield a distinctive national ideology."[44] As a result, the government institutionalized State Shintō and issued the Imperial Rescript on Education in 1890. This document declared in Confucian terms the Emperor as the father of Japan and his subjects his children. As a result, wrote Joseph A. Kitagawa, "Christianity came under severe attack as an unpatriotic religion."[45] The golden era of Western Christianity was over in Japan.

Meanwhile, after issuing the Manifesto of 1890 that formally declared an end to the practice of plural marriage in the United States (and thus enjoying the subsequent decline in federal prosecution), Church leaders looked abroad for missionary opportunities. Thanks in part to seven additional articles published in the *Juvenile Instructor* in the 1890s, Japan was still positioned in the forefront of the Saints' international conscience.[46] In 1893 an author of one of the seven articles predicted the gospel would soon reach Japan:

> The day is not far distant when the gospel of the Lord Jesus Christ will be introduced among this intelligent and progressive people. The door is already open for admission, at least in a limited extent, and greater opportunities for the promulgation of truth will gradually be

provided until the extreme limits of the empire shall be reached by the Elders who may be sent as representatives of the Church.[47]

Although Christianity was falling rapidly out of favor in Japan, the country was increasingly viewed as a progressive nation and an emerging world power. This provided the Meiji government the leverage to renegotiate the inequalities of the earlier Harris and Ansei commercial treaties. Furthermore, Japan displayed its military might when it shocked the world by crushing China during the Sino-Japanese War of 1895.[48] George Q. Cannon editorialized:

> Among the many surprising events which have occurred of late there is nothing that has aroused the attention of the world equal to the success of the Japanese in their recent war with China. . . . [M]any have entertained the opinion that they were inferior in many respects to the Chinese. . . . In this contest, however, they have exhibited qualities that have called forth the respect and admiration of the nations of Europe.[49]

Growing economic interests at this time fortuitously coincided with the Saints' economic interests. The Church was able to negotiate a second attempt to open the Japan Mission, which again failed. During the economically trying 1890s, Church leaders tried to improve Utah's economy:[50] in 1895, Elder Abraham H. Cannon[51] (illus. 2-3) and his fellow leaders decided to exploit Utah coal and iron deposits, expand railroad infrastructure throughout the territory, and construct a regional railroad from Salt Lake City to Los Angeles.[52] They named their proposed route the

Courtesy Church Archives, The Church of Jesus Christ of Latter-day Saints

Illus. 2-3. Abraham H. Cannon. In 1895, Elder Cannon proposed to Church leaders a plan for a railroad linking Utah with San Diego making it easier for missionaries to reach ships bound for Japan.

Utah and California Railroad.[53] Once the projected tracks were laid, it was hoped, the Saints would benefit by shipping coal and coke from Cedar City and Coalville to southern California at a fraction of its current cost.[54]

Elder Cannon's coal and railroad dream was partially shared by Robert Brewster Stanton, a California mining promoter. Years earlier, Stanton researched whether a "water-level railroad" could be built along the Colorado River from Grand Junction, Colorado, south to the Gulf of California or from Yuma, Arizona, west to his hometown of San Diego, California. When he learned that the route to San Diego was possible, however, he lacked financing. Stanton began promoting a smaller railroad from the Virgin River down the Colorado River to Yuma, Arizona, and then west to San Diego.[55] In 1895, Stanton met Cannon and proposed a merger of their railroad dreams. He confided that the Japanese government was then selecting a Pacific seaport for its country's expanding trade and national shipping line. According to Stanton, the Japanese favored San Diego. Would Church leaders be interested in constructing a railroad linking San Diego and the lucrative coal deposits of Utah?

Stanton's proposal offered the Church temporal and spiritual opportunity: the new railroad might simultaneously improve Utah's depressed economy and open the door for Latter-day Saint missionaries in Japan. On August 8, 1895, Elder Cannon shared Stanton's proposal with the First Presidency and the Quorum of the Twelve. Elder Heber J. Grant, who as a member of the Twelve was present, reported that the business proposal was discussed but the Japan Mission question postponed.[56] Although the discussion was delayed, Elder Grant, at the time, appears to have believed he might lead the mission.[57]

Elder Cannon later traveled to San Francisco to meet Stanton and his associate Walter Smith. Smith, the *San Francisco Chronicle*'s war correspondent in the Sino-Japanese War, had been assigned to the Japanese commander-in-chief. In this capacity he had learned of the Japanese government's business plans. Cannon recorded:

> Mr. Smith feels sure that we could induce the great Japanese steamship company, Nippon Yusen Kisha [sic] to make San Diego its American terminus, providing we can assure them that a railway will be built to that place which will have connection with the eastern

part of the United States. If such a connection can be made it will be very successful in a financial way.[58]

Stanton and Smith next introduced Cannon to Koya Saburo, the Japanese consul. Cannon reported that "[Koya] received us cordially. . . . He seemed a little reserved at first but gradually warmed up, and spoke freely on railway and other matters."[59] Koya was familiar with the Church and with Utah, having previously traveled to Salt Lake City and read the Iwakura Mission's positive account of their short stay. He was also aware that Itō Hirobumi, the current Japanese prime minister, was impressed with the Saints.

Elder Cannon took this opportunity to broach the subject of sending Mormon missionaries to Japan. He reported:

> Mr. Koya thought it very probable that we might secure permission to preach the Gospel in Japan without any government interference; in fact his people are anxious to hear the Christian religion proclaimed, as they have an idea that the success of the English-speaking people is due to their language and their religion.

Koya suggested something else that seemed to offer a favorable prospect: the recently negotiated Anglo-Japanese Treaty established that in 1899 "all the ports as well as the interior of Japan [would] be thrown open to the commerce of the world." Finally, Koya disclosed that the Japanese parliament was going to meet soon to allocate the Chinese war indemnity. The Japanese navy would be strengthened first, but the government also planned to expand the Nippon Yusen Kaisha shipping line. To further this last goal, Koya suggested that his government was indeed interested in San Diego and invited Cannon to attend sessions of the Japanese parliament to be held the following month.[60]

Elder Cannon returned to Utah optimistic about both missionary and business plans. Within a week, he dictated a report to Church leaders who expressed a "very strong" feeling that a member of the Twelve should soon open Japan to missionary labor "at no distant day."[62] Attending the Salt Lake Fifth Ward, Cannon spoke "for about an hour on the missionary work . . . and the opening which seems now to [the Church] offered by Japan."[62] Continuing his enthusiasm, Cannon wrote an article in the Church periodical *Contributor* that expressed the growing hope of Church leaders to open Japan to proselytizing.

"The authorities of the Church," he wrote, "have of late had their minds more or less exercised in regard to Japan as [a] country in which the Gospel might be profitably preached." He shared Koya's sentiments that "Japan would warmly welcome our Elders to labor as missionaries among the people" and that "any reluctance on our part to send missionaries to Japan for fear of the disastrous consequences, could be easily removed by our application to the parliament and ministers for permission to preach the Gospel."[63]

Although Cannon did not travel to Japan to lobby the Utah-California Railroad with members of the Japanese parliament, he and his partners nevertheless moved forward with the project and by the following summer "appeared ready for success."[64] The partners retained engineer Henry Maxwell McCartney to make financial estimates and a final survey. However, their plans were derailed by the intervention of James J. Hill, owner of the Great Northern Railroad. Hill, also seeking an Asian steamship partner to complement his railroad empire, proposed Seattle—instead of San Diego—to the Japanese government as a port for the *Nippon Yusen Kaisha*.[65] Unfortunately for the Cannon-Stanton proposal, Japanese leaders accepted Hill's proposal on July 11, 1896.[66] To compound the setback, eight days later Elder Cannon passed away. The plans for the Utah-California Railroad and the Japan Mission expired as President Wilford Woodruff and other Church leaders soon focused their attention on more pressing political issues,[67] and later that year Utah finally achieved statehood.

President Lorenzo Snow's Administration and the Japan Mission

President Woodruff died September 2, 1898. Days later the Quorum of the Twelve sustained eighty-four-year-old Lorenzo Snow as the fifth President of the Church (illus. 2-4). President Snow selected George Q. Cannon and Joseph F. Smith as counselors.[68] President Snow's administration was marked by the Church's improving financial position and higher international profile.

At the time of President Snow's sustaining, the Church owed an almost overwhelming $2.3 million to creditors. This debt was the result of the U.S. government's seizure and mismanagement of Church property during the antipolygamy Edmunds-Tucker Act episode and due to

Illus. 2-4. Lorenzo Snow. During the administration of President Snow, the Church leaders increased their attention toward Japan.

debt-financed public work projects in the 1890s. Seeking a solution to the difficulty, President Snow toured the settlements of southern Utah in 1899 and was inspired to reemphasize the paying of tithes. By the time of his death in 1901, the Church's financial position had improved dramatically and a mission to Japan was financially feasible.[69]

During President Snow's administration, the Church became better prepared to enter Japan organizationally as well. "After the financial difficulties of the church were put in the way of adjustment [President Snow's] mind seemed to revert to this world-wide extension idea of the gospel," wrote Church historian B. H. Roberts.[70] As the Church entered the twentieth century, it had 283,765 members, 967 wards and branches, 43 stakes, and 4 temples, and these were almost entirely U.S. based.[71] Hundreds of missionaries served in thirteen missions, the majority of which were located in the United States. Desiring to expand internationally, President Snow increased attention on foreign nations and regions such as Russia, Austria, South America—and Japan.[72] To President Snow, the central responsibility of the members of the Quorum of the Twelve was "to warn the nations of the earth and prepare the world for the coming of the Savior," not to overly busy themselves with stake and ward duties, which were the responsibilities of stake presidents and bishops.[73]

By summer 1900, the ill and weakening President Snow was increasingly dependent upon the administrative skills of George Q. Cannon, who believed that the Church should review and possibly reallocate its missionary resources. As historian Davis Bitton pointed out, "The golden days of the early mass conversions seemed to be over."[74] To combat this decline, Cannon drafted a resolution outlining a new missionary course:

> That our policy be to stop sending Elders to the Southern States and Great Britain, unless it be in cases where Elders are specifically needed; and that in those and other English-speaking countries where our Elders are in too great numbers, we reduce the number; and that the Elders, where they were laboring in places without results, be encouraged to push into new fields.[75]

This new policy had important consequences for Latter-day Saint missionary work in the South Pacific and Pacific Rim region, which included Japan. Although elders in the Pacific and Asia areas represented only a tiny portion of the Church's missionary force, clearly the Church was taking more notice of the region.[76]

Finally, on February 14, 1901, during a weekly meeting of the First Presidency and the Quorum of the Twelve Apostles, George Q. Cannon, on behalf of President Lorenzo Snow, stated that it was the mind of the First Presidency to open the Japan Mission with Elder Heber J. Grant as its first president. Church leaders had learned that Elder Grant was free from "financial embarrassments" and was hoping to fulfill a long-considered apostolic tour of the world. In light of his situation, they felt it appropriate that he preside over the new Japan Mission and fulfill his proper role as an Apostle to the nations.[77] Although it had been discussed before that Elder Grant would lead the missionary work in Japan and Grant himself had been impressed he would lead the mission, he was nevertheless surprised by the timing and suddenness of his call, which he accepted without hesitation. The wishes and heartfelt prayers of William Wood, Angus M. Cannon, Lorenzo Snow, George Q. Cannon, William Willes, Abraham H. Cannon, and many others were answered with the creation of the Japan Mission.

An earlier version of this article appeared as Reid L. Neilson, "The Japanese Missionary Journals of Elder Alma O. Taylor, 1901–10" (master's thesis, Brigham Young University, 2001; BYU Studies and Joseph Fielding Smith Institute for Latter-day Saint History, 2001), chapter 2.

Notes

1. Leonard J. Arrington, "Historical Development of International Mormonism," *Religious Studies and Theology* 7 (January 1987): 9.
2. Eugene E. Campbell, *Establishing Zion: The Mormon Church in the American West, 1847–1869* (Salt Lake City: Signature Books, 1988), 174.
3. For a history of early Latter-day Saint missionary efforts in Asia, see R. Lanier Britsch, *From the East: The History of the Latter-day Saints in Asia, 1851–1996* (Salt Lake City: Deseret Book, 1998), 8–42.
4. Kenneth B. Pyle, *The Making of Modern Japan* (Lexington, Mass.: D. C. Heath and Company, 1996), 57–60.
5. "Opening of Japan," *Millennial Star* 16 (September 2, 1854): 552.
6. Wilford Woodruff, *Wilford Woodruff's Journal, 1833–1898, Typescript*, ed. Scott G. Kenney, 9 vols. (Midvale, Utah: Signature Books, 1985), March 22, 1857, 5:41. Brigham Young used the word "liberate" to refer to spiritual darkness; he hoped the Japanese would receive gospel teachings and ordinances.
7. Pyle, *The Making of Modern Japan*, 65.
8. Woodruff, *Journal*, December 31, 1858, 5:263. Two years earlier, on November 18, 1856, Elder Woodruff recorded, "I spent the evening in reading Comodore Perrys visit to Jappan."
9. "William Wood—Pioneer," in *Our Pioneer Heritage*, comp. Kate B. Carter (Salt Lake City: Daughters of Utah Pioneers, 1970), 13:264. See also William G. Hartley, "Adventures of a Young British Seaman, 1852–1862," *New Era* 10 (March 1980): 38–47.
10. "William Wood—Pioneer," 13:264.
11. Jacob Adler and Gwynn Barrett, eds., *The Diaries of Walter Murray Gibson, 1886, 1887* (Honolulu: The University Press of Hawaii, 1973), ix–x.
12. Jacob Adler and Robert M. Kamins, *The Fantastic Life of Walter Murray Gibson: Hawaii's Minister of Everything* (Honolulu: University of Hawaii Press, 1986), 45–46.
13. Woodruff, *Journal*, November 4, 1860, 5:515.
14. Adler and Kamins, *Life of Walter Murray Gibson*, 48.
15. Brigham Young Office Journals—Excerpts, 1853–62, November 13, 1860, New Mormon Studies CD-ROM (Smith Research Associates, 1998).
16. Adler and Kamins, *Life of Walter Murray Gibson*, 49. Wilford Woodruff also recorded the event: "In the afternoon Capt Walter M Gibson . . . spoke followed by President Brigham Young. Brother Gibson said that He was about to take another mission. Was going to Jappan, Siam, & the Malay Islands. He has had an invitation by the Historian of Jappan to visit that Land. Is intimately acquainted with the King of Siam & has been Strongly invited by the princes & Chiefs of the Malay Islands to visit them. He seems to have been raised up as an

instrument in the Hands of God to open the way among those Nations for the receptions of the gospel." Woodruff, *Journal*, November 18, 1860, 5:519.

17. Brigham Young Office Journals, November 20, 1860.

18. For a further treatment of Gibson's activities and interaction with the Latter-day Saints, see R. Lanier Britsch, *Moramona: The Mormons in Hawaii* (Laie, Hawaii: Institute for Polynesian Studies, 1989), 50–58 and Adler, *Life of Walter Murray Gibson*, 44–68.

19. Pyle, *The Making of Modern Japan*, 71.

20. "Itō Hirobumi," *Japan: An Illustrated Encyclopedia* (Tokyo: Kodansha, 1993), 1:637.

21. "Opening of a Mission in Japan," *Deseret News*, April 6, 1901, 9.

22. For a treatment of the Iwakura Mission's stay in Salt Lake City, see Wendy Butler, "The Iwakura Mission and Its Stay in Salt Lake City," *Utah Historical Quarterly* 66 (Winter 1998): 26–47, reprinted herein.

23. Butler, "The Iwakura Mission," 29.

24. See Butler, "The Iwakura Mission," 24–47.

25. Britsch, *From the East*, 47.

26. "Opening of a Mission in Japan," 9.

27. When the Japan Mission was opened in 1901, Cannon provided letters of introduction for Heber J. Grant to meet Itō, who was then prime minister. However, the anticipated Grant-Itō meeting likely never happened due to pressures from other Christian missionaries living in Tokyo. "Opening of a Mission in Japan," 9; Alma O. Taylor, Journal, October 19, 1909, L. Tom Perry Special Collections, Harold B. Lee Library, Brigham Young University, Provo, Utah. See also, Ronald W. Walker, "Strangers in a Strange Land: Heber J. Grant and the Opening of the Japan Mission," *Journal of Mormon History* 13 (1986–87): 20–43, reprinted herein.

28. "Opening of a Mission in Japan," 9.

29. George Q. Cannon, "Editorial Thoughts," *Juvenile Instructor* 8 (February 17, 1872): 28.

30. See "The Japanese Troupe," *Deseret News*, April 25 and 27, 1870. After one show, Elder Woodruff thought the Japanese accomplished "the most wonderful feats" he had ever seen. Woodruff, *Journal*, April 27, 1870.

31. "A Japanese Idol," *Juvenile Instructor* 8 (May 10, 1872): 73–74; "A Country Scene in Japan," *Juvenile Instructor* 8 (October 25, 1873): 169–70; "Festival of the Idol Tengou in Japan," *Juvenile Instructor* 9 (February 28, 1874): 49; "Japanese Peasant in Winter Costume," *Juvenile Instructor* 9 (March 23, 1874): 81; "Japanese Amusements," *Juvenile Instructor* 10 (August 21, 1875): 193–94; "Japanese Customs," *Juvenile Instructor* 11 (January 15, 1876): 18–20; "Japanese Temple," *Juvenile Instructor* 11 (June 1, 1876): 127–28; "A Japan Shoe Store," *Juve-*

nile Instructor 13 (June 15, 1878): 133–34; "Japanese Children," *Juvenile Instructor* 13 (November 1, 1878): 245.

32. "A Japanese Idol," 74.

33. "A Country Scene in Japan," 170. "Japanese Temple" chronicles young Japanese noblemen who are being educated in the United States, and it closes, "Let us hope some of them may hear of the gospel that has been restored to the earth in our day, and carry the 'glad tidings' to the land of the rising sun." "Japanese Temple," 127–28.

34. "Japanese Soldiers," *Juvenile Instructor* 17 (May 1, 1882): 138–39; George Q. Cannon, "Editorial Thoughts," *Juvenile Instructor* 18 (January 15, 1883): 24; "A Japanese Tea-House," *Juvenile Instructor* 18 (March 15, 1883): 81–82; George Q. Cannon, "Editorial Thoughts," *Juvenile Instructor* 18 (June 1, 1883): 168; "A Japanese Meal," *Juvenile Instructor* 19 (March 15, 1884): 81–82; "A Japanese Execution," *Juvenile Instructor* 19 (April 15, 1884): 126–27; "Varieties: A Word for the Japanese," *Juvenile Instructor* 19 (May 15, 1884): 149; William Willes, "Tidings from Japan and China," *Juvenile Instructor* 19 (October 1, 1884): 291–92; "The City of Yokohama, Japan," *Juvenile Instructor* 20 (June 15, 1885): 177–78; "The Metropolis of Japan," *Juvenile Instructor* 22 (November 15, 1887): 337–38; and "A Japanese Traveling Equipage," *Juvenile Instructor* 23 (April 15, 1888): 113.

35. George Q. Cannon, "Editorial Thoughts," 168.

36. "The Metropolis of Japan," 337.

37. See R. Lanier Britsch, *Nothing More Heroic: The Compelling Story of the First Latter-day Saint Missionaries in India* (Salt Lake City: Deseret Book, 1999).

38. William Willes, Journal, June 17, 1884, in Charleen Cutler, ed., *The Life of William Willes: From His Own Personal Journals and Writings* (Provo, Utah: Family Footprints, 2000).

39. Willes, Journal, June 14, 1884.

40. William Willes, "Tidings from Japan and China," 291–92.

41. Willes, Journal, July 1, 1884.

42. Willes, "Tidings from Japan and China," 292.

43. Pyle, *The Making of Modern Japan*, 125.

44. Pyle, *The Making of Modern Japan*, 126–27.

45. Joseph M. Kitagawa, *Religion in Japanese History* (New York: Columbia University Press, 1990), 243.

46. Vidi, "A Progressive People," *Juvenile Instructor* 28 (October 1, 1893): 595–97; "The Parliament of Religions," *Juvenile Instructor* 28 (October 1, 1893): 605–8; "A Commercial City of Japan," *Juvenile Instructor* 30 (January 15, 1895): 41–42; Editor, "Strength in Unity, Not in Numbers," *Juvenile Instructor* 30 (June 1, 1895): 341–43; "Japan," *Juvenile Instructor* 31 (January 1, 1896): 9–12; Edi-

tor, "Japanese Progress," *Juvenile Instructor* 32 (June 1, 1897): 354–55; and "In the Land of the Mikado," *Juvenile Instructor* 33 (December 15, 1898): 809–11.

47. Vidi, "A Progressive People," 597.

48. In April 1895, the victorious Japanese forced the humbled Chinese government to sign the Treaty of Shimonoseki. Negotiated by Itō Hirobumi, the treaty forced China to recognize the sovereignty of Korea, give up Taiwan and the Pescadores Islands, pay an indemnity equal to 230 million taels, and enter a commercial agreement with Japan.

49. Editor, "Strength in Unity, Not in Numbers," 341–42.

50. Leonard J. Arrington, *Great Basin Kingdom: An Economic History of the Latter-day Saints, 1830–1900*, reprint (Salt Lake City: University of Utah Press and Tanner Trust Fund, 1993), 399–400.

51. Born in 1859, Abraham H. Cannon was ordained a member of the Twelve in 1889, thereby joining his father, George Q. Cannon (by then a member of the First Presidency), in the highest councils of the Church. Blessed with familial contacts, tremendous energy, and business acumen, Abraham became involved in the leadership of the Bullion-Beck mining company; State Bank of Utah; Utah Loan and Trust Co.; ZCMI; George Q. Cannon & Sons Co.; Co-operative Furniture Co.; Salt Lake Chamber of Commerce; *Deseret News; Contributor;* and various Utah railroads. See Andrew Jenson, *Latter-day Saint Biographical Encyclopedia: A Compilation of Biographical Sketches of Prominent Men and Women in The Church of Jesus Christ of Latter-day Saints*, 4 vols. (Salt Lake City: Andrew Jenson History Co. and Andrew Jenson Memorial Association, 1901–1936), 1:167–68.

52. The Church provided at least $100,000 in preliminary financing but received little return. Arrington, *Great Basin Kingdom*, 399–400.

53. See Edward Leo Lyman, "From the City of Angeles to the City of Saints: The Struggle to Build a Railroad from Los Angeles to Salt Lake City," *California History* 10 (Spring 1991): 76–93.

54. See Brian D. Corcoran, "'My Father's Business': Thomas Taylor and Mormon Frontier Economic Enterprise," *Dialogue: A Journal of Mormon Thought* 28 (Spring 1995): 105–41.

55. Dwight L. Smith, "The Engineer and the Canyon," *Utah Historical Quarterly* 28 (July 1960): 273; Dwight L. Smith, "Robert B. Stanton's Plan for the Far Southwest," *Arizona and the West* 4 (Winter 1962): 369–72.

56. "There was some negotiations pending to try and arrange a connection with the proposed Railroad company which is to be built to the coast by the Utah company making connection with a Japan Steam Ship Co. to have a line of steamers from Japan to San Diego. As this matter was now before the First Presidency the matter of a mission being opened up in Japan was allowed to

pass from the present." Diary Excerpts of Heber J. Grant, 1887–1899, Internally Dated, August 8, 1895, New Mormon Studies CD-ROM (Smith Research Associates, 1998).

57. Elder Grant seems to have been "delighted with such a mission" and was eager to "get freed of debt so he can labor more among the saints or go on a foreign mission." Diary Excerpts of Heber J. Grant, August 8, 1895.

58. Abraham H. Cannon, Journal, August 19, 1895, Abraham H. Cannon Collection, L. Tom Perry Special Collections, Brigham Young University, Provo, Utah.

59. Abraham H. Cannon, Journal, August 19, 1895.

60. Abraham H. Cannon, Journal, August 19, 1895.

61. Abraham H. Cannon, Journal, October 3, 1895.

62. Abraham H. Cannon, Journal, September 1, 1895. See also September 5 and 8, 1895.

63. Abraham H. Cannon, "A Future Mission Field," *Contributor* 16 (October 1895): 764–65.

64. Lyman, "From the City of Angeles to the City of Saints," 85.

65. Michael P. Malone, *James J. Hill: Empire Builder of the Northwest* (Norman: University of Oklahoma Press, 1996), 164. See also Albro Martin, *James J. Hill and the Opening of the Northwest* (New York: Oxford University Press, 1976), 471–74.

66. E. Mowbray Tate, *Transpacific Steam: The Story of Steam Navigation from the Pacific Coast of North America to the Far East and the Antipodes, 1867–1941* (New York: Cornwall Books, 1986), 121.

67. Although his attention was elsewhere, President Woodruff retained his interest in Japan. On April 22, 1896, he attended a lecture on Japan given in Salt Lake City by Frank G. Carpenter. The following year, President Woodruff allowed Senator Frank J. Cannon to speak on his recent trip to Japan and China to a large crowd in the Church's Tabernacle. See Woodruff, *Journal,* April 22, 1896, and "Some People of the Far East," *Deseret News,* November 29, 1897.

68. Davis Bitton, *George Q. Cannon: A Biography* (Salt Lake City: Deseret Book, 1999), 423.

69. Maureen Ursenbach Beecher and Paul Thomas Smith, "Lorenzo Snow," *Encyclopedia of Mormonism*, 3:1369–70.

70. B. H. Roberts, *A Comprehensive History of The Church of Jesus Christ of Latter-day Saints, Century One*, 6 vols. (Provo, Utah: Corporation of the President, The Church of Jesus Christ of Latter-day Saints, 1965), 6:375.

71. *Our Heritage: A Brief History of The Church of Jesus Christ of Latter-day Saints* (Salt Lake City: The Church of Jesus Christ of Latter-day Saints, 1996), 104.

72. On September 28, 1901, Lorenzo Snow made the following statement, later quoted by Joseph F. Smith: "We have started in this direction by sending Brother Grant over to Japan, but this is only a start. Things seem to be going favorably with him; but whether he will accomplish much or not matters not in one sense; it is for the Apostles to show to the Lord that they are His witnesses to all the nations, and that they are doing the best they can." Joseph F. Smith, "The Last Days of President Snow," *Juvenile Instructor* 36 (November 15, 1901): 689–90.

73. Joseph F. Smith, "The Last Days of President Snow," 690. See also Richard O. Cowan, *The Church in the Twentieth Century* (Salt Lake City: Bookcraft, 1985), 20; and Francis M. Gibbons, *Lorenzo Snow: Spiritual Giant, Prophet of God* (Salt Lake City: Deseret Book, 1982), 230–31.

74. Bitton, *George Q. Cannon,* 436.

75. George Q. Cannon Journal, September 6, 1900, as quoted in Bitton, *George Q. Cannon,* 436–37.

76. Gordon Irving, "Numerical Strength and Geographical Distribution of the LDS Missionary Force, 1830–1974," *Task Papers in LDS History,* No. 1 (Salt Lake City: Historical Department of the Church of Jesus Christ of Latter-day Saints, 1975), 11. Irving defines "Pacific-Asia" as "Australasian, Australian, East Indies, Japanese, New Zealand, Samoan, Sandwich Islands/Hawaiian, and Society Islands."

77. Heber J. Grant, *A Japanese Journal,* comp., Gordon A. Madsen, (n.p.: By the compiler, 1970), February 14, 1901; Rudger Clawson, *A Ministry of Meetings: The Apostolic Diaries of Rudger Clawson,* ed. Stan Larson (Salt Lake City: Signature Books, 1993), 247.

3

The Iwakura Mission and Its Stay in Salt Lake City

Wendy Butler

Early on the blustery morning of February 3, 1872, more than one hundred Japanese arrived by train from the west in Ogden, Utah Territory. Kume Kunitake, whose responsibility it was to keep the group's official journal, wrote:

> To the east there are mountains and to the west there are mountains. Ogden has three thousand people and the Weber River runs through it. Because of the great snowfall in the Rocky Mountains, the rail lines are buried in snow. The railroad company sent several thousand men to clear it, but it is still not clear. We took the Utah Central Railroad to Salt Lake City.[1]

This group represented the lion's share of Japan's new Meiji government. Just four years earlier, in 1868, the country had experienced the Meiji Restoration. Its main objective was to overthrow the military government, the Tokugawa Shogunate, that had ruled feudal Japan since 1600. The Meiji Restoration theoretically restored power to the emperor, but Meiji Japan was actually governed by an oligarchy of former samurai and a court noble. Half of this oligarchy and two-thirds of the high-level bureaucrats left Japan in winter 1872 to tour the world for a year and a half while a caretaker government was left in charge. Historians call this group the Iwakura Mission because of its top-ranking member, Iwakura Tomomi, who as Minister of the Right and second in rank behind the emperor was the only court noble in the oligarchy (illus. 3-1).

Other high-ranking officials included Iwakura's deputies, Kido Takayoshi and Okubo Toshimichi. These two were former leading samurai from Chōshō and Satsuma, domains that had been instrumental in the overthrow of the Tokugawa Shogunate. They also played influential roles as leaders of Japan's push for modernization after the Iwakura Mission. Other members, like Itō Hirobumi, were younger, unproven statesmen who would later affect Japanese politics for decades. The mission also included Japan's top bureaucrats and military leaders.

The prestigious makeup of the embassy was extraordinary. Most striking, it showed a high level of confidence—first, that the government would survive so soon after a major change and for an extended length of time without most of its leaders at home; and second, that the tour was necessary and important. Japan's early Meiji leaders had high expectations that they would gain useful facts and insights from the Western world that would affect the future of Japan.

The Iwakura Mission was also the largest and most influential assembly of Japanese statesmen ever to leave that country. There had been much smaller shogunate missions to the West in the 1860s, but none compared with the Iwakura Mission. It had forty-nine official members, and as many as fifty-eight others traveled with the embassy. Interpreters, baggage handlers, students, and samurai retainers swelled the ranks to more than twice its official size.

The Salt Lake City portion of the Iwakura Mission's world tour has been overlooked primarily because it was unplanned. It was, and still is, seen as an unfortunate delay. Consequently, historians have neglected to search the sources available for information on this stay and have continued to rely on incorrect observations made in previous works. These errors range from general assumptions that the stay was unimportant to specific errors about events and controversial occurrences. Not only will this paper attempt to correct these inaccuracies, but it will also show how the postponement in Salt Lake City shaped the attitudes of the Japanese and influenced the Iwakura Mission.

The Purpose

Historians do not discount the Iwakura Mission's impact on the shaping of modern Japan, yet confusion exists concerning the Mission's purpose. Historians today cite a combination of three

Courtesy Church Archives, The Church of Jesus Christ of Latter-day Saints

Illus. 3-1. Iwakura Tomomi. In 1872, Iwakura Tomomi, Japan's Minister of the Right, led a group of Japanese government officials on a year and a half tour of the United States. The Iwakura Mission, as it would become known, made an unplanned stop in Salt Lake City in February 1872.

reasons for the convening of the Iwakura Mission: to display the new Meiji government's control of power, to renegotiate unequal treaties with Western powers, and to gather information about the West and its modernization.[2]

Marlene J. Mayo, who has written extensively on the Iwakura Mission, emphasized treaty revision as a purpose in her article titled "Rationality in the Meiji Restoration: The Iwakura Embassy."[3] In a later piece, "The Western Education of Kume Kunitake: 1871–6," her focus was solely on the information-gathering aspect of the mission. Furthermore, the latter article lacks a discussion of diplomacy, even in a section called "Military Matters and Diplomacy." Mayo acknowledged the multiplicity of opinions on the purpose of the mission, noting that "the confusion has been compounded by the failure of scholars to refer to one another's conclusions or to clarify the reasons for conflicts of opinion."[4] Unfortunately, the confusion lingers.

I suggest that the Iwakura Mission was formed for the sole purpose of studying the society and institutions of the West but that its Salt Lake City stay caused the members to alter their original focus. Their lengthy stay in Salt Lake City made Iwakura and his associates see the United States as not as unified or as technologically advanced as they had supposed. They decided to enter into treaty negotiations once they reached Washington, D.C.—negotiations that were not part of their original plan. Even though Japan was unhappy with its current treaties with the West, its leaders perceived that their country was not strong enough, nor were they themselves experienced enough, to bargain with Western powers.[5] One need only to look at the makeup of the Iwakura Mission to conclude that its objective was fact-gathering. If treaty revision had been a prominent motive, the mission would have looked strikingly different. It would have included men more experienced with foreign affairs and diplomacy. Instead, besides the leading politicians already mentioned, the mission included representatives of most of the bureaucratic agencies and departments of Meiji Japan.

The Foreign Department was the most widely represented, with Vice-Ambassador Yamaguchi Masouka, three first secretaries, three second secretaries, one third secretary, one fourth secretary, and one attaché—ten officials in all. It was crucial that key Foreign Department officials become quickly tutored in diplomatic affairs of the West.

The Treasury Department sent one first secretary, one commissioner (who was also in charge of the Bureau of the Census), and six officers. The Education Department was well represented with a fourth secretary, a chief clerk, and five officers. The War Department had Yamada Akiyoshi, who was a brigadier general of the Imperial Army, and an officer. An acting commissioner and four official attachés represented the Judicial Department. The Public Works Department sent two officers plus the commissioner of dockyards and public works. One prefectural governor and the secretary of another governor accompanied the mission. The Imperial Court sent five representatives as well as Prince Iwakura Tomomi. A mission intent on renegotiation treaties would not have been weighed down with these extra personnel from diverse government divisions. A streamlined group of diplomats would have been more effective. Their highly defined objective would be carried out by a few diplomats with specific instructions and the historical record of imperial sanction would not be silent.

Not only would the makeup of a diplomatic mission have been different, but its itinerary would have been organized differently. The tour would have been structured almost exclusively around world political centers rather than the inspection of trade, agricultural, and industrial centers.

The Iwakura Mission was created in order to find answers to profound questions that required much observation, debate, and consideration. How was the Meiji government to organize its military, its political system, and the education of its youth? Did Japan need to alter its culture and its class system, or did these need to be discarded altogether in the quest for modernization? Japanese officials confidently set out to answer these questions, but they did so with caution. Knowing that Japan was reluctant to reject its culture, which was largely based on Confucian thought, they carefully considered what they observed. While the mission was in England, for example, Iwakura stated that its members intended to take with them only that which was good in the West and to "avoid the evils that seem everywhere to have followed the advance of civilization."[6] The religious and philosophical background of the Japanese acted as a barrier to the wholesale acceptance of Western secular and religious ideas.

The Japanese Arrive in Utah

Sailing from Yokohama harbor on December 23, 1871, the Iwakura Mission was to tour for eighteen months, visiting the United States, Great Britain, France, Belgium, Holland, Germany, Switzerland, Italy, Austria, Russia, Malaya, Indochina, and British Hong Kong. The first stop in the United States was San Francisco, where the company rested before continuing by train across the continent.

Stopping in Salt Lake City was not part of the itinerary. The group had been informed by the Union Pacific Railroad that the Rocky Mountain passes were open and that the Mission could travel to the East Coast without delay. However, winter 1872 was severe across much of the continent. Frequent, heavy snowstorms plagued the Mountain West, blocking the passes and often stranding passengers traveling both east and west on the infant transcontinental railroad. On February 3, the train carrying the Japanese officials was forced to stop at Ogden. When the passes were cleared, more than two weeks after the arrival of the Japanese, the Salt Lake City papers reported that on several snow-blocked trains passengers had experienced severe cold temperatures, near-starvation, and general sickness from exposure. On one stranded car there was even a fatality.[7] The huge delegation from Japan was fortunate to have been spared these calamities, but it was stranded in Salt Lake City for nineteen days—longer than it was to stay in any North American city other than Washington, D.C.

An official welcoming committee from Salt Lake City met the members of the Iwakura Mission as they disembarked in Ogden. The committee escorted them by rail to the capital city and settled them into the city's best hotel, the Townsend House. The committee's responsibility also included organizing the official functions for the Japanese, such as tours, receptions, and banquets. Just as they would in nearly every city they visited on their world tour, the Japanese saw the usual military review, visited schools for children, and attended numerous receptions and banquets.

The Salt Lake City portion of the Iwakura Mission's world tour has been most often regarded in a negative manner. Many Americans of the day saw the stranding of this large and influential delegation in the heart of Brigham Young's empire as an embarrassment. They wondered what impression the Japanese would get of the United States by observing the polygamous Latter-day Saints in Utah Territory. Recently, one historian described the stay as a "setback,"[8] while other writers have mentioned the stay only as an excuse to relate amusing anecdotes.[9]

Of peripheral importance, a study of the Salt Lake City stay also tells us much about the city and about Utah Territory in 1872, and it provides a remarkable opportunity to observe how Americans of European ancestry and Asians encountered each other on the Western frontier. The perceptions of the two groups in this interplay of cultures—especially racial and social attitudes held by the people of Salt Lake City, the Japanese, and those of the rest of the country—are insightful and important.

The Japanese visitors observed that which was unique to Utah. They saw the newly built Tabernacle and were impressed by its acoustics, size, and construction. Their diarist recorded a lengthy description of the dimensions and capacity of the building and added, "we are told that ... when a sermon is delivered from the pulpit, even a person sitting in the last row can hear the speaker's voice without missing a word."[10] Even if this anecdote is lacking the famous pin dropped on the pulpit, we see that as early as 1872 an explanation of the excellent acoustics was part of the set tour of the Tabernacle. The group visited a nearby museum run by Brigham Young's son, John W. Young, and they commented on the foundation that was being built for the Salt Lake Temple.[11] They also met with members of the Utah Territorial Legislature and Supreme Court and with city officials.

At all these locations, welcome speeches were pro forma. Almost all the speeches centered on industrial progress in the Western world. Many speakers complimented the United States on its rapid industrialization and settlement of Western lands. Some speeches lauded both the technological advances and speed with which Utahns had built a city in the midst of a "howling wilderness."[12] At a banquet on February 12, T. H. Bates said,

> And here in the heart of our continent, where we have seen lonely desolations changed to busy scenes of commerce and industry; where we have seen the haunts of savage aborigines transferred to happy homes, and evidences of peace and prosperity, and remember that nowhere is the indomitable energy, enterprise and intelligence

of the Anglo-Saxon race more strikingly illustrated than here, by the lofty mountains of Utah.[13]

On the whole, the speeches the Japanese heard each day promulgated the notion that advanced civilization had always rested in the Western tradition. More than one speaker congratulated the Japanese on their farsightedness in starting their fact-gathering tour with the United States, which was praised as "the most active and most powerful of all civilizations of the earth."[14] Another speaker suggested that nations should be measured not by their age but by how much they have accomplished. "From this standpoint," he stated, "the United States is the mightiest of all nations."[15] These self-congratulatory statements could be viewed as inhospitable to the Japanese; however, they are consistent with the nineteenth-century American pride in progress that was tied to expansionism.[16]

It is only fair to note that a few speakers honored their guests by focusing on the Japanese nation, its history, and its aspirations for the future. For the most part, such thoughts were expressed by Americans who had lived in Japan and were traveling with the Iwakura Mission, including U.S. Ambassador to Japan Charles E. DeLong (illus. 3-2) and the delegation's interpreter, N. E. Rice.

One other speech clearly stood out as an exception. It is unclear who wrote or delivered it, but the speech was signed by Lorenzo Snow, president of the Council of the Utah Territorial Legislature, and Orson Pratt, speaker of the House of Representatives.[17] The speech praised the Japanese nation for its long history of twenty-five centuries and enumerated the many world civilizations that had risen and fallen during that time. While some of these countries, the speaker stated, had "destroyed and desolated nations, to gratify their desires of conquest and their lust of gain, you have been contented with your own lot, and cultivated the arts of peace."[18] This speech also stands apart from the others because it emphasized what Americans could learn from the Japanese instead of what Japan could gain from the United States. The speaker thoughtfully expressed:

> We feel honored by your visit, and bid you share with us all that is good, useful and interesting, and would ask at your hands some lessons in civil polity, in jurisprudence, in the art of science of government that

Courtesy Church Archives, The Church of Jesus Christ of Latter-day Saints

Illus. 3-2.　Charles E. DeLong. As U.S. ambassador to Japan, DeLong traveled with the Iwakura Mission's tour of the United States, which included a stop in Salt Lake City and a visit with Brigham Young.

we may be enabled to perpetuate principles conducive to the best interests of humanity on this vast continent.[19]

The largest public event for the Japanese during their nearly three-week stay was a grand banquet and ball held on February 12. Tickets were distributed to city, territorial, military, and religious dignitaries, and there was much politicking to secure the coveted tickets. For days after the occasion the newspapers billed the ball as the largest and most elaborate event ever held in Utah. All three Salt Lake City newspapers—the *Deseret News,* the *Salt Lake Daily Herald,* and the *Salt Lake Tribune*—ran long articles describing in detail the attire of the most notable ladies. In the center of attraction were five young, kimono-clad Japanese girls who accompanied the embassy at the request of the emperor. These girls were headed to private schools on the East Coast to be the first Japanese females to study in the United States.

Even though official functions filled most of their visit, the embassy members found time to explore the city. They took walks around the city, marveling at the sights. Vice-Ambassador Kido wrote in his journal that "the mountains on all four sides were covered with silvery snow; it was a superb scene." And, "We took a stroll through the downtown area . . . the whole world was as glittering jewels; the snow-covered landscape is superb."[20] Kume Kunitake, perhaps reflecting his responsibility as official journalist, wrote about the city in less romantic terms:

> The roads are muddy after it rains or snows. The sidewalks before the stores are of wood that have been laid down. The streets are not lit by gas as in San Francisco, but the main intersections have large wick lanterns. People's houses are primarily made out of wood. As for Mormon men, after they marry each wife they add a window. Though the city is very wide, there are only three or four main streets.[21]

In the evenings, members of the embassy enjoyed the city's cultural offerings, seeing such plays as *Neck and Neck* and *Pizarro, or the Death of Rolla.* Salt Lake City resident Elizabeth A. Howard went to the theater on February 6 and noted in her diary that the embassy occupied the first circle directly above the handsomely fitted box for the Latter-day Saint prophet and that Chinese lanterns decorated the theater in their honor.[22] Some of the Japanese also attended a speech given by an itinerant lecturer whose topic was appropriately titled, "The World, Its Antiquity, Development, Progress in Civilization, and Man's Destiny."

Utahns' Perceptions of the Japanese

What perceptions of the Japanese did the people of Salt Lake City gain? Surprisingly, although more than a hundred Japanese dignitaries stayed in the city for more than two weeks, few people wrote of the visitors in their diaries. Those who did write recorded primarily factual statements that were devoid of description or elaboration. For example, Samuel Parker Richards noted in his journal on February 6, 1872, "At eleven o'clock I went down to the city hall to see the Japanese embassy, as they were having a reception of the various officers of the city and county, and military, and the legislative members."[23] Wilford Woodruff made this brisk record in his journal: "In the evening I had an interview with the President of the Board of Agriculture of Japan. He was at the Townsend House."[24] One diarist recorded, "Today I am 36 years old. Today the Japanese Embassy arived in the City."[25]

If diaries were devoid of remarks about the Japanese, newspapers were not. Reporters, whose job it was to notice and write about such things, educated their readers by writing extensively about the Japanese. Newspapers did not merely report their whereabouts and activities but scrutinized the differences between Japanese and Caucasians. One journalist enlightened and entertained his readers about this country newly opened to the world. He wrote of Japan's geographical size, describing it as fourfold the size of Utah Territory. He explained Japanese methods of farming and suggested that the farms were "models of order and neatness." He said that the Japanese were intelligent and progressive people. He spoke in glowing terms of the wealth of Japan and said that its north had minerals in abundance and "that there is also located there a continuous bed of gold, silver and copper."[26] Later in the same article he inserted another sensational morsel of information that was surely a popular subject of conversation in many Utah homes the day it was printed:

> The gentlemen of the embassy are "two sword" men, enjoying the peculiar privileges of their high nobility, among which is that of cutting off the heads of any of the lower classes who might offend them,

without being held to answer for other than a limited offence which the payment of a fine would cover.[27]

The reporters also wrote about the physical appearance of the Japanese. The day after the embassy reached Salt Lake City, the *Salt Lake Tribune* carried an article headlined "Arrival of the Embassy" that described the Japanese as distinguished visitors who appeared to be "very intelligent" and "highly cultivated." The reporter also noted that "the men are dressed in full American costume and they wear the Yankee toggery with as much grace and dignity as Europeans."[28] This statement must have gratified Iwakura and his associates. The Tokugawa Shogunate had sent a smaller embassy in 1860 that had been ridiculed in the American press because the Japanese officials' off-the-rack suits did not fit their smaller stature. Because of this, Prince Iwakura had insisted that those who could afford the cost wait to have their Western suits tailor-made in San Francisco. However, the Japanese could not entirely escape editorial comments about their size. After a military inspection at Camp Douglas a reporter wrote,

> Our Japanese friends must have observed, as did all present, the marked difference in stature between General Yamada, of the Imperial army of Japan, and General Morrow, in command of the United States forces here, as both gentlemen passed down the line at the review yesterday. The former is, probably, not to exceed five feet in height, and weighs not over 100 pounds; the latter must be nearly a foot taller and a hundred pounds heavier. We all know General Morrow is a handsome man, after the Anglo-Saxon order, and we are not surprised to learn that Yamada is looked upon as fine-looking by a nation whose peers and princes are almost invariably of small stature. Small as Yamada is, he looked every inch a soldier in his uniform and his martial bearing was the subject of general remark.[29]

Reporters in Salt Lake City struggled to categorize these distinguished Asians. Cautioning Salt Lake City residents to treat the Japanese with courtesy and respect, one reporter told his readers that these foreign visitors were "an extremely intelligent body of men . . . with an utter absence of Orientalism."[30] In essence, he said that even though the Japanese were Asian, they should be treated as though they were not. To many Americans of the late nineteenth century, the terms

Oriental and *Asian* did not denote a member of a race so much as it did a degenerate.[31]

Another newspaper reporter tried to give his readers a sense of the dignity of these foreigners by comparing them to the Chinese, a nationality that Americans generally held in low esteem.

> There is little if any similarity between the Japanese and the Chinese. While the latter belong to a race that is marked with evidences of decay, and show but little if any disposition to adopt the progressive institutions of the age, the latter [the reporter obviously meant to write former] show the energy and spirit of a young and healthy race, destined to play an important part in the future civilization of the world. Japan, with its 30,000,000 of population, crowding forward to take its place among the civilized and enlightened nations, has unquestionably a great future.[32]

It is not difficult to see from this statement that Americans viewed the Far East as declining or backward. Residents of Salt Lake City were being asked to separate "good" Asians from "bad" Asians, most likely a difficult and confusing task.

Japanese Impressions of Utahns

The two cultures did not meet on an equal footing. For most people living in Salt Lake City, this was their first encounter with any Japanese.[33] Many of these Japanese, on the other hand, had been acquainted with and worked with Americans and Europeans for years, if not decades. Some had studied in the United States, and for a few this was a second excursion to the Western Hemisphere. Accordingly, the perspectives of each group were unique. Citizens of Salt Lake City were curious about a country that was just beginning to gain world prominence and a people whose customs and appearance were alien to their own. In contrast, these Japanese had already formed general impressions of Americans. This visit was specifically to see America's institutions and to understand how they affected the lives of its people. The Japanese had the advantage in this meeting of cultures.

What impression did the Iwakura Mission gather of Salt Lake City and its inhabitants? Because its members were highly educated, cultured, and part of an aristocracy that valued reserve and delicacy in their dealings with others, they were extremely polite and formal in all their conversations. Their answers to their hosts' inquiries were always solicitous and seldom revealed the intense scrutiny that the visitors were giving to all aspects of society. To discover the impressions they gained of Salt Lake City and of its people, one must turn to their diaries and to memoirs written in later life.

A recurrent theme of the diaries was the natural scenery of the region, especially the snow-covered mountains. Kido spoke of the mountains as being "naturally different from anything we see in Japan."[34] Even before they arrived in the Salt Lake Valley, the visitors were struck by the majesty of the region's mountains. As their train neared Utah and the inevitable closure of the rails at Ogden, they crowded around the windows to see "the moonlight shining on the cliff edges and mountains . . . like the glint from the edge of a sword."[35] The Japanese saw the mountains as holders of great strength and power and likened them to a symbol of Japanese power—the samurai sword.

The Japanese also observed the people of Salt Lake City. The delegation's enforced stay allowed them to form attitudes of Americans based on numerous interactions over their nineteen-day visit. In no other city did the Japanese have an opportunity to turn acquaintances into friendships. They saw the city's leading citizens in formal and relaxed settings, and they had the time to discuss detailed issues with bureaucrats and politicians.[36] They also had many chances to observe the general populace, a luxury they did not have after they left the Rocky Mountains. After the embassy's stay in Salt Lake City, its pace picked up as it quickly traveled from one city to the next, stopping long enough to take lodgings in a hotel, observe industries, visit institutions, or view the beauty of a unique landscape. In Chicago, for example, it stayed less than twenty-four hours.

An interesting influence on the visitors' formation of opinions was that the Japanese saw the Latter-day Saints of Utah as Americans—something that the rest of the country generally denied and that many continued to deny even after the territory was granted statehood nearly a quarter of a century later. While other Americans used differences in religion to classify Latter-day Saints as unacceptable, the Japanese, as outsiders, were not inclined to view these differences as defining factors of American identity.

The members of the Iwakura Mission did not make remarks about Utahns that showed they perceived them as anything but Americans. They did make general observations about polygamy, but their remarks carried no hint of judgment or opinion. In fact, when the Japanese made disparaging remarks about Utahns, they were similar to those they made about Americans in other cities. For instance, while in San Francisco the Japanese disapprovingly acknowledged that men and women openly displayed affection toward one another. In Salt Lake City they commented that some Utahns became too rowdy at a late-night social affair.

While the Japanese recognized that the Latter-day Saints had been driven to live in the wilderness by those who had objected to their religion, they saw them as an example of the religious zeal found in Western civilization rather than an exceptional case. After seeing Temple Square, Kume Kunitake wrote, "There are 200,000 believers and they are building such a large temple in the midst of the mountains in a desolate place. That Westerners believe in religion and do not begrudge paying considerable money for such a temple can be readily observed in this site."[37]

One Sunday many of the Japanese attended Latter-day Saint religious services in the Tabernacle; they were curious to see how this religion, perceived by many Americans as so different from other American churches, conducted its services. In the official mission diary, Kume Kunitake wrote,

> We went to the Mormon Church to hear some doctrine. Part of the sermon was taken from the New Testament concerning the doctrine that people from the corners of the four seas are all one people and are thus brothers. On the whole the service sounded much like other Protestant Churches.[38]

This excerpt shows that the Japanese did not view the Latter-day Saints as significantly different from other Americans but, in fact, as very much the same. The following quote shows that members of the Iwakura Mission understood the existence of enmity toward the Saints, even if the diarist misunderstood some Church doctrines, but it gives no indication that the visitors had come to the same conclusions.

> Mormonism is a branch of Christianity. The westerners see it as being heretical. One of the primary teachings is that if one man

> does not have seven wives or more, he will not get into Heaven. . . .
> All Americans hate this religion. The government has decided that
> proselytizing must stop and guards are placed around his [Brigham
> Young's] house.[39]

It is important not to misinterpret this nonjudgmental stance as a policy of Iwakura and his associates. The entire purpose of this world tour was to analyze Western society, and to that end they liberally acknowledged and discussed cultural and social issues that they witnessed as they traveled the globe. Interestingly, polygamy was not an issue that disturbed them, probably because of the East-Asian tradition of multiple wives.

Members of the embassy also learned about the history of The Church of Jesus Christ of Latter-day Saints along with Utah Territory. On his first night in Salt Lake City, Kido Takayoshi wrote in his journal that a former territorial governor, Frank Fuller, had told him the history of the territory:

> In 1847 the Mormons were driven out of the United States; and in
> their flight, Young led 144 people (including 3 women) to this place.
> They carried their belongings on their backs for 1100 or 1200 miles
> from any human habitation. At that time this was Mexican territory;
> but the next year Mexicans fought and lost a war to the United States,
> and so ceded this land.[40]

The embassy also examined the politics of the region. They noted the differences between a state, which enjoyed full privileges, and a territory, which did not. Kume's diary indicates that they understood that a territory could not govern its own affairs, have a constitution, choose its own governor, or send a voting representative to Congress.[41]

American Media Coverage

While Salt Lake City wined and dined the one-hundred-plus Japanese for nineteen days in February 1872, the rest of the country looked on. Many wondered what image the Japanese were gathering of Americans while they were stranded in the Mormon city. Because of polygamy, the nation's eyes were already turned toward Utah. At the same time, Utahns were making a serious bid for statehood. While the Japanese were in Salt Lake City, the territory elected a delegate to Congress, voted to uphold the Constitution of the United States, and voted to petition Congress to accept Utah as a state. Any political or social fiasco could tip the already precarious situation against Utah. Because the elections went entirely to what many voters called the "Mormon Ticket" and because the territory allowed female suffrage, the national press called the elections a fraud and a mockery. A California paper said that they "hoped the Japanese had access to a competent Philadelphia lawyer to explain to them the affairs in Mormondom."[42]

One event in particular caused embarrassing media coverage for the embassy and their hosts. Two days after arriving in Salt Lake City, Ambassador DeLong and prominent members of the embassy called on Brigham Young at his residence. The Latter-day Saint prophet was being held without bail on a murder charge, a prisoner in his home under guard of a U.S. marshal.[43] The visit to Young created a controversy that spread, via telegraph, from the local press to many newspapers across the country. Even though Brigham Young was the most important figure in the territory, many Americans thought that the embassy should not have visited a religious leader who held no political office and who was under arrest.

The controversy centered on how the decision to see Young had been made. The *Salt Lake Tribune* told the story this way: The day before the visit, Iwakura received Young's messenger at his hotel who asked that the principal members of the embassy call on the Church leader. Iwakura reportedly replied that etiquette required Young to call on him. The messenger then informed Iwakura that Young was eager to meet the Japanese but that he could not make calls since he was confined to his room in the charge of a federal officer. Iwakura supposedly "saw the point at once and with a frown, said: We came to the United States to see the President of this great nation; we do not know how he would like for us to call on a man who had broken the laws of his country and was under arrest."[44]

Historians of the Iwakura Mission have relied solely on this *Tribune* article when relating this colorful incident. Thus, they deny that a visit to Brigham Young took place and emphasize that the Latter-day Saint prophet was rejected by the Japanese prince. A 1995 work, for example, stated that during the Salt Lake stay "the only event of note was that Iwakura refused an invitation to call on Brigham Young, on the grounds that it would be politically improper."[45] However, there is evidence that the *Tribune* article was incorrect and that a delegation did meet with Brigham Young. Not only have other sources been neglected, but the conflict in the local press between the *Tribune* and the Church-influenced *Deseret News* has not been considered as a cause of misinformation about the visit. The *Deseret News*'s depiction of the event, published the same day, was markedly different from the *Tribune*'s:

> The Embassy, having expressed a great desire to see President Young . . . took the earliest opportunity of visiting him at his mansion, he being the first of our citizens to whom they paid their respects. The interview was an exceedingly agreeable one, the members of the Embassy evincing great interest in learning that all the improvements in the Territory had been accomplished within 25 years.[46]

In addition to the *Deseret News* account, the embassy's own record contradicts the *Tribune*'s version. Kido Takayoshi's diary entry for February 5 gives an account of the visit that has been overlooked. He casually recorded that the visit to the Tabernacle was followed by a visit to Brigham Young, whose home was located in the next city block. This entry makes one realize how natural this sequence of events was. The Japanese had toured the Tabernacle and the Salt Lake Temple construction site then walked the short distance to the Mormon leader's home. After seeing the prophet, they visited a nearby museum run by his son. This was unquestionably the obligatory Church tour.

Besides the preponderance of sources that substantiate the occurrence of the visit, there is another reason to doubt the authenticity of the *Tribune* story. Iwakura, because of his high political and courtly rank, would not have received messengers such as the one supposedly sent by Brigham Young. Ambassador DeLong was responsible for arranging all the embassy's official functions while they were in the United States. Indeed, Kido noted in his diary that DeLong had arranged for the visit "beforehand."[47]

The visit outraged people in Salt Lake City who were not affiliated with the Church. Some who had received invitations to the grand banquet and ball to be given for the Japanese on February 12 returned their tickets in protest. The story of the supposed invitation refusal was reported in the *Tribune* two days after it occurred and was telegraphed to other papers around the country four to five days later. A number of papers reprinted versions of the *Tribune* story. The amusing twist to this affair is that the banquet was too tempting a prize to forego. Those who had given up their tickets asked for them back after Eastern papers reported that DeLong, when questioned about taking the Japanese to see Brigham Young, had adroitly answered that he "did not know where the party was being taken."[48] The excuse, though probably untrue, was adequate enough to allow the protestors to reclaim their tickets and attend the ball.

The visit to Brigham Young caused such a commotion that the local papers were still jousting over it a week later. The *Deseret News* updated its readers with "The Latest" on February 13: "The latest donkeyism of the sensation[al] telegraphic dispatches from this city to the west is that the heavens are likely to fall because the Japanese Embassy visited President B. Young. Well, let them fall, if that is all that holds them up."[49]

Even ten days after the visit, the editor of the *Tribune* considered the issue current news:

> A number of the Japan commissioners connected with the Embassy called on the prophet, who received them kindly and, after describing to them his journey across the plains in 47, presented them with a few copies of the Book of Mormon. The visitors were, no doubt, anxious to compare the prophet of the West with the Mikado, and we understand, that they prefer their own High Priest. The difference between the two seems to be that the Mikado is pressing forward to grasp the civilization of modern times, while the prophet, with his Book of Mormon, is endeavoring to get back to the habits and customs of barbarous times.[50]

The Brigham Young episode may have generated more headlines in newspapers across the country, but the more significant embarrassment for the United States was the inability of the Union Pacific Railroad to transport the stranded Iwakura Mission. Not only was the new and highly touted transcontinental railroad proving ineffective for winter travel, but those involved in trade worried that commerce with Asia would suffer because the Union Pacific could not keep the trains running. Ambassador DeLong was quoted in several Eastern papers as stating that millions of dollars would be lost to the transcontinental route because the Japanese would report unfavorably on shipping anything across the United States in winter.[51]

Many wondered if the Japanese would opt to ship their goods across Panama rather than risk costly delays in the Rocky Mountains. The *New York Times* thought that this was highly likely given the ineptitude of the Union Pacific in handling the snow blockade.[52] Indeed, on February 14, several Americans stranded in Utah returned to San Francisco, hoping to get to New York faster via the Panama Railroad.[53] The *Chicago Tribune* took Union Pacific officials to task:

> The experiences of the passengers differ, but the majority denounce the management of the Union Pacific without stint, saying there is no excuse for such long delay and hardships; that with reasonable energy and determination of officials who understood their business the blockade could have been raised or passed two weeks ago.[54]

Several passengers who had been stranded in the mountains in snow-blocked passenger cars threatened to sue the company; a few even threatened to lynch the superintendent of the railroad.[55]

The rest of the country were desperate to get the Japanese out of Utah. The governor of Illinois offered to pay for a special train that would take the entire embassy back to San Francisco, where they could take a ship to Panama and travel across the isthmus.[56] Even Ambassador DeLong grew impatient. After eleven days in the city, he questioned a stagecoach entrepreneur about moving the entire delegation some two hundred miles over the passes in sleighs. The businessman estimated that it would take sixty days at one thousand dollars per day.[57]

Treaty Negotiation

As Americans fretted about the delay in the Rocky Mountains, the Japanese started to brood over what they would face once they reached Washington. The delay, however difficult, afforded time and confidence for one delegate to press the United States for treaty revision. Itō Hirobumi spent several evenings writing three memoranda on the upcoming meetings with Secretary of State Hamilton Fish. The first memorandum acknowledged that the present group was not authorized to conclude new treaties but was expected to discuss the advantages and disadvantages of the present treaty that Japan saw as unfair to its rights as a sovereign nation. The successive memoranda went further toward suggesting that the embassy might try to draft a new treaty and hold binding discussions with the secretary of state.[58]

Itō Hirobumi's argument must have been persuasive. Iwakura and the other ranking officials accepted the proposals when he presented them in an evening meeting on February 20 in one of their hotel rooms at the Townsend House. They decided to press for treaty revision while in Washington. Thus, in Salt Lake City the embassy moved from expecting to meet and hold informal discussions with diplomatic officials to pressing for treaty revision as full diplomatic ambassadors.

The Salt Lake City stay changed the defining purpose of the Iwakura Mission even if the efforts at treaty revision proved to be a dismal failure. During their meetings in Washington, Hamilton Fish determined that, even though the embassy was made up of the highest-ranking government officials, it still lacked the papers necessary to enter into diplomatic negotiations. After Fish informed Iwakura of this, Iwakura sent Okubo and Itō back to Japan to convince the emperor to issue the appropriate documents. By the time these two men returned from Japan with the credentials, Iwakura had become so frustrated with Fish and the laborious negotiation process that he decided to depart immediately for Europe.

This unfavorable experience arose from the extra time the embassy members had on their hands in Salt Lake City. They had the leisure to think, meet, fret, and discuss with each other their concerns about their meetings on the other side of the Rocky Mountains. What made them make such a momentous decision? Why did they decide to enter into treaty negotiations when they had previously said that they were not yet ready to do so? Perhaps it was because of their experiences in the American West. The embassy embarked on this world tour with definite images of countries and their people. The United States, though young, was seen as a powerful, unified nation with national goals and ideals. Its institutions were well respected, and it had made great advances in industrialization.

Lessons Learned by the Japanese

One can speculate that the Japanese saw that the United States was not as exemplary as they had supposed. In Salt Lake City they saw that Americans were anything but unified. They quarreled over religious differences and used these differences to influence politics and judicial matters. The flaws of the country's technology were shown when the famed transcontinental railroad could not keep its trains moving through the mountain passes. In both Salt Lake City and San Francisco, extended contact with Western Americans, who were not as socially reserved as East Coast Americans, likely caused the Japanese to conclude that they could succeed at treaty negotiations. The delegates had been extremely well accepted, their experiences in communicating at official functions were highly positive, and, other than the transportation delay, the trip was going very smoothly. America welcomed them and accepted them as they were—the dignified ambassadors of the emperor of Japan. The delegation did not know that they were to meet their match with Hamilton Fish.

Itō Hirobumi presented his proposals just two days before the mission departed Salt Lake City. After several false reports that the passes were open, a specially outfitted train arrived in Ogden from the East Coast on February 21. The embassy left Salt Lake City early the next morning and continued its world tour.

As has been shown, the Salt Lake City stay shaped the Iwakura Mission. Without this lengthy stay, Iwakura, Okubo, and Kido might not have been swayed by Itō Hirobumi's arguments in favor of treaty negotiations.[59] In Washington, Kido wrote in his diary that Itō had been rash in his arguments that swayed the oligarchs. Early in the negotiation process he noted that there was "very little advantage to us" in Itō's treaty.[60] Kido concluded that it had been a mistake to listen to Itō in Salt Lake City. Kido saw his group of negotiators giving up everything to the Americans and gaining nothing for Japan. He sadly concluded that Japan could not yet compete with Western powers in the art of diplomacy even though for a time it looked as if they could.

An earlier version of this article appeared as Wendy Butler, "The Iwakura Mission and Its Stay in Salt Lake City," Utah Historical Quarterly *66 (Winter 1998): 26–47.*

Notes

1. Kume Kunitake, *Tokumei zenken taishi: Bejo kairan jikki* (A True account of the tour in America and Europe of the special embassy), 5 vols. (Tokyo: Iwanami Shoten, 1977), 137–38.
2. See W. G. Beasley, *Japan Encounters the Barbarian: Japanese Travelers in America and Europe* (New Haven: Yale University Press, 1995), 157; *Kodansha Encyclopedia of Japan* (Tokyo: Kodansha, 1983), s.v. "Iwakura Mission," 358; and Eugene Soviak, "On the Nature of Western Progress: The Journal of the Iwakura Embassy," in *Tradition and Modernization in Japanese Culture*, ed. Donald H. Shively (Princeton, N.J.: Princeton University Press, 1971), 7.
3. Marlene J. Mayo, "Rationality in the Meiji Restoration: The Iwakura Embassy," in *Modern Japanese Leadership*, ed. Bernard S. Silberman and Harry D. Harootunian (Tucson: University of Arizona Press, 1966), 324.
4. Marlene J. Mayo, "The Western Education of Kume Kunitake: 1871–6" *Monumenta Nipponica* 27, no. 1 (1973): 3–67.
5. Japan had signed several unequal treaties with Western powers in 1858, beginning with the Harris Treaty with the United States in July. These treaties were highly unfavorable for Japan. They opened several key Japanese cities to foreign trade, set Japanese tariffs and import duties at low levels that could only be regulated under international control, and allowed extraterritoriality for foreign residents in Japan.
6. W. G. Beasley, "The Iwakura Mission in Britain, 1872," *History Today* 31 (October 1981): 33.
7. *Salt Lake Tribune*, February 17, 1872.
8. Beasley, *Japan Encounters the Barbarian*, 163.
9. Mayo, "The Western Education of Kume Kunitake," 54.
10. Kido Takayoshi, *The Diary of Kido Takayoshi, Vol. II: 1871–1874*, trans. Sidney Devere Brown and Akiko Hirota (Tokyo: University of Tokyo Press, 1985), 123.
11. Kume, *Tokumei zenken taishi*, 140–41.
12. *Deseret News*, February 9, 1872.
13. *Salt Lake Daily Herald*, February 13, 1872.
14. *Deseret News*, February 8, 1872.
15. *Salt Lake Daily Herald*, February 11, 1872.
16. For an excellent discussion of this theme, see the chapter, "The Pleasing Awfulness," in Sandra L. Myres, *Westering Women and the Frontier Experience, 1800–1915* (Albuquerque: University of New Mexico Press, 1982).
17. Both Lorenzo Snow and Orson Pratt were also at this time members of the Quorum of the Twelve Apostles. Snow was later President of the Church from 1898 until his death in 1901.

18. Utah Territorial Legislature, Address of the Legislative Assembly to the Japanese Embassy, February, 16, 1872, Journal History of the Church, February 16, 1872, Church Archives, The Church of Jesus Christ of Latter-day Saints, Salt Lake City, microfilm copy in Harold B. Lee Library, Brigham Young University, Provo, Utah.

19. Utah Territorial Legislature, Address of the Legislative Assembly to the Japanese Embassy, February, 16, 1872, Journal History of the Church.

20. Kido, *Diary of Kido Takayoshi*, 127.

21. Kume, *Tokumei zenken taishi*, 139. When Kume wrote his memoirs at an advanced age, he clarified this statement by saying that when one walked down a street in Salt Lake City, one could see the number of wives a man had by how many windows he had in his home. It is unclear how Kume received this incorrect impression.

22. Elizabeth A. Howard, "Diary," February, L. Tom Perry Special Collections, Harold B. Lee Library, Brigham Young University, Provo, Utah.

23. Samuel Parker Richards, "Journal," February 6, 1872, Church Archives.

24. Wilford Woodruff, *Wilford Woodruff's Journal*, ed. Scott G. Kenney 9 vols. (Midvale, Utah: Signature Books, 1985), 7:61.

25. Brigham Young Hampton, "Journal," February 4, 1872, Church Archives.

26. *Salt Lake Daily Herald*, February 5, 1872.

27. *Salt Lake Daily Herald*, February 5, 1872. A seventeenth-century edict made this technically true, but it is a simplistic characterization. *Kokushi daijiten* (Dictionary of the history of Japan) (Tokyo: Yoshikawa Kōbunkan, 1979–97), 4:443. By 1876 the Meiji government eliminated samurai privileges and made all Japanese citizens equal. Kenneth B. Pyle, *The Making of Modern Japan*, 2nd ed. (Lexington, MA: D. C. Heath, 1996), 105.

28. "Arrival of the Embassy," *Salt Lake Tribune*, February 5, 1872.

29. *Salt Lake Daily Herald*, February 7, 1872.

30. *Salt Lake Tribune*, February 5, 1872.

31. Roger Daniels, a leading immigration historian, has said that the Japanese "automatically inherited the prejudices already established against [the] Chinese." See his "Majority Images–Minority Realities: A Perspective on Anti-Orientalism in the United States," in *Nativism, Discrimination, and Images of Immigrants*, ed. George E. Pozzetta, vol. 15 of American Immigration and Ethnicity (New York: Garland, 1991), 107–8.

32. *Salt Lake Daily Herald*, February 7, 1872.

33. A Japanese acrobatic troop had performed in Salt Lake City in spring 1870. See *Deseret News*, April 27, 1870.

34. Kido, *Diary of Kido Takayoshi*, 127.

35. As quoted in Mayo, "The Western Education of Kume Kunitake," 59.

36. See Dean W. Collinwood, Ryoichi Yamamoto, Dazue Matsui-Haag, *Samurais in Salt Lake: Diary of the First Diplomatic Japanese Delegation to Visit Utah, 1872* (Salt Lake City: US-Japan Center, 1996), 23.

37. Kume, *Tokumei zenkin taishi*, 140–41.

38. Kume, *Tokumei zenkin taishi*, 146.

39. Kume, *Tokumei zenkin taishi*, 141–44.

40. Kido, *Diary of Kido Takayoshi*, 123.

41. Kume, *Tokumei zenken taishi*, 140.

42. Quoted in *Deseret News*, February 14, 1872.

43. See Leonard J. Arrington, *Brigham Young, American Moses* (New York: Alfred A. Knopf, 1985), 372–73; and Thomas G. Alexander, *Utah: The Right Place* (Salt Lake City: Gibbs Smith, 1995), 175–76.

44. *Salt Lake Tribune*, February 7, 1872.

45. Beasley, *Japan Encounters the Barbarian*, 163.

46. *Deseret News*, February 7, 1872.

47. Kido, *Diary of Kido Takayoshi*, 124.

48. *Salt Lake Daily Herald*, February 16, 1872.

49. "The Latest," *Deseret News*, February 13, 1872.

50. *Salt Lake Tribune*, February 15, 1872.

51. *Chicago Tribune*, February 5, 1872.

52. *New York Times*, February 5, 1872.

53. *Chicago Tribune*, February 14, 1872.

54. *Chicago Tribune*, February 19, 1872.

55. *Chicago Tribune*, February 19, 1872.

56. *Chicago Tribune*, February 15, 1872.

57. *Salt Lake Tribune*, February 14, 1872.

58. Marlene J. Mayo, "A Catechism of Western Diplomacy: The Japanese and Hamilton Fish, 1872," *Journal of Asian Studies* 26 (1967): 391.

59. Kido, *Diary of Kido Takayoshi*, 180.

60. Kido, *Diary of Kido Takayoshi*, 142.

4

Tomizo and Tokujiro: The First Japanese Mormons

Shinji Takagi

In August 1901, Heber J. Grant and his companions arrived in Japan to open the first permanent mission in Asia and begin their difficult proselytizing labors among the Japanese.[1] It took them almost seven long months to claim the first fruit of their labors. On March 8, 1902, on the shore of Omori in Tokyo Bay, Hajime Nakazawa, a professed Shinto priest, was baptized, confirmed, and ordained an elder. This event was symbolic indeed. For one thing, Nakazawa was presumably affiliated with a religious sect whose roots went back to the ancient indigenous religion of Japan.[2] For another, more interestingly, the name *Hajime* signifies "beginning" or "first" in Japanese.

Although the baptism of Hajime Nakazawa undoubtedly is the first of the missionary fruits to be claimed in Japan, it hardly represents the first fruit of the Church among the Japanese. Frequent contacts between Japanese and Latter-day Saints prior to the opening of the mission in Japan in 1901 are well documented. Following the completion of the transcontinental railroad in 1869, Ogden, Utah, became an important railroad junction, where just about every Japanese traveler stopped on his way to much of the United States and Europe.[3] Some even stayed in Utah and its surrounding regions.[4] Contacts were also made in Hawaii, where, following the beginning of large-scale Japanese emigration in 1885,[5] frequent contacts were reported in Laie and other places. Some of the Japanese people so contacted affiliated themselves with the Mormons well before 1901.[6]

This paper will tell the stories of two such people, Tomizo Katsunuma (1863–1950) and Tokujiro Sato (ca. 1851–1919). Both were born in Japan during the final days of the Tokugawa or Edo period (1603–1868)[7] and came in the latter half of the nineteenth century to what is now part of the United States. Tomizo received the best education available in Japan, became a veterinarian, came to the United States in part to pursue further studies in veterinary science, and spent most of his life as a United States immigration officer, veterinarian, and prominent citizen in Hawaii. In contrast, Tokujiro had little formal education, came to Hawaii at a young age as a contractual immigrant worker, married a native Hawaiian, and earned his living as a carpenter, butcher, cook, and taro farmer. The purpose of this article is to cast their lives against the economic, political, and social conditions of their day and to appreciate their struggles as pioneers in a strange land.

Tomizo Katsunuma

In 1937, Edward L. Clissold[8] began his summary of notable events in the ministry of the Church among the Japanese people of Hawaii in these words:

> Any story of the Japanese members of the Church of Jesus Christ of Latter-day Saints in the Hawaiian Islands should begin with the arrival in Hawaii in 1898 of Dr. T. Katsunuma, a then recent graduate of the Utah State Agricultural College [sic], and a member of the Church holding the office of a priest in the Aaronic Priesthood.[9]

Tomizo Katsunuma (illus. 4-1) was a prominent and respected man of some influence in the Japanese and non-Japanese communities of Hawaii during the first half of the twentieth century, when the Japanese constituted about 40 percent of the total population.[10]

Tomizo, who was a veterinarian by training and practice, worked for the United States government as an immigration inspector in Honolulu from 1898 to 1924. Because of this role and because he was responsible for initiating the emigration of Japanese to Hawaii from his home prefecture of Fukushima, he was honored as the Father of Immigrants. Among Mormons in Hawaii, he was respected as one of the Church's first documented members of Japanese ancestry.

Early Years in Japan. Tomizo Katsunuma was born on October 6 in the third year of Bunkyu (or November 16, 1863)[11] in the castle town of Miharu, Banshu (now Fukushima Prefecture). He was the third son (and fourth child) of Naochika Katogi,[12] a samurai of the Miharu clan, and his wife Yo (or Yoko).[13] After studying the Chinese classics at the clan school, he entered an elementary school in Miharu, where he was in the first graduating class under the new educational system of the Meiji period (1868–1912).[14] He then went on to study Chinese books and Western learning at a newly opened middle school in Miharu until 1878, when at age fifteen he was enrolled in the Sendai Foreign Language School in the principal city of Sendai, where he studied English reading and writing.

In 1880, Tomizo moved to Tokyo and entered the Preparatory School of the University of Tokyo in Hitotsubashi. There he completed three years of study in liberal arts.[15] However, he gave up the idea of pursuing a higher education because of a lack of funds. After returning home, he took a job for meager pay at a silk-reeling factory, then as the principal of an elementary school in the village of Michiwatashi for a monthly wage of ten yen. When a middle school was opened in the village of Tatsuta, he was appointed as assistant professor to teach English.

This area of the country (Tamura County) was a breeding center for horses, and a need was felt to train a resident veterinarian with county funds. In 1885, Tomizo was requested by the county commissioner to attend the Tokyo School of Veterinary Science[16] for a monthly allowance of fifteen yen. He subsequently transferred to the department of veterinary science at the Imperial College of Agriculture in Komaba and, upon graduation in 1888, was appointed assistant researcher at the school.

Courtesy June Stageberg

Illus. 4-1. Tomizo Katsunuma (1863–1950).

Arrival in the United States. In the late 1880s, there was a sort of emigration fervor in Japan. In part, this reflected the depressed state of the economy. Following the Satsuma Rebellion (armed uprisings carried out by former samurai of the Satsuma clan) of 1877 and the inflationary consequence of financing the war, the Meiji government began to pursue a deflationary policy in the early 1880s under the leadership of Finance Minister Masayoshi Matsukata. The agrarian distress created by the deflationary policy of the 1880s was so severe that the government changed its previously cautious attitude toward emigration and instituted a program of supervised emigration to Hawaii in 1885.[17] At the same time, the Chinese Exclusion Act of 1882, which halted the immigration of Chinese laborers, had created a demand for Japanese workers in the United States. In this atmosphere, Tomizo determined to look for a chance to emigrate.

The chance came rather quickly. Upon hearing that one of his elder brothers, Shigenori, was going to the United States to survey the electric power industry, Tomizo decided to go along. On April 25, 1889, the two dream-filled brothers departed in a steamboat for America, leaving behind a Meiji Japan agitated over the establishment of the National Diet. Tomizo was twenty-five years old and had been married to Endo Mine[18] for less than a month, the wedding having taken place on March 30. According to his biographer, Mine nevertheless encouraged his decision, allowing her husband to move ahead in pursuit of his purpose and dream.[19]

On May 10, 1889, the two brothers arrived in San Francisco. After staying with Tomizo for several days, Shigenori traveled on the transcontinental railroad to observe electricity-related enterprises in the East and remained in the United States until January 1890.[20] Being left alone, Tomizo stayed in the vicinity of San Francisco, visiting the ranches in the surrounding communities with the help of Sutemi Chinda, the Japanese Consul in San Francisco.[21] He subsequently engaged in raising sheep and cattle at a large-scale vineyard managed by a Japanese man by the name of Nagasawa in Santa Rosa, California.[22]

In those days, there was an association of Japanese in San Francisco called the Patriotic League, whose principal members included the founder, Yoshizo Kasuya (later the speaker of the House of Representatives), and others who would also become prominent in

Japanese politics. In the 1880s, Japan was swept by a nationwide popular political movement called the Popular Rights Movement, in which certain dissatisfied elements of society were demanding a reform of the Meiji government along Western democratic lines. The government dealt forcefully with the movement, imprisoning many of its leaders and executing a few. The Patriotic League was initially organized in January 1888 by dissident leaders who had fled the country, although it is not clear how much of that political zeal remained once the Meiji constitution (with a nominal democracy) was promulgated in 1889. Under these circumstances, Tomizo was invited to join the League, became involved in its work, and participated in political discussions with his compatriots.

Encounter with the Mormons. Tomizo's introduction to Mormonism came as a direct consequence of his connection with the Patriotic League. In the early 1890s, members of the League established the business of providing mail handling, remittance, translation, letter writing, and other services to Japanese immigrant workers.[23] The first subcontractor was a man by the name of Tadashichi Tanaka, who set up his office in 1891 in Nampa, Idaho, and staffed it with student laborers from San Francisco. As one of the student laborers supplied by the Patriotic League, Tomizo worked in Tanaka's Idaho office as his right-hand man. Because Tanaka had earlier managed a house of ill repute in the railroad town of Ogden, Utah, it is possible that Tomizo first went to Utah in 1890 before moving to Nampa in 1891.[24]

Tomizo's business and other activities in the early 1890s must have taken him to places in Idaho, Utah, and other Western states and territories. In 1891, another brother, Shutaro, came to the United States to study dairy farming at the Agricultural College of Utah (now Utah State University). During his studies, Shutaro made trips to Salt Lake City to conduct experiments in sericulture,[25] almost certainly accompanied by Tomizo. Although it is not known how Tomizo ended up in Logan, Utah (where he would be baptized into the Church), it is likely that his departure from Idaho was triggered by Tanaka's dismissal as the field agent in spring 1893, on charges that wages withheld from the workers on the Oregon Short Line were mishandled.[26] The decision to relocate to Logan may have been a joint decision with his brother. Shutaro stayed in the Idaho-Utah area from 1891 to about 1895.[27]

While in Logan, Tomizo first entered Brigham Young College, a Mormon academy, and completed a course in "theology," probably religious education. His enrollment at Brigham Young College may have been inspired by his desire to study Mormonism or may have been only a precursor (in terms of mastering the English language) to his studies in veterinary medicine at the Agricultural College. The registrar's office at Utah State University has records of Tomizo's enrollment for the academic years 1895 and 1896. It is not clear, therefore, if he actually graduated from a degree-granting program. According to his biographer, however, he completed the course of study in agriculture in three years, upon which he became an assistant for a Dr. Fischer, a German professor in veterinary science.[28]

While in Logan, Tomizo naturally had frequent contacts with Mormons, prominent among whom was Carl Christian Amussen, a wealthy Danish convert to the Church and the father, with his third wife, Barbara McIsaac Smith, of Flora Amussen, the wife of Ezra Taft Benson, the thirteenth President of the Church. After retiring from his successful jewelry business in Salt Lake City, Amussen was living in a two-story, French-style villa in Logan, with "marble fireplaces, a great winding stairway in solid mahogany with turned balustrades, two grand porticos, one facing each street, a steam heating plant, and modern plumbing."[29] His initial contact with Tomizo was likely related to the fact that Amussen was a horseman who was proud of his white Arabian horses. It may be recalled that, even before coming to Logan, Tomizo was a veterinarian skilled in the handling of horses.

As Amussen was a wealthy man, he spent his winters in Santa Barbara or the Monterey Peninsula in California. During those winter months, according to the Amussen family historian,

> he entrusted his house to a Japanese student by the name of Katsunuma. Before he left Logan, the Japanese friend had been converted to the Church, typifying and exemplifying the missionary zeal which characterized the entire life of Carl Christian Amussen from the time of his conversion until the day of his death.[30]

Tomizo was baptized by Guy W. Thatcher and confirmed a member of the Church by Joseph E. Lewis on August 8, 1895. He was subsequently ordained a deacon by R. M. Lewis on January 25, 1896.[31] It was also during his Logan years that Tomizo became a naturalized U.S. citizen—

citizenship was possibly granted in recognition of his service in the Utah National Guard[32]—and in 1896 cast his first vote, for Democratic presidential candidate William Jennings Bryan.

Relocation in Hawaii. In 1894 the Japanese government terminated its program of supervised emigration to Hawaii.[33] In response, there was a rise of private emigration companies that recruited laborers for profits. In 1898, for example, there were nine such companies, which shipped 12,293 laborers abroad, mostly to sugar plantations in Hawaii.[34] While in Utah, Tomizo was recruited by one of those companies, the Hiroshima Emigration Company. The Hiroshima Emigration Company had had a long-standing relationship with the Patriotic League and hired some of the League members as its executives. Tsutau Sugawara, a prominent member of the Patriotic League, was one of them, and he had set up an office in Honolulu in 1895.[35] The recruitment of Tomizo may have been initiated more directly by Tatsusaburo Matsuoka, Tomizo's office mate in Nampa, who also became an executive of the Hiroshima Emigration Company upon his return to Japan in 1897. Accepting the Hiroshima company's offer, Tomizo left Utah for the Pacific and arrived in Honolulu on January 15, 1898.

However, Tomizo's involvement with the Hiroshima Emigration Company was apparently brief because, in the early spring of the same year, he made his first trip home under contract with the Kumamoto Emigration Company.[36] Until that time, most of the immigrants to Hawaii had come from the regions in western Japan, including Kumamoto, Fukuoka, Yamaguchi, and Hiroshima. The Kumamoto Emigration Company was the first of the major emigration companies to pay attention to the Tohoku region, and the charge given to Tomizo was to recruit emigrants from that region, including from his home prefecture of Fukushima. Upon his return home, he gave stirring speeches in his Tohoku accent and inspired many to emigrate to Hawaii.[37] Tomizo returned to Hawaii on July 26, 1898, accompanied by a group of about one hundred Fukushima immigrants.[38]

Obviously, the highlight of his first trip home was the reunion with his wife, Mine, whom he had not seen for almost ten years. He had not even seen their son, Katsumi, who was born in Miharu following Tomizo's departure for the United States. For a few months in the first half of 1898, they lived in a detached room in the eastern part of the

Endo house in their hometown of Miharu. Thus, Tomizo indisputably became the first Japanese Mormon to live in Japan.[39] Their union was not to be disrupted again by a long absence. Soon after the birth of the second child, Kiyomi (in January 1899), the family traveled to Hawaii to be with Tomizo.[40]

Life in Hawaii. Upon his permanent settlement in Hawaii, Tomizo became an immigration officer of the U.S. government. Given his earlier connections with Japanese emigration companies, his U.S. citizenship and his ability to speak English (though not without a strong accent) must have been important factors in this appointment, as Hawaii was being annexed to the United States at the time of his appointment (the process of annexation was completed in August 1898) and was to become a full territory of the United States in June 1900. With this changed status of Hawaii, the period of contractual immigration ended, only to be succeeded by a period of free immigration. A flood of Japanese immigrants continued to come, and the U.S. government needed someone of Tomizo's background to handle the arrival of those immigrants, which averaged about sixty per ship.[41]

Whenever a group of Japanese immigrants arrived, Tomizo, as an immigration inspector for the U.S. government took a launch with customs officers to the ship, which was temporarily anchored awaiting their arrival. The team would then make a preliminary check of passengers as the ship was being docked along the pier. Things would generally move smoothly for the first-class passengers. Immigrants and other third-class passengers would be housed in the Immigration Department to go through the necessary investigation. Tomizo worked in this capacity until June 30, 1924, the day before the Johnson-Reid Immigration Act, which barred from entry all aliens ineligible for citizenship, took effect.

During that period, hardly a single Japanese immigrant landed in Hawaii without being inspected by Tomizo. Because of that status, he was well respected in the Japanese community, and many, including those who arrived as picture brides (in other words, women whose marriages to resident immigrants were arranged across the Pacific through the exchange of photographs), came seeking his advice even on personal matters.[42] He was called "Doctor Katsunuma" or sometimes simply "Doctor" in the Japanese community, not because he had a doctorate (which he did not), but out of respect for his professional training in veterinary medicine, which he continued to practice and which he continued to regard as his true vocation in life.[43]

He was known for his sharp wit, humor, and jovial personality. According to historian Yukiko Kimura, he was "unconventional, unpretentious, and had an open and direct way of doing things. . . . Japanese residents of Hawaii, rural and urban, accepted him with affection and respect because of these characteristics."[44] Yasutaro Soga, a friend and a prominent figure in the Japanese community of Hawaii, wrote:

> Dr. Katsunuma, who was always called "Roko"[45] among us and "Dr. Party" among the people, was a popular figure in the society circles of Honolulu. This was true not only among us the Japanese, but also among the White, Chinese, Kanaka (native Hawaiian), and Portuguese peoples. Regardless of race, religion, social status or age, he would talk to any acquaintance he might meet on the streets of Honolulu with the same familiarity. Whenever I was with him, his conversation with an acquaintance would become so long that I was sometimes distressed. . . .
>
> Like myself, he did not drink much. At parties, however, he was famous for his Japanese limerick, which went something like "it is human to have facial pits, horses don't have them." At Rotary Club socials and other functions, he would make people burst into laughter by imitating a cock crow or a horse laughter. In this manner, Dr. Katsunuma was a unique personality among us, his associates in Hawaii.[46]

Arriving immigrants were sometimes dumbfounded by the words that came out of Tomizo's mouth, which were spoken with a Tohoku accent and were full of humor and wit. Toward the immigrants from Fukushima Prefecture, his paternalistic feelings were sometimes manifested violently, particularly when he was young. His biographer cites one eyewitness account:

> It [The man] was a Matsumoto or something like that from Adachi County. When we arrived at Honolulu harbor, Mr. Katsunuma told us to gather together, so we all went upon the deck. This man came up considerably late. He was wearing an unlined summer kimono with splashed patterns, and walked up pattering his wooden clogs of medium height, with a tobacco case hanging down from his

waist. Even we could tell that he was in trouble. Furious with anger, Mr. Katsunuma ran up to that man, kicked him with the shoe, trampled on him two or three times when he fell, yelling, "Where do you think you are? You are a disgrace to Fukushima."

The biographer interpreted Tomizo's behavior as reflecting "his constant passion for the improvement of younger immigrants."[47]

A Community Leader. With no propensity for smoking or drinking, Tomizo had as a favorite pastime reading and writing. In 1907, when the old and deteriorating Japanese Consulate building (purchased by the first consul in 1886) was put on sale, Tomizo purchased the building, moved it to Metcalf Street, and, upon renovation, called it Bashoan after his pen name, Basho.[48] He was often found reading a book in a wisteria chair on the verandah of the house. His writings reveal that he was an avid reader, knowledgeable about many things, both East and West, old and new.[49] For example, he wrote on such diverse subjects as the Japanese beetle, tattoos, and the contemporary Japanese *haiku* poet Meisetsu Naito.

Writing almost became his profession. With the printing press and movable types that he had shipped from his brother in Tokyo, he upgraded the *Yamato Shinbun* (a mimeographed newspaper with which he was associated from the earliest days) to a printed daily paper. In 1906, Yasutaro Soga (originally of Tokyo) was invited to become the president and editor-in-chief, and the title was changed to the *Nippu Jiji* (later the name would change again, to the *Hawaii Times*). Tomizo supported the newspaper company by serving as vice president and by frequently writing columns that enjoyed wide readership and commanded considerable influence among the Japanese-reading public. Tomizo obviously loved the newspaper business because he was engaged in it until just before his death.

In describing Tomizo's writing style, Soga expressed himself in these words: "[Dr. Katsunuma] had an inquisitive mind, had passion for newspapers, and had a first class style of his own when it came to writing. His 'Tohoku' accent even manifested itself in writing. Because 'e' and 'i' were reversed, we were always troubled."[50]

A collection of Tomizo's essays that appeared regularly in the Sunday columns of the *Nippu Jiji* from April 1922 to June 1924 was later published as a book under the title of *Kansho no Shiborikasu* (Strained lees of sugarcanes), with ten thousand copies printed by the Nippu Jiji Company. This three-hundred-page book not only is revealing of Tomizo's witty character but is also a great source of information on the social history of Japanese immigrants in Hawaii.

Tomizo often acted as an arbitrator in public or private disputes. In 1900, when a number of Chinese workers were killed in a major collision, the Japanese offenders were sentenced to death. Tomizo resolutely stood up in their defense and eventually succeeded in reducing the sentence. From this time on, Tomizo became a great advocate of the Japanese community in Hawaii. In 1909, Tomizo and his newspaper repeatedly demanded that the working conditions of Japanese plantation workers be improved, and they supported the strike of seven thousand plantation workers. When an incident of serious consequence occurred in the Japanese community, Tomizo was often called to intervene and find a peaceful settlement.[51]

For many years, Tomizo was a confidant of Japanese consuls stationed in Honolulu. When a Japanese consul was preparing for the festivities of the first emperor's birthday (to be held on November 3, 1900) after Hawaii had become a U.S. territory, he recognized the need to be sensitive and requested that Tomizo become a member of the planning committee. Tomizo was also a charter (and the first non-Caucasian) member of the Rotary Club of Honolulu. He was involved in many community functions and activities, including the management of the Japanese hospital; the March 26, 1922, reunion of the first Japanese immigrants (called *gan-nen-mono*) and their descendants[52]; and the festivities held on February 8, 1935, in celebration of the fiftieth anniversary of the commencement of the government-supervised program of emigration. He had a close association with both Christian and Buddhist leaders of the Japanese community, and Japanese dignitaries visiting Hawaii often called on him.

As a leader of the Japanese community in Hawaii, Tomizo twice represented the community in attending the imperial coronation ceremonies in Japan. The first time was in September 1915 when Tomizo made his third trip home,[53] leading a group of about fifty people. Before traveling west to Kyoto to attend the coronation of Emperor Taisho, the group was invited by Marquis Shigenobu Okuma, then prime minister of Japan, to his residence in Tokyo, where Tomizo is said to have "mystified Marquis Okuma by giving a formal reply which was both relevant and witty."[54] The second occasion was in 1928, when he made his fourth and last trip home to attend the coronation of Emperor Showa (or Hirohito), which was held on November 13.

Early Association with the Church. Writing in 1937, Clissold explained that when Tomizo first arrived in Hawaii almost forty years earlier, he

> attended services regularly at Auwaiolimu (in Honolulu) for several months. As the services were held entirely in Hawaiian, however, he became discouraged and for many years attended church only at conference time. During these periods of inactivity, he continued to claim membership and never hesitated to admit that he was a Mormon.[55]

The festivities of the fiftieth anniversary celebration of the Hawaiian Mission, which were held in December 1900, might have been one of those occasions when Tomizo attended church. A picture taken on that occasion features Tomizo with George Q. Cannon, one of the first missionaries to Hawaii, who returned to represent the First Presidency.[56]

According to Clissold, Tomizo also met with Heber J. Grant, then a member of the Quorum of the Twelve:

> When President Heber J. Grant passed through Hawaii on his way to preside over the Japanese Mission, Dr. Katsunuma met him and offered his services as missionary. For some reason he was not called to the mission field and continued to live in Hawaii as the only Japanese member.[57]

The statement that Elder Grant passed through Hawaii on his way to Japan is obviously incorrect, as the *Empress of India,* which carried the first missionaries to Japan in August 1901, did not visit Honolulu.[58] The timing of Tomizo's meeting with Elder Grant must have been in March 1902, when the Apostle did visit the Hawaiian Mission on his way back from Japan to attend the April general conference.[59] Whether Tomizo at that time was the only Japanese member in Hawaii, as Clissold says in his statement, is also subject to question.[60]

Apparently, Elder Grant and his companions knew about Tomizo from the earliest days of their mission in Japan. It is possible that they had heard about him from George Q. Cannon while they were still in Utah. Alma O. Taylor, one of the first missionaries to Japan, writes that on August 19, 1901, they received at their boarding house in Yokohama a man by the name of Ushida, "who at one time went to school for about 4 months in the L.D.S. College . . . and was well acquainted with Thomaz Katsunuma who now lives in Honolulu, H.I. and is a member of the Church." On the same day, the missionaries received a letter from "Mr. Katogi the Brother of T. Katsunuma . . . [who] had been in Salt Lake City and appreciated the kindness of the Mormons in helping him in the raising of silk."[61] Shutaro Katogi, who must have found out about the arrival of the Mormon missionaries by reading newspaper accounts, invited Elder Grant to come to see him in Tokyo and offered some assistance to the Church. On August 25, the editors of the Tokyo newspaper *Shakai Shimpo* came to interview the missionaries in Yokohama, as recorded in Taylor's journal:

> They brought with them a letter of introduction from Mr. Katogi with whom Bro. Grant had become acquainted while in Tokio a few days ago. . . . These gentlemen told us that . . . if we would go to Tokio that they wanted to call a large meeting and give us the opportunity of addressing through an interpreter, the Japanese people. They also said that the proprietor of their paper Mr. Oda told them that he would take great delight in introducing us to the people of his country. They also were the bearers of a message from Mr. Matsuoka, . . . telling us that he would furnish us a house without charging rent if we would only come to Tokio.[62]

During his second trip home in 1904, Tomizo himself sought out and visited the mission home in Tokyo. Taylor describes the visit:

> Learned upon returning to headquarters that Bro. Katsunuma from Hawaii had visited Prest. E[nsign] on Monday the 4th [of April 1904]. Bro. Katsunuma is the first Japanese to join the Church in all the world. He was converted in Utah many years ago. He has become an American citizen and is now in the civil service at Hawaii. He having received a month's furlough, is in Japan visiting friends & relatives. He sought "Mormons" out the first thing and seemed pleased with what they had accomplished & were doing. He was glad to see some Latter-day Saint Hymns in his native language and gave the sect. of the Mission ¥[yen] 10.00 towards further translation.[63]

A Japanese Mormon in Hawaii. During the early years in Hawaii, in addition to the language difficulty, his wife's attitude toward religion may also have played a part in Tomizo's general inactivity in the Church. She was a staunch Methodist and did not think much of the Mormons.[64] The rest of the family apparently attended the Methodist Church. As English increasingly became a dominant language in Hawaii, however, Tomizo must have become a more active participant in Latter-day Saint services. Certainly by the early 1920s, Tomizo was an active participant. In a Sunday newspaper column published on November 6, 1921, he talks about the visit of an English professor from Utah and mentions that they became acquainted with each other because of their association in the Church.[65]

In the early 1930s, Tomizo was instrumental in the organization of a Japanese Sunday School class in the Kalihi (Honolulu) Branch in May 1934 and the subsequent establishment of the Japanese Mission in Hawaii. In the critical meeting of key individuals held in the Hawaiian Mission home on April 6, 1934, Tomizo was present, along with Castle H. Murphy (mission president) and Edward L. Clissold, and offered the opening prayer.[66] In connection with the First Presidency visit in Hawaii in summer 1935, J. Reuben Clark Jr. writes that "among the Japanese Saints in Honolulu [is] . . . Dr. Tomizo Katsunuma, who at one time attended college in Utah."[67] In Clark's account, Tomizo was undoubtedly a member of the group of Japanese Saints who "gave to President Grant and his group a delicious dinner and afterward a delightful entertainment of song, dance, instrumental music and recitation."[68]

Writing in 1939 about the establishment of the Japanese Mission in Hawaii in February 1937, John A. Widtsoe mentions Tomizo as one of the seventeen Church members of Japanese ancestry found by Hilton A. Robertson, the incoming mission president.[69] On October 1, 1939, following the establishment of the Japanese Mission, Tomizo was ordained an elder by Robertson.[70] Widtsoe describes Tomizo as "a student of Brigham Young College and the Utah State Agricultural College [sic], and the first Japanese baptized into the Church" and as "active in the service of the mission in Honolulu."[71] He goes on to say that there is "much friendliness among the Japanese for our work" and that the "Japanese daily, *Nippu Jiji* of Honolulu, under the able leadership of Mr. Yasutaro Soga . . . made frequent timely references to the work of the Latter-day Saints among the Japanese." This is to be expected. Soga was one of Tomizo's closest friends, and Tomizo himself was involved in the editorial work of the *Nippu Jiji*.

After retiring from the Immigration Department in 1924, Tomizo returned to his real vocation as a veterinarian and continued the pleasant pastime of writing. Such retirement days were quietly spent until summer 1950, when he was hospitalized at Kuakini Hospital. He gradually weakened because of advancing age and, on September 11, closed his colorful life of almost eighty-seven years. His wife and other close relatives were at his bedside. The funeral was solemnly held on September 13 at the Church's large tabernacle on Beretania Street, with Edward L. Clissold conducting. The tabernacle was filled with flowers, and many dignitaries were in attendance. The memorial addresses were given by Yasutaro Soga and Chomatsu Tsukiyama (president of the Senate). It was said to be the largest funeral held there in many years, with no room left even to stand.[72] An obituary appeared in the English-language *Honolulu Advertiser*, under the large headline "Dr. Katsunuma, first Japanese Mormon, Dies."[73]

Tokujiro Sato

Tokujiro Sato (illus. 4-2), also known in Hawaii as Toko, Toku, or Sasaki,[74] is another person who has a claim to being the first Japanese Mormon. Unlike Tomizo Katsunuma, however, very little is known, let alone written, about him. However, the contrast with Tomizo goes beyond the availability of reliable information. In all likelihood, Tokujiro was a person of humble means and little education.

An Eyewitness Account. The best place to begin is the only published eyewitness account of him, which describes the 1919 encounter of Tokujiro or Toko with Elias Wesley Smith, the son of Joseph F. Smith and president of the Hawaiian Mission:

> During my recent visit, through the different conferences on the Islands of Maui and Hawaii, I had the privilege of meeting the first Japanese convert to the Church of Jesus Christ of Latter-day Saints, who is now living at Kukuihaele, Hawaii. We held an interesting meeting in his home and spent the night there.
>
> Becoming interested in Brother Toko, I learned that he was born in Tokio, Japan, in the year 1849 [sic]. At the age of seventeen [sic] he worked his way to Hawaii, arriving here in 1866 [sic]. In 1879 [sic]

he married a Hawaiian by the name of Kalala, and they have happily passed their ruby anniversary. He joined the Church in 1892 [sic], and has been and is still a faithful member.

He related to me many interesting incidents that took place here many years ago, among which was the Walter Murray Gibson trouble, and how he witnessed Gibson's unlawful rise to power, and his dishonorable failure....

Brother Toko is now seventy [sic] years of age, hale and hearty, and able to work six days a week raising Kalo (a Hawaiian vegetable used in making poi) for the market. In this way he earns an honest living. He has a large family of bright children.[75]

Illus. 4-2. Tokujiro Sato (ca. 1851–1919).
Courtesy June Stageberg

Smith's statement is extremely valuable as a starting reference, not because it is entirely correct (which it is not), but because it raises so many questions. For one thing, the arrival date of 1866 means that Tokujiro left Japan when the country was still under Tokugawa rule. Could he have left then? Very likely the dates of both his birth and arrival, if not anything else, are incorrect.[76] Moreover, even if we take those dates at face value, how is it possible for someone who arrived in Hawaii in 1866 and joined the Church in 1892 to witness the Walter Murray Gibson trouble of 1861–64, if the statement refers to Gibson's unlawful administration of Lanai, the gathering place for the Hawaiian Saints?[77] Maybe Smith was putting his own words into Tokujiro's mouth, when Tokujiro was thinking of something else.

Smith's statement, however, convincingly demonstrates that in Kukuihaele on the island of Hawaii there was a Japanese man who claimed to have arrived in Hawaii long before the government-supervised program of emigration began in 1885 and whom a Church leader regarded as belonging to the Church, the man having been baptized before the opening of missionary work in Japan in 1901. Furthermore, Smith's encounter with Tokujiro is entirely probable. Smith arrived in Honolulu on June 25, 1919, replacing Samuel Edwin Woolley, who had served as mission president for twenty-four years from 1895 to 1919.[78] Thus, the new president was in need of quickly acquainting himself with the conditions prevailing in various parts of the islands. Because Smith was born in Laie during his father's exile (1885–87)[79] and had himself filled a mission to Hawaii from 1907 to 1910, he spoke Hawaiian fluently, as did Tokujiro (albeit with a Japanese accent). So the conversations, which must have taken place between June 25 and October 22 (when the report was filed),[80] were undoubtedly conducted in that language.

Gan-nen-mono. As previously mentioned, organized immigration of Japanese workers to Hawaii did not begin until early 1885, when the Japanese government initiated a supervised program of emigration under a provisional agreement with the Kingdom of Hawaii. The first group of 948 Japanese immigrants arrived in Hawaii aboard the *City of Tokyo* on February 8, 1885, to work mostly on sugar plantations. Tokujiro Sato's arrival in Hawaii predates the first group of government immigrants by almost twenty years, because he came in 1868 (not 1866, as stated by E. Wesley Smith) as a member of the only group of immigrants who left Japan before the commencement of government emigration.[81] As the year 1868 was the first year of Meiji,[82] this group came to be called collectively "first year men," or *gan-nen-mono* in Japanese.

With declining population[83] and the emergence of sugar, pineapple, and other agricultural industries, Hawaii was eager, at least from the early 1850s, to receive foreign workers to cover the shortfall of labor.[84] Desiring to secure Japanese workers and knowing Japan was opening to international intercourse in the late 1850s, the Hawaiian authorities approached the Tokugawa shogunate about the matter in 1865 by appointing Eugene M. Van Reed, a Dutch-American businessman living in Yokohama, as Hawaii's consul in Japan. No formal agreement could be secured because the shogunate objected not only to the idea of emigration itself but also to a businessman acting in a diplomatic capacity. However, on April 22, 1868,[85] Van Reed was finally successful in obtaining the permission of the shogunate to recruit up to 350 Japanese immigrants to work on sugar plantations in Hawaii for three years.

Van Reed contracted with Japanese agents to recruit immigrant workers on the streets of Edo (present-day Tokyo) and Yokohama. The recruitees were mainly city dwellers, who had little experience in farming. Perhaps about half of the group were vagabonds, coolies, gamblers, drunkards, and other troublemakers who infected the urban streets of Japan during that period of great political and social unrest. Some were the second and third sons of small merchant houses, struggling in the economic depression of the time. Others were carpenters, plasterers, and other construction workers who had been employed in the rapidly developing open-treaty port of Yokohama. An overwhelming majority of them were young, over two-thirds of them being in their late teens and twenties.

Their contract was for three years (counting from the date of arrival in Hawaii), during which time they would be required to work twenty-six days a month for four dollars (or three dollars in the case of women). Transportation, food, lodging, and medical care would be provided by the employers, free of charge. The recruitees responded to these terms, thinking that they would be rich when they returned home in three years. Uneducated as they were, they had no idea what *Hawaii* meant, let alone where the country was located. They called the place *tenjiku*, the ancient name for India, or simply a faraway place.

The fourth year of Keio (1868) was the year during which political power was transferred from the Tokugawa shogunate to the new imperial government of Emperor Meiji. The transfer of power was far from peaceful, however. Early in the year, following the declaration of imperial rule at the Imperial Palace in Kyoto, a civil war broke out. Strengthened by their victories in earlier battles, the imperial (now government) forces were marching toward Edo just about the time the immigrants were being recruited on the streets. Unfortunately for Van Reed and his party of immigrants, the Meiji government completely took over the political control of the port of Yokohama on May 9, 1868,[86] just about the time the chartered British ship *Scioto*[87] was preparing to leave with the immigrants on board. On May 6,[88] the immigrants had already begun boarding, upon the satisfactory completion of a medical examination.[89]

The new authorities stationed in Yokohama disapproved the shogunate's earlier agreement to allow its subjects to emigrate to Hawaii as contractual workers. Van Reed protested, saying that it would be a breach of diplomatic protocol not to honor the international agreement of a previous regime. On their part, the Meiji authorities argued that Hawaii was not a commercial treaty partner. Furthermore, they did not think that the terms of the contract were satisfactory and objected to the credentials of Van Reed as Hawaiian consul. They were also aware of the prevailing public opinion that the immigrant workers would be made slaves once they reached Hawaii.

Seeing the intransigence of the Japanese authorities, Van Reed appealed to the last resort measure. On the early morning of May 17, 1868,[90] with customs clearance from the British (but not Japanese) authorities,[91] he allowed the *Scioto,* carrying 150 Japanese immigrants (144 men and 6 women), to leave Yokohama harbor under the cover of darkness.[92] As the ship slowly moved out to the open sea, there was much rejoicing among the passengers because they were finally freed from the lingering fear that they would be arrested and punished by the government authorities. The immigrants had generally been ignorant of the intricacy of either politics or diplomacy but understood only that their departure was in question and their lives were possibly in danger.

The ship arrived in Honolulu on June 19. On the following day, the 149 immigrants (one had died at sea) were allowed to go ashore. While on board, all the men, except for two who would do so later, had had their characteristic topknots chopped off on board as a token of gratitude for having survived the voyage across rough seas and also possibly as a symbol of their severance from their old world. After two weeks of vacation in Honolulu, the immigrants were assigned to different employers, who were required to pay seventy dollars per immigrant to the government and to make an advance of ten dollars in cash to each immigrant, which would then be deducted from monthly wages.

In the meantime, the unauthorized departure of the *Scioto* had become a diplomatic embarrassment for the newly established government. To restore national dignity, the government tried in vain to work with the resident diplomatic community to explore ways of punishing Van Reed and to secure the return of the immigrants. Just at that time, complaints of mistreatment, poor diet, and other hardships began to surface among the immigrants in Hawaii. For one thing, the immigrants were city dwellers unaccustomed to a rural lifestyle, let alone farming. Besides, their working conditions were severe, as they were made to work twelve straight hours a day under the heat of sun. There were at least two natural deaths and one suicide. There were also complaints of inadequate pay, particularly when half the wages were withheld for deferred payment upon their return home. These and other problems were undoubtedly compounded by language difficulties. The plight of the Japanese immigrants reached the Japanese consul in San Francisco, and several letters arrived from Tomisaburo Makino, the leader of the immigrants in Hawaii, requesting the Japanese government to intervene on their behalf.

In consequence, the Japanese government decided to send twenty-five-year-old Kagenori Ueno as special envoy to Hawaii. Traveling by way of San Francisco, Ambassador Ueno arrived in Honolulu on December 27, 1869,[93] and immediately began to investigate the situation and to negotiate with the Hawaiian authorities.[94] Ueno proposed two alternatives. One was that all immigrants be returned to Japan immediately at the expense of the Japanese government. The other was that only those wishing to return immediately be returned at the expense of the Japanese government but the remainder be returned at the end of the three-year contract period at the expense of the Hawaiian government. On January 10, 1870,[95] the Hawaiian government accepted the second of the two proposals, subject to the condition that the agreement was "limited by the general law of all nations and of this country [and] by the fact that should any desire to remain the Hawaiian Government has no authority to compel them to go."[96] In the event, forty-two immigrants returned to Japan, and the rest (including two women) remained.[97] The working conditions and general treatment of the remaining immigrants were also improved so that no more serious complaints were reported during the rest of the initial contract period.

Life in Japan. Because the unauthorized departure of the *Scioto* in 1868 was a major diplomatic incident, there exist several government and semiofficial records that detail the names, ages, and, in some cases, occupations of the immigrants. The trouble, however, is that much discrepancy exists across different records, owing not only to poor record keeping but more importantly to the fact that the immigrants (with the exception of four or possibly five) were commoners without surnames. During the Tokugawa period, there was a definite hierarchical ordering of society based on occupational categories consisting of samurai (including aristocrats and clergymen), peasants, artisans, merchants, and undercaste people. To have a surname was a privilege reserved for samurai, some landed farmers, and favored townspeople, including artisans and merchants of wealth and distinction. Only 4 of the 150 gan-nen-mono had surnames, and the rest frequently changed their names after arriving in Hawaii, making it difficult to trace individual immigrants through time.

The various records show that there were two immigrants by the name of Tokujiro (with no surname). The statement of E. Wesley Smith, however, establishes that the Tokujiro we seek is listed as eighteen years old when he boarded the ship, the other Tokujiro being listed as twenty-seven years old.[98] In the old Japanese way of counting age,[99] this means that he was born during the fourth year of Kaei (or the twelve-month period from February 1, 1851, to January 29, 1852, and not 1849 as Smith claims) and that he was sixteen or seventeen years old in terms of Western counting when he came to Hawaii, depending on the exact date of his birth.[100] It is almost certain that Tokujiro was not of the samurai class, despite the claim of the family oral history to the contrary.[101] For one thing, he did not have a surname, or at least it is not recorded that he did. For another, Tatami-machi (or Tatami-cho), which is believed to have been his place of residence,[102] was in the Kyobashi section of Edo,[103] a small area southeast of Edo Castle, and was where artisans specializing in the making of *tatami* (mat extensively used in the furnishing of Japanese-style houses) were concentrated. Given the definite demarcation that existed between the sections for samurai and townsmen, no samurai could have possibly lived in that part of town.[104]

By the time he left home at the age of sixteen or seventeen, Tokujiro may well have already been an accomplished tatami maker in his own right. Family oral history has it that he was skilled in carpentry and helped build houses in the Waipio Valley on the northeastern coast of the island of Hawaii.[105] That he was a skilled carpenter cannot be disputed, as the house which he built for himself more than one hundred years ago still stands in the early twenty-first century.[106] These carpentry skills could have been acquired as part of his apprenticeship in tatami making, which involves mastering the use of carpentry tools. His supposed samurai status, undoubtedly of his own or his family's concoction, may be traced to the possible contractual relationship that his shop had with one of the hatamoto (Tokugawa retainer) families. Tatami-machi was linked by a bridge over the outer moat to the cluster of large hatamoto houses, which faced the inner moat of the castle. Tatami makers were placed in that precise location for the very purpose of serving the needs of those households and even the Tokugawa household itself.

In 1868 the town that Tokujiro was leaving behind was in a state of economic and social chaos. With the opening of Japan to international trade in the late 1850s, the relative prices of basic commodities began to change, resulting in a sharp redistribution of wealth. With trade came a rise in the relative prices of exportables such as silk and tea, while those of importables such as sugar and cotton fell. The wholesale merchants of Edo were particularly hard hit, as the flow of commodities was diverted to Yokohama and new merchants emerged to exploit the new business opportunities created by the opening of trade. To make matters worse, the Tokugawa shogunate began to stockpile rice and other essential commodities in preparation for the impending showdown with the antishogunate forces. With shortage and inflation, poverty was rampant.[107] The Keio period (1865–68) was a period of great social unrest, during which there were at least five major riots in Edo.

In spring 1868, it was under these economic and social conditions that the townspeople of Edo heard that the imperial forces were coming to destroy the city. Although Edo Castle was handed over to the imperial forces on May 3[108] in a peaceful settlement and the city was spared from being burned, the people in general were not fully informed of these developments. For some time, the streets remained filled with people carrying household effects in their attempt to flee the city. For Tokujiro and the other newly recruited immigrants from Edo, the call for laborers to work in Hawaii was not only an opportunity for life in a new land but also an opportunity to escape from economic depression and possible death in the old land. This sense of terror and urgency to escape is captured by the following quote from the (not-so-reliable) family oral history of Tokujiro:

> Tokujiro and thirteen other [sic] of his fellow samurai [were told that] if they were caught by the Imperial forces they would be beheaded. Seeing that they could not escape death if they remained

in Japan, their leader suggested them to find a way to run away to some far away country. Until Tokujiro and his fellow guards could find a way to escape they had to stay in hiding to prevent being captured by the Imperial forces.[109]

What is remarkable about this story, which Tokujiro must have told his family members in one form or another, is its seeming resemblance to the well-known story of a group of immigrants from Edo called *Imado-gumi,* headed by Komekichi Sakuma. The Imado-gumi group of twenty-five immigrants left the street of Imado in the Asakusa section of Edo on May 7[110] for their thirty-mile journey toward Yokohama. Heading south, they walked through the chaotic downtown streets of Edo and came to Takanawa, when they saw a large army of government soldiers marching into town. Caught by terror, they suddenly stopped and hid themselves in a grove of trees upon a hill in Shinagawa[111] and remained there until the last of the soldiers was seen walking up north to the central part of Edo. Other than the samurai reference, the resemblance between the two stories is so striking that one wonders whether Tokujiro was a member of Imado-gumi, with Komekichi being the leader. Or perhaps, the Imado-gumi story is only representative of a similar scene experienced by all the forty or so immigrants from Edo.

Life in Hawaii. The records filed by the gan-nen-mono chief Makino indicate that, when the time came to allocate the 148 immigrants (excluding one infant) among different employers, 51 were sent to Oahu, 71 to Maui (of this, 51 went to Haiku Sugar Company alone), 20 to Kauai, and 4 to Lanai (under the employ of W. M. Gibson).[112] E. Wesley Smith's statement that Tokujiro witnessed the Walter Murray Gibson trouble may well mean, if taken literally, that he was one of the four immigrants assigned to Lanai in the employ of Gibson. By 1868 the Gibson trouble had been long over, but Gibson still lived in Lanai. We know from a different source that, of the four assigned to Lanai, three (including a married couple) returned home in connection with the visit of Ambassador Ueno in early 1870.[113] The fourth immigrant assigned to Lanai might have been Tokujiro.

Or just as easily, Tokujiro could have been sent to Maui. After all, almost half the people were sent there. Lanai, particularly the valley of Palawai, where Gibson likely lived, was only a short distance from Lahaina, Maui, across the channel. As Lanai lacked most amenities of life, Gibson must have frequented Maui to purchase basic supplies. Even in Maui, Tokujiro and others could easily have had opportunities to see Gibson from time to time. In fact, the family oral history states that Tokujiro was first sent to Maui. Yet again, it is also possible that he first went to Lanai but moved to Maui in conjunction with the promise of the Hawaiian government, made with Ambassador Ueno, to improve the working conditions of the Japanese immigrants. He would not have stayed in Lanai if the conditions there had been so bad that three out of the four initial immigrants decided to leave.[114]

Interestingly, the list of gan-nen-mono filed on May 21, 1871, by Makino with the Hawaiian government designates "Toku Jilo" as desiring to go to the United States after the conclusion of the initial three-year contract period.[115] In early 1871, in response to an inquiry by Makino, the Japanese government authorized the remaining one hundred or so immigrants to return home, remain in Hawaii, or go to the United States without penalty. Judging from what we know about his later life experiences as well as his generally limited ability to speak English, however, it is almost certain that Tokujiro did not go to the United States when the contract was fulfilled in June 1871. As he was prepared to leave whatever place he was in, he may well have left for the island of Hawaii at that time.

With the enactment in Japan of the Household Register Law in 1871, it may have been around this time that Tokujiro took the surname Sato. Initially, when he arrived in Hawaii, he chose to be called Toku or Toko. Shortening of Japanese names to adapt to the Hawaiian manner of speech was an extremely common practice in those days.[116] When the time came to pick a surname, he could have easily adopted the name chosen by his family in Tokyo. When we recognize that he claimed that he was from Tatachi-machi, Kyobashi-ku, Tokyo, and that the Kyobashi section of Tokyo became a *ku* (city ward) only in November 1878,[117] we can be reasonably sure that he maintained some contact with his family at least until some time after that date. Alternatively, the fact that he also used the surname Sasaki at least for a while may indicate that he chose the name Sasaki first, only to find out later that his family had adopted a different name.

Whether by choice or by assignment, Tokujiro's years in Maui were followed by a permanent move to the island of Hawaii. According to one source, Tokujiro went to Waipio on the northeastern coast to work as a butcher and to farm taro.[118] On the other hand, the family oral history states that he went to Waimea (on the highland about ten miles south of Waipio) to work for Samuel Parker at his ranch as a carpenter and a cook and that the two developed a friendship that lasted a lifetime.[119] Samuel Parker (1852–1920) was the flamboyant grandson of John Palmer Parker (1790–1868), who jumped ship in Hawaii, befriended King Kamehameha I, and built a large and prosperous ranch on the Waimea plain. Whether Tokujiro first went to Waipio or Waimea, he finally ended up in Kukuihaele (about five miles south of Waipio along the Pacific coast), where he built his own home and spent his final years. Information is so scanty that we cannot possibly reconstruct the sequence of his life in Hawaii. One thing we know for sure is that his entire life on the island of Hawaii was spent in a relatively small triangular region connecting Waimea, Waipio, and Kukuihaele. His life in the three principal locations may well have been overlapping and not necessarily sequential.

Sometime after arriving on the island of Hawaii, Tokujiro married Kalala Keliihananui Kamekona, a Hawaiian with mixed Irish and Chinese lineage. According to family sources, Kalala Keliihananui Kamekona was the daughter of Kamekona (from the Waipio Valley) and Kaiahua (from the neighboring Waimanu Valley).[120] She is said to have been born in Mana or Waipio circa 1851, but this date cannot be correct because it would make her fifty-five or fifty-six years old when the last child, Kaniela, was born in February 1907. According to E. Wesley Smith's account, Tokujiro and Kalala were married in 1879 and had "happily passed their ruby anniversary" by 1919. The reference to the ruby anniversary must be Smith's creation and not Tokujiro's comment because it is difficult (though not impossible) to believe that she did not have children for almost ten years after marriage (until the latter half of the 1880s) when she was fertile enough to give birth to ten children during her lifetime.[121] These considerations seem to suggest that Tokujiro's marriage to Kalala took place in the middle of the 1880s and that Tokujiro was then in his early thirties and Kalala in her early twenties (having been born around 1862).

Kalala's possible birthplace of Mana is interesting because, in all likelihood, it refers to Mana Hale (in Hawaiian, House of the Spirit), the house built by John Palmer Parker outside of Waimea on the lower slope of 13,796-foot-high Mauna Kea. Undoubtedly, *Mana* later began to mean the whole compound of the Parker home or even the whole community of ranchers, workers, and their families working on Parker Ranch.[122] Samuel Parker and his royal wife, Harriet Panana Napela, had a lavish lifestyle, alternating their residence between Mana and the king's palace in Honolulu. They were part of Hawaii's high society and regularly entertained "world travelers and socialities." Their parties are said to have "rivalled even those of King Kalakaua, a close friend of theirs."[123] Kalakaua was on the throne from 1874 to 1891. During 1878–87, the king's close confidant and advisor was Walter Murray Gibson, who, after being excommunicated from the Church in 1864, tried his hand in Hawaiian politics and served as the premier and minister of foreign affairs before being forced to flee the country for a life of exile in California. No doubt, Gibson was one of those distinguished guests at Parker's home in Mana, and Tokujiro had plenty of opportunities in his capacity as the family chef to get to know Gibson. In this light, Tokujiro's presumed witness of Gibson's rise and fall takes on a new meaning.

Given Tokujiro's work and Kalala's family connection in Mana, it is possible that the two met and were married in Mana. Tokujiro may have obtained work as a cook at Parker Ranch because of his previous experience as a butcher in Waipio. Or his Parker Ranch job may have been his first in Hawaii. At any rate, after being married, the couple must have spent much of their married life in Waipio,[124] where Tokujiro raised taro, built homes as a carpenter, and after 1885, when Japanese immigrants began to arrive in Hawaii, helped them with the Hawaiian language and Hawaiian culture. A story is told of Sentaro Kawashima, a young Japanese immigrant, who was taught by Tokujiro to speak Hawaiian and English, farm taro, and make poi and *okolehau* (homemade Hawaiian whiskey).[125] Tokujiro had become fluent in the Hawaiian language so that sometimes he was asked by a court of law to act as an interpreter.[126] Such an assignment was not unusual for the gan-nen-mono who stayed in the Hawaiian islands, because, with very few or even no other Japanese around, they had to assimilate into the Hawaiian community.

It is said that when Tokujiro moved to Kukuihaele and built a house for his own family, he carried lumber from the Waipio Valley on an ox wagon.[127] Kukuihaele is only a short distance from Waipio, but it is located at least a few hundred feet above the valley. To carry the lumber up the steep hill must have been a strenuous and arduous task, a task that cannot possibly be carried out by someone in his old age. Thus when the house was built in Kukuihaele, he was perhaps in his late thirties or early forties (in other words, the house was probably built sometime during the 1890s). It is almost certain that the house was built by 1901, because Tokujiro was there when Kawashima arrived at the Kukuihaele plantation during that year.[128] In Kukuihaele, Tokujiro raised taro (as he had done or possibly continued to do in Waipio) on an irrigated farm adjacent to the back of his house. The farm was about half an acre in size and stretched out on a moderate slope overlooking the Pacific ocean. For a time, the couple had a store, selling *poi* or taro and beef. The beef might have been procured through his old connection with Samuel Parker, indicating that Tomizo's association with him was a long one.[129]

Association with the Church. According to E. Wesley Smith's statement, Tokujiro supposedly joined the Church in 1892 and had been and was still a faithful member of the Church when they met in 1919. Tokujiro may well have joined the Church, but there is no record to support the claim that his baptism took place in 1892. It is difficult to have faith in the validity of that date, when every other date in Smith's statement has turned out to be incorrect. Moreover, even the descendants of Tokujiro generally are skeptical of the claim that he was a member of the Church, although they do not deny the possibility.[130] However, a handful of Church records do exist to establish his association, if not affiliation, with the Church.

The membership records of the Waipio Branch in the Northern Hawaii District do list Tokujiro (as Toko Sr. born circa 1845), although no baptism information is given. His wife, Kalala, is also listed (as Clara Toko baptized in Mana), although no date is given for either birth or baptism. The children's baptisms, when they did occur, are more accurately recorded. The records show that at least six of the nine children were baptized: Mary Melelaulani and Hana on December 7, 1902; John (listed as Toko Jr.) on December 9, 1902; Pula on March 6, 1904; Willard Matsu (Kanuka) on November 1913; and Kaniela on April 17, 1919. No records exist, however, for the other three children, Ohumukini, Emily, and Fukui.[131]

Given the very fact that membership records exist for Tokujiro, that almost all his children were baptized, and that the visiting mission authority considered him a faithful member, the weight of the evidence seems to suggest that Tokujiro was a baptized member of the Church.[132] Considering that, when the first three of the children were baptized in December 1902, the oldest child (Mary) was fifteen years old, there is a reasonable basis for believing that Tokujiro was baptized prior to her eighth birthday, namely, August 29, 1895, if he was baptized at all. Otherwise, Tokujiro and Mary (then over eight years old) would have been baptized at the same time. On the other hand, to believe that he was baptized after Mary is difficult (though not impossible) because then the baptism would have more likely been recorded, given the better record-keeping practice in later years. This conjecture provides some credibility to E. Wesley Smith's statement that Tokujiro was baptized in 1892. If Tokujiro's baptism was during the latter part of the period preceding Mary's eighth birthday, it was remarkably close to Tomizo Katsunuma's baptism date of August 8, 1895. It may be that Tokujiro was baptized along with the eldest daughter Ohumukini, whose baptism information is not available but who is considered to have been a member.[133]

The Tokujiro Sato family, however, was far from being the typical Mormon family of contemporary America. Their religious understanding and practice were constrained both by the cultural settings of the day and by the different expectations that the Church had of its members. The descendants remember Kalala as fond of drinking *okolehau* and as being "cranky" most of the time, possibly because of her drinking habit.[134] In his later years, perhaps with the increasing population of Japanese, Tokujiro came to emphasize his Japanese identity. Although he exclusively spoke Hawaiian to his children, he spoke Japanese to some of the grandchildren as they developed proficiency in that language; he also apparently encouraged at least one of his daughters to marry a Japanese and gave up one of his sons for adoption to a Japanese family.[135]

For one reason or another, none of the children took the name Sato, although his son John and grandson Albert each carried it as their middle name. After all, Sato was a name foreign to Tokujiro. John took the name Toko, Willard (who was given up for adoption) carried the name Yamamoto, and the two youngest sons decided to use their mother's honored Hawaiian name of Kamekona. Whatever shortcomings Tokujiro and Kalala might have had as Mormon parents, a host of practicing Latter-day Saints are found among their descendants today, particularly those who have come through the Ohumukini, Fukui, and Kaniela lines.

Tokujiro died in his home shortly after his meeting with E. Wesley Smith in 1919,[136] and after a funeral held presumably at a Latter-day Saint chapel, he was buried in a cemetery located on the Pacific shore.[137] His grave no longer exists because it was washed away in a tidal wave. His house, however, still stands on the same spot, and the legacy of hard work and perseverance that he exhibited throughout his life continues.

Conclusion

Tomizo Katsunuma and Tokujiro Sato each has a legitimate claim to being the first Japanese Mormon. Both happened to be at the crossroads of some major historical transformations making their conversion possible. First, with the western frontiers secured, the United States was becoming a Pacific military and economic power, eventually annexing the peaceful and independent kingdom of Hawaii. Second, following the opening of the country to international intercourse, Japan itself was rapidly developing into a modern nation-state, and a host of adventurous Japanese were venturing out of the country to explore opportunities abroad. Finally, against these major transpacific political developments in the background, the Mormons were trying to solidify their base in the Intermountain West and were engaged in an aggressive proselytizing program. Without the changes created by these currents in the surrounding power and opportunity structures, neither Tomizo nor Tokujiro would have been freed from the shackles of tradition to embrace a new religion in a new land and to be Mormon pioneers of Japanese ancestry.

Some may challenge the use of the term "pioneer" to describe these early members, at least in the usual sense in which the term is understood. After all, they never walked the plains for a thousand miles. They were never harassed for their religious beliefs. They never helped, at least in a major way, the institutional establishment of the Church in their community, let alone in their native land. They held no leadership positions in the Church to speak of. In some ways, they were marginal affiliates of Mormonism.

Perhaps they can more appropriately be called path breakers, a special type of pioneers separated from the binding root of a certain cultural tradition and serving as a bridge between the real pioneers (who are to come) and their old world.[138] Indeed, neither Tomizo nor Tokujiro may have been stalwart converts in the full sense of the word; they may have been marginal affiliates of the Church. However, path breakers they were—even pioneers in their internal struggle to reconcile the tenets of the gospel with the demands of Japanese culture, the same struggle that has continued to this day among their fellow Latter-day Saints of Japanese ancestry.

Appendix
Children of Tomizo and Tokujiro

Children of Tomizo and Mine[139]

Katsumi, son, born on May 12, 1890, Miharu, Fukushima.
Kiyomi, daughter, born on January 24, 1899, Miharu, Fukushima.
Takeo, son, born on February 20, 1902, Honolulu.
Yasuko, daughter, born on May 13, 1904, Honolulu.
Yoshiko, daughter, born on September 8, 1906, Tokyo.
Woodrow, son, born on March 9, 1913, Honolulu.

Children of Tokujiro and Kalala[140]

Ohumukini, daughter, birthdate unknown, Hawaii.
Mary Melelaulani, daughter, born in 1887, Hawaii.
Hana, daughter, born in 1889, Waipio, Hawaii.
John, son, born in 1892, Waipio, Hawaii.
Pula, son, born in 1895, Waipio, Hawaii.
Emily, daughter, birthdate unknown, Hawaii.
Fukui, son, born in 1901, Hawaii.
Willard Matsu (Kanuka), son, born in 1904, Waipio, Hawaii.
Kaniela (Daniel), son, born in 1907, Waipio, Hawaii.

This article originally appeared as Shinji Takagi, "Tomizo and Tokujiro: The First Japanese Mormons," BYU Studies 39, no. 2 (2000): 73–106.

Notes

1. The most comprehensive treatment of Mormon labors in the Japan Mission (1901–24) is found in Shinji Takagi and William McIntyre, *Nihon Matsujitsu Seito Shi, 1850–1980* (Japan Latter-day Saints history, 1850–1980) (Kobe, Japan: Beehive Shuppan, 1996), chapters 1–5. For a shorter treatment in English, see Ronald W. Walker, "Strangers in a Strange Land: Heber J. Grant and the Opening of the Japanese Mission," *Journal of Mormon History* 13 (1986–87): 21–43, reprinted herein. The formal name of the mission established in Japan in 1901 was the Japan Mission, although it was frequently referred to as the Japanese Mission. The missions established later in Hawaii (in 1937) and in postwar Japan (in 1948) were both officially called the Japanese Mission.

2. Judging from the circumstances surrounding his contact with the Church, however, it does not seem appropriate to consider him a ceremonial priest of a Shinto shrine. More likely, he held a pastoral office in a religious organization based in part on Shinto principles. In Japanese religious terminology, such Shinto offshoot groups are collectively called Sect Shinto (of which there were thirteen sects during the Meiji period), as opposed to State Shinto. See Takagi and McIntyre, *Nihon Matsujitsu Seito Shi*, 69–70.

3. Given the frequency of transpacific and transatlantic passenger service and the timely railroad connections, the most convenient and often fastest way to travel to Europe was via the transcontinental railroad in the United States, even after the completion of the Suez Canal in 1869.

4. The U.S. Census of 1890 reported 2,039 Japanese residents in the United States, of whom about half were in California. From 1891 to 1900, 27,440 Japanese were admitted to the United States. Yuji Ichioka, *The Issei: The World of the First Generation Japanese Immigrants, 1885–1924* (New York: Free Press, 1988), 8, 51.

5. During the initial ten years (1885–94) alone, almost thirty thousand Japanese emigrated to Hawaii. Ichioka, *First Generation Japanese Immigrants*, 40.

6. The first recorded contact was made at the Church school in Laie in the late 1880s, when several Japanese pupils were enrolled. Church membership records suggest that there was a baptism of a Japanese woman by the name of Miki in Maui. See Andrew Jenson, comp., *The History of the Hawaiian Mission of The Church of Jesus Christ of Latter-day Saints*, as quoted in Russel T. Clement and Sheng-Luen Tsai, "East Wind to Hawaii: Contributions and History of Chinese and Japanese Mormons in Hawaii," in *Proceedings, the Second Annual Conference of the Mormon Pacific Historical Society*, 1981, typescript, in

possession of the author, reprinted in *Voyages of Faith: Explorations in Mormon Pacific History*, ed. Grant Underwood (Provo, UT: Brigham Young University Press, 2000), 89–106.

7. Having received the title of *shogun* (military general) from the emperor, the Tokugawa family, or the shogunate, ruled Japan from its castle in Edo (present-day Tokyo) during this period. The inherent contradiction of the Tokugawa regime, namely, the system of rule by one dominant clan over less dominant yet competing clans, became evident when Japan was dragged into contact with foreign powers in the early nineteenth century. It was simply not possible for the Tokugawa family to assume the role of government of a modern nation-state based on the revenue from its fiefs alone. In early 1868, the Tokugawa family was obliged to return the right to rule to the imperial family in what is known as the Meiji Restoration.

8. A prominent Church member in Oahu, Edward L. Clissold was particularly active in Church affairs among the Japanese. At various times, he served as president of the Waikiki Branch, chairman of the Oahu District Council, counselor in the presidency and president of the Oahu Stake, acting president of the Japanese Mission (in Hawaii), and thrice president of the Hawaiian Temple. From 1948 to 1949, he served as the first president of the Japanese Mission (in Japan) after its reestablishment following the conclusion of World War II. As the quoted summary of the beginning of work among the Japanese in Hawaii appears at the beginning of the president's reports concerning the newly created Japanese Mission (in Hawaii), Clissold was apparently writing at the request of the incoming mission president, Hilton A. Robertson, to summarize some of the notable events in the history of the Church among the Japanese people of Hawaii up to that time. For more information on the Japanese Mission, see Shinji Takagi, "Riding on the Eagle's Wings: The Japanese Mission under American Occupation, 1948–52," *Journal of Mormon History* 29 (2003): 200–232.

9. Edward L. Clissold, "Missionary Work among the Japanese in the Hawaiian Islands," in the Central Pacific (Japanese) Mission, Mission President's Reports, 1937–49, University Archives, BYU–Hawaii, Laie, Hawaii, 1937. At the time Tomizo attended, the school was called the Agricultural College of Utah.

10. Stephan Thernstrom, ed., *Harvard Encyclopedia of American Ethnic Groups* (Cambridge: Harvard University Press, 1980), 561–62.

11. Japan was on the lunar calendar until December 2 in the fifth year of Meiji (or December 31, 1872). For this reason, an attempt will be made throughout this article to list both Japanese and Western dates for important events and incidents within Japan through the end of 1872. Several different dates

have appeared in various documents for Tomizo's birthday, including October 6 (Church membership records; Tsuyoshi Ebihara, *Katogi Yasuji no Jinsei Techo* [Memoirs of Katogi Yasuji] [Yokohama, 1977]), November 1 (Kanji Takahashi, *Imin no Chichi Katsunuma Tomizo Sensei* [The life of Dr. Katsunuma Tomizo, the father of immigrants] [Honolulu: Bunkichi Suda, 1953]; Hatsutaro Yunojiri, *Katogi San Rokyodai* [The three venerable Katogi brothers] [Tokyo: Denki-no-tomo, 1932]), November 11 (the obituary in the *Hawaii Times,* September 12, 1950), and November 18 (the obituary in the *Honolulu Advertiser,* September 12, 1950). It is likely that October 6 was the correct (lunar) date and that the November dates are wrong solar transformations of that lunar date. Unless otherwise noted, the biographical information in this section comes from Yunojiri, *Katogi San Rokyodai;* and Takahashi, *Imin no Chichi Katsunuma Tomizo Sensei.*

12. Naochika was born in Taira on September 15 in the fourth year of Tempo (1833) as the fourth son of Isota Katsunuma, a retainer of Tsushimamori Ando, the lord of the Taira clan. For a long time, he was a teacher of Toda-school judo. At the persistent request of the lord of the neighboring Miharu clan, Naochika made the decision to move to Miharu and transferred the charge of the judo school to his most trusted disciple. At that time, according to the wishes of the Miharu clan, Naochika succeeded the old Katogi family and formally became the clan's judo teacher. As Naochika could not face the prospect of losing his Katsunuma name, Naochika asked the youngest son Tomizo to retain the Katusnuma name.

13. Yo was the daughter of Koroku Hanazawa, a retainer of the Taira clan.

14. The Meiji period under the reign of Emperor Meiji began when the restoration of direct imperial rule was proclaimed in early 1868.

15. At that time, students completing the three-year course of study in liberal arts at the Preparatory School were offered admission to the University of Tokyo to study law, letters, and science. Because of this privilege, admission to the Preparatory School was extremely competitive and was based on an entrance examination covering many subjects. See University of Tokyo, *Tokyo Daigaku Hyakunen Shi* (Centennial history of the University of Tokyo), vol. 1 (Tokyo: University of Tokyo Press, 1984), 551–600.

16. The Imperial College of Agriculture was founded in 1878 by the Ministry of Home Affairs and became a part of the Imperial University (later Tokyo Imperial University) in 1890, when the University of Tokyo (with programs in law, letters, science, and medicine) was upgraded to become a comprehensive university with the addition of agriculture, engineering, and the Graduate School. See the University of Tokyo, *Tokyo Daigaku Hyakunen Shi,* 742–83.

17. A preliminary agreement with the Kingdom of Hawaii was signed in 1884, succeeded by the formal Immigration Convention of 1886.

18. Mine was the eldest daughter of Tsuneshi Endo, senior clerk of the Tamura County government.

19. Takahashi, *Imin no Chichi Katsunuma Tomizo Sensei*, 6.

20. After returning to Japan, Katogi Shigenori became an engineer at the Miyoshi Electric Factory and, during his spare time, published a magazine called *Denki no Tomo* (literally, *Friends of Electricity*). He later became independent, established a company called Denyu-sha, and was engaged in business in the Ginza district of Tokyo.

21. Ebihara, *Katogi Yasuji no Jinsei Techo*, 252. Chinda later served as Japan's Ambassador to the United States.

22. Tomizo Katsunuma, *Kansho no Shiborikasu* (Strained lees of sugarcanes) (Honolulu: Katsunuma Kinen Shuppan Koenkai, 1924), 113.

23. A commercial firm called the Japan-U.S. Contracting Company was established in 1892, and a formal agreement was signed with the Hiroshima Emigration Company for the provision of immigrant labor. See Ichioka, *First Generation Japanese Immigrants*, 48–51. However, it is likely that the business itself was established much before 1892.

24. Ichioka, *First Generation Japanese Immigrants*, 49–50. According to Takahashi, *Imin no Chichi Katsunuma Tomizo Sensei*, 7, Tanaka lived in Salt Lake City and, in 1890, invited Tomizo to come to manage his business of distributing everyday necessities to railroad workers and receiving orders from them. The designation of Salt Lake City as the place of Tanaka's residence is probably wrong, but if the year 1890 is right, Tomizo must have lived in Ogden, Utah, at least for a while. According to Ebihara, *Katogi Yasuji no Jinsei Techo*, 239, when Shutaro Katogi, the elder brother of Tomizo, arrived in the United States in fall 1891, Tomizo was already in Idaho. Shutaro's specific purpose in coming to the United States was to acquire skills in dairy farming, but he had to first study English for about eighteen months until April 1893. This latter date coincides with the dismissal of Tanaka as the labor contractor for the Oregon Short Line. See the paragraph immediately below.

25. Ebihara claims that Shutaro met with Brigham Young on one of his visits to Salt Lake City. Ebihara, *Katogi Yasuji no Jinsei Techo*, 239–40. Of course, this cannot be true as Brigham Young had been dead for over ten years, prompting one to question the authenticity of some of the historical events discussed in his book.

26. Ichioka, *First Generation Japanese Immigrants*, 74.

27. During this time, the two brothers visited the Columbia Exposition (the so-called Chicago World Fair) of 1893 and New York City. In summer 1894, they traveled from Logan to Salt Lake City to visit His Imperial Highness Prince Yorihito, who was on his way home from France by way of the United States.

Katsunuma, *Kansho no Shiborikasu*, 152. After leaving Logan, Shutaro spent a year in Wyoming learning cattle-raising techniques before going back to Japan in 1896. Upon his return, he attempted a large American-style dairy operation but failed. See Ebihara, *Katogi Yasuji no Jinsei Techo*, 240–41.

28. Yunojiri, *Katogi San Rokyodai*, 63.

29. David A. Burton, "Carl Christian Amussen," prepared for the family reunion of the Ezra Taft Benson family, July 1978.

30. Burton, "Carl Christian Amussen."

31. Deceased member records, 1941–88, Church Archives, The Church of Jesus Christ of Latter-day Saints, Salt Lake City. However, no other Aaronic Priesthood ordinations are recorded.

32. Although the generally accepted interpretation of naturalization laws at the time was that Japanese were ineligible for citizenship, the final interpretation was in the hands of local officials, and according to one estimate, as many as 460 Japanese were granted citizenship by local judges. This flexibility was abolished, however, in 1922 when the Supreme Court ruled that naturalization was limited to "free white persons and to aliens of African nativity and to persons of African descent." Japanese remained as "aliens ineligible to citizenship" until the passage of the McCarran-Walter Immigration and Nationality Act in 1952. See William K. Hosokawa, *Nisei: The Quiet Americans* (New York: William Morrow, 1969), 89–91; and Yukiko Kimura, *Issei: Japanese Immigrants in Hawaii* (Honolulu: University of Hawaii Press, 1988), 40. Incidentally, the obituary on Tomizo published in the September 12, 1950, issue of the English-language *Honolulu Advertiser* states that he was granted citizenship because the judge thought he was a Caucasian. The author considers this to be a rather farfetched explanation.

33. The last ship carrying contractual immigrants under government supervision arrived in Honolulu on June 28, 1894. Under this program, a total of 29,139 individuals traveled from Japan to Hawaii between 1885 and 1894. See Soen Yamashita, *Nippon Hawaii Koryushi* (History of Japanese-Hawaiian exchanges) (Tokyo: Daito Shuppansha, 1943), 19.

34. Ichioka, *First Generation Japanese Immigrants*, 48.

35. Ichioka, *First Generation Japanese Immigrants*, 51–52.

36. Kimura, *Japanese Immigrants in Hawaii*, 33.

37. According to Tomizo's own account, when he "returned home for the first time in the spring of the 31st year of Meiji, [he] became an agent of the Kumamoto Emigration Company and recruited emigrants to Hawaii in the Tohoku region." *Nippu Jiji*, January 13, 1934. The author's translation of the Japanese original.

38. Kimura, *Japanese Immigrants in Hawaii*, 33.

39. Alma O. Taylor, Journal, August 19, 1901, L. Tom Perry Special Collections, Harold B. Lee Library, Brigham Young University, Provo, Utah. He was not the first Mormon to live in Japan, however. In a journal entry on August 14, 1901, Alma O. Taylor, one of the first missionaries to Japan, wrote about visiting the widow of the late Mr. Ponseforte, who "had at one time lived in Salt Lake City and was a member of the Church." This man "apostatised before leaving the U.S." and "some twenty or twenty five years ago . . . came to Japan and married a Japanese woman."

40. The claim of Kimura that the family traveled together (Kimura, *Japanese Immigrants in Hawaii*, 33) is obviously incorrect, as Kiyomi was born in Miharu. In an interview with the author, Kiyomi said that Tomizo had called the family to Hawaii only after getting a permanent job as an immigration officer. Kiyomi Katsunuma Suzuki, interview by author, Honolulu, Oahu, February 1, 1997. Although the exact time cannot be ascertained, the family must have joined Tomizo relatively soon, as a picture taken in December 1900 shows Tomizo and Mine together. The couple's second son Takeo was born in Honolulu in February 1902.

41. Takahashi, *Imin no Chichi Katsunuma Tomizo Sensei*, 13. From July 1894 to 1908 (when the U.S.–Japan Gentlemen's Agreement, which severely restricted the entry of Japanese laborers, came into force), a total of 108,534 contractual or free immigrants traveled from Japan to Hawaii under private (nongovernmental) schemes. From 1908 to 1924 (when the Johnson-Reid Immigration Act, which prohibited the immigration of Japanese nationals, came into force), a total of 62,277 immigrants (many of whom were "picture brides") traveled to Hawaii by invitation only. See Yamashita, *Nippon Hawaii Koryushi*, 19, 339–40.

42. Kimura, *Japanese Immigrants in Hawaii*, 40.

43. A story is told that, when His Imperial Highness Prince Sadachika made a visit to Honolulu on his way back from the United States, one of the fine horses on board given as a gift to the imperial family fell sick. Tomizo was called and successfully treated the sick horse. See Takahashi, *Imin no Chichi Katsunuma Tomizo Sensei*, 16; and Katsunuma, *Kansho no Shiborikasu*, 232.

44. Kimura, *Japanese Immigrants in Hawaii*, 42.

45. *Roko* is an honorific title used to address an elderly person.

46. Takahashi, *Imin no Chichi Katsunuma Tomizo Sensei*, preface; author's translation.

47. Takahashi, *Imin no Chichi Katsunuma Tomizo Sensei*, 13–14; author's translation.

48. *Basho*, in this configuration of Chinese characters, literally means "horse laughter," no doubt intended as a pun for the great seventeenth-century *haiku* poet Basho Matsuo.

49. See, for example, Katsunuma, *Kansho no Shiborikasu*.

50. Takahashi, *Imin no Chichi Katsunuma Tomizo Sensei*, preface; author's translation.

51. Takahashi, *Imin no Chichi Katsunuma Tomizo Sensei*, 16–17.

52. For *gan-nen-mono*, see the second part of this article on Tokujiro Sato. On this occasion, all four surviving members of the first group were present. If Tokujiro had lived a few more years, there would have been a meeting of Tomizo and Tokujiro, the main characters of our story. Katsunuma, *Kansho no Shiborikasu*, 1–4.

53. The second trip was made in 1904, during which Tomizo visited the mission home in Tokyo. See the last section of this part of the article.

54. Takahashi, *Imin no Chichi Katsunuma Tomizo Sensei*, 18; author's translation.

55. Clissold, "Missionary Work." Writing about the Japanese Mission in Hawaii in 1939, John A. Widtsoe used almost identical sentences to describe Tomizo, indicating that he relied on Clissold for the information. John A. Widtsoe, "The Japanese Mission in Action," *Improvement Era* 42 (February 1939), 88–89, 125.

56. Clement and Tsai, "East Wind to Hawaii"; R. Lanier Britsch, *Moramona: The Mormons in Hawaii* (Laie, Hawaii: Institute for Polynesian Studies, 1989), 114–16.

57. Clissold, "Missionary Work."

58. *Empress of India* was a steamship of the Canadian Pacific fleet, which did not include a stop in Honolulu in its transpacific passenger service between Vancouver and Yokohama.

59. In a letter addressed to President Samuel E. Wooley of the Hawaiian Mission, dated April 21, 1902, Horace Ensign, secretary of the Japan Mission in Tokyo, acknowledged the receipt of money and writes, "We trust that the time spent with our beloved President, Apostle Grant, was profitable." Japan Mission Letterpress Copybooks, 1901–23, Church Archives.

60. See the second part of this article on Tokujiro Sato.

61. Taylor, Journal, August 19, 1901.

62. Taylor, Journal, August 25, 1901.

63. Taylor, Journal, April 9, 1904. Ten yen was exactly five dollars when converted at the gold parity (both Japan and the United States were on the gold standard at that time). One yen was more than twice the average monthly newspaper subscription rate and would be more than three thousand yen when converted to current yen in purchasing power terms. Hence, in very rough terms, ten yen would be now equivalent to around three hundred U.S. dollars, which was a considerable sum, given the much lower level of wages. See Takagi and McIntyre, *Nihon Matsujitsu Seito Shi*, 104–6.

64. Suzuki, interview.

65. Katsunuma, *Kansho no Shiborikasu*, 8–9.

66. Clissold, "Missionary Work."

67. J. Reuben Clark Jr., "The Outpost in Mid-Pacific," *Improvement Era* 38 (September 1935): 533.

68. Clark, "Outpost in Mid-Pacific," 533.

69. In his *Improvement Era* article, Widtsoe erroneously writes that the Japanese Mission in Hawaii was organized in February 1936. The correct year is 1937. Widtsoe, "Japanese Mission in Action," 88.

70. Deceased member records, 1941–88.

71. Widtsoe, "Japanese Mission in Action," 88, 125.

72. "Bashoan Tomizo Katsunuma Dies," *Hawaii Times* (Japanese), September 12, 1950, 3; Yasutaro Soga, "Memories of the Late Dr. Tomizo Katsunuma," *Hawaii Times* (Japanese), September 16, 1950, n.p.

73. "Dr. Katsunuma, First Japanese Mormon, Dies," *Honolulu Advertiser*, September 12, 1950, n.p.

74. Yasuo Baron Goto, *Children of Gan-nen-mono: The First-Year Men* (Honolulu: Bishop Museum Press, 1968), n.p.

75. E. Wesley Smith, "The First Japanese Convert to the Church," *Improvement Era* 23 (December 1919): 177.

76. Unfortunately, some Mormon writers have taken the wrong dates at face value without checking them against available historical fact. See, for example, Clement and Tsai, "East Wind to Hawaii"; and Sharlene B. C. L. Furuto, "Japanese Saints in Hawaii and Japan: Values and Implications for Baptism," *Proceedings, the Eleventh Annual Conference of the Mormon Pacific Historical Society*, 1990, typescript, in possession of the author, 1–15.

77. After missionaries were removed in 1857, Walter Murray Gibson appointed himself leader of the Church and seized Church property in Hawaii. See *1997–1998 Church Almanac* (Salt Lake City: Deseret News, 1996), 210. Unless otherwise noted all information concerning Gibson in this article comes from the following sources: Frank W. McGhie, "The Life and Intrigues of Walter Murray Gibson" (master's thesis, Brigham Young University, 1958); Esther Leonore Ferreira Sousa, "Walter Murray Gibson's Rise to Power in Hawaii" (master's thesis, University of Hawaii, 1942); R. Lanier Britsch, *Unto the Islands of the Sea: A History of the Latter-day Saints in the Pacific* (Salt Lake City: Deseret Book, 1986), chapter 7; "Tabernacle," *Deseret News,* November 21, 1860, 297, as quoted in McGhie, "Walter Murray Gibson," 70; R. Lanier Britsch, *Moramona: The Mormons in Hawaii* (Laie, Hawaii: Institute for Polynesian Studies, 1989).

78. Britsch, *Mormons in Hawaii*. Smith is credited for moving the headquarters of the mission from Laie to Honolulu.

79. Joseph F. Smith, Second Counselor in the First Presidency since 1880, came to Hawaii to escape the harassments of U.S. marshals associated with polygamy and remained in Laie from February 1885 to June 1887. In late June, he left Hawaii for Utah upon hearing of the ill health of John Taylor, who subsequently died in July 1887. R. Lanier Britsch, *Unto the Islands of the Sea*, 141–43.

80. This fact convincingly refutes the family oral tradition that Tokujiro died on November 11, 1918.

81. In addition, about a dozen Japanese are said to have come to Hawaii as individual immigrants prior to 1885. The information on *gan-nen-mono* comes from Soen Yamashita, *Gan-nen-mono no Omokage* (Vestiges of the first-year men) (Tokyo: Hawaiian Society of Japan, 1968); supplemented by Roy M. Shinsato, "The Gannen Mono: Great Expectations of the Earliest Japanese Immigrants of Hawaii," *Hawaii Historical Review* 1 (January 1965): 180–94; Yamashita, *Nippon Hawaii Koryushi*; Hiroshi Shimaoka, *Hawai Imin No Rekishi* (History of Hawaiian emigration) (Tokyo: Tosho Kankokai, 1978); and others.

82. The new era of Meiji was declared on September 8 of the fourth year of Keio (according to the lunar calendar), or October 23, 1868, and made retroactive to January 1 of that (lunar) year.

83. The population of Hawaii, which stood at 130,313 in the 1832 census, declined to 84,165 in 1850, and then to 69,000 in 1860. Shinsato, "Gannen Mono," 181.

84. The initial importation of Chinese workers began in 1852, followed by, among others, Polynesians (1859), Japanese (1868), Portuguese and Micronesians (1878), Puerto Ricans (1900), and Koreans (1903). See Yamashita, *Nippon Hawaii Koryushi*, 20.

85. Or March 31, according to the lunar calendar.

86. Or April 17, according to the lunar calendar.

87. Although the ship was built in 1849 at Brunswick, Maine, and was owned by George F. Lovett of Boston, it flew the British flag, having been registered in Gibraltar under British law. Goto, *Children of Gan-nen-mono*, n.p.

88. Or April 14, according to the lunar calendar.

89. Because of the generally poor health of the people then, only 141 people out of some 400 applicants passed the medical examination. Because the ship left in a hurry, the quota of 350 immigrants was not used up. Nine of the rejected applicants smuggled onto the ship, making the total 150. See Yamashita, *Gan-nen-mono no Omokage*, 30–31.

90. Or April 25, according to the lunar calendar.

91. Under the terms of the Ansei commercial treaties, Western powers, including Britain, France, Russia, the Netherlands, and the United States, were given extraterritorial privileges in Japan.

92. An alternative figure for the number of immigrants, 153, is widely accepted among Japanese historians. The ship's American physician, David J. Lee reported the figure of 148. Goto, *Children of Gan-nen-mono*, n.p. Based on admittedly secondary evidence presented by various authors, the present author is satisfied that the most reasonable figure is 150.

93. Or November 25, according to the lunar calendar.

94. Shinsato, "Gannen Mono," 186.

95. Or December 10 of the second year of Meiji, according to the lunar calendar.

96. As quoted in Shinsato, "Gannen Mono," 186–87.

97. When the initial three-year contract period ended, twelve immigrants (including one born in Hawaii) returned to Japan at the Hawaiian government's expense, about forty moved to the continental United States, and about fifty remained in Hawaii as *gan-nen-mono*. Because one of the two remaining women left for Japan, only one woman remained in Hawaii as a *gan-nen-mono*.

98. Yamashita, *Gan-nen-mono no Omokage*, 70–71.

99. In the old Japanese system, a child is one year old when he or she is born, and a year is added on each New Year's day.

100. Hence, Tokujiro was around sixty-eight years old (not seventy years old) when he met E. Wesley Smith in 1919.

101. The oral history, as summarized in Joelle Segawa Kane, "Gan-nen-mono," n.d., states that Tokujiro was "a samurai of the Hatamoto class, which was the rank of the loyal guards of the Tokugawa Shogun."

102. Yamashita, *Gan-nen-mono no Omokage*, 73. This fact is corroborated by the family portrait of Tokujiro, on which it is stated (most likely by Tokujiro himself) that he is from Tatami-machi, Kyobashi-ku, Tokyo.

103. The Kyobashi section of Edo is now part of several large city blocks located in Kyobashi 3-chome, Chuo-ku, Tokyo, a short distance southeast of the Yaesu entrance of Tokyo station. See Tokyo City Government, Planning Bureau, *Tokyo-shi Chomei Enkaku Shi* (Chronicle of town name changes in Tokyo City), vol. 1 (Tokyo: Tokyo City Government, 1938), 60–61.

104. Two additional facts from the Hawaii period add strength to our conjecture that Tokujiro was not of the samurai class. First, later in Hawaii, Tokujiro was engaged in the butchery business, considered to be the most despicable profession in Tokugawa Japan. Second, before settling on Sato, he chose two surnames, Sato and Sasaki, as if he did not know which one to keep.

105. Albert Sato Toko, interview by author, Kamuela, Hawaii, June 12, 1999. Toko is the grandson of Tokujiro.

106. In an interview with the author, Leslie Lactaoen, the current resident of the house, testified of the solid construction of the house, which has stood

the test of time. Leslie P. and Renee Lactaoen, interview by author, Kukuihaele, Hawaii, June 12, 1999.

107. According to an incomplete survey conducted in the fourth year of Keio (1868), there were about seventy-four thousand people in Edo who were considered destitute. Of this figure, about two thousand were in the Kyobashi area. Another source states that there were about three hundred thousand people in poverty in the second year of Meiji (1869). See Hiromichi Ishizuka, *Tokyo no Shakai Keizai Shi* (Social and economic history of Tokyo) (Tokyo: Kinokuniya Shoten, 1977), 21–24.

108. Or April 11, according to the lunar calendar.

109. Kane (not dated).

110. Or April 15, according to the lunar calendar.

111. Yamashita, *Gan-nen-mono no Omokage*, 16–18.

112. Yamashita, *Gan-nen-mono no Omokage*, 38–39. There are different accounts of their allocation.

113. Makino's report filed on January 29, 1870. See Yamashita, *Nippon Hawaii Koryushi*, 217–19.

114. In a personal interview, one of the descendants of Tokujiro told the author that Tokujiro might have fathered children in Maui.

115. Shinsato, "Gannen Mono," 192–93.

116. As another example, the *gan-nen-mono* leader Tomisaburo Makino (Makino being his samurai surname) chose to be called Tomi Saburo, as if Saburo was his surname. Sometimes, he signed his name T. Saburo. Yamashita, *Gan-nen-mono no Omokage*, 66.

117. Kyobashi Kyokai, comp., *Kyobashi Hansho Ki* (Prosperity history of Kyobashi) (Tokyo: the author, 1912), 7.

118. Jiro Nakano, "Sentaro Kawashima: Japanese Settlers of Waipio Valley," *Hawaii Herald*, June 20, 1986, 14–15.

119. Kane, "Gan-nen-mono," 4. A shorter version was published in the *Hamakua Times*, June 1999.

120. Kamekona family records, provided by Noelani Kamekona, Pearl City, Hawaii.

121. This statement should be qualified by the possibility that the unnamed child who died in infancy had been the first child and was born much earlier.

122. The headquarters of Parker Ranch moved in 1879, when John Parker II, the son of Jon Palmer Parker and the uncle of Samuel, moved to a more central location in Waimea. Samuel, however, continued to live in Mana. See Parker Ranch Foundation Trust, "Parker Ranch Historic Homes," n.d., Parker Ranch Visitor's Center, Kamuela, Hawaii.

123. Jackie Kido, "Hawaii's Ranching Dynasty: Parker Ranch," *Spirit of Hawaii* (July 1997): 10.

124. The predominant population of Waipio consisted of Hawaiians and Chinese, with a few Japanese. There were no plantations, but rice was cultivated on its fertile soil. Toko, interview.

125. Nakano, "Japanese Settlers of Waipio Valley," 14.

126. Toko, interview; Clara Toshiko Taise, interview by author, Naalehu, Hawaii, February 7, 1999.

127. Lactaoen, interview.

128. According to Nakano, "Japanese Settlers of Waipio Valley," 14, Tokujiro told Kawashima to quit the plantation and to farm taro in Waipio and he served as a go-between in arranging a marriage with a Hawaiian woman named Kainoa. Apparently, Tokujiro maintained two residences, one each in Waipio and Kukuihaele, through the early years of the twentieth century.

129. In an interview with the author, Albert Sato Toko, the grandson of Tokujiro, recalled a story told by his father John to the effect that he (John) had one day left school to go to see his father in a mountain home. As John Toko was born in 1892, this story must mean that Tokujiro still worked at Parker's mountain compound in the 1900s. Albert also speculated that, as Tokujiro and Kalala were thus physically separated during periods of substantial length, Kalala was unfaithful and gave birth to children of other men.

130. Taise, interview; Toko, interview.

131. See the appendix for the list of children in order of birth. According to Kaniela, the youngest son, as told by his daughter, all the children of Tokujiro were baptized as children except for Fukui. However, even Fukui later joined the Church, as he married an active Hawaiian Latter-day Saint.

132. As an interesting sidelight, Sentaro Kawashima, Tokujiro's student in taro farming and the Hawaiian way of life in general, later joined the Church on March 7, 1927, and was ordained an elder on October 24, 1929. He is said to have remained a well-respected and stalwart member of the Church until his death on October 17, 1956. Nakano, "Japanese Settlers of Waipio Valley," n.p.; deceased member records, 1941–88.

133. Noelani Vera Kamekona, interview by author, Pearl City, Oahu, February 7, 1999.

134. Taise, interview; Toko, interview.

135. Taise, interview.

136. Based on Kaniela's best recollection, it has been believed that Tokujiro died in Kukuihaele on November 11, 1918. This date cannot be correct, because we know that he was alive when Wesley Smith came to see him in 1919.

137. Kamekona, interview.

138. Armand L. Mauss, letter to author, August 7, 1999; Armand L. Mauss, email message to author, October 21, 1999.

139. Hatsutaro Yunojiri, *Katogi San Rokyodai* (The Three Venerable Katogi Brothers) (Tokyo: Denki-no-tomo, 1932), 67. Katsumi's reported birthday of May 12, 1890, more than a full year after the departure of Tomizo for the United States on April 25, 1889, may be an error.

140. Family sources, supplemented by Yasuo Baron Goto, *Children of Gannen-mono: The First-Year Men* (Honolulu: Bishop Museum Press, 1968); Membership records, Waipio Branch, Northern Hawaii District, Church Archives. As there are discrepancies across different sources, the years of birth are only approximate. In addition, there was another child who died in infancy.

5

Translator or Translated?
The Portrayal of The Church of Jesus Christ of Latter-day Saints in Print in Meiji Japan

Sarah Cox Smith

By the time missionaries from The Church of Jesus Christ of Latter-day Saints arrived in Japan in August 1901, they were forty-two years behind the first Christian missionaries who had come to the country following the expulsion of Catholic missionaries in the early 1600s. The first of this new wave of Christian missionaries arrived in 1859 from Catholic, Episcopal, and Presbyterian churches, and from the Dutch Reformed Church in America.[1] By 1883 there were at least eighteen different Protestant missions in Japan.[2]

These pioneering missionaries performed a marvelous work in promulgating the tenets of Christianity in a country that was by no means waiting to hear the gospel. The Japanese were not ready in large part because a strong anti-foreign sentiment persisted in that country throughout the 1860s and beyond.[3] Christianity had been officially outlawed in Japan since 1614, when a nationwide ban on the religion was issued—a ban that was not lifted until 1873. Even then, Christianity was not officially legalized until 1889. Although foreign missionaries were eventually allowed to come to Japan in the mid-1800s before the ban on Christianity was lifted, like other foreigners these missionaries were segregated from the general population in foreign enclaves and were not authorized to proselytize. As late as 1868, 110 Japanese Christians—including women and children—were brought from the Nagasaki area to the small town of Tsuwano, where they were imprisoned and tortured because of their faith. Thirty-six were martyred for refusing to renounce their beliefs.[4]

Once the prohibition against Christianity was lifted, however, missionaries confronted a new problem of communication, more specifically, of translation. In the 1850s and 1860s, there were very few printed works available in Japan, religious or otherwise, that had been translated from European languages into Japanese.[5] Consequently, early missionaries had very few Japanese texts available for their proselytizing efforts, and most missionaries lacked the knowledge to translate their message not only into a foreign tongue but also into a foreign culture. These pioneering missionaries set out to remedy the situation as quickly as they could, but their early translations were almost uniformly incomprehensible, or at least offensive to native ears.

One difficulty in translation proved to be learning the Japanese language, especially the written language, without the aid of modern lexicons and texts and with a limited understanding of culture, indigenous religious, and social mores. In fact, an early Japanese Protestant and pastor of the Fujimi-chō church, Uemura Masahira, remarked about an early hymn translation made by foreign missionaries that "the devout spirits God was able to comfort through such clumsy, slipshod song were no doubt very few."[6] Even when the signifying words were right, the signified ideas were often foreign to the Japanese people.

Meiji translator and theorist Chiba Kikukō (1870–1938) compared translation to taking a flower from a garden and making it bloom elsewhere. One needs an intimate understanding not simply of the color and variety of the flower itself, he claimed, but also of the characteristics of the garden into which it is being transplanted.[7] Early Christian missionaries found that not only were their printed works misunderstood but also their messages and motives as they were translated into a foreign language and culture. This was partly due to the missionaries' faulty understanding of the "garden" into which the works were transplanted and partly due to the Japanese people's faulty understanding of the "flower" the missionaries brought with them. This study examines the problem of translation in its broadest sense, the carrying over of something foreign to a new place and a new cultural context where it risks being misunderstood.

Church Representations in Print

The Church of Jesus Christ of Latter-day Saints was represented in print in Japan long before any official representative arrived, but these descriptions, many published by other Christian sects, were rarely flattering and usually focused on the practice of polygamy. Whereas many other Christian sects cooperated with each other in preaching and teaching, they often warned against the Latter-day Saint Church and its teachings. The religion was portrayed as ridiculous and indeed laughable in its doctrine but with an uncanny, almost eerie, power to attract believers. Many perceived it to be a threat to Japanese culture. In a sense, the Latter-day Saint doctrines had been translated—or rather, mistranslated—by Japanese and resident Christian writers long before the missionaries ever set foot on Japanese soil. It was against these beliefs and perceptions that the early Latter-day Saint missionaries had to perform their monumental task of translation, not just of their written materials, but also of their mission.

There was an overwhelming sense in many of these writings by other Christian authors that the coming of the Latter-day Saints would do harm to the country and in particular to the precarious status of the country's women, so recently emerging from a system that fostered, or at least allowed, abuse and exploitation. Most importantly, however, the Church and its practice of polygamy were depicted as a threat to *bunmei kaika*, the Meiji ideal of civilization and enlightenment.

Of course, many in Japan had certainly heard of Utah and the Mormons through the stay of the Iwakura delegation in Salt Lake City in February 1872. It is likely that another of the earliest introductions in print that Japan had to Mormonism came through the 1879 Japanese translation of Jules Verne's *Around the World in 80 Days*. Passepartout, the naive servant through whose eyes the tale was told, heard a lecture on the tenets of Mormonism, including "the custom of polygamy, which is its foundation [sic]."[8] He wondered at the polygamist women in Salt Lake City, who seemed to be "neither well nor happy," and he was afraid that they were eyeing him as a potential mate.[9] The biologist-cum-poet Yatabe Ryōkichi (1851–99) knew at least the name Joseph Smith to include in his introduction to the 1882 collection of new-style verse, *Shintaishishō*, perhaps from his studies at Cornell University in the 1870s or Passepartout's description.

Magazine articles broadened the scope of knowledge about the Church. These articles focused primarily on polygamy and the dangers it posed for the society, and especially the women, of a country that reformers hoped would someday become a Westernized country.

Many Westerners—as well as many native writers and speakers—had condemned the Japanese practice of polygamy, or more accurately, concubinage, a legal practice in Japan in the late nineteenth century. In one famous example, the German geologist Edmund Naumann casually remarked in an 1886 article in the Munich *Allgemeine Zeitung* that princes and flag bearers (his incorrect translation of *hatamoto* or "officers of the flag") were allowed multiple wives in Tokugawa Japan, implying that the practice was still common in the 1880s. Well-known author Mori Ōgai (1862–1922), in 1886 still a virtually unknown student of public health, replied hotly:

> I assert that the present regime has no connection whatsoever with the Tokugawa family, and the customs of Iyeyasu's rule are irrelevant in a discussion of modern laws and practices.... That the Japanese are and were monogamists is evidenced in the different designations for wife (*tsuma*) and concubine (*sobame*).... In contemporary Japan a married man has a concubine only rarely, and he is not considered the more respectable for doing so. But here I will refrain from drawing examples from obvious similarities in modern Europe.[10]

Throughout his article, Ōgai tried to prove that his country was not backward and simple-minded but that it stood on a par intellectually and morally with the great powers of Europe. He concluded about Naumann's rash assertions that "appearing in one of Germany's most widely read papers, such an incorrect summary could be fatal to the status which the Japanese people are gradually beginning to enjoy in Europe."[11] Ōgai's concern here was almost entirely for the way Japan was perceived by the outside world. He and other non-Christian thinkers in Japan at the end of the nineteenth century desired to distance themselves and their country from the practice of polygamy for purely political reasons in order to foster Japan's ability to enter into a global society as an equal participant with other, more "civilized," countries.

The Japanese antipathy toward polygamy can also be traced to the efforts of foreign missionaries to overhaul the moral climate in Japan and, in particular, to make the country a place that prohibited the sexual exploitation of women. Christian missionaries were often convinced from travelogues and other media representations that Japan was not only a pagan country but an immoral one in need of complete social reform. These missionaries, almost exclusively from Protestant sects, established local chapters of the Women's Christian Temperance Union throughout Japan, founded schools (often schools with the express charge to educate women), and worked diligently for the abolition of prostitution. The Japanese people, and in particular Japanese men, were often seen by these missionaries as intemperate and sexually promiscuous. The practice of polygamy would, in their minds, run counter to their mission of improving the moral climate of the country.

Early Western and native reformers were not solely interested in preventing polygamy, but they worked for an improvement of the status of women in general as an antidote to the traditional value of *danson johi*—"revere men, despise women." For example, in its short-lived history, the *Meiroku Zasshi*, a journal of social reform supported by such Meiji luminaries as Fukuzawa Yukichi (1834–1901) and Mori Arinori (1847–89), published several articles on concubinage, prostitution, native marriage practices, and marriage laws and customs that discriminated against women.[12] Reformers believed that improving the status of women would improve the status of the nation not only at home but also in the eyes of the world. Like Ōgai, the reformers did not want their country to appear barbaric to outsiders, whose gaze had so recently turned to them.

Similarly, Wakamatsu Shizuko[13] (1864–96), a female Christian writer and translator, lamented the humiliation Japan would have to experience in relation to other nations in "The Condition of Woman in Japan," an article she composed in English for the *Japan Evangelist* in 1887. She wrote that

> the opening of the country to mixed residency, has been seriously contemplated, and it will, no doubt, be accomplished at no distant date. Perhaps, this may happen simultaneously with Japan taking her position with the European nations, in the dignity of a constitutional monarchy. This opening of the country, viewed from the point of the present low degree of culture together with the humiliating position of woman in her relation to man, has justly been deemed equivalent to inviting the people of the West to the exhibition of the nakedness of barbarism. Especially humiliating must be the criticism of Christian nations whose criterion of civilization is woman's positions at home and in society![14]

Although Wakamatsu Shizuko does not directly address the question of polygamy, she clearly believes that Japan occupies a position inferior to the rest of the civilized world—an inferiority occasioned by Japan's neglect of its female citizens.

It is fitting, then, that one early article about the Church appeared in a journal dedicated to raising women's status in Japan, the Christian magazine *Jogaku Zasshi* (The journal of women's education). Founded in 1885 by Iwamoto Yoshiharu (also known as Iwamoto Zenji, 1863–1942) and others, the journal was the first Japanese mass-market periodical addressing women's issues and aimed at women readers. The journal enjoyed a large circulation and appealed both to women and to reform-minded men.[15] Iwamoto's goal in publishing the journal was to refresh the moral climate of Japan by educating women, raising their status, and revamping the Japanese model of home and family to give women and children a safe moral and social environment. To that end, he solicited and often wrote articles on etiquette, home management, and fashion; history and literature; as well as social reform, women's rights, and the necessity of educating women.

The article "Morumon-shū" (The Mormon religion) appeared in *Jogaku Zasshi* in October 1890 in direct response to President Wilford Woodruff's injunction on September 24 of that same year to the members of the Church to "refrain from contracting any marriage forbidden by the laws of the land."[16] The announcement led to a lengthy argument against and condemnation of polygamy eleven years before Latter-day Saint missionaries entered the country. But the article introducing the policy of this strange new religion also required a rehearsal of the history and doctrine and a characterization of people who could be so deluded as to join. The articles proved to be not only an introduction to the Church but also a condemnation of it as a religion not fitting for "true" or "civilized" Christians.

The strongest arguments against polygamy given in this *Jogaku Zasshi* article were made on behalf of women. The author, presumably editor Iwamoto Yoshiharu, boldly claimed that in polygamy "one man divides his love among many women, while many women give all their love to one man,"[17] and in his mind, this was to the advantage of the man. He identified this situation as a "travesty of pure love and human feeling,"[18] making wives mistresses and husbands kings. Iwamoto's notions of sealing also worked to the advantage of men: he defined sealing[19] as "standing in for the dead husband, marrying the widow."[20] The widow, he claimed, will one day die and go to heaven. Until she rejoins her husband there, she gives her sealed husband his "selfish marriage," becoming his "temporary wife"[21] while on earth.

Iwamoto believed that the lust of men, given free rein in polygamy, would disrupt the sacredly appointed home. He identified Joseph Smith, who took multiple wives, as a "slave to carnal passion."[22] Brigham Young got slightly more sympathetic treatment. His stand on polygamy was given a doctrinal basis, as Iwamoto reports:

> Young claimed . . . [that] a union of just one man and one woman is contrary to the will of God. Man must have as many children as possible to give homes to the spirits waiting for them. Not fulfilling this responsibility is a sin. Those who do not fulfill this responsibility will be imperfect, like birds without wings, or like a body without a spirit.[23]

Iwamoto claimed that Brigham Young saw life as a paradise, where men's desires were the law, and mistook lust for something sacred. It was, of course, always men who were portrayed as giving in to carnal lust. This lust led, Iwamoto continued, to destruction of the home and consequently damage to the women and children in the home.

Iwamoto and others published in *Jogaku Zasshi* were particularly wary of any people or practice that threatened the home since their mission was to encourage the establishment of a home with one husband and one wife, where men and women respected each other and treated each other well. Iwamoto claimed a man coming home to many wives enters a "temple of *shura*,"[24] a home full of struggle, jealousy, and suffering, instead of a home that was not of this world.[25] Ideal marital relations in the *Jogaku Zasshi* schema were sacred, a pledge of spirit and eternal life, not a matter of the flesh.[26] Iwamoto ended his article by vividly contrasting Milton's "perfect *pair*" of Adam and Eve with a polygamous couple, "mere contractors of carnal lust" who were no better than herds of swine and flocks of chickens.[27] Clearly the reformers at *Jogaku Zasshi* saw polygamy as a threat to the concept of home and the status of women that they had tried to build.

The article did not, however, unilaterally condemn the Latter-day Saints. Their diligence and sincerity were praised as the moral forces that sustained them when their enemies drove them from their homes and destroyed their meetingplaces. The Saints had tamed the wilderness of "Ootah" into a verdant and arable land. Iwamoto claimed that "although we sorrow for the mistakes in their belief, still we feel pity for their being persecuted for the differences of their religion."[28] Similarly, the Latter-day Saints' work ethic was lauded along with their self-sufficiency, their honesty, and their love toward one another. These favorable traits served to make the religion appealing but deceptively so. The article clearly condemned the Church as a religion that could only appeal to the most gullible and backward of people, certainly not to educated Christians.

The genesis of the Church, and especially the translation of the Book of Mormon, was veiled in mystery and suspicion in this article and in other articles that appeared shortly before and after the arrival of the Latter-day Saint missionaries. The *Jogaku Zasshi* article reports that the Church was established sixty-seven years earlier in North America

> by Smith, who was young in years but terribly clever, with ambition to become a great priest. He spoke of strange visions, and on September 21, 1823, received a grand vision telling him that certain people had separated themselves from ancient Israel and had left for North America. He was told that the last of these was Mormon. Mormon's son Moroni had gathered the revelations, recorded them in stone, and buried them in a place about three English *ri* [leagues] from Palmyra. The next morning Smith went to that place and, reading the words on the stone, discovered they were "new Egyptian." He kept reading and translated the work. No one else saw the record, yet twelve testified that Smith had seen it. After Smith had read it, the record in stone spontaneously vanished without a trace. He divided the translation into twelve volumes and in 1830 made it public as scripture of the Mormon religion.[29]

This account accorded with later accounts published in newspapers and periodicals with much larger circulations when news of the Latter-day Saint missionaries' impending arrival reached Japan in 1901. For example, one newspaper account read as follows:

> Mormonism is not an ancient religion but an extremely recent one. The farmer Joseph Smith was born in Sharon in the state of Vermont

in 1805. In 1820 through a revelation from God he became aware that the Book of Mormon, a Christian holy book[30] that contained the ancient history of America, had been recorded on golden plates and was buried in the ground. He discovered these plates three years later on a hill four *ri* [leagues] from Palmyra in the state of Ontario, but at that time he was not yet permitted to read the writing. In 1807 [*sic*] he was once again visited by an angel. He returned to the place and, receiving from God a type of spectacle device, read the plates. When he did, he found that the characters were reformed Egyptian. These told that there was, long ago, a prophet named Mormon who diligently tried to promulgate Christianity. Eventually Mormon, upon receiving direction from God, transferred the things he had received to many plates of gold measuring 8″ in length and 7″ in width. By the same divine instruction he buried them in the ground. This holy book Joseph Smith translated in the space of one night [*sic*] and, using the book as a foundation, established with six others a new religion, what in other words is today's Mormon religion.[31]

In both of these accounts, the religion was identified as new and perhaps unproven. Joseph Smith was viewed as a slightly suspicious, sometimes sneaky, and deceptive man: he was purportedly "terribly clever," with "great ambition," and he saw "strange visions." He was given attributes (the ability to translate the entire Book of Mormon in one night, for example) that made his claims seem all the more ludicrous. The inaccuracies in both accounts (for example, the notion in the first account that the book was engraved on stone rather than gold) suggest that the sources were unreliable, the authors' grasp of the English language was insufficient, or the story simply was unbelievable.

The *Jogaku Zasshi* article identified other divergences of Latter-day Saint doctrine with mainstream Japanese Protestant Christianity. Iwamoto seemed determined to point out that the Church was clearly not a Christian religion, was certainly not one suited to a civilized society, and in fact was perhaps a danger to civilization. He took issue with seven of the doctrines of the Church that set it off from other Christian sects. Iwamoto summarized these doctrines as follows:

1. God is like humankind with flesh and form.

2. Human beings are one manifestation of *shintai* [a Shintō term defined as "An object of worship in which the spirit of a deity is

believed to reside. A symbol or medium of the spirit of deity"[32]] and one day will become gods.

3. Human beings were not made by God but have existed eternally.

4. Human beings have no original sin; they bring sin upon themselves by the actions they commit.

5. In the universe there are many beings of spirit and flesh. Just as on earth, they inhabit a number of dwelling places. Earth is just one of these dwelling places.

6. God is the head of those who have eternal life and beneath Him are four types of beings: (a) *shoshin* [a Shintō term referring to the collection of various gods], or beings of flesh and spirit made perfect. When humankind progresses they become *shoshin*, (b) servants of heaven (angels) who are not yet gods. They follow laws and are free to roam the earth, (c) humankind, and (d) spirits who have not yet received the bodies they must occupy. They float about in space.

7. Human beings, through matrimony, may someday become gods, and their family will be in [their] service in heaven.[33]

These doctrines were described as "side-splittingly laughable." Iwamoto claimed that no right-thinking person would believe anything so ridiculous, but he conceded that the religion appealed to new immigrants to the United States for whom teachings about the future and the heavens were much more appealing than their familiar and perhaps uncomfortable present reality.[34] Iwamoto was not just condemning the Church for taking advantage of people whose situation made them gullible, he was also suggesting that this religion appealed to those who were backward, underdeveloped, and uneducated. He tacitly contrasted people like this to his countrymen, who were presumably civilized enough to recognize the religion as ridiculous.

The greatest threat Iwamoto identified was to *bunmei kaika*. As the logic went, if the Latter-day Saints and their strange doctrine and their misogynist practices found place in the civilized United States, what harm could they cause in Japan, which was relatively new to notions of modernization and enlightenment? Iwamoto warned, "They have infiltrated the very center of the United States, a country founded on enlightenment [*bunmei*]. They have poisoned and stained with evil the home of those civilized ones [*kaikajin*] of strict ethics and morality."[35] He continued to caution that the strongest powers of government were powerless before the Saints: "The [American] president has tried time and again to destroy this evil influence, even trying military force which met strong resistance. He tried litigation, and tried legislation, but this despicable, filthy, evil practice still exists as it did before."[36] Latter-day Saints, in the *Jogaku Zasshi* schema, were tenacious and dangerous. They would presumably come to destroy what Iwamoto and his associates had worked for if they were allowed entry into the country.

Church Representation by Latter-day Saint Missionaries

The Latter-day Saint missionaries themselves saw their work as distinctly different. Alma O. Taylor reports in an undated draft of a speech or tract:

> Watakushi-domo wa Batsujitsu Seito Iesu Kirisuto Kyōkai no kenri wo tekitō ni uke, sono daihyōsha toshite ten ni mashimasu ikeru kami yori Josefu Sumisu ni arawashitamaishi sukui to inochi no michi wo oshie Nihon e mairimashita. [We, having received the proper authority from The Church of Jesus Christ of Latter-day Saints, as representatives of the same, have come to Japan to preach the way of life and salvation as revealed to Joseph Smith by our living God in heaven.][37]

Taylor and the other missionaries came not to corrupt the women nor to threaten the civilization but to teach the way of life and salvation. Despite their profound belief in their message, however, the missionaries had to present it within a context of the notions the Japanese had already formed about the Latter-day Saints through the written word.[38]

The missionaries spent considerable effort countering the assumption that the Church was based on the practice of polygamy. The Japanese translation of Anderson's *A Brief History of the Church of Jesus Christ of Latter-day Saints,* for example, included a chapter on polygamy not present in the English version, emphasizing the fact that the Church no longer sanctioned the practice. Eventually the efforts of the mission turned to what was perhaps the most effective means to present the doctrines and aims of the Church: translating the entire text of the Book of Mormon into Japanese.

The missionaries who were engaged in the work of translation encountered many of the same problems other foreign Christian translators had faced: they arrived in Japan with almost no knowledge of the language or the culture and in particular, no knowledge of the written language (including the differences between the written and spoken languages). Latter-day Saint missionaries met an additional hurdle: they had received so much negative press from both resident foreigners and natives that they initially had trouble finding native speakers willing to help them improve their language skills. It is not surprising, then, that the work of translating the Book of Mormon commenced in 1904 and continued through 1909, taking almost six years in total.

Initially, mission president Horace S. Ensign requested that each elder in the mission spend his spare moments translating bits and pieces of the Book of Mormon that would eventually be compiled, reviewed, and then published. Seven months later, the entire work of translation was assigned to Alma O. Taylor, who worked full time until its completion.

Elder Taylor finished his Romanized translation, written in the colloquial style, in 1906, after one year and nine months of steady work. Had the work then been transcribed into *kana* (phonetic pronunciation) and *kanji* (Chinese characters) and been published, it quite likely would have been subject to some of the same shortcomings as other early translated works by foreigners, such as the hymnal cited by Pastor Uemura Masahira. The care taken in revision, however, was the key to presenting the Church to Japan as an intelligent, civilized entity. The next eighteen months were spent re-reading the translation for grammatical coherence, comparing the text to the English for doctrinal soundness, then again re-reading it for smoothness. Taylor reflected, "In view of the time [the re-reading and revision] took and the amount of labor it required, it would be more proper to call it a new translation."[39] Three native speakers served as scribes in the work, identified by Taylor as Brother Chiba Yasubeie and Messrs. Mori Hachirō and Sakuraba Takeshirō. Elder Frederick A. Caine also assisted in reading and comparing the manuscript with the English version.

As the re-reading and revision progressed, Taylor sought additional native speakers to help polish the composition style. He searched out the best help he could find to refine the style of the translation, writing in his history of the work that "this criticism was absolutely necessary, for my Japanese was all too imperfect to produce a translation worthy of the approval and respectful consideration of the public."[42] Taylor clearly recognized early in the translation and editing process that the work had to be written in a way that it could not only be understood but also be accepted by a native audience as a work worthy of serious consideration.

His first requests for help in 1906 were declined by Hirai Kinza, a man Taylor believed had both integrity and ability and was one of four delegates to the World's Parliament of Religions held in conjunction with the World's Columbian Exposition in Chicago in 1893. Taylor then asked for reviews from Noguchi Zenshirō of Kōbe, another of the delegates to the World's Parliament, and Suzuki Genta of Sendai, a friend of the Sendai missionaries.[41] Both recommended, to Taylor's dismay, that the style be changed from the colloquial *genbun'itchi* to what he called *bunshō*, a more elegant literary style. They claimed that "all efforts at putting force and dignity into the translation as it stood in 'gembunitchi' had proved unsuccessful."[42]

In 1906, when Taylor was seeking advice about the style of the Book of Mormon translation, Japan was still negotiating the differences between its written and spoken languages. *Genbun'itchi* or *genbun'itchi-tai* were generic terms referring to a written style developed around the end of the nineteenth century mimicking to one degree or another colloquial Japanese. *Bunshō-tai,* on the other hand, referred to a collection of styles that existed only in written Japanese and that usually relied heavily on classical Japanese and Chinese grammar and vocabulary. Although virtually all Japanese narratives written prior to and immediately following the Meiji Restoration were styled in bunshō-tai, over the last two decades of the nineteenth century genbun'itchi developed a hold on literature to the point that by 1905, 78 percent of all Japanese novels were written in colloquial style; in 1906 the number increased to 91 percent, in 1907 to 98 percent, and in 1908 to 100 percent.[43] Outside the literary world, however, more formal writing styles prevailed. Not until World War I did historical, scientific, and critical writings begin to adopt the colloquial style, and many official documents used bunshō styles until after World War II.[44] Taylor's advisors both perhaps considered the Book of Mormon a nonfiction, historical, or even philosophical document rather than a literary work and thus a work unsuited for colloquial style. Taylor himself reported that "it has developed that there are only two or three men in all Japan to-day whose 'gembunitchi' writings truly merit public praise," perhaps another motivation for changing the style of the work.[45]

Consequently, Taylor had to find an author capable of changing the style of the translation. Hirai Kinza's brother Hirai Hirogoro, a lecturer at Waseda University, was hired and eventually fired before he could complete the work. His place was taken by Chōkō Ikuta[46] (1882–1936), the Christian translator of Nietzche, after the post was refused by Natsume Sōseki[47] (1876–1916), who was then perhaps the best-known author in Japan, and another prominent author, Tsubouchi Shōyō[48] (1859–1935), who had been introduced to the missionaries by poet and novelist Iwano Hōmei (1873–1920). Chōkō was a student of Natsume Sōseki.

Taylor was not, however, satisfied with Chōkō's skill simply by the recommendation of Japan's leading literary man. He tested Chōkō's ability by asking him to review Hirai's work and make any changes he felt necessary in pencil. Without revealing the author of the changes, Taylor returned with the sample of Chōkō's work to Tsubouchi Shōyō and Iwano Hōmei,[49] as well as to another leading poet, Kawai Suimei[50] (1874–1965), asking if Chōkō's changes improved the style and tone. All the authors agreed that they did, and after ascertaining Chōkō's character and disposition as well, Taylor employed him as the main reviser beginning in July 1908. Before turning Hirai's work over to Chōkō, Taylor checked it one more time himself, comparing it to the romanized version (Hirai had written in kana phonetic pronunciation for all the Chinese kanji so that Taylor could read and comprehend the work), and then employed four more native copyists[51] to make a clean copy from which Chōkō could work.

Chōkō finished his work in May 1909. Taylor reviewed the changes once again himself and then delivered the manuscript, now in bunshō style, to Kawai Suimei for a final reading after having Chōkō's last changes transcribed onto a clean copy by Namekawa Hiroyuki. The final corrections were completed on July 24, 1909. Chiba Yasubeie and Elder Caine re-read the work a last time before it was sent to the printer, and Taylor double-checked the references not only in the translation but also in the original romanized version, making several corrections. The first few volumes of the manuscripts were left at the printers in January 1909, and proofs began arriving in February of that year. Taylor describes the painstaking reading of the proofs as follows:

> The first proof was always read aloud by Mr. Hiroyuki Namekawa and Elder Caine followed the reading with the printer's manuscript in hand, while I followed with the manuscript from which the printers manuscript was copied. The references were also read at this time. Either Elder Caine or Mr. Namekawa read aloud from the proof sheets while one followed with the printer's manuscript and I followed with the English text before me. After this reading by three of us, either Elder Caine or I carefully read them once alone before sending them back. The second proofs were always read alone by Mr. Namekawa first, then reviewed by either Elder Caine or me to see if all the corrections in the first proofs had been properly made. After this review, either Elder Caine or I carefully read the proofs through once more. The third proofs were always read first by Mr. Namekawa and then compared with the second proofs by Elder Caine or me to see if any changes had been omitted or improperly made. The fourth, fifth, sixth and seventh proofs were examined in the same manner as the third proofs.[52]

The first installment of printed copies appeared on October 11, 1909, and the initial printing eventually totaled almost five thousand copies, including specially bound editions for the emperor and empress, crown prince and princess, and various government leaders.

Taylor and the other early missionaries had a clear sense of their mission of education and enlightenment when they came to Japan. They were faced with the difficulty of entering into a fairly hostile environment where news of their mission as Latter-day Saints and of their religion had already been socially translated and to a large degree misunderstood, or rather mistranslated. The missionaries' care in making translations, and particularly the extreme care taken with the first translation of the Book of Mormon, showed them to be civilized men who could converse with and appeal to the most educated and enlightened Japanese people. Taylor read the entire original romanized version five times and the translation nine. Other critics read the manuscript in various incarnations seven times. And the missionaries sought help not just from native speakers but from the most important writers they could find—some of the finest authors of the time. The translators were keenly aware not only of their message but also of how it had to be delivered. Despite the many months of exhaustively detailed work of revision and editing required, the choice of a formal translation language rather than genbun'itchi was consistent with the "force and dignity" of the message they carried.

The translation did not become a literary bestseller. It did not directly address the Japanese mistrust of the religion that had once preached and practiced polygamy, but the fact that the translation was carried out with such thoughtful care shows that the Mormon missionaries were not willing to be translated merely by their native hosts and to risk having their mission and their church's doctrine misunderstood. They undertook the Herculean task of translation to set the record straight and present themselves as builders of civilization and enlightenment rather than as its destroyers.

This paper was presented at "A Centennial Celebration: The LDS Church in Japan, 1901–2001," October 13, 2001, Brigham Young University, Provo, Utah.

Notes

1. J. Liggins and C. M. Williams were sent to Nagasaki from their missions in China in 1859 by the Domestic and Foreign Missionary Society of the Protestant Episcopal Church in the United States. Physician James C. Hepburn and his wife, who had also been serving in China and Singapore, came to Kanagawa in October 1859 representing the Presbyterian church. And S. R. Brown, D. B. Simmons, and G. F. Verbeck reached Nagasaki in November of that year, representing the Dutch Reformed Church in America. Their wives joined them the next month. In addition, Jonathan Goble, one of the members of Commodore Perry's famous expedition, came to Kanagawa Japan as a missionary for the American Baptist Free Mission Society in 1860. Winburn T. Thomas, *Protestant Beginnings in Japan: The First Three Decades, 1859–1889* (Tokyo and Rutland, Vt.: Charles E. Tuttle Company, 1959), 76–77.

2. Thomas, *Protestant Beginnings*, 79.

3. Statesman Ii Naosuke, for example, was murdered in 1860 by angry fellow countrymen for his pro-foreign policies.

4. The town of Tsuwano, in present-day Shimane Prefecture, claims that these were the last Christian martyrs in Japan.

5. A survey of early missionary work in Japan reports that there were 432 "Christian items" (including parts of the Bible, commentaries, tracts, songbooks, etc., both translations and original works) published in Japanese prior to 1882. Of these, only 10 were published prior to 1855, and an additional 70 prior to 1872. The big translation boom in religious works came at the same time as the boom in literary translations, with 352 Christian works (primarily translations) published in the decade after 1872 and 453 in the 1880s and with 40 periodicals devoted to Christian topics in circulation by 1894. Thomas, *Protestant Beginnings*, 122–25.

6. Cited in Akiyama Yūzō, *Umoreta Hon'yaku: Kindai Bungaku no Kaitakusha* (Tokyo: Shindokushosha, 1998), 42.

7. Chiba Kikukō, "Chūjitsu ni shite shikōshite jiyū naru hon'yaku" (Faithful yet free translation), *Bunshō sekai* 4, no. 13 (1909): 35.

8. Jules Verne, *Around the World in 80 Days*, trans. Geo. M. Fowle (Philadelphia: Porter & Coates, 1873), 222.

9. Verne, *Around the World in 80 Days*, 228–29.

10. Mori Ōgai, "Die Wahrheit Ueber Japan" (The truth about Japan), in *Ōgai Zenshū*, (Tokyo: Iwanami Shoten, 1973), 26:616.

11. Mori Ōgai, "Noch Einmal 'Die Wahrheit Ueber Japan'" ("The truth about Japan" revisited), in *Ōgai Zenshū*, 26:608.

12. Mori Arinori serialized a discussion of Japanese marriage traditions, "On Wives and Concubines," in the journal from 1874 to 1875, deploring the slave-like status of women in relation to their husbands and calling for a more equal and fair marriage model and more responsible and moral behavior on the part of Japanese men. Other authors such as Katō Hiroyuki and Tsuda Mamichi wrote in favor of rights for women, including the right to enter into a marriage free of the threat of husbands taking concubines. Mori Arinori, "On Wives and Concubines," in *Meiroku Zasshi: Journal of the Japanese Enlightenment*, trans. William Reynolds Braisted (Cambridge, Mass.: Harvard University Press, 1976), 104–5, 143–45, 189–91, 252–53, 331–33.

13. The pseudonym for Shimada Kashiko, who became Iwamoto Kashiko after her marriage to *Jogaku Zasshi* editor Iwamoto Yoshiharu. She was also a regular contributor to the journal and is perhaps best known as the translator of *Little Lord Fauntleroy* into Japanese.

14. *In Memory of Mrs. Kashi Iwamoto: The First Graduate of Ferris Seminary, with a Collection of her English Writings* (Yokohama: Yokohama Seishi Bunsha, n.d.), 136–37.

15. *Jogaku Zasshi* eventually evolved into two magazines, *Jogaku Zasshi* and the influential journal of the Japanese Romantic movement, *Bungakkai*. *Jogaku*

Zasshi focused primarily on women's education and *Bungakkai* on literature informed by Christian and Romantic notions.

16. Andrew Jenson, *Church Chronology: A Record of Important Events Pertaining to The Church of Jesus Christ of Latter-day Saints*, 2d ed. (Salt Lake City, Deseret News, 1914), 188. The articles that appeared in newspapers all over the country upon the arrival of missionaries in 1901 also spoke overwhelmingly of the Church's practice—by that time former practice—of polygamy. It was a topic of great interest to many Japanese, at home and abroad. These contemporary articles tended to reflect in large measure the ideas and sentiments being published in the foreign English press at the time, and, in fact, many of the Japanese articles appear to be translations or at least paraphrases of the same. See Shinji Takagi, "Mormons in the Press: Reactions to the 1901 Opening of the Japan Mission," *BYU Studies* 40, no. 1 (2000): 141–75, reprinted herein.

17. "Morumon shū," *Jogaku Zasshi* 235 (October 11, 1890): 251, translated by the author.

18. "Morumon shū," 251.

19. Once transliterated *shiiru* (to seal) in *katakana* next to the *kanji* for *fūyaku* (combined meaning *fū* [to seal hermetically] and *yaku* [promise]); later usages moved to the standard reading of the characters as *fūyaku*.

20. "Morumon shū," 249.

21. *Kari no tsuma*.

22. "Morumon shū," 248.

23. "Morumon shū," 248.

24. *Shura* is a shortened form of *Ashura*, the Indian king equated with demons.

25. "Morumon shū," 251.

26. "Morumon shū," 250.

27. "Morumon shū," 251.

28. "Morumon shū," 248.

29. "Morumon shū," 247.

30. *Yaso no o-kyō*.

31. "A Strange Phenomenon from the Current Religious World," *Yamato Shimbun*, August 18, 1901.

32. *Basic Terms of Shintō*, rev. ed. (Tokyo: Kokugakuin University Institute for Japanese Culture and Classics, 1985), 58.

33. "Morumon shū," 248.

34. "Morumon shū," 248.

35. "Morumon shū," 250.

36. "Morumon shū," 250.

37. Alma O. Taylor, Journals 1901–1946, L. Tom Perry Special Collections, Harold B. Lee Library, Brigham Young University, Provo, Utah. The original draft is written almost entirely in *katakana* (phonetic syllabary).

38. The Japanese were not the only ones to construct a context that had to be taken into account. Taylor later wrote home about the difficulty of putting the word of God into a "pagan language." Taylor identified Japanese as a "pagan language" in a previous letter home, before he arrived in Japan. He saw his task as bringing Christian enlightenment to a country that had no Christian context and so no way of even speaking of Christian concepts.

39. Taylor, Journals, "The History of the Japanese Translation of the Book of Mormon," 2, Perry Special Collections.

40. Taylor, Journals, "The History of the Japanese Translation of the Book of Mormon," 3.

41. Suzuki was also the editor of the *Kahoku Shimpō* newspaper.

42. Taylor, Journals, "The History of the Japanese Translation of the Book of Mormon," 4.

43. Nanette Twine, "The Genbunitchi Movement: Its Origin, Development, and Conclusion," *Monumenta Nipponica* 33, no. 3 (1978): 354.

44. Twine, 355.

45. Taylor, Journals, "The History of the Japanese Translation of the Book of Mormon," 4.

46. Pen name of Ikuta Hiroharu.

47. Pen name of Natsume Kinnosuke.

48. Pen name of Tsubouchi Yūjirō.

49. Pen name of Iwano Yoshie. Iwano is not identified by his full name in Taylor's journals or in his history, but Iwano is once referred to as "Y. Iwano" and is presumably the famous writer. He had assisted the elders in translating the first volume of hymns.

50. Pen name of Kawai Kōsaburō.

51. Identified as Kawanaka Aritatsu, Mori Hachiro, Kuga Eisaburo, and Mr. Nakamura Yoneji. Taylor, Journals, "The History of the Japanese Translation of the Book of Mormon," 11.

52. Taylor, Journals, "The History of the Japanese Translation of the Book of Mormon," 12.

6

Strangers in a Strange Land: Heber J. Grant and the Opening of the Japan Mission

Ronald W. Walker

Look!
In a world circumscribed by iron
a poor dynamo is panting momentarily
Set in a white circle.

(Murano Shiro, "Hammer Throw")

When Heber J. Grant returned from a two-week vacation in Pacific Grove, California, in February 1901, the news he heard at first seemed favorable. One of his associates in the Quorum of the Twelve, Francis M. Lyman, had been asked to preside over the Church's European Mission. Elder Grant congratulated himself that "missionary lightning had once more escaped me," "heaved a sigh of relief," and embraced Lyman in mock celebration.[1]

Since Grant's appointment as a General Authority almost two decades earlier, rumors had often circulated about a forthcoming proselytizing mission. Each time, however, the reports died stillborn. During the 1880s, the Church and its opponents warred relentlessly on theological, political, and even commercial terrain, and Elder Grant's business acumen was repeatedly deemed too important to the Utah scene to allow a foreign assignment.

The repose given to Elder Grant by Lyman's assignment to the Liverpool office was short-lived. Two days after his return from California, during the General Authorities' regular temple meeting, Grant heard George Q. Cannon, First Counselor in the First Presidency, announce the decision to open a new mission in Japan. "The moment he made this remark," Grant later recalled, "I felt impressed that I would be called to open up this mission."

Preparing for a Mission

This prescience, however, brought a flood of reasons why he should reject the call. The Panic of 1893 and its subsequent depression had crippled his finances. He calculated his net worth to be a negative $30,000. Moreover, he had co-signed financial notes making him responsible for another $100,000 in personal debt. Because of his straitened circumstance, neither of his wives had a home of her own, while his mother's house was mortgaged to assist with his obligations.[2]

As President Cannon continued for twenty-five minutes, Grant quietly weighed financial and religious commitments. Then came the call he expected from Cannon: "We hear that Brother Grant has overcome all his great financial difficulties and has announced that he is going to take a trip around the world to celebrate his financial freedom, and we have decided to stop him half way around at Japan, to preside."[3]

Having extended a call to Grant, Cannon yielded to President Lorenzo Snow, who, since becoming the Church's prophet, seer, and revelator in 1898, had slashed at every unnecessary expenditure to save money. Fearing that Elder Grant's precarious finances might somehow encumber the Church, President Snow had some specific questions in mind.[4] First he wanted to know whether President Cannon had accurately quoted the Apostle about touring the world.

"Heber, did you make that statement?"

"Yes, I did, but there was an extra word in it, and the word was 'if.'" Grant had no plans to leave if he was unable to retire the rest of his debt.

"Well, then, you are not free?"

"No, I am not free, I owe a few dollars."

President Snow wanted specifics. "Well, what are you making?"

"A little better than $5,000 a year."

"Can you afford to lose that $5,000 for three years while you are in Japan?"

"Yes, I can."

In later years, Grant's memory of this incident remained very much alive. "[President Snow] tried for ten minutes to get something out of me [about my debts] and could not do it," Grant remembered.

> Finally I said, "President Snow, with the blessing of the Lord I think I can arrange all my affairs to go on this mission, . . . and it will be time enough for me to come and tell you I cannot when I feel in my heart I can't."
>
> "The Lord bless you, my boy," said President Snow, obviously pleased. "We will give you a whole year. You go right to work and fix up your affairs to go on this mission."[5]

As the meeting concluded, President Snow assured Grant that if he worked diligently, he "would accomplish a greater labor than any I had ever accomplished before in my life" and hinted that China might soon be opened for proselytizing as well as Japan.[6]

At the time of his selection, Elder Grant was forty-four years old, the husband of two plural wives (a third had died seven years earlier), and a leading businessman. He was president of the State Bank of Utah, the Salt Lake Theatre Company, three insurance companies, and the Cooperative Wagon and Machine Company—one of the largest retail outlets in the territory. In addition, he served as chairman of the Utah Sugar Company and Zion's Cooperative Mercantile Institution, two leading Utah businesses, and he was a board or committee member of a half-dozen other organizations.

Grant had left school while a teenager, and the hectic pace of his business life had subsequently given him little opportunity for reading and reflection. At the time of his call, he was the only member of the Twelve who had not served a regular proselytizing mission.[7] Most had served several. All these circumstances left Grant feeling unprepared and inadequate. "I do not know when anything has struck me much harder than being called to Japan," he confided. "I really dreaded being called to the British mission . . . , but I look upon the European mission in comparison to opening up the work in Japan, as a picnic on the one hand and a great labor on the other. However, I shall go and do the best I possibly can."[8]

Part of Elder Grant's hesitancy, of course, could be explained by his finances, which he tried to improve within an hour or two after the meeting of the Twelve. Locking his bedroom door, he prayed for relief. "I told the Lord I did not want to wait until tomorrow morning to make some money, but I wanted to put in that afternoon making a little." An impression came. "Get the Sugar Company to pay a stock dividend, that they can pay the same [money] dividend on the watered stock as they were doing on the original."

The Utah Sugar Company, founded only a decade earlier to provide Utah's farmers with a much needed cash crop, was at last reaping large profits, which in turn fueled ever increasing stock splits, higher dividends, and feverish speculation. Although the company's reserves hardly warranted the action, Grant hoped for another round of share splitting and dividend boosting. With the board scheduled to meet the following day, the timing was exquisite.

After concluding his meditation, he hired a buggy and went to meet the Salt Lake City–based directors, informing them of his mission call to Japan and pointedly reminding them how in the early 1890s he had gone into debt to support the company, only to face the onslaught of the great panic. The next day the board unanimously approved Grant's proposals and his securities jumped $16,000, an increase that temporarily left him astounded. Catching his breath, during the next several weeks he further speculated in the stock and reaped enough profit to pay all his debts, including a $13,000 note that had been owing for over twenty years.[9]

Organizing the Japan Mission

With his finances under control, Grant turned to organizing his mission. He handpicked three men to go with him. First, he requested the twenty-nine-year-old Horace S. Ensign, who had earlier served as his private secretary and most recently had returned from a three-year mission in Colorado. In addition to his business and Church experience, Ensign possessed a magnificent baritone voice that Grant hoped would attract Japanese attention.[10] Second, he selected the mustachioed, bespectacled Louis A. Kelsch, who, after his conversion to the Church, had filled missions to the Southern States, the Pacific Northwest, England, and Germany. Since 1896 he had presided over the Northern States Mission, whose headquarters were in Chicago. Elder Kelsch accepted Grant's invitation with alacrity.[11] Finally, Grant asked Alma O. Taylor, an eighteen-year-old living within the boundaries of his own Salt Lake City congregation, to join the mission. Taylor, who was cherubic-faced but serious-minded, had studied at Chicago Harvey Medical College and worked in his family's undertaking business. Upon receipt of his call, he sought Japanese-language textbooks and began studying Buddhist philosophy.[12]

These four men constituted what became known as the "Japanese Quartet," the first wave of the intended Latter-day Saint missionary force to Japan (illus. 6-1). It was hoped that they would "go on ahead," Grant noted, "look over the country, see what we can do, and if everything is all right and conditions are propitious we will then send for our wives and will probably need more Elders."[13] During this first stage, the missionaries planned to spend a year learning the language and then begin proselytizing.[14]

Grant approached his mission in his usual ambitious style. He first planned to ask his business and banking friends in New York to prevail

Courtesy Church Archives, The Church of Jesus Christ of Latter-day Saints

Illus. 6-1. The first four missionaries to Japan at a missionary benefit dinner in Salt Lake City in summer 1901. Standing *(left to right)*: Horace S. Ensign, Alma O. Taylor. Seated *(left to right)*: Heber J. Grant, Louis A. Kelsch.

on United States President William McKinley to speak to the Japanese ambassador on his behalf. Perhaps the ambassador would in turn write favorable letters of recommendation. As another idea still more bold, Grant considered the possibility of getting himself appointed to head the American legation in Tokyo.[15] But his fellow General Authorities vetoed these and other ideas as too extravagant, requesting that the mission start out in a "humble way."[16]

Shortly after 11:00 PM on July 24, 1901, Grant and his companions boarded the train for Portland, en route to Japan. The date had not come by chance. Suggestive of the weight that the Latter-day Saint community placed upon the mission, Grant had chosen to start on Pioneer Day, the anniversary of Brigham Young's 1847 entrance into the Salt Lake Valley. Because of the possibility of cohabitation prosecution, neither of Grant's wives was there to see him off. There was, however, a crowd of one hundred and fifty friends and relatives, including Grant's mother, Rachel, eight of his ten children, and six General Authorities, all of whom partially compensated for his wives' absence. As the train pulled away from the station, Grant claimed he had never been happier in his life. He was now, with the support and love of hundreds of friends and relatives, off to introduce the gospel of Jesus Christ to Japan.[17]

Months before Elder Grant's arrival, the mainline Protestant clergy had planned a major campaign to mark the turn of the new century in Japan. In early 1901 they began with a series of neighborhood prayer meetings in the nation's largest cities. These failed to stir enthusiasm. But when the Whitsunday festivals began in early summer, their program gained momentum. To advertise their planned revivals, the staid ministers adopted the flamboyant methods of the Salvation Army, which had entered Japan only recently. The Protestants placed notices of their meetings in newspapers and posted eye-catching placards. They canvassed house-to-house, extending special invitations to those who were thought to be open to Christian influence. Capping their preparations, an hour or two before their scheduled meeting, they hoisted banners and lanterns along the street, loudly chanted Christian hymns, and distributed broadsides.

While the Protestants' "Forward Evangelistic Campaign" earned a relatively small harvest for a nation of forty million, most clergymen were buoyed. They had been about their task since at least the mid-1870s, when the government had granted Christians religious tolerance, but gains were always hard won. During the last decade, progress had become still more difficult. Part of the problem lay with Meiji policy. When the nation ended its self-imposed isolation and embraced Western culture, some government leaders equated Christianity with material progress and had looked upon the ministers with favor. But by the 1890s, Japan again turned inward. The popular watchwords of the time became: "Down with frivolous Europeanization!" "Keep to our national heritage!" and "Japan for the Japanese!"[18]

These were not the only conditions working against the missionaries. The setting of rural Japan was especially restrictive. There, tenant farmers, who comprised half of the nation's population until the middle of the twentieth century, were fettered by feudal social structures and the historic family system, both of which were reformulated and given new life during the period of anti-Christian reaction. Religious and social change became increasingly difficult, with many Christian congregations—which had begun optimistically only a few years earlier—waning and eventually closing. Even in the more fluid urban society, there were challenges. By the beginning of the twentieth century, the nation's military expenditures exacted heavy and impoverishing levies. Under this burden, some former Christian converts, who had hoped that their new faith would assist them in getting ahead, recanted. Thus, at the very time that the Latter-day Saints launched their mission, despite the Protestants' public clamor and mass rallies, the Christian churches were afflicted by decreased attendance at their mission schools, slower conversion rates, and widespread apostasy.[19]

Part of the problem lay with the Christian missionaries themselves, who too often failed to separate their own Western and national ways from their Christian message. Many Japanese bridled under such ethnocentrism, complaining that the Christian churches were "mere importations," with titles, organizations, methods, and teachings that had "nothing to do with the interests or needs of the Japanese."[20] All this created stony soil. When Grant and his companions approached Japan, Christianity had at best a toehold. The Greek Orthodox denomination may have had thirty thousand Japanese members; the Roman Catholics, fifty-five thousand (many of these descended from families who had practiced Christianity underground for three hundred years); and the Protestants, who had been most active since the Meiji Restoration, seventy thousand. Taken together, the Christian population constituted only a little more than one-third of 1 percent, and, given the ephemeral discipleship of many Japanese, even these figures were probably inflated.[21]

Yet this did not stop Grant and his fellow laborers. Early in the morning of August 12, land was sighted, and at 10:00 AM the *Empress of India* dropped anchor at Yokohama on the western coast of Tokyo Bay's expansive waters. Quarantine checks required about an hour, following which the "Japanese Quartet" took a steam launch for shore. For Grant, their arrival came none too soon. "I said good bye to the *Empress* without any regrets," he said.[22] He had been seasick much of the way.

Working with the Press in Japan

Several days after landing, the missionaries found themselves in the center of a growing controversy. Learning that a local boardinghouse had turned them away because they were Mormons, a Yokohama newspaper charged the innkeeper with religious "fanaticism." Another journal quickly defended the act, with charges and countercharges soon filling the press.[23] "A heavy war is raging," wrote Alma Taylor only eight days after the missionaries' arrival. While many of the newspaper features were "severe" or "slanderous" against the missionaries, the dispute, in Taylor's mind, nevertheless brought invaluable publicity.[24]

During the following weeks, Grant worked long hours defending the Church in the press. Not understanding the toil involved in composition, he grew frustrated that his writing required time-consuming draft after time-consuming draft. "I have never felt my own lack of literary knowledge so keenly as since I came here," he confided to his Utah friends.[25] And as he had so often expressed since the beginning of his mission, he also lamented his unfamiliarity with the finer points of Latter-day Saint theology. He found topics such as original sin and the Church's view of premortal life "difficult to fully explain."[26]

With newspaper publicity came letters and visitors, the receipt of which soon began to be a part of the missionaries' daily routine. While claiming a lively interest in the missionaries' religious message, many of their visitors, once their motives were searched more deeply, seemed merely curious about the Americans. Others revealed what appeared to be a crass self-interest, seeking position, salary, or the opportunity to sharpen their English language skills.

This experience was certainly a factor in Grant's decision to vacate Yokohama for Tokyo, which, it was reported, had "fewer foreigners, a higher class of natives, a more religious sentiment, and by far better instructors in the language and much cheaper living."[27] Thus, two months after the missionaries had debarked, they secured accommodations in Tokyo's leading hotel, the eleven-year-old Metropole, and settled into an established routine.[28]

Proselytizing in Japan

During his mission, Grant studied as he had never before. He read and reread the scriptures, Church history and apologetics, Christian homilies, and several books dealing with Japanese history and culture. In candid moments he admitted that such a steady diet of studying was "just about the hardest thing on earth for me to do," though on other occasions he put forward the best possible face.[29]

But no amount of good cheer could camouflage the distress he felt over the Japanese language; its unusual syntax and thousands of Chinese ideographs posed a massive challenge for Grant.[30] Though he toiled hundreds of hours studying the language and eventually compiled a detailed, one-hundred-page notebook filled with Japanese vocabulary, his progress was virtually nil.[31] "I do not seem to be able to remember anything that I learn and even the words that I have learned when I hear someone else use them I do not recognize," he complained. For an achievement-oriented man who preached the universal virtue of pluck and application, the unyielding, flint-hard language exacted a heavy emotional toil. With considerable pain, he finally reconciled himself to his language failure and devoted himself to what seemed more profitable pursuits.[32]

Yet the language study of his colleagues continued, and on the missionaries' move to Tokyo, Grant hired their prime Japanese investigator, Hiroi T., whom they had met in Yokohama, to serve as tutor. But the man's talents failed to speed the younger men's progress, and Taylor and Ensign argued for living among the Japanese in order to learn the language. Grant was reluctant. From the beginning, he had hoped that the mission could "start at the top" with the country's more influential citizenry. That would require learning "standard" or literary Japanese and not the dialects of the people.[33]

The tension between the missionaries and their leader unsettled Grant. He slept fitfully four nights in the middle of November, and he admitted to friends back in Utah that, while he seldom was attacked with "the blues," he could "almost get up an attack this morning and not half try."[34] With Ensign and Taylor increasingly restive and even demanding, Grant finally yielded to having the missionaries learn the language among the people though the decision went against his better judgment.

Grant's decision was confirmed the next day by what seemed a cold and distant letter from the First Presidency that appeared to contradict everything the missionaries had done since arriving in Japan. The missionaries were told to avoid newspaper controversy and to mingle among the people, and, in Elder Grant's case, pointedly instructed to resume language study.[35] "I would have appreciated ONE word of approval," he lamented, "but as it was not written I had to accept it as an evidence that there was none to give."[36] His reaction probably owed as much to his own emotional state as to the letter's actual contents. Obviously written in haste and without full attention to Grant's various reports, it gave offense where none was intended. Nevertheless, he hastened to implement its directions. "I know that to obey is the only way for an apostle," he told a friend.[37] He and Kelsch secured accommodations at a nearby boardinghouse, while Ensign and Taylor moved to a hotel catering to the Japanese trade.

Before their separation, the missionaries had entertained at Hiroi's request two men of unusual demeanor, Miyazaki Toranosuke and Takahashi Gorō. Miyazaki, the scion of a prominent family, would later distinguish himself as the self-proclaimed "Messiah-Buddhist," a spiritual leader who mixed Christian primitivism with the native culture.[38] But it was Takahashi who clearly attracted Grant's eye. He had already gained the Saints' confidence by publishing on his own initiative a defense of their mission in the *Sun*, a leading Japanese periodical.[39] Takahashi spoke English well, read Hebrew and French, and even understood some Egyptian. He had distinguished himself as an educator, a lexicographer, a translator of the Protestant New Testament edition, and a prominent Christian polemicist.[40] While resisting Grant's pleas to convert, Takahashi volunteered to write a book introducing the Latter-day Saint missionaries and their message to the Japanese public.[41]

There were other impressive investigators, too. In mid-February 1902, Grant and the other missionaries dined at the home of Ichiki S., who, according to Taylor, had "figured prominently in many of the wars in Japan especially during the troubles of the Meiji restoration." Also present were Miyasaki and a Mr. Suyenaga, a newspaper editor. The Japanese appeared drawn to Latter-day Saint teachings, especially to the missionaries' description of Mormon economics and group life in the many villages established in the Intermountain West. Ichiki and his friends promised to arrange a hearing for the Utahns before a group of literati drawn from the national press and members of the lower house of the national Diet.[42]

Ichiki's presence was obviously formidable. Hiroi, who claimed to know him well, noted that in his circle Ichiki "speaks and the rest obey" and reported that the man "executes whatever he decides to do no matter how hard or what the odds." Takahashi, obviously overwhelmed, found Ichiki to be "a man such as is rarely found in Japan."[43]

Suddenly, almost in spite of themselves and certainly contrary to the low-profile language-training mission they had at first conceived, the missionaries seemed on the verge of considerable success. The momentum continued when Nakazawa Hajime, who described himself as a Shintō priest with influence over fifteen hundred followers, appeared at Grant's room. In previous visits, Nakazawa had expressed dissatisfaction with his religion and voiced a desire to investigate the Church. When his superiors learned of his conduct, they severely rebuked him and eventually expelled him from his order.[44] This hastened his search for truth. On March 8, 1902, Nakazawa became the missionaries' first formal convert, baptized along the shoreline of Tokyo Bay.

Other candidates were also petitioning for baptism. Attracted by the newspaper publicity, men who knew little of the missionaries' beliefs sought baptism, and Grant found that the chance for adding names to the Church's rolls was ample if he merely accepted every request made of him. But in each case he put them off, demanding they receive formal instruction.⁴⁵ Some candidates had impressive credentials. Mr. Koshiishi, editor of the newly established *Tokyo Shimbun* and apparently a compeer of Ichiki, petitioned Grant several days after Nakazawa's conversion, but a catechizing of the applicant found that he knew "practically nothing of the gospel" and that he would be "stepping blindly into the church." Like others before him, Koshiishi was refused.⁴⁶

More persistent in the quest for baptism was Kikuchi Saburō, a Christian preacher who, the missionaries were informed, held open-air meetings in Ueno Park attended by five hundred to fifteen hundred people. Unlike others before him, Kikuchi would not be dissuaded, declaring his determination by vaingloriously offering himself to be crucified, if necessary, for the faith. Grant yielded before such ardor. Two days after Nakazawa's rite, the missionaries rowed into the nearby bay and baptized Kikuchi. In keeping with Latter-day Saint practice of conferring priesthood authority on its male laity, both converts were ordained to the office of elder.⁴⁷

Kelsch, Ensign, and Taylor must have observed these events with troubled feelings because of a major change that was in the offing. The day before Nakazawa's baptism, just as the mission appeared to be gaining success, they learned that Grant would be returning to Salt Lake City for a visit. When Ensign woke Taylor with the news, the zealous youth could hardly believe it. "The idea, I thought to myself, of Bro. Grant thinking of returning home. Why he has only been here it seems for a week or two."⁴⁸ However, the time had not passed so quickly for Grant. Imprisoned by his inability to learn the language and ill-fitted by temperament to the slow, almost monastic life of his mission, he greeted the opportunity to return home as a welcome relief. Moreover, with his eldest daughter announcing her engagement and a new Church president about to be sustained, Grant also had personal and official reasons for leaving. He sailed for America in March 1902.

Nearly a half-year later, Heber J. Grant was back in Japan, accompanied by nine new missionaries. Four were unmarried: Frederick A. Caine, Erastus L. Jarvis, John W. Stoker, and Sandford Wells Hedges (illus. 6-2). The other five were married or had family ties: Marie and Joseph Featherstone had just been sealed; Mary Ensign was called to join her husband, while Grant looked forward to the companionship

Illus. 6-2. The unmarried missionaries called to Japan in 1902. Left to right: John W. Stoker, Erastus L. Jarvis, unidentified woman, Frederick A. Caine, and Sanford W. Hedges. Photograph taken ca. 1902.

of Augusta and their daughter, Mary (illus. 6-3). The presence of the women, he thought, would add a sense of permanence to the mission.[49]

Elder Grant used a highly personal reason to secure permission for Augusta to travel with him to Japan. Though his three wives had borne him an even dozen children, Grant's only two sons had died. In the Church's turn-of-the-century patriarchal society, the prospect of having his name "blotted out when I die" was deeply distressing.[50] Accordingly, he had appealed to his superiors that Augusta "will soon be past all hope [of bearing a son] . . . , unless in the near future we can be together."[51] But even this chance was slim. Their only child, Mary, had been born thirteen years earlier.

Perhaps for the first time since their marriage eighteen years earlier, Augusta and Grant now experienced what could be described as a normal and unhurried relationship. Each evening, they strolled through

Illus. 6-3.   Left to right: Heber J. Grant, Mary Grant (daughter), and Augusta Grant (plural wife) in Japan, ca. 1902.

the neighborhood, walking across the parade ground or maybe down close to an adjoining railroad track.[52] The couple noticed new things about each other. For one thing, Augusta sensed that Grant's patience did not run as deep as she had supposed. Grant readily conceded the point. "When a man is at his office and away from the little annoying things that come in a home almost every hour, he may be very patient," he reflected. "But the change comes when he has his office [in his home] and these things [are] with him all the time."[53] Augusta found it strange to see her husband study, take so much rest, and, for that matter, be so closely tied to the mission home and its domestic concerns. Once she discovered him scrubbing the kitchen floor, an act that caused an offended domestic servant immediately to halt.[54]

Elder Grant had hoped that the literarily inclined Augusta could assist with his official mission correspondence, but the newspaper controversy had lapsed during his absence in Salt Lake City so her assistance was not greatly needed. Augusta's writing ability, however, did fill an important function. Her many letters to friends and relatives in Utah chronicled their everyday life. After one rain shower, she found their shoes "moss grown," while their clothing had "patches of mould . . . that looked like small vegetable gardens." The offending articles of clothing had to be brushed, shaken, and sunned. "The houses smell mouldy," she complained; "every one that I have been in has the same smell and the ground is never dry around the yard. When we get into bed the sheets and clothing feel perfectly wet, as all our clothing does when we put it on in the morning."[55]

The carnivorous mosquitoes were especially troublesome to Augusta. On her first night in Japan, she set aside her protective netting. As a result, the insects kept her awake most of the night, and upon arising she was a "perfect sight." There were numerous other pests, "strange and marvelous."

> When we keep the mosquitoes out the fleas have their turn, and we saw outside our windows three immense spiders. . . . One night a rat ran across the net over the bed, and then there was a great scrimmage to catch it, and the bravest man who was "not afraid of a rat," skipped up on the bed in a hurry when the pest ran over his bare foot.

There seemed to be no end to such afflictions. Once, she insisted, the men in the mission home caught in the dead of night "two of the strangest looking great big things" imaginable, which they took outside and tied to a tree. According to Augusta's excited and perhaps imaginative report, some of the irritating creatures had forked tails, while others had long horns or hoods over their heads. Still others had a "thousand legs."[56]

The unmarried elders joined Alma Taylor at a Japanese hotel that provided room accommodations and one Western and two Japanese meals a day for fifteen dollars a month. The married missionaries, including Grant, secured a "semi-Japanese" house, only a block or two from the residence of the crown prince, that had five Westernized rooms and six Japanese ones.[57] While the Japanese section was clean and pleasant, its sliding doors and shutters seemed too confining to the Americans. When walking through this part of the house, they felt as though they were "in a box" and consequently used it only for storage.[58]

The mission headquarters was surrounded by a high board fence and sat on a small hill. Immediately outside the front gate was a rickshaw stall, which was normally occupied by half a dozen cabmen waiting for fares. Still further beyond, situated immediately in front of the house, lay a four-hundred-acre Japanese army parade ground, with barracks in the distance.[59] From their vantage on the hill, the missionaries could observe the soldiers, who sometimes drilled from dawn to dusk. During the summer season, the troops wore white duck suits with contrasting navy blue caps trimmed in red. Augusta thought the young recruits picturesque, sitting as they often did "on the green grass, their guns stacked and [their] bugles hanging on them."[60] The troops were preparing for the nation's impending conflict with Russia.

As the months progressed, the missionaries developed an established Sunday regimen. They reserved mornings for themselves, when the entire contingent gathered at the Grant home for Sunday School. These services were conducted in English, with a choir, consisting of everyone present, lending musical counterpoint (Grant joined Caine, Ensign, and the women in establishing the melody).[61] At 2:00 PM, the Saints invited the Japanese to worship with them, and six to a dozen usually did so. The visitors, who were often different young male students every week, closely observed the missionaries' mannerisms, inquired about Western music and culture, and asked occasional questions about religion. To place them at ease, the Americans eventually held this meeting in the Japanese part of their home, trading chairs for native floor cushions and forgoing the use of the Western piano (illus. 6-4).[62]

Such low-key and low-profile dealings with the Japanese were a major change from the excited and publicized moments that had followed the missionaries' first arrival. Not only had the newspaper controversy passed but also the opportunity to teach Ichiki and his supposedly influential friends. During Grant's absence in the United States, Japanese authorities had placed them under arrest, possibly as a result of their political beliefs or activity. Chagrined by having had contact with men who had become felons and apparently fearing adverse publicity, Elder Grant accepted their imprisonment as prima facie evidence of insincerity. "I have to smile when I think of the important men we thought we had made friends with, now being under arrest," he wrote. He made no further effort to contact or teach them.[63]

Efforts to introduce the gospel in Japan were beginning to unravel: the leading Japanese who had befriended the missionaries were now in prison. And there were other signs of unraveling. Despite his initial

Illus. 6-4. Alma O. Taylor *(far left)*, Heber J. Grant *(center)*, and others enjoying a traditional Japanese dinner.

expressions of interest and sympathy, Hiroi, the missionaries' salaried translator, had grown increasingly aloof and uncooperative. He was eventually dismissed with two months' notice and what was hoped to be an assuaging dinner at the Metropole Hotel.[64] The missionaries' converts were even less satisfying. Shortly after his baptism, Kikuchi proposed that the Americans underwrite his venture to sell patent medicine. When they declined, the Japanese proselyte announced the need to "set aside religious duties for a time." He was seen rarely again by the missionaries.[65] Nakazawa Hajime seemed similarly mercenary. Following his conversion, he requested fifteen hundred dollars to start a printing office. When his proposition was rejected, Nakazawa threatened to revert to his Shintō vocation unless the missionaries employed him. Begrudgingly, Elder Grant extended to him a loan, but when Nakazawa's wife sought further monetary support, the missionary declined. "My impression is that the only interest either one of . . . [the Nakazawas] have in the Church or us is to try and get some money," he confided to his diary.[66] Months later, events appeared to confirm Grant's judgment; Nakazawa was captured while attempting to burglarize the mission home.

With several converts being similarly unproductive, Grant's overall assessment was dour. "I think we have had some fearfully poor material join the Church," he concluded.[67] "The way some Japanese jump at the gospel and then drop it as soon as they learn there is no pay in it or no employment is really amusing."[68] Undoubtedly, the Japanese view of the matter was different. Accustomed to the Protestant practice of allowing some of their converts active and often paid leadership roles, they saw no inconsistency between religious quest and personal advancement. Indeed, many Japanese Christians expected it.

This certainly was the case of Takahashi Gorō, the scholarly polemicist and self-styled Church advisor and critic. He hotly criticized Grant for not supporting Nakazawa's printing venture, and following the burglary of the mission headquarters, he compared Nakazawa with Victor Hugo's tragically impoverished Jean Valjean:

> Of course, speaking intellectually, you have no responsibility for . . . [Nakazawa's] doing, but intellect is not all and all. Everybody knows that Nakazawa lost his lucrative profession for sympathizing with Mormonism. . . . But Mr. Grant quite cold bloodily has left him destitute of help.[69]

The missionaries were not swayed by Takahashi's argument, preferring to believe that the scholar's scorn reflected his own failed ambition. Elder Taylor had a plausible explanation: because President Grant had first entertained the Japanese scholar at the prestigious Metropole Hotel and talked expansively about the Church's past achievements, Takahashi had assumed that they intended to spend millions of dollars funding Japanese charitable projects, which might in turn provide him a sinecure. According to Taylor, Takahashi "dreamed himself into the position of [the Church's] chief Japanese advisor, director, or something else with a mint and a name."[70]

In the missionaries' eyes, Takahashi had been treated fairly. Shortly after their initial meeting, Elder Grant had advanced Takahashi about four hundred yen (two hundred dollars) for his proposed book, after which Takahashi had further exposed himself by borrowing against his royalties. When the book failed to sell, he sought another loan from Grant. Rather than advance more money, Grant at length decided to relieve the man's financial embarrassment by buying most of the

700-volume run. Eventually the missionaries placed 362 books with members of the National Diet's House of Peers and another 8 to high-level functionaries. The rest were apparently used in their proselytizing.[71]

Takahashi's *Morumonkyō to Morumon kyōto* (Mormons and Mormonism) was, in fact, an able, several-hundred-page work that introduced the basic story and history of the Church to the Japanese audience, but it was also filled with archaeological and philological excursions, a philosophical defense of polygamy, and an extended discussion of the Church's ability to meet modern social ills. These topics gave the volume a heavy quality that no doubt dampened sales in a market that already found Mormon topics passé.[72]

The failure of *Morumonkyō to Morumon kyōto* and the younger missionaries' growing estrangement from their former contacts failed to dampen their enthusiasm. During a conference in early 1903, they politely challenged Grant's cautious policy.that more time and preparation were required before active proselytizing could begin. Describing himself as "surprised and pleased" by their attitude, Grant immediately rescinded his request to tour Latter-day Saint churches in Samoa, New Zealand, and Australia—a long-standing personal goal—and began preparation for the start of formal preaching of the gospel.[73]

After producing a tract that introduced the Church to the Japanese public in broad terms, Grant hired the Kinki Kan Hall for the formal inauguration of Latter-day Saint preaching in Japan. The history-conscious missionaries carefully recorded their proceedings. Two of them tried to deliver their message in Japanese. Caine's effort drew muffled titters, but Taylor flawlessly recited the content of the their new tract. Then Grant followed with a sixty-five-minute sermon. Setting aside his carefully selected Bible references, the mission leader spoke with "very good liberty" on such basic themes as the mission of Joseph Smith and the Articles of Faith.[74] Hearty applause followed each song and talk, despite the missionaries' initial protests; when the crowd learned that an English text of Taylor's remarks was available, the response was immediate. According to Grant, "there was a rush like those trying to get to a bargain counter at a Z. C. M. I. special sale."[75]

Several weeks later, the elders were dispatched to their fields of labor. Two went to Naoetsu on the Japan Sea coast, two were assigned to Nagano, where Grant had toured during his first months in Japan, and four, including Grant himself, remained in or near Tokyo.[76] The day after he and his companion began distributing tracts, Ensign reported himself "very happy."[77] But such enthusiasm was hard to sustain. At one location, the missionaries learned that imposters calling themselves Mormons had already preceded them, leaving behind "a bad record" and a ruined image. Elsewhere rumors circulated that the Mormons were Russian spies, which may have partially accounted for the people's sometimes hostile behavior.[78] After distributing tracts in a small village, Elder Hedges reported that initial receptivity had quickly turned negative. At one house, "the door was slammed so quickly in my face that I did not know what struck me."[79]

The missionaries' lack of success deeply troubled Grant and brought on one of his periodic dark moods. He wondered if the lack of discernible progress could be traced to a possible failure in his leadership, and though the First Presidency had long released him from the mandate of learning Japanese, he still brooded over his inability to grasp the language. "To the end of my life I may feel that I have not done what He expected of me, and what I was sent here to do," he complained.[80]

His increasing isolation may have contributed to his negative feelings. With his elders now in the field and his own movement restricted by the barriers of language and culture, Grant, in the words of Taylor, "irked at the leash, as any man of energy and action would do."[81] During late spring and early summer 1903, his emotions oscillated widely, sometimes within the narrow range of a single letter. He might first petition the First Presidency for eight or ten more missionaries, for he clearly hoped for concrete results before leaving his mission.[82] Then, a paragraph or two later, as the reality of the Japanese mission once again imposed itself, his steadfastness wavered. Wasn't his time "being thrown away"? Couldn't he be more productive elsewhere? Such ruminations about leaving were probably encouraged by his half-brother Brigham F., or "B. F.", and by others who repeatedly assured him of his imminent release.[83]

Grant himself may have precipitated this prospect but in a way consistent with his sense of duty. In early May 1903 he had written to Anthon H. Lund, President Joseph F. Smith's newly called counselor in the First Presidency, hinting of his availability to succeed Francis M. Lyman as head of the European Mission. Grant did not wish the

Presidency to think that he was calling himself on a mission or releasing himself from another. "I am well and happy and as contented as I ever was in my life, and feel that I can live here for years with pleasure," he wrote. Still, he made his point explicit: "I would love to be where I could have something to do."[84]

He was not prepared to leave the question entirely in the hands of the First Presidency. Frustrated and anguished, he retired to some woods for prayer.

> I told the Lord that whenever He was through with me . . . [in Japan], where I was accomplishing nothing, I would be very glad and thankful if He would call me home and send me to Europe to preside over the European mission.

By his own account, it was only the second time during his life that he had sought a Church position (the other was an earlier plea to serve on the board of the Young Men's Mutual Improvement Association to serve the youth).[85]

Presumably Grant's personal struggle was kept from most of his missionary associates, who, in contrast to his own self-doubts, seemed to think favorably of his accomplishments. Certainly his leadership often left them moved.[86] Once, after Elder Stoker had turned his ankle and the sprain discolored with infection, Grant suggested that the missionaries fast and pray in Stoker's behalf. He called them into a meeting, where he began with singing and more prayer. Then he and others spoke of the spiritual healing that they had witnessed. "The feeling that characterized the meeting grew stronger & stronger," Stoker reported. "I was almost overcome." Elder Ensign then took some consecrated oil and rubbed it on the afflicted limb and asked for an immediate healing as a "testimony" for all present. As the final act, Grant laid his hands on Stoker's head and promised the "free & perfect usage" of the foot. As he spoke, Stoker sensed a movement within the limb and a snapping sound. The conclusion was spectacular: the missionary "involuntarily" stood on his feet and walked for the first time in ten days.[87]

Despite his accomplishments, Grant was ready to move on. Yet by the third week of August, Grant had surrendered any hope that he might soon leave the country. A recent letter from Abraham O. Woodruff, his associate in the Quorum of the Twelve, carried no intimation of a release, despite an earlier request for discreet information.

News from Grant's family was more to the point. These sources suggested that while President Smith had not yet decided the timing of his return, the most likely possibility was not until early 1904—the next year. Grant claimed himself "not in the least disappointed" with this information. With his sense of duty again paramount, he expressed the hope for six more months of service in order to get things moving.[88]

To avoid the extremes of the Tokyo summer and position himself in what appeared the mission's most promising area, Grant took his family to Hojo, a seaside resort in Chiba Prefecture. There, on August 23, he received a registered letter informing him that a cable was being held in Yokohama. Its contents could only be relayed to him in Tokyo. He left for Tokyo at once, arriving at the Metropole sometime after midnight. The decoded message left him stunned. "You are now released," it cryptically read. "Leave the business in the hands of Ensign," wrote the First Presidency.[89] Rather than the emotional relief that Grant had long assumed his release would bring, he now felt deep and painful regret. His tearful prayers that evening contrasted the seeming "failure" of his mission with the larger-than-life successes of his apostolic predecessors. It was 5:00 AM before he was able to set aside his thoughts and fall asleep.[90]

Two hours later he was somewhat refreshed and had a more objective view. Writing several letters, he acknowledged the success of his earlier ministry and was also confident about upcoming events. "I have a willing heart," he reflected, and "know that I will do more [good work]." But his mind clearly remained troubled. "I am in hopes that I am not released, . . . that it is only a call to come home," he wrote the First Presidency. But his resolve vanished before he ended his sentence. "I have done so little here," he concluded, "it may be felt that it is better to use me in some other field where I can do more good."[91]

Grant already knew that there was only one available steamer that could get him to America in time for the October 1903 general conference, and he quickly booked passage. He also requested that all the missionaries return to mission headquarters for a two-week farewell conference, the highlight of which took place in the wooded terrain above Yokohama harbor. Commemorating the dedication of the mission exactly two years earlier, the missionaries rehearsed their original program, repeating the same hymns and reading an outline of

Elder Grant's dedicatory prayer (illus. 6-5). There was, however, a significance to the site that was probably unknown to any of the group besides Grant himself. At the beginning of the mission, he explained to the group, he had often come to the place to dissipate his melancholy in prayer.[92]

The three-hour meeting, in Grant's words, was "the one meeting of all meetings ever held in this land." While all twelve missionaries were "blessed with remarkable demonstrations of the Spirit," he seemed specially endowed. Invoking his apostolic authority, he blessed his missionaries and reminded them of their duty. "I never saw a man that was as full of the Spirit of God as he was then," recounted one of the young men.[93]

Eight days later, Augusta, Mary, and Grant embarked on

Courtesy John W. Welch

Illus. 6-5. Horace S. Ensign, Louis A. Kelsch, and Heber J. Grant at the dedication site in Yokohama, Japan, 1901. Alma O. Taylor probably took the photograph.

the SS *Aki Maru*. Grant left with a surprisingly high view of the Japanese. From his many contacts and experiences, he sensed the nation's great military potential. Moreover, he saw the Japanese as "patriotic beyond any people" he had ever known, and described them as "workers." Their ambition and curiosity seemed limitless except, lamentably, on the paramount matter of religion.[94] Yet there was something within Grant that suggested that he himself had not experienced the last chapter. To the end of his career, he would remember the emotion he had felt during the pronouncement of his dedicatory prayer. "I feel impressed that there is yet a great work to be accomplished there. . . . How soon this may come I do not know."[95]

He departed with the hope of returning someday. His experience, he realized, had not been entirely negative. He had placed on his frame a precious fifteen pounds, and his quieted nerves once again permitted Spenserian writing. Moreover, he had outfitted himself with a pair of spectacles that corrected an astigmatism that for many years had hindered reading and studying.[96] Nevertheless, despite listing all the positive things he could muster, he knew that Japan had aged him "at least ten years" although he had spent only two in the land of the Mikado.[97]

As the ship departed, his missionary friends walked to the edge of the bund to see him off. At first they shouted pleasantries across the mooring. Then, as the *Aki Maru* gradually steamed from port, they waved handkerchiefs until the passengers could no longer be seen.[98]

This paper was presented at "A Centennial Celebration: The LDS Church in Japan, 1901–2001," October 13, 2001, Brigham Young University, Provo, Utah. An earlier version of this article was originally published in Journal of Mormon History *13 (1986–87): 20–43.*

Notes

1. Heber J. Grant (hereafter Grant) to Louis A. Kelsch, March 2, 1901, Grant Letterpress Copybooks 31:373, Grant Papers, Church Archives, The Church of Jesus Christ of Latter-day Saints, Salt Lake City. Also see Grant to Rachel Ivins Grant, February 16, 1901, Letterpress Copybooks 31:321. I have supplied box and folder information only when access to materials cannot be established by using the Heber J. Grant register. All such specific references pertain to the Grant Papers.

2. Undated and untitled memorandum, box 145, folder 4, Grant Papers. See also Grant Typed Diary, February 14 and 16, 1901, Grant Papers; Grant to Rachel Ivins Grant, February 16, 1901, Letterpress Copybooks 31:321; Grant, "Ram in the Thicket," *Improvement Era* 44 (December 1941): 713.

3. Grant, "Ram in the Thicket," 713. Nearly identical wording is found in Undated and untitled memorandum, 1. Also see Grant Typed Diary, February 14, 1901.

4. Précis of First Presidency proceedings, Journal History of The Church, February 12, 1901, 1, Church Archives (hereafter cited as Journal History).

5. Undated and untitled memorandum, 3. Grant provided variations of this dialogue in several published reminiscences. See Grant, "Response," *Improvement Era* 44 (October 1941): 585, and Grant, "Ram in the Thicket," 713.

Opening of the Japan Mission 171

6. Grant Typed Diary, February 14, 1901. The Mormon press subsequently confirmed the possibility of a Chinese mission, "Missions to the Orient," *Deseret Evening News,* February 16, 1901, 4 and "Opening of a Mission in Japan," *Deseret Evening News,* April 6, 1901, 9.

7. Alma O. Taylor, "Memories of Far-off Japan: President Grant's First Foreign Mission, 1901 to 1903," *Improvement Era* 39 (November 1936): 690.

8. Grant to Anthony W. Ivins, February 15, 1901, Letterpress Copybooks 31:315.

9. Grant, Remarks at New York Chapel, May 22, 1938, Box 156, Folder 4; Undated and untitled memorandum, 7; Grant Typed Diary, February 23, 1901.

10. Ensign had been before the Salt Lake City public as a singer since the age of ten. "Opening of a Mission in Japan," 9, provides a biographical sketch. See also Grant to Joseph A. McRae, n.d. but about March 18, 1904, Letterpress Copybooks 38:468, and Biographical Sketch contained in Letterpress Copybooks 33.

11. "Opening of a Mission in Japan," 9, and Biographical Sketch, Letterpress Copybooks 33. A copy of Kelsch's *A Practical Reference Arranged Especially for Missionaries of The Church of Jesus Christ of Latter-day Saints* can be found in box 194, folder 1, Grant Papers. For his reaction to the call, see Kelsch to Grant, March 11, 1901, Letterpress Copybooks 31:419.

12. Grant Typed Diary, May 10, 1901; Biographical Sketch, Letterpress Copybooks 33; Grant, *Seventy-fourth Semi-Annual Conference of The Church of Jesus Christ of Latter-day Saints* (Salt Lake City: The Church of Jesus Christ of Latter-day Saints, 1903), 12; Grant to Joseph E. Taylor, June 2, 1912, Letterpress Copybooks 45:463; Grant to Francis Grant, February 10, 1934, Family Correspondence, Grant Papers.

13. "Opening of a Mission in Japan," 9; Grant to Anthony W. Ivins, September 15, 1901, and Grant to Frederick Beesley, March 29, 1901, Letterpress Copybooks 33:233 and 423 respectively; and Lucy Grant Cannon, Diary, March 14, 1901, excerpts in possession of author.

14. Alma O. Taylor to his mother, contained in Alma O. Taylor, October 3, 1901, "Journals, 1901–1946," L. Tom Perry Special Collections, Harold B. Lee Library, Brigham Young University, Provo, Utah.

15. Grant to Junius F. Wells, September 30, 1901, Letterpress Copybooks 33:267.

16. Grant to Louis A. Kelsch, March 18, 1901, Letterpress Copybooks 31:421; Grant to Junius F. Wells, September 30, 1901, Letterpress Copybooks 33:267.

17. Grant Diary entries inserted in Letterpress Copybooks 34:1, July 25, 1901.

18. Masaharu Anesaki, *History of Japanese Religion* (Rutland, Vermont & Tokyo, Japan: Charles E. Tuttle Company, 1971), 360; Kishimoto Hideo, *Japanese Religion in the Meiji Era,* trans. and adapted by John F. Howes, Centenary Culture Council Series (Tokyo: Obunsha, 1956), 251–52, 255–57.

19. Drummond, *History of Christianity in Japan,* 220–21; Kishimoto, *Japanese Religion,* 259.

20. Anesaki, *History of Japanese Religion,* 405. See also Kishimoto, *Japanese Religion,* 296–97; and Joseph M. Kitagawa, *Religion in Japanese History* (New York: Columbia University Press, 1966), 241.

21. Otis Cary, *History of Christianity in Japan,* 2 vols. (New York: Fleming H. Revell Company, 1909), 1:359; Kiyoshi and Fujio, "Christianity," 308. These estimates are extrapolated from 1907 and 1909 estimates.

22. Grant Diary, August 12, 1901, Letterpress Copybooks 34:8.

23. Cary, *History of Christianity in Japan* 1:309–10.

24. Taylor, Journal, August 20, 1901; Alma O. Taylor, "Memories of Far-Off Japan," *Improvement Era* 39 (November 1936): 690–91. The controversy is best chronicled in Frederick R. Brady, "The Japanese Reaction to Mormonism and the Translation of Mormon Scripture into Japanese" (master's thesis, Sophia University, 1979).

25. Grant to Joseph F. Smith, October 14, 1901, Letterpress Copybooks 33:287–89.

26. Grant to B. F. Grant, August 24, 1901, Letterpress Copybooks 33:149.

27. Taylor, Journal, August 28, 1901.

28. Edward Seidensticker, *Low City, High City: Tokyo From Edo to the Earthquake* (New York: Alfred A. Knopf, 1983), 42; Grant to Brother Hull, October 18, 1901, Letterpress Copybooks 33:292.

29. Grant to Francis M. Lyman, March 6, 1903, General Correspondence.

30. Protestant missionaries also found the Japanese language to be formidable. "Sherwood Eddy concluded, on the basis of his long experience with missionaries in every part of the world, that if one were to include reading and writing as well as speaking, Japanese is probably the most difficult language in the world for a foreigner to learn." Drummond, *History of Christianity in Japan,* 148, footnote. The language-gifted Alma Taylor described the task of learning Japanese akin to "striking a pick against flint rock." Taylor to Grant, May 22, 1902, General Correspondence.

31. Richard L. Evans, "Strange Language," *Improvement Era* 45 (November 1942): 709.

32. Grant Diary, September 18–20, 1901 [single entry], Letterpress Copybooks 34:36.

33. Grant to Junius F. Wells, September 30, 1901, Letterpress Copybooks 33:268.

34. Grant Diary, November 5–17, 1901 [single entry], Letterpress Copybooks 34:76; Grant to Francis M. Lyman, November 15, 1901, Letterpress Copybooks 34:427–30.

35. General Authorities to Grant, November 8, 1901, Letterpress Copybooks 34:108.

36. When Anthon H. Lund, a newly called counselor in the First Presidency, wrote a softer letter to Grant several weeks later, Grant's emotion was still not spent. He told Lund that he took the Presidency's letter as "a polite way of telling me I had been wasting my time in the past" and then complained, "When a man is thousands of miles away from home and done his best and all that he has done has been done with the full approval of his associates a letter like the one I got from you is appreciated more than words can tell, especially when it came in connection with the official letter of the Presidency which gently but kindly 'sat on me.'" Had parts of the original letter been written by George Gibbs, the Presidency's sharp-tongued secretary, Grant claimed that he would have merely dismissed its contents with the thought, "Confound Gibbs' sarcasm." Grant to Anthon H. Lund, December 22, 1901, Letterpress Copybooks 34:149–50.

37. Grant to Francis M. Lyman, February 21, 1902, Letterpress Copybooks 35:2.

38. Anesaki, *History of Japanese Religion*, 385–86.

39. Grant, in *Seventy-second Annual Conference of The Church of Jesus Christ of Latter-day Saints* (Salt Lake City: The Church of Jesus Christ of Latter-day Saints, 1902), 47–48.

40. Senichi Hisamatsu, "Kambara Ariake," *Biographical Dictionary of Japanese Literature* (Tokyo: Kodansha International Ltd., 1976), 276; Cary, *History of Christianity in Japan* 1:148–49; G. B. Sansom, *The Western World and Japan: A Study in the Interaction of European and Asiatic Cultures* (New York: Alfred A. Knopf, 1951), 480. In the several years prior to the coming of the Mormons, Takahashi had published the *Japanese Alphabetical Dictionary with Chinese & English Equivalents* and a second volume, *A New Pocket Dictionary of the Japanese and English Languages*. In 1869 he may also have been the first Christian converted in Tokyo if Drummond, *History of Christianity in Japan*, 165, typographically errs in giving "Toru Takahashi" the honor.

41. Grant, in *Seventy-second Annual Conference*, 47–48; Grant to Gorō Takahashi, December 13, 1901, Letterpress Copybooks 34:140; Grant Diary, December 7–19, 1901 [single entry], Letterpress Copybooks 34:145.

42. Taylor, Journal, February 13 and 16, 1902.

43. Taylor, Journal, February 16, 1902.

44. Taylor, Journal, February 23, 1902.

45. Occasionally Grant recorded such incidents. See Grant Diary, December 7–19, 1901, Letterpress Copybooks 34:447.

46. Taylor, Journal, March 10, 1902. After Grant's refusal to approve the request, several of Koshiishi's associates described Grant as insincere and self-seeking.

47. S. C. Richardson notebooks, Church Archives; Grant to Kelsch, Ensign, & Taylor, April 4, 1902, Letterpress Copybooks 32:192; Grant, in *Seventy-second Annual Conference,* 45–46.

48. Taylor, Journal, February 12, 1902.

49. Grant to Nakazawa Hajime, May [?] 2, 1902, Letterpress Copybooks 35:204.

50. Grant to Charles W. Nibley, March 4, 1905, Letterpress Copybooks 39:418; Grant to Ellen Stoddard Eccles, December 17, 1912, Letterpress Copybooks 48:43; Grant to B. H. Roberts, December 16, 1922, Letterpress Copybooks 60:57.

51. Grant to Joseph F. Smith, October 14, 1901, Letterpress Copybooks 33:287–89.

52. Augusta Grant to "All the Dear Folks at Home," July 29, 1902, Letterpress Copybooks 35:427–29.

53. Grant to Lucy Grant Cannon, December 1, 1905, Letterpress Copybooks 40:592.

54. Augusta Grant to "My Dear People," September 17, 1902, Letterpress Copybooks 35:480.

55. Augusta Grant to the "Folks at Home," August 8, 1902, Letterpress Copybooks 35:442–43.

56. Augusta Grant to the "Folks at Home," August 8, 1902, Letterpress Copybooks 35:442–43. Reading Augusta's description before it was posted, Heber and Mary complained that the account suggested the Japanese pests were as "big as cows." Augusta refused to budge. "I tell them to write their [own] version."

57. Grant to Smith, Winder, and Lund, n.d., excerpts in Grant Diary, July 23, 1902; Grant to "All the Loved Ones at Home," July 20, 1902, Letterpress Copybooks 35:362; Augusta Grant to "My Dear People," September 17, 1902, Letterpress Copybooks 35:478; Grant to B. F. Grant, July 24, 1902, Letterpress Copybooks 35:365.

58. Augusta Grant to "All the Dear Folks at Home," July 29, 1902, Letterpress Copybooks 35:427–29.

59. Augusta Grant to "All the Dear Folks at Home," July 29, 1902, Letterpress Copybooks 35:427–29, August 8, 1902, Letterpress Copybooks 35:442–43.

60. Augusta Grant to "Family at Home[?]," May 11, 1903, General Correspondence.

61. "The Work in Japan," *Deseret Evening News,* June 5, 1903, 4; Grant Typed Diary, March 1–10, 1903; Mary Grant to Fannie Gardiner, August 10, 1902, Letterpress Copybooks 35:446.

62. Grant to Sandford W. Hedges, May 19, 1903, Japanese Mission Letterpress Copybook 1:39, Church Archives; Letter of Augusta Grant, May 11, 1903, Family Correspondence; Grant Diary, May 24, 1903, Letterpress Copybooks 36:320.

63. Grant to Kelsch, Ensign, and Taylor, June 18, 1902, Letterpress Copybooks 35:260; also Grant to Joseph F. Smith, John R. Winder, and Anthon H. Lund, October 1, 1902, General Correspondence.

64. Taylor, Journal, May 17–19 [single entry], 1902; Grant to Kelsch, Ensign, and Taylor, April 16, June 18, and June 28, 1902, Letterpress Copybooks 35:146, 260, and 441. Grant responded to Hiroi's demands with an even hand. "We did all we could to make things pleasant for you while you were in our employ," he wrote.

> Surely you must not blame us that you could not get the employment that you wished at the time you stopped teaching us, neither must you blame us for what people say. We never gave any one to understand that you had joined our Church. We would have been proud to have had you do so, had you been converted to the truths which we have to offer, but as you know we have no desire to have any one join with us unless they have become convinced that we have in very deed the plan of life and salvation as again restored to earth direct from heaven.

Almost two decades later, Hiroi, who at the time was studying in New York, sought a $1,000 loan from Grant, claiming a monied and influential group now supported him. T. Hiroi to Grant, June 23, 1920, General Correspondence.

65. Taylor, Journal, October 20, 1903, and February 28, 1904; Grant, in *Seventy-fourth Semi-Annual Conference,* 13.

66. Grant, in *Seventy-fourth Semi-Annual Conference,* 13; Grant Typed Diary, March 11–20 [single entry], 1903; Grant Diary, July 2, 1903, Letterpress Copybooks 36:490.

67. Grant to Horace S. Ensign, January 20, 1905, Letterpress Copybooks 39:269–70.

68. Grant Manuscript Diary, June 22, 1903, Grant Papers.

69. Gorō Takahashi to Horace Ensign, December 20, 1903, Taylor Diary of the same date.

70. Taylor Diary, December 20, 1903.

71. Grant to Joseph F. Smith, John R. Winder, and Anthon H. Lund, January 20, 1903, General Correspondence; Taylor, Journal, March 22, 1906; Brady, "Japanese Reaction to Mormonism," 165. The distribution of *Morumonkyō to Morumon kyōto* (Mormons and Mormonism) to Diet members did not occur until 1906, three years after Grant's departure from Japan.

72. Brady, "The Japanese Reaction to Mormonism," translates large portions of *Morumonkyō to Morumon kyōto*. Brady also discusses the first Japanese book about Mormonism, *Morumon Shō*, a 94-page, pocket-sized volume written by Uchida Akira under the pen name Uchida Yu. Rough translations of several chapters of Takahashi's work are found in box 148, folder 2. For Takahashi's proposed ten-chapter table of contents, see Grant, in *Seventy-second Annual Conference*, 48.

73. Grant Typed Diary, February 1–28, 1903 [single entry]; Grant to Joseph F. Smith, John R. Winder, and Anthon H. Lund, February 19, 1903, General Correspondence.

74. Grant Diary, April 18, 1903, Letterpress Copybooks 36:149; Grant to Joseph F. Smith, John R. Winder, and Anthon H. Lund, April 20, 1903, Letterpress Copybooks 36:61–62; Grant to J. Golden Kimball, April 23, 1903, Letterpress Copybooks 36:81–83. Grant variously estimated the size of the crowd to be as high as 650.

75. Grant to Joseph J. Cannon, April 25, 1903, Letterpress Copybooks 36:102.

76. Grant to Joseph F. Smith, John R. Winder, and Anthon H. Lund, and Grant to J. Golden Kimball, April 20 and 23, Letterpress Copybooks 36:61–62, 81–83; Taylor, Journal, April 9–22 [single entry], 1903.

77. Grant Diary, April 30, 1903, Letterpress Copybooks 36:155; Grant Manuscript Diary, May 9, 1903.

78. Grant to Horace Ensign and Frederick Caine, May 22, 1903, Letterpress Copybooks 36:300; Grant Manuscript Diary, May 9, 1903.

79. Sandford Wells Hedges, "Scenery and Customs of Japan," *Improvement Era* 6 (September 1903): 818–19.

80. Grant to Francis M. Lyman, November 15, 1901, Letterpress Copybooks 34:430; Grant to Matthias F. Cowley, May 12, 1903, Letterpress Copybooks 36:239–41.

81. Alma O. Taylor, "Memories of Far-Off Japan: President Grant's First Foreign Mission, 1901 to 1903," *Improvement Era* 39 (November 1936): 691.

82. Grant to Francis M. Lyman, June 10, 1903, Letterpress Copybooks 36:385–86; Grant to Joseph F. Smith, John R. Winder, and Anthon H. Lund, June 10, 1903, Letterpress Copybooks 36:394–95.

83. Grant to Matthias F. Cowley, May 12, 1903, Letterpress Copybooks 36:240; Grant to "Brother" Tanner, July 15, 1903, General Correspondence; Grant to Frederick Caine and Sandford Hedges, July 17, 1903, General Correspondence; Grant to Rachel Grant, July 28, 1903, Family Correspondence.

84. Grant to Anthon H. Lund, May 8, 1903, Letterpress Copybooks 36:205.

85. Grant, "Greetings Across the Sea," *Improvement Era* 40 (July 1937): 405.

86. John W. Stoker Diary, July 20, 1902, John W. Stoker Papers, 1902–35, Church Archives.

87. Stoker Diary, March 11, 1903; Horace S. Ensign, "Incidents Connected with the Japan Mission," April 12, 1904, box 147, folder 11; Mary Grant to "My Dear Sisters," March 14, 1903, box 126, folder 8; Grant Typed Diary, March 11 to 20, 1903; Grant to Joseph F. Smith, John R. Winder, and Anthon H. Lund, March 19, 1903, General Correspondence.

88. Grant to Anthony W. Ivins, April 24, 1903, Letterpress Copybooks 36:84; Grant to Abraham O. Woodruff, August 17, 1903, General Correspondence; Grant Manuscript Diary, August 20, 1903; Grant to Rachel Grant, September 2, 1903, Family Correspondence.

89. Grant to Horace S. Ensign, August 24, 1903, General Correspondence; Grant Manuscript Diary, August 23, 1903; Taylor Diary, July 11 to August 31, 1903 [single entry].

90. Grant Manuscript Diary, August 23 and 24, 1903; Grant to Joseph F. Smith, John R. Winder, and Anthon H. Lund, August 24, 1903, General Correspondence; Grant to Rachel Grant, August 24, 1903, Family Correspondence.

91. Grant to Joseph F. Smith, John R. Winder, and Anthon H. Lund, April 24, 1903, General Correspondence; Grant to Rachel Grant, August 24, 1903, Family Correspondence.

92. Horace Ensign to Joseph H. Felt, September 12, 1903, General Correspondence; Taylor, Journal, September 1, 1903.

93. Stoker Diary, September 1, 1903; Horace Ensign to Joseph H. Felt, September 12, 1903, General Correspondence; Ensign, "Incidents Connected with the Japan Mission," April 12, 1904, copy in Box 147, Folder 11.

94. Grant to Anthony W. Ivins, June 20, 1904, Letterpress Copybooks 38:635.

95. For early expressions of this sentiment, see Grant to Joseph E. Taylor and Alma O. Taylor, January 25, 1904, and September 28, 1905, Letterpress Copybooks 38:217 and 40:312.

96. Remarks of Rachel Grant, February 13, 1902, Relief Society Minute Book B, 1898–1902, Thirteenth Ward Papers, Church Archives; Grant to Junius F. Wells, September 30, 1901, Letterpress Copybooks 33:267–68; Grant to Eva[?] Grant Moss, January 10, 1915, Letterpress Copybooks 50:478.

97. Grant to J. Wilford Booth, March 1, 1906, Letterpress Copybooks 40:912.

98. Stoker Diary, September 8, 1903.

7

Mormons in the Press: Reactions to the 1901 Opening of the Japan Mission

Shinji Takagi

On Monday, August 12, 1901, Heber J. Grant, a member of the Quorum of the Twelve Apostles of The Church of Jesus Christ of Latter-day Saints, arrived in Tokyo Bay aboard the *Empress of India*, a steamship operated by the Canadian Pacific Railway Company.[1] Accompanied by missionaries Horace S. Ensign, Louis A. Kelsch, and Alma O. Taylor, Grant intended to organize in Japan the first permanent mission of the Church in Asia.[2] After passing quarantine, this "quartet"[3] took a steam launch for the Grand Hotel in the Yokohama Foreign Settlement.[4] When the four missionaries checked in at the elegant hotel, which professed to be the "largest and most complete hotel in the Far East," "second to none either in Europe or America,"[5] they obviously had no conception of the extensive coverage they would receive in the Japanese press.

The amount of press coverage given the Mormon missionaries during the next month or so was unprecedented and has not been surpassed in the subsequent history of the Church in Japan. More than a dozen newspapers in the capital city of Tokyo, two nationally influential newspapers in the dominant commercial city of Osaka, and no less than twenty major regional newspapers throughout the country devoted considerable space—often on front pages—to articles and editorials reporting or otherwise commenting on the arrival of this new Christian sect with unusual doctrines (for a list of newspapers, see the appendix to this chapter).[6] From August 13, the day after the missionaries' arrival, to September 10, not a day went by without something about

Mormons being printed somewhere in Japan. During this time, no less than 160 articles, editorials, and letters appeared in the Japanese press. The scope of this massive newspaper coverage was reinforced and given greater permanency by articles about the missionaries' arrival that were published in two of the most influential national magazines, the *Chuo Koron* (Central Review) and the *Taiyo* (Sun).[7]

This paper presents a review and analysis of the press coverage of the arrival of Mormon missionaries in Japan during the ensuing month. The intention is (1) to show that the press spread knowledge throughout Japanese society of this important event in the history of the Church[8] and (2) to provide the historical and social context within which Mormon missionary work began in Japan. Specifically, the unusual degree to which Mormonism was discussed in the Japanese press was related to the nature and role of the resident foreign press, the competitive nature of the newspaper industry with its propensity toward sensationalism, and, most importantly, Japan's own internal conflict regarding its social institutions.

Japan at the Turn of the Twentieth Century

After many years of political difficulties associated with the practice of plural marriage, the Saints in the United States had finally received some relief in part as a result of the Manifesto of 1890 and the granting of statehood in 1896. Perhaps for these and other reasons, Church leaders could afford to devote more attention and resources to missionary work outside the then established missions of the Church.[9] The leaders must have noted the spectacular rise of Japan to the ranks of the more progressive nations of the world, propelled as it was by the promulgation of a written constitution in 1889 with guaranteed religious freedom and parliamentary representation, the defeat of China in the Sino-Japanese War of 1894–95, and the subsequent adoption of the gold standard in 1897.[10] In fact, upon the announcement of his mission call at the April 1901 general conference, Heber J. Grant commented on his very positive impression: "The Japanese are a wonderfully progressive people. . . . Of the Oriental races they are without doubt the most enterprising and intelligent. . . . Some authorities say that when it comes to absorbing knowledge they eclipse any people in the world today."[11]

Perhaps little appreciated by the Church leadership at the time was a legal development of major significance to prospective Mormon missionary work in Japan. In 1894 the Japanese government agreed to revise the series of commercial treaties, collectively called the Ansei treaties, that the Tokugawa shogunate had signed with eleven Western nations in the late 1850s and the early 1860s.[12] The Ansei treaties not only allowed the signatory countries access to major ports and commercial cities[13] for trading purposes, but also gave their nationals the right to be tried in a consular court according to their own laws. In exchange for these extraterritorial privileges, however, the Ansei treaties and the associated domestic statutes limited foreigners freedom of access in Japan. In principle, foreigners were not allowed to travel in Japan without explicit permission and were required to live in designated foreign settlements established in the treaty ports and cities, most notably Yokohama, Kobe, and Tokyo.[14] The foreign settlements were restricted areas, in which the Japanese government strictly controlled entrance by Japanese and exit by foreigners.

Attempts to change the Ansei treaties began a few years after the imperial government took over the governance of Japan from the Tokugawa shogunate in 1868. The new government of Emperor Meiji commenced the seemingly fruitless effort of renegotiating with the foreign powers the terms of what it had started calling the Unequal Treaties because of the system of extraterritoriality enjoyed by the foreigners in Japan. The revision of the fifteen Ansei treaties[15] remained the single most important objective of Japanese foreign policy during the subsequent quarter of a century. The end of extraterritoriality, even a modification of it, was opposed by the treaty port communities.[16] They generally took a hostile and condescending attitude toward the natives and wanted to maintain their privileges and freedom from Japanese law. On the other hand, the Protestant missionaries were in favor of a modification. They were eager to proselytize in the interior without resorting to subterfuge or fearing harassment from the police.[17]

The system of extraterritoriality was beset with problems and was not a sustainable arrangement anyway.[18] First, in some countries, such as the United States, the constitutionality of consular courts was questioned. Second, there was a lack of experienced officers to administer justice. Third, the appeals process was so costly that many (mostly

Japanese) were effectively deprived of justice. For example, those tried in consular courts had to file an appeal with a higher court located in foreign countries, such as Shanghai (Britain) or Saigon (France). Some serious crimes such as murder could not be tried in Japan in the first place. Fourth, some countries did not maintain consuls in Japan. Fifth, problems occurred when jurisdictions overlapped (as would happen when a case involved a Frenchman and a Dutchman). For these and other reasons, extraterritoriality in Japan was becoming increasingly unworkable by the late 1880s.[19] Thus, the treaty powers were prepared to make concessions in return for commercial advantages, such as access to the Japanese market. In part to ease the apprehension of the foreign powers, the Japanese government took a series of measures to reform its legal system along Western lines, including its criminal, commercial, and civil codes.

After several failed attempts, Japan finally secured an agreement in 1894 with the British government that would abolish extraterritoriality in exchange for allowing foreign merchants to have access to Japan outside the treaty ports and cities. With the decisive British agreement in hand, the Meiji government succeeded in convincing the other countries to sign similar agreements, beginning with the United States in 1895. The revised treaties came into force for all fifteen treaty powers in summer 1899 amid some domestic furor over the prospect of allowing foreigners, especially Christian missionaries, to move freely among the populace.[20]

Heber J. Grant and his associates arrived in Yokohama just two years after the foreign settlement there had been legally abolished and foreigners could live and travel in Japan as they pleased. This is not to say that missionary work could not have been conducted in Japan prior to 1899. In fact, several mainstream Christian denominations had already been established in Japan and had met with some success.[21] However, their method of proselytizing was not the kind Mormons generally employed. Mainstream churches had established their bases of operation in the foreign settlements, notably in Yokohama, Tokyo, and Osaka,[22] and had reached the Japanese by building mission schools, where religion could be mixed with secular instruction. Christianity was also spread by foreign teachers employed in Japanese schools; these teachers were given somewhat greater freedom of movement within the country. Most of the notable Christian converts of the Meiji period were social elites who were influenced by Christian teachers while studying at some of the country's most prestigious institutions of secondary or higher education. Given the limited financial and human resources of The Church of Jesus Christ of Latter-day Saints in the second half of the nineteenth century, however, building schools probably would not have been possible for the missionaries in Japan.

Reactions of the English-Language Press

When Grant and his associates arrived two years after the segregation of foreigners had been lifted, Yokohama possessed a thriving foreign community along the harbor in the original settlement as well as in a newer settlement upon a hill overlooking the harbor. To meet the needs of the foreign community, estimated at between 2,000 and 2,400 in number,[23] Yokohama maintained several foreign-language newspapers, including the *Japan Advertiser,* the *Japan Herald,* and the *Japan Mail.*[24] Of these, the *Japan Advertiser* (founded in 1890) was the only notable newspaper under American management. Unfortunately, because all of these newspapers had a circulation of at most only several hundred, no known copies from this period exist in any Japanese public library. Thus, for information regarding the foreign press in Japan, we must rely on newspaper clippings in Elder Alma O. Taylor's scrapbook, references in his diaries, and some weekly mail editions that have been kept in major libraries overseas.[25]

The English-language press in Yokohama reacted immediately to the arrival of the Mormon missionaries. By this time, the Protestant missionaries, who were an important component of the foreign community in Yokohama, had already been informed by their headquarters that the Mormon missionaries would shortly be arriving in Japan.[26] The elders' arrival on August 12 was reported in the *Japan Advertiser* on the following day, with a comment that the Mormons would "find the native apparel better than their wares."[27] This rather unkind reaction of the *Japan Advertiser* possibly reflected the fact that the paper was at that time under the editorship of a Unitarian missionary, Arthur M. Knapp (editor, 1899–1902), who might have traveled on the same ship as the Mormon missionaries.[28] The *Advertiser*'s reaction, however, may have exaggerated any lack of civility on the part of the Unitarian missionary, for Elder Grant wrote the following in his journal a few days later:

> I got a letter to the editor of the *Advertiser,* Mr. Napp [sic], and called on him. He received us very kindly and promised us fair treatment at the hands of his paper. He published the address to the Japanese people and wrote an editorial that we need not look for much success in this land but said we would be kindly received by the Japanese people.[29]

The significance of the *Japan Advertiser* reaction lies not so much in its message as in the fact that it was the first to report the arrival of the Mormon missionaries and consequently gave rise to a proliferation of newspaper reports, articles, and editorials on Mormonism during the following month.

At that time, both in terms of influence and readership, the *Japan Mail* and the *Japan Herald* were much more important in Yokohama and elsewhere in Japan.[30] Of the two, the *Japan Herald* was more hospitable to the Mormons. On August 14, Grant visited the office of the *Japan Herald* and received a warm reception. The editor said that he would like to write a story about the Mormon missionaries and agreed to publish an eight-hundred-word official statement that Elder Grant had prepared. As the editor had promised, the next day's *Japan Herald* carried the entire transcript, unedited, of Grant's "Address to the Great and Progressive Nation of Japan," which in part reads:

> In company with my associates sent to you from the headquarters of the Church of Jesus Christ of Latter-day Saints, in Salt Lake City, Utah, an Apostle and minister of the Most High God, I salute you and invite you to consider the important message we bear. We do not come to you for the purpose of trying to deprive you of any truth in which you believe, or any light that you have been privileged to enjoy. We bring you greater light, more truth and advanced knowledge, which we offer you freely.[31]

An account of the interview with Grant was published on the same day (August 15). After quoting the thirteen Articles of Faith in their entirety, the account explained the missionary program of the Church (in which some 1,600 missionaries worked without remuneration), the proper name of the Church (with *Mormons* being a nickname), its belief in the Book of Mormon, the termination of polygamy with President Wilford Woodruff's Manifesto, and the secular accomplishments of Utah Mormons. Grant wrote in his journal: "The Herald report of my interview is very fair indeed and the next day after its publication I called and thanked Mr. Harrison for it."[32] At that time, J. H. Brooke was both the owner and the editor of the *Japan Herald*;[33] Harrison may well have been his subordinate. The elders' cordial relationship with Harrison appears to have lasted for a long time, as Alma O. Taylor suggested in his journal on February 2, 1902: "In the evening [we] entertained at supper Mr. Harrison the editor of the Japan Herald."

The *Japan Mail*, on the other hand, was not so hospitable but took a consistently hostile position towards the Mormons. For example, it accused the Mormons of participating in polygamy and thereby degrading women, of coming to Japan "in the guise of Christianity" to carry men to "the days of Lot and Abraham," and of being "corruptors of morality" and "enemies of pure happiness"; it equated plural marriage with concubinage; it belittled the letters to the editor written by Grant; and it reprinted a rather lengthy anti-Mormon article entitled "The Mormon Menace," written by a non-Mormon resident of Utah.[34] At that time, the *Mail* was both owned and edited by Captain F. Brinkley, a retired British army officer who was connected somehow with the Japanese government.[35] As will be explained more fully below, the *Mail*'s anti-Mormon stance reflected its Protestant missionary clientele. The *Mail*'s stance may also have been a reflection of its usual anti-American sentiment, which was quite strong in the foreign settlement community at that time.[36] On August 17, the *Mail* called the *Herald* the "champion of the Mormon Mission" because of its favorable views of the Mormons. In response, that evening the *Herald* called the *Mail*'s editor "an amateur journalist." The *Mail* asserted that the Mormons should not be allowed to remain in Japan to preach, a position echoed by the Japanese-managed *Japan Times* of Tokyo in its August 20 editorial.[37]

From the vantage point of faraway Kobe, another large foreign settlement immediately west of Osaka, some 350 miles southwest of Tokyo,[38] the editor of the *Kobe Chronicle*[39] wrote this perspective on the press war in Yokohama:

> [The] arrival of a Salt Lake City Apostle with a number of elders has aroused some attention in Japan, though it seems to have caused far more stir among the foreign newspapers than among the Japanese, who naturally regard the establishment of one more sect in Japan with more or less indifference. As was to be expected, the missionaries already established in this country are not pleased at such an encroachment on their preserves, and one ex-missionary now conducting a boarding-house in Yokohama even refused to give the Mormon missionaries accommodation. A Yokohama foreign journal which may be taken as representing the missionaries even went so far as to advocate that the preaching of these missionaries should be officially forbidden.

The editor then goes on to criticize the *Japan Times:*

> It is not very surprising, perhaps, that such intolerance should be advocated by a foreign journal in touch with missionaries already established in the country, but we certainly were surprised to find the *Japan Times,* published in Tokyo and edited by a Japanese, taking up the same attitude a day or two later, and urging that the teaching of Mormon doctrines should be prohibited in this country.

Predicting that the Mormons "will find [that] their efforts at proselytisation in Japan will be received with stolid indifference," the *Chronicle* editor concluded by calling for religious tolerance:

> It is to be hoped that religious intolerance is not one of the innovations from the West which is to be introduced into Japan.... [We] hope that the Government will not be misled by the efforts of rival propagandists into a departure from the attitude of tolerance which has been so honourable a feature of the Meiji era, and in which Japan has set such a fine example to Christendom.[40]

Strictly on rational grounds, the editor, probably an American named Robert Young, was not fond of Christianity.[41] Thus, his opposition to Christianity in general was translated into his fair treatment of the Mormon missionaries who were being ill treated by Protestant missionaries.

The more substantive problem with the foreign press in Yokohama was the lack of professionalism, compounded by the small size of the foreign community itself. According to historian James Hoare, the "invective of the Yokohama papers became notorious not only in Japan but far outside the country. The lack of real news often meant that editors had little better to fill their papers with than personal attacks on their rivals. The smallness of the foreign communities meant that no such attacks could be ignored and so the cycle went on."[42] Moreover, the smallness of the foreign communities also meant that the newspapers depended heavily on subscribers for operating funds. Consequently, maintaining an impartial view on issues was difficult, and "switches in editorial policy, even under the same editor, were . . . a marked feature" of what has been called "treaty port journalism."[43] The controversy with which the Mormon missionaries were accosted by the Yokohama foreign press was a product of treaty port journalism, the very type of newspaper controversy the elders were later counseled by the First Presidency to avoid.[44]

Reactions in the Japanese Press

Despite the *Kobe Chronicle*'s claim that the Mormons had been met with "indifference," the elders also received wide, though by no means universal, coverage in the Japanese press. Likely, the Japanese press obtained the news of the arrival from the August 13 issue of either the *Japan Advertiser* or the *Japan Herald*.[45] The *Jiji Shinpo* of Tokyo quickly responded on August 14 by noting the arrival. The *Yamato Shinbun* (also of Tokyo) published a similar report the following day. At the turn of the twentieth century, Tokyo had over a dozen competing newspapers, among which the *Yorozu Choho* had the largest circulation (at close to one hundred thousand),[46] followed by such papers as the *Hochi Shinbun*, the *Niroku Shinpo*, and the *Chuo Shinbun*.[47] The *Kokumin Shinbun*, the *Tokyo Asahi Shinbun*, and the *Miyako Shinbun* were also important. With a circulation of only about ten thousand, the *Jiji Shinpo* was considered to be a first-rate newspaper and was extremely influential because its readership was concentrated in the business community.[48]

Beginning on August 16, the story of the elders' arrival was picked up by a number of regional newspapers throughout the country. Probably the news was obtained from the wire services or from the papers' Tokyo correspondents, who could communicate via telephone or telegraph, which had connected most major points of the country by that time.[49] The *Niigata Shinbun* and the *Tohoku Nippo* (Niigata), the *Kobe Yushin Nippo,* and the *Shizuoka Minyu Shinbun* were the first regional papers to report the news. They were followed by the *Osaka Asahi Shinbun,* the *Kyoto Hinode Shinbun,* and the *Hokkoku Shinbun* (Kanazawa) on August 17. Subsequently, reports, articles, and editorials relating to the Mormon missionaries and their message were published extensively in many of the country's major newspapers, including the *Ryukyu Shinpo* of Naha, Okinawa.

In Tokyo, correspondents of the *Jiji Shinpo* and the *Niroku Shinpo* both reported accounts of interviews with the Mormon missionaries. On August 16, the *Jiji* devoted the top two-thirds of page four (illus. 7-1) to an interview with Elder Grant held at the Grand Hotel. The interview summarized Grant's business career and explained the history and beliefs of the Mormons, including their persecution, industry, and polygamy. This interview was picked up by the *Kyoto Hinode Shinbun* on August 18 and by the influential *Kahoku Shinpo* (Sendai), which published it in two parts on August 18 and 20. Another interview, conducted by a *Niroku Shinpo*'s reporter, was published in that newspaper in five parts on August 17, 18, 19, 21, and 23, again summarizing the history

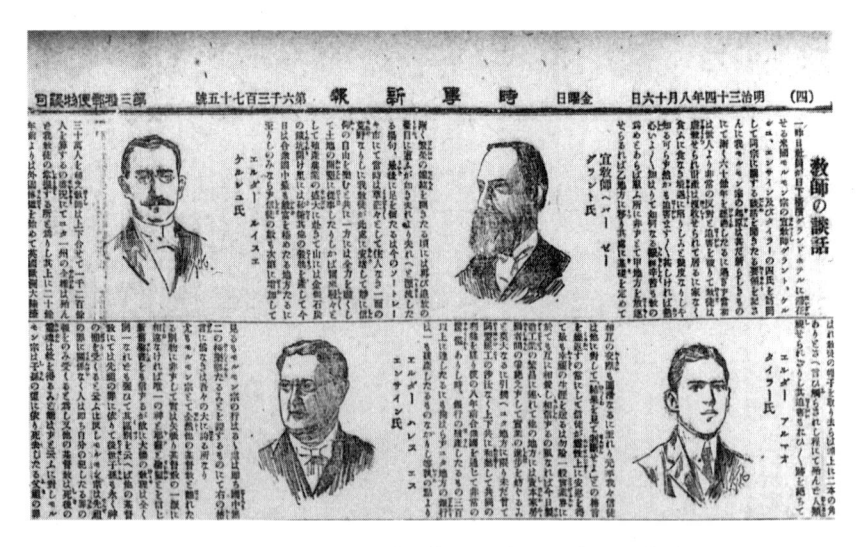

Illus. 7-1. On August 16, 1901, Tokyo's *Jiji Shinpo* devoted almost an entire page to an interview of the Mormon missionaries by its reporter; the missionaries' portraits accompanied the article. *Left to right:* (top row) Louis A. Kelsch, Heber J. Grant; (bottom row) Horace S. Ensign, Alma O. Taylor. All photographs courtesy Shinji Takagi.

Illus. 7-2. On August 19, 1901, Tokyo's *Niroku Shinpo* published a cartoon depicting the four Mormon missionaries as the "Mormon *bodhisattva* (Buddhist saints)" with halos, and with a group of prominent Japanese gentlemen (presumably including Hirobumi Ito) worshipping them. In view of the presumed practice of polygamy among the Mormons, the cartoon was evidently alluding to the practice of concubinage prevalent among the leading men of Japan.

and beliefs of Mormonism. The *Niroku* also published on August 19 a cartoon depicting the four elders (illus. 7-2) and, more significantly, the entire English-language text of Elder Grant's "Address to the Great and Progressive Nation of Japan," with a Japanese translation, on August 19 and 20 (illus. 7-3a, 7-3b). All in all, at least fifteen Tokyo-based newspapers reported in one form or another the arrival of the Mormon missionaries during the months of August and September 1901.[50]

Fairly extensive commentary including an exposition on Church history and doctrines was also found in the *Kobe Yushin Nippo* (August 16), the *Yamato Shinbun* (August 17–22, 24–27), the *Osaka Asahi Shinbun* (August 19), the *Osaka Mainichi Shinbun* (August 21, 23–24), the *Moji Shinpo* (August 22), the *Kyochu Nippo* of Kofu (August 24, 27–28), and the Tokyo *Mainichi Shinbun* (September 5–6 and 8). The *Kyochu Nippo*

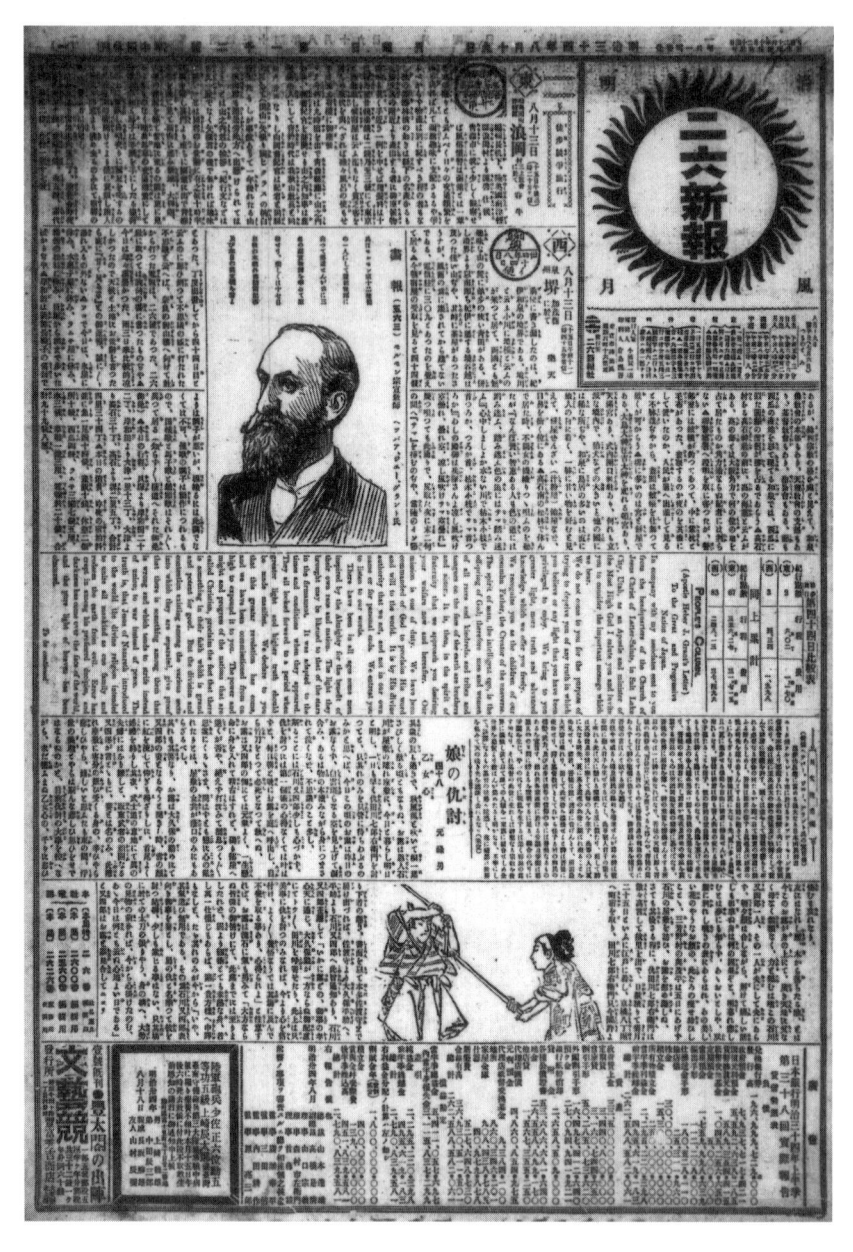

Illus. 7-3a. Front page of the *Niroku*, August 19, 1901. The *Niroku* published in two parts, the entire text of Elder Grant's "Address to the Great and Progressive Nation of Japan," accompanied by a Japanese translation of the text, a portrait of Elder Grant, and a portrait of Joseph Smith.

Illus. 7-3b. Front page of the *Niroku*, August 20, 1901.

series was a verbatim copy of the *Osaka Mainichi* series. Except for the *Osaka Asahi* article—which presented the thirteen Articles of Faith (see discussion below) and discussed in a factual manner the nature of the Book of Mormon, the proper name of the Church, the place of secular pursuits in Mormon religious life, and the reasons for and practice and termination of polygamy—all the rest were anti-Mormon in tone. For example, all but *Yamato* referred to the Spaulding theory as a credible explanation for the origin of the Book of Mormon. Other frequently referenced topics included claims about fraudulent banking practices in Kirtland, the immoral and questionable character of Joseph Smith, the political ambition of the Church to establish an independent kingdom, the founding of a secret society to protect Joseph Smith's life, the execution of oaths to demand absolute obedience to authority, the Mountain Meadows massacre, and other usual fares of anti-Mormon literature. The *Mainichi* (Tokyo) called the Mormon religion "superstitious," "dubious," "unworthy of an educated person's attention," and its teachings "incompatible with civilization."

One religious newspaper gave particularly extensive coverage to the Mormons. The *Kyogaku Hochi* of Kyoto published at least twenty-nine articles on Mormon themes between August 18 and September 24. Founded by a Buddhist priest in 1897, the *Kyogaku Hochi* was informally affiliated with the Jodo-shinshu sect of Buddhism.[51] Significantly, it was read not only by Kyoto's citizenry but also by subscribing temples and other religious institutions throughout the country.

The newspapers contained translations of Mormon terms and texts that remained in the Japanese Church vocabulary for years. Of particular significance was the August 19 issue of the *Osaka Asahi,* in which the thirteen Articles of Faith and the expression *Latter-day Saints* were translated into Japanese. In the choice of words and sentence structure, the translation of the Articles of Faith is almost identical to the one the Church would subsequently adopt, indicating the possibility that the Church translator, Goro Takahashi, consulted the *Osaka Asahi* translation.[52] The translation of the phrase "Latter-day Saints" *(Batsujitsu Seito),* is also the same as the one which was subsequently to be used by the Church.[53] The *Osaka Asahi*'s translation of the Articles of Faith was reprinted in the August 26 issue of the *Yamato Shinbun* and the August 29 issue of the *Ryukyu Shinpo*. In the August 18 issue of the

Yamato Shinbun, the expression "Book of Mormon" was translated as *Morumon Kei*, the same wording that would be used by the Church for over ninety years.

Next to the arrival of the LDS missionaries, the most widely reported event was the refusal of a Yokohama boardinghouse keeper—an ex-Protestant missionary named Staniland—to admit them. This event was described in Alma O. Taylor's journal entry for August 13 as follows:

> During this afternoon we had been hunting for a place to board which would be cheaper than at the hotel and at one place to which Bro[ther] Kelsch, Bro[ther] Grant and Bro[ther] Ensign were directed they found suitable rooms but when they were about to accept them, the landlord said: "We had been expecting some Mormon preachers from Utah." The Brethren said that they were the ones and had just arrived the day before on the steamer Empress of India. "Oh!" said he, "I cannot take you under any consideration.["] After talking with him a few moments during which they asked him if he would not like to hear the other side of Mormonism, he said that he did not and would not have anything to do with them or their money, so they left him and sought elsewhere for acomidations.[54]

This incident was first reported by the English-language newspapers. The *Japan Mail* covered the event on August 16 in a condescending manner by saying that the paper was "given to understand that the Mormon elders who recently arrived in Japan are not staying at Beverly House, No. 2, Bluff," to which the *Japan Herald* sharply reacted in its evening edition. The *Herald* accused the "tenant of the premises in question" for appearing "to glory in his indefensible conduct" by reporting the incident to "the all too complaisant *Mail*," and concluded that "to save trouble to future applicants for rooms, advertisements emanating from No. 2, Bluff, should be worded after this fashion: 'Lodging to let, but only to persons deemed by the letter, to hold correct opinions. . . . Particulars to be had on the premises, at No. 2, also at the *Japan Mail* Office.'" The Associated Press carried the news with a commentary that the Mormon missionaries had received "a sample of the lack of Catholicity which characterises Christian workers in the Orient, and of the sectarian feeling which vitiates their work."[55]

Starting August 19, the boardinghouse incident was picked up by Japanese newspapers in Tokyo, Nagoya, Osaka, Kyoto, Fukuoka, Moji, and Okinawa.[56] For some reason, the story became distorted by the Japanese press to the effect that Staniland had admitted the missionaries but his wife, finding that they were Mormons, kicked them out. Some editorials, such as those in the *Mainichi* (Tokyo) on August 21 and in the *Jiji* on August 25, capitalized on this version, arguing that the sexual immorality of Japanese men was reinforced by the blind obedience of Japanese women, who should be more like American women. Undergirding the reaction of the *Mainichi* and other papers to the Staniland incident was the antiprostitution movement, a major social force at that time, as well as the conflict in Japanese society over the proper role of women.[57]

The Question of Polygamy

The Mormon missionaries, representing a religion whose recent history included belief in and practice of polygamy, arrived during a time of national debate over antiprostitution and monogamy. From the mid-1880s on, Christians led a movement to abolish the system of licensed prostitution in Japan, in part responding to a similar movement in leading countries of the world.[58] Earlier, in 1872, the Meiji Government had abolished the system of licensed prostitution that involved slavery by issuing the Anti-Slavery Law and the Prostitute Liberalization Law. The following year, however, yielding to pressure from brothel owners, the government allowed prostitutes to engage in the profession of their own free will and brothel owners to offer their facilities to such prostitutes.[59]

The antiprostitution movement regained momentum in 1885, when a women's magazine called *Jogaku Zasshi* was inaugurated and began campaigning against licensed prostitution. In December 1886, the Tokyo Women's Temperance Union was founded with the broader objective of promoting the liberalization of women and a charter that included (1) promoting the establishment of a wholesome association between husband and wife, (2) improving the status of women in the family, (3) abolishing prostitution, and (4) establishing the system of monogamy. Three years later, it filed a petition with the government, stating that the prevalent practice of concubinage was adultery. Also, in 1890, a move toward consolidation began. Local antiprostitution organizations joined together to establish the National Anti-Prostitution

League, and in 1893 the Tokyo Women's Temperance Union absorbed other Christian women's organizations throughout the country to become the Japan Women's Christian Temperance Union.[60] By the late 1890s, the antiprostitution movement was a major national movement and a significant social force.[61]

In this social movement, a significant role was played by the *Mainichi* of Tokyo and the Salvation Army, which had arrived in Japan in 1895. The *Mainichi,* an antiprostitution newspaper, set up a daily column in which it reported the names of prostitutes who left the profession.[62] The Salvation Army, on its part, preached against the evils of prostitution in the August 1, 1900, issue of its magazine *Toki no Koe* (War cry), calling for licensed prostitutes to leave the profession and offering assistance and asylum to those who did so.[63] On August 5, as a group of Salvation Army volunteers were walking through the red light districts of Tokyo with copies of the magazine, they were attacked by mobs hired by brothel owners. This incident was reported in newspapers throughout the country.[64]

Thus, the Mormon missionaries arrived in Japan at a time when Japanese society was debating the evils of its social institutions that subjugated women, including licensed prostitution and, more broadly, the marital relationship between husband and wife. In this light, it is easy to understand why almost all of the editorials on Mormon themes published in Japanese newspapers at that time discussed the Japanese practice of concubinage in the context of Mormon polygamy. For example, in a two-part front-page editorial published August 16–17, the *Yamato Shinbun*[65] made a far-fetched suggestion that the people of nobility (who frequently practiced concubinage) should all become Mormons and that the commoners be forbidden to become Mormons. This way, the editorial argued, the evil practice of concubinage could be eliminated in Japan. On August 21, the Tokyo *Mainichi Shinbun* wrote a front-page editorial entitled "Foreign Mormonism and Domestic Mormonism," arguing that Japan's elite society did not have the moral qualification to reject Mormonism and that the practice of concubinage should be abolished. Other negative editorials were even introspective. For example, on August 24, the *Kyoto Hinode Shinbun* published an editorial stating that prohibiting the preaching of Mormonism by legal means would be useless unless the system of monogamy was firmly established first. Otherwise, a "type of Mormonism" would continue to flourish in Japan.

Heber J. Grant fought the perception that the Mormons had come to preach polygamy. In his interviews with the Japanese press as well as in his letters to the editors of the *Japan Mail* and the *Japan Herald*, he vehemently denied any suggestion that the Mormon missionaries had come to preach polygamy, referring to the Manifesto of 1890. He was not entirely persuasive, however. For one thing, he simultaneously made rather laudatory remarks about polygamy, including the logic behind the Mormon practice of polygamy, phrases such as "beautiful" polygamist families, and comments about the social and biological virtues of such practice. Perhaps more importantly, Grant admitted that he himself was a polygamist.[66] Probably for these and other reasons, many newspaper articles continued to claim that the Mormons still believed in polygamy, while fully acknowledging the official termination of the practice in the Manifesto.

The image of the Church as a polygamist institution lingered for years. In October 1901, Kajiko Yajima, the president of the Japan Women's Temperance Union, and Chiseko Seda, the president of the Tokyo Women's Temperance Union, filed with the Home Ministry a petition to ban the preaching of Mormonism on the grounds that the Mormons still believed in polygamy and that there were still polygamists in Utah.[67] As late as March 1907, Alma O. Taylor, then the president of the Japan Mission, felt compelled to write for the *Jiji Shinpo* an article stating there was "no fear of polygamy."[68] Likewise, E. D. Thomas, who succeeded Taylor, devoted considerable space to the topic of polygamy in an article published in the May 1911 issue of the *Seiko* (Success), a monthly magazine.[69]

Hirobumi Ito and the Legal Prostitution Controversy

The Mormon elders carried at least one letter of introduction to Hirobumi Ito (1841–1909), perhaps the single most important political leader of the Meiji period and one of the founding fathers of modern Japan.[70] The letter was written by Angus M. Cannon, the younger brother of George Q. Cannon and the manager of the *Deseret News* office during 1867–74.[71] Cannon's association with Ito resulted from the visits Ito made to the United States in 1870 as a part of his responsibility at the Ministry of Finance to study the monetary system of the United States and in 1872 as a member of the mission led by Prince Tomomi Iwakura, Junior Prime Minister, to begin preliminary renegotiations of treaty revision with the treaty powers and to study their modern institutions.[72]

One thing Elder Grant had not been informed of was the fact that Hirobumi Ito was known in Japan as a womanizer and an advocate of licensed prostitution.[73] In 1896, in an interview with the Tokyo correspondent of the *London Daily News,* Ito stated that he supported licensed prostitution as a realistic way of controlling vice and protecting the public. A summary of this interview was published in the September issue of the *Fujin Shinpo,* the monthly magazine of the Tokyo Women's Temperance Union, and Ito's position on prostitution became widely known in Japanese society.[74] Thus, the August 24, 1901, issue of the *Yonezawa Shinbun* called Ito "a Mormon in deed" and a "good representative of Mormonism in the Orient." The August 27 issue of the *Yamato Shinbun,* referring to Grant's letters of introduction to Ito, stated that Ito was the "overlord of the sexual world, and the supreme ruler of carnal desire." The fact that Grant had a letter of introduction to Ito sent a wrong and unintended signal to the Japanese public.

Apparently, Elder Grant had every intention of meeting Ito upon his arrival in Japan. His intentions were implied in a short *Deseret Evening News* article under the headline "Arrive at Yokohama, Apostle Grant and Companions Now in the Mikado's Empire." The article stated:

> President Snow received a cablegram today from Apostle Heber J. Grant announcing that he and his companions arrived safely at Yokohama last midnight. The cablegram merely stated the fact, giving no further particulars but those who are familiar with his plans say that Apostle Grant will first call on the highest government officials including the mikado himself, and will lose no time in getting the work started in Japan.[75]

The Japanese press was more explicit. The August 16 issue of the *Jiji Shinpo* quoted Grant as saying that he would visit Ito with letters of introduction. On the same day, the *Shizuoka Minyu Shinbun* speculated that Ito might be the first person to be baptized by the Mormons.[76]

However, Elder Grant was probably unsuccessful in meeting Ito in Tokyo. According to the August 21 entry of the journal of the Japan

Mission, "President Grant went to Tokyo again, not having been successful in meeting the parties yesterday for whom he has letters."[77] On January 19, 1902, Alma O. Taylor wrote in his journal, "Another [of the Japanese students who visited us was] the nephew of Marquis Ito to whom we have letters of introduction from Bro[ther] Angus Cannon, who, with his Brother Geo[rge] Q. Cannon, had met the Marquis a number of times." The fact that the missionaries still possessed the letters from Angus Cannon seems to suggest that as of January 1902 the letters had not yet been given to Ito. A more definitive statement comes from the October 19, 1909, journal entry of Alma O. Taylor:

> After dinner we were favored with a call from Mr. Akimoto a Japanese who has been engaged in beet raising in Idaho for a long time. . . . A friend of his who is a high official in the government told him that when Apostle Grant and his companions came to Japan, Marquis (now Prince) Ito proposed welcoming officially, by public reception, the Mormon missionaries. All Buddhist and Shinto sects approved the suggestion but the Christians (?) were unanimous in their opposition and said they could not accept an invitation to such a reception. This manifestation of ill will caused the Marquis to withdraw his proposal.[78]

If this story is true, it establishes that Ito was willing to see Grant but, for reasons unknown, did not.

Constitutional and Legal Questions

Another topic frequently treated in the newspapers concerned the limits to the freedom of religion guaranteed by the Meiji Constitution. Chapter 3 article 28 of the constitution reads, "Japanese subjects shall, within limits not prejudicial to peace and order, and not antagonistic to their duties as subjects, enjoy freedom of religious belief."[79] The key expression is "peace and order," which can restrict the exercise of religious freedom. Many newspaper articles and editorials used this restriction to argue that the government should prohibit the preaching of Mormonism. The first newspaper to take this line of reasoning was the *Japan Mail*, which argued in its August 17 issue that the Mormons should be officially forbidden to preach in Japan because their teaching threatened peace and order. Over subsequent days, this position was adopted by Japanese newspapers, including the *Chugoku, Hinode, Osaka Mainichi, Moji Shinpo, Kyushu Shinbun,* and *Yonezawa Shinbun.*[80]

These arguments may have some validity as a Home Ministry ordinance stipulated that a religious organization must file an application before it could be authorized to preach. On August 24, the *Tokyo Asahi* and the *Osaka Asahi* (both under the same management) became the first newspapers to take a look at this issue, noting that the Mormons had not yet filed an application with the authorities. Possibly in response to this *Asahi* report, which was picked up by the *Japan Herald* in the evening, Elder Grant decided to go to Tokyo on August 27 to consult with the Home Ministry about securing a permit to preach and to distribute tracts in Japan.[81] He returned again to Tokyo on September 2–3, in order to "attend to some business with the Home Department."[82]

As Elder Grant discovered, the procedure to secure a permit was quite simple, requiring only that an application be filed with the local authorities, in this case, with the Kanagawa Prefectural Government. The press closely followed the actions of the Mormon missionaries in this matter. Between August 25 and 29, the newspapers frequently made references to the possible decisions of the authorities.[83] Curiously, the only thing which the Ito-affiliated *Tokyo Nichinichi* reported during August was the fact that, as of August 28, the Mormons had not filed an application. The *Tokyo Nichinichi* may have considered it wise to distance itself from the controversy surrounding the possible relationship between Ito and the Mormon missionaries.

Elder Grant and his companions continued their attempts to meet the legal requirements. On September 6, they visited the chief of the Kanagawa Police Department to determine the requirements of the law. The chief told them he would consult with the governor before informing them of the particulars. This incident was noted in the September 10 issue of the *Kyogaku Hochi.*[84] In the event, on September 17, application was made to the governor to preach the gospel. On September 20, the missionaries received a communication from the governor's office, requesting them to reappear and answer questions regarding their intentions. On September 21, when they called again at the governor's office, they were told that they "did not have to make such an extensive application as [they] had done in order to get permission to preach and establish a mission, and that there were some points which the law required that had not been mentioned in the application."[85] These developments were reported in the September 21 issue of the *Tokyo Nichinichi,* the September 23 and 24 issues of the *Kyogaku Hochi,* and possibly other newspapers, as well as the October issue of the nationally influential *Chuo Koron* magazine.[86] On October 5, after a few more attempts, the missionaries completed the bureaucratic formalities.[87]

The Osaka Controversy

As previously noted, some of the newspaper editorials used the arrival of the Mormon missionaries as an occasion to discuss the contemporary social issues of Japanese society. Other editorials, however, took definite positions for or against the idea of allowing the Mormon missionaries to preach in Japan, with the Japanese press being roughly split between antagonists and defenders. The antagonists were led by the influential *Jiji Shinpo,* which on August 20 argued that Mormonism was a "perverse" religion and should be banned in Japan "as in the United States." On August 23, the *Chuo Shinbun* likewise argued that Mormonism should be banned in Japan as the Mormons had not truthfully given up the practice of polygamy. These articles were followed by the August 27 issue of the *Kyushu Nippo,* which supported the idea of banning Mormonism for being against Japan's morals.[88]

There were defenders of Mormonism as well. On August 21, the day after the *Jiji* published its devastating editorial, the *Shizuoka Minyu Shinbun* defended the right of the Mormons as a Christian sect to preach in Japan, saying that the mysterious stories associated with Mormonism were not unusual in religion. On August 25, the *Dokuritsu Shinbun,* noting the earnestness of the Mormon missionaries in traveling thousands of miles to come to a country with a totally different culture, stated that complacent Japanese religionists could learn much from Mormonism. The *Chukyo Shinpo* of August 27 devoted part of its front page to appeal to those who were advocating the idea of banning Mormonism, saying that the Mormon missionaries could not be so stupid as to preach the illegal practice of polygamy. It went on to say that what should be feared was not foreign Mormonism but domestic Mormonism, namely, those wealthy Japanese gentlemen who practiced the evil of concubinage.

The most spectacular debate took place in the commercial city of Osaka between its nationally influential *Osaka Asahi* and *Osaka Mainichi*, which fiercely competed with each other and were often known to take opposite positions on issues that came up. The debate began on August 20, 1901, when the *Asahi* devoted two front-page columns to an editorial entitled "Mormon Missionaries Arrive," which read in part:

> Mormonism is distinguished by its practice of polygamy. Although it professes to uphold Christian teachings, it is despised by other Christians.... Several years ago, the United States Government enacted a law to prohibit [polygamy], but the practice has not yet disappeared. Its teachings still approve [polygamy], and the state of Utah, in which the headquarters are located, is a stain in the United States of America. Now, the missionaries of a religion which is considered perverse, feared and despised by the people of America and Europe, have come to Japan and set out to preach.

The writer then went on to say that he objected to Mormonism because the polygamy it promoted could "degrade the public morals of Japan." As Japanese society was just beginning to recognize the evils of concubinage and public opinion was rising against such practice, he continued, allowing a polygamist religion to be preached might "rekindle" the dying practice. He recognized the constitutional freedom of religion but argued that the freedom of religion was guaranteed only insofar as religious practice did not violate the law. Inasmuch as polygamy was prohibited by law, it was constitutional to prohibit the preaching of Mormonism in Japan. "Hence," he wrote, "Mormonism is a perverse religion that disrupts social ethics and endangers public peace. It is thus appropriate from the standpoint of national policy to prohibit it today and to cut off the penetration of the vicious practice before it spreads."

The *Mainichi* immediately responded to the editorial. On August 21, it devoted two front-page columns to an editorial entitled "What in the World Should Prevent Them?" After noting the wide coverage the Mormon missionaries had received in the Western-language newspapers in Yokohama and others in Tokyo and Osaka, the editor stated:

> I believe that there is no need to prohibit the preaching of Mormonism.... Inasmuch as it recently made a public declaration

that it would give up polygamy, by the order of the U.S. Government, there should be no fear that it will dare to break the law of the land even in Japan. Moreover, although our ancient custom may allow concubines to be kept, it does not permit the stupid act of having several legal wives. How could the teachings of the Mormon sect change it by themselves?

The editor then explained the existence of many religions in Japan by saying, "It is because the Japanese people are broad-minded and do not show particular dislike for any of them. Why should the Mormon sect be the only exception?" Although the editor noted the Mormon "tactics" of resorting to supernatural phenomena, he brushed them away by saying that Mormonism was not different from any other Christian, Buddhist, or Shintoist religion in this regard. He did not necessarily compliment Mormonism, however, because he said it was a foolish religion. He simply argued that education, and not legal sanction, should be used to make sure that such a religion not be accepted by the ignorant populace. As to the right of the Mormon missionaries to preach, however, his position is clear:

> Constitutionally, Japan upholds the freedom of religion. As long as it is not prejudicial to public peace, any religion is permissible, be it Buddhism or Christianity. Among the ignorant public, even Tenrikyo or Renmonkyo is allowed to exist. Then, what in the world should prevent the coming of Mormonism?

The impact of this debate should not be underestimated for at least three reasons. First, Osaka was (and, to a lesser extent, still is) an important economic center of Japan, the principal city of the historic Kansai region extending from Kyoto to Kobe. During the pre-WWII period, the economic might of Osaka was unmatched by any city, including Tokyo, in terms of manufacturing and finance. Second, the *Osaka Asahi* and the *Osaka Mainichi* were both newspapers of national significance. Their influence went beyond the fact that they were both read widely within the greater Kansai region. In 1888, the *Osaka Asahi* had expanded to the Tokyo market by purchasing the *Mezamashi Shinbun* and changing the name to the *Tokyo Asahi Shinbun*.[89] Although in 1901 the *Osaka Mainichi* did not have an explicit Tokyo presence, its management and editorial board included nationally prominent figures.

Third, the Osaka newspapers were the first in Japan to assume a modern corporate form of management and, as such, quickly expanded their scale of operations, aided by their efficient sales and advertisement departments.[90] In 1897, for example, the *Osaka Asahi* had begun to subscribe to the Reuter wire service. In response, in 1897, the *Osaka Mainichi* appointed Kei Hara, a prominent diplomat and future prime minister, to become the editor-in-chief (and, later, president of the company).[91] Hara used his diplomatic connections to appoint foreign correspondents in various parts of the world. At the turn of the twentieth century, the *Asahi* had a readership of about 120,000, while the *Mainichi* claimed 100,000.[92]

A Voice of Reason: Eitaro Okano

One member of the press who was particularly helpful to the Mormon missionaries' cause was Eitaro Okano, a prominent journalist[93] and the English-language editor of the *Niroku Shinpo*. The *Niroku Shinpo* promoted social justice and, as such, naturally defended the rights of prostitutes to leave the confinement of forced servitude.[94] The *Niroku* also had a tendency towards sensationalism and quickly gained in readership after it was restarted in 1900. By the end of 1903, it had the largest circulation in Tokyo, with a peak readership of about 150,000 people.[95]

Okano first visited the missionaries on August 14, 1901, when they were still at the Grand Hotel.[96] Elder Taylor's journal entry on that day states, "In the evening a Japanese editor of the largest Japanese newspaper in Japan published at Tokyo came from Tokyo to interview us." It has already been mentioned that, as a result, the *Niroku* published a five-part article based on that interview plus the full text of Elder Grant's address to the people of Japan.

Apparently, the relationship between Okano and the missionaries became even more cordial. On August 23, Elder Taylor recorded:

> We found two representatives from the "Niroku Shinpo" [sic] newspaper published in Tokio. These gentlemen had called to learn more concerning our doctrines than what [they had] published already.... They had come to learn particularly of the difference in doctrine between our Faith and the beliefs of other Christians.

It was also Okano who arranged and assisted Elder Grant's initial meeting with the Home Ministry official in charge of the religion bureau.[97] It is possible that his association with the missionaries continued for some time.

Okano's greatest contribution to Mormon proselytizing work, however, was the editorial[98] he published on August 22. Amid the frenzy caused by the voices of the influential *Jiji* and *Osaka Asahi* calling on August 20 for the authorities to prohibit the preaching of Mormonism, Okano defended the rights of the Mormons and encouraged readers to look at positive aspects of Mormonism. He began by reminding readers of the finiteness of human wisdom, so that only unlearned people are "proud of the low level of our present civilization and are satisfied with the shallow state of our present knowledge." He then went on to say:

> It may be that what a majority calls good is evil and what a majority calls evil is good. . . . I am not advocating an unnecessarily skeptic view. . . . I am only a man who cannot blindly follow the opinion of a majority. . . . Mormons have come. They have come for the first time since the opening of Japan. I welcome them. We must first find out [what they believe]. During the sixty some years since the establishment of their religion, they have withstood extreme opposition and persecution and now claim the membership of 300,000 and 1,200 teachers. They virtually control the entire state of Utah, which has come to be called the most prosperous region in the United States. This is a fact. In [Mormonism], there must be something that is appealing. . . . Four missionaries have come across the vast ocean to enter Japan, which has been influenced by the civilization of Christian nations of the West for a long time. We must say that they are brave. As we hear, they are supporting themselves with their own funds. Their spirits are to be admired. I cannot bear mistreating them with a bitter face. I will instead welcome them with a smile of good will, and desire to listen to their doctrines.

Undoubtedly, Okano's August 23 visit to the missionaries was a fulfillment of his own public declaration. His was indeed a voice of reason amid the hysteria of the day.[99]

Conclusion

From mid-August to mid-September 1901, at least forty newspapers throughout the country devoted considerable space to articles and editorials on issues surrounding the arrival of Mormon missionaries. When we recognize that there were only about one hundred respectable newspapers in Japan at that time[100] and that the arrival of the Mormon missionaries was also covered by two of the leading national magazines,[101] we realize that the extent of the press coverage was massive indeed.

To be sure, the extensive press coverage was initially triggered by the generally hostile resident foreign press, which received much of its subscription revenue from the Protestant missionary community. Fuel was added by the culture of the treaty-port newspapers, which were managed by amateur journalists who took delight in petty arguments among themselves. The resident foreign press was frequently used as a source of foreign news; as such, the foreign language newspapers in Japan at that time exerted greater influence than the number of subscribers might have indicated. The foreign press's story of the arrival of Mormon missionaries was quickly picked up by the Japanese press. The ensuing fervor with which the subject of Mormonism was treated in the Japanese press was undoubtedly related to the tendency of Japanese newspapers toward sensationalism (designed to outrival their competitors) as well as to the sheer curiosity of the Japanese public concerning the Mormon practice of polygamy.

On a more fundamental level, however, the zeal with which the arrival of the Mormon missionaries was covered emanated from Japanese society's own internal conflict regarding the morality of its own marital and related social institutions, which was a major social issue dividing the country at the turn of the twentieth century. In this respect, the reaction of Japanese society to the arrival of the Mormon missionaries, as reflected in its press coverage, provides a means of understanding the fabric and dynamics of that society. Against the dominant sentiment calling the authorities to ban the preaching of Mormonism, there were voices of reason and fairness, which indicated the (increasingly) pluralistic nature of Japanese society.

In terms of proselytizing work, the impact of the extensive press coverage was likely more positive than negative, if there was any effect at all. For one thing, the Japanese public was by then quite tolerant of religious diversity and probably did not care one way or another what the Mormons believed or practiced. Hence, whatever the negative message the press coverage might have contained, it was more than offset by the positive benefit of mere publicity. Second, responding to this publicity, there were some positive developments for the Church, such as an offer of speaking opportunities for the missionaries and the publication of a major treatise on Mormonism entitled "Morumonkyo to Ramakyo (Mormonism and Lamaism)" by an influential Christian writer named Goro Takahashi.[102] Third, as another consequence of the publicity, the Mormon missionaries received numerous letters and visitors from all over the country. Although these visitors did not immediately result in convert baptisms, the missionaries did, as a result, meet in late August with Tatsutaro Hiroi, who agreed to serve as their translator, interpreter, and Japanese teacher.[103] Be that as it may, when newness wore off, the interest in Mormonism waned. Nonetheless, through both newspapers and magazines, the press was instrumental in making sure that the news of the arrival of Mormonism in Japan penetrated every region and sounded in virtually every ear.

Appendix
A Partial List of 1901 Japanese Newspapers and Magazines That Discussed the Mormons, with Their Depositories

Tokyo Newspapers

Chuo Shinbun, National Diet Library, Tokyo
Dokuritsu Shinbun, National Diet Library, Tokyo
Hochi Shinbun, National Diet Library, Tokyo
Japan Times, National Diet Library, Tokyo
Jiji Shinpo, National Diet Library, Tokyo
Mainichi Shinbun, National Diet Library, Tokyo
Miyako Shinbun, National Diet Library, Tokyo
Niroku Shinpo, National Diet Library, Tokyo
Tokyo Asahi Shinbun, National Diet Library, Tokyo
Tokyo Nichinichi Shinbun, National Diet Library, Tokyo
Yamato Shinbun, National Diet Library, Tokyo
Yomiuri Shinbun, National Diet Library, Tokyo
Yorozu Choho, National Diet Library, Tokyo

Osaka Newspapers

Osaka Asahi Shinbun, Osaka University Library, Osaka
Osaka Mainichi Shinbun, Osaka University Library, Osaka

Regional Newspapers

Chugoku, National Diet Library, Tokyo
Chukyo Shinpo, National Diet Library, Tokyo
Hokkoku Shinbun, National Diet Library, Tokyo
Kahoku Shinpo, Kahoku Shinposha, Sendai
Kobe Yushin Nippo, Kobe Municipal Library, Kobe
Kyochu Nippo, Yamanashi Prefectural Library, Kofu
Kyogaku Hochi, Ryukoku University Library, Kyoto
Kyoto Hinode Shinbun, National Diet Library, Tokyo
Kyushu Nichinichi Shinbun, Kumamoto Prefectural Library, Kumamoto
Kyushu Nippo, Fukuoka Municipal Library, Fukuoka
Kyushu Shinbun, Kumamoto Prefectural Library, Kumamoto
Moji Shinpo, Kitakyushu Municipal Library, Kitakyushu
Niigata Shinbun, Niigata Prefectural Library, Niigata
Ryukyu Shinpo, Okinawa Prefectural Library, Naha
Shinano Mainichi Shinbun, Matsumoto Municipal Library, Matsumoto
Shizuoka Minyu Shinbun, National Diet Library, Tokyo
Tohoku Nippo, Niigata Prefectural Library, Niigata
Yamanashi Nichinichi Shinbun, Yamanashi Prefectural Library, Kofu
Yonezawa Shinbun, Yamagata Prefectural Library, Yamagata

Magazines

Chuo Koron, monthly, National Diet Library, Tokyo
Taiyo, monthly, National Diet Library, Tokyo

This article originally appeared as Shinji Takagi, "Mormons in the Press: Reactions to the 1901 Opening of the Japan Mission," BYU Studies 40, no. 1 (2000): 141–75.

Notes

1. At that time, the Canadian Pacific fleet consisted of three ships—the *Empress of India,* the *Empress of Japan,* and the *Empress of China*—and

connected Vancouver and Hong Kong, via Victoria, Yokohama, Kobe, Nagasaki, and Shanghai. See the newspaper advertisement that frequently appeared in those days, for example, the *Japan Times,* August 8, 1901.

2. Although the Church had earlier sent missionaries to such places as China, India, and Thailand, the efforts were short-lived and did not result in the establishment of a permanent mission. See "Minutes of Conference," *Deseret Evening News,* September 18, 1852, 4, for the names of fourteen missionaries sent to Asia in 1852.

3. The expression "quartet" was first used by Augusta, the plural wife of Heber J. Grant, in a letter addressed to her husband in Japan. See Alma O. Taylor, Journal, December 25, 1901, L. Tom Perry Special Collections, Harold B. Lee Library, Brigham Young University, Provo, Utah.

4. Currently, on this location stands the Yokohama Doll House.

5. See the newspaper advertisement that frequently appeared in those days, for example, the *Japan Times,* August 8, 1901. See also Heber J. Grant, "A Japanese Journal," comp. Gordon A. Madsen, August 12, 1901, Perry Special Collections.

6. See Frederick R. Brady, "The Japanese Reaction to Mormonism and the Translation of Mormon Scripture into Japanese" (master's thesis: International College, Sophia University, 1979); and Murray L. Nichols, "History of the Japan Mission of the L.D.S. Church 1901–1924" (master's thesis: Brigham Young University, 1957). The present study expands the scope of analysis in these earlier studies and offers a sociohistorical explanation for the newspaper coverage of the first Mormon missionaries, a view first sketched in Shinji Takagi and William McIntyre, *Nihon Matsujitsu Seito Shi, 1850–1980* (Japan Latter-day Saint history, 1850–1980) (Kobe, Japan: Beehive Shuppan, 1996).

7. A brief editorial and a brief communication, respectively, appeared in the September issue (dated September 1) and the October issue (dated October 1) of the *Chuo Koron* (Central Review), and a two-page article by a religious commentator was published in the September 5 issue of the *Taiyo* (Sun). Along with the *Nihonjin* (Japanese), the *Chuo Koron* and the *Taiyo* were considered to be the three leading national magazines of the period. See Taketoshi Nishida, *Meiji Jidai no Shinbun to Zasshi* (Newspapers and magazines of the Meiji period) (Tokyo: Shibundo, 1961), 262. Nothing, however, was written on the Mormons in the *Nihonjin* during the months of August and September.

8. Although no hard figure is available, it can be reasonably assumed that no less than half of Japan's 44 million people were literate at the beginning of the twentieth century. This conjecture is based on the following two pieces of indirect evidence. First, by the end of the Tokugawa period, Japan already had a highly literate society which "compared favourably . . . with some

contemporary European countries." Practically every samurai was literate, as were "the majority of town-dwellers with a settled occupation" and "a good proportion of the farmers of middling status." In 1868 somewhat more than 40 percent of boys and about 10 percent of girls were receiving some kind of formal education, meaning that at least 25 percent of the population were literate. See R. P. Dore, *Education in Tokugawa Japan* (Berkeley and Los Angeles: University of California Press, 1965), 2–3, 254, 291. Second, in 1902, thirty years after a government-directed program of school construction began in 1872, the rate of primary school enrollment was 90 percent, and less than 20 percent of draft-age males were illiterate. See Takenori Inoki, *Gakko to Kojo: Nippon no Jinteki Shihon* (Schools and factories: Human capital in Japan) (Tokyo: Yomiuri Shinbunsha, 1996), 25–27.

9. For a general overview of the Church at the turn of the nineteenth century, see James B. Allen and Glen M. Leonard, *The Story of the Latter-day Saints* (Salt Lake City: Deseret Book, 1976), 435–65.

10. For a general overview of nineteenth-century Japanese history, see, for example, W. G. Beasley, *The Modern History of Japan* (London: Weidenfeld and Nicolson, 1981).

11. "Opening of the Mission in Japan," *Deseret Evening News,* April 6, 1901, 9.

12. The earlier treaties signed with the United States (the Kanagawa treaty negotiated by Commodore Matthew C. Perry), Russia, Britain, and the Netherlands during 1854–55 were not commercial treaties and obliged Japan only to open Hakodate, Shimoda, and Nagasaki for the provision of coal, water, and food; to allow consuls to be stationed; and to grant most favored nation status and the right to be tried in a consular court. It should be noted that, in these (as well as Ansei) treaties, the slight individual differences in terms that might have existed across treaties were immaterial because the best terms were to be applied to all countries because of the most favored nation status clause. For this reason, they could collectively be treated as a single treaty for all intents and purposes. See Shigeru Yamamoto, *Joyaku Kaiseishi* (A history of the treaty revision) (Tokyo: Takayama Shoin, 1943), 27–55.

13. The major ports were Shimoda, Hakodate, Nagasaki, Kanagawa, Niigata, and Hyogo. Shimoda was to be closed six months after the opening of Kanagawa. The commercial cities were Edo and Osaka.

14. Yokohama was opened in lieu of Kanagawa, and Kobe in lieu of Hyogo. Edo was renamed Tokyo in 1868.

15. Eleven of the treaties were inherited from the Tokugawa regime, and four additional ones were signed after the Meiji restoration.

16. James Edward Hoare, "The Japanese Treaty Ports, 1868–1899: A Study of the Foreign Settlements" (PhD thesis, University of London, 1970), 213.

17. Fearing the reactions of the Western diplomatic community, the government's attitude toward the work of Christian missionaries in the interior was equivocal. For example, local officials would display open opposition, which might then be overruled by the central government. Moreover, the enforcement of restrictions on Christian missionary activities differed in intensity from period to period and from place to place. See Charles W. Iglehart, *A Century of Protestant Christianity in Japan* (Rutland, Vt., and Tokyo: Charles E. Tuttle, 1959), 60.

18. Hoare, "Japanese Treaty Ports," 157–59, 165–70.

19. Hoare, "Japanese Treaty Ports," 212.

20. Of the fifteen treaty powers, the revised treaties came into force on July 17, 1899, for thirteen of them and on August 4 for the remaining two, namely, France and Austria. For Germany, the revised treaty came into force on July 17, but the right to a consular trial was retained until August 3. See Yamamoto, *Joyaku Kaiseishi*, 621.

21. It is estimated that, at the turn of the twentieth century, there were about 130,000 Christians in Japan (against the population of 44,000,000), including some 54,000 Roman Catholic and 30,000 Orthodox members. See Otis Cary, *A History of Christianity in Japan: Roman Catholic and Greek Orthodox Missions* (Rutland, Vt., and Tokyo: Charles E. Tuttle, 1976), 355, 423; and Otis Cary, *A History of Christianity in Japan: Protestant Missions* (Rutland, Vt., and Tokyo: Charles E. Tuttle, 1976), 296. Among the many Protestant denominations that had come to Japan by far the most prominent were the Congregational, Presbyterian-Reformed, Methodist, Anglican-Episcopal, and Baptist churches, which were collectively called the "Big Five." See Iglehart, *Century of Protestant Christianity*, 80–82.

22. With the completion of the railroad between Kobe and Osaka in 1874, most merchants in Osaka moved to Kobe. In Tokyo, foreigners were permitted to live outside the settlement. Thus, it is said that virtually all the residents of the Tokyo and Osaka settlements ended up being Christian missionaries. Akio Hotta and Tadashi Nishiguchi, eds., *Osaka Kawaguchi Kyoryuchi no Kenkyu* (A study of the Osaka Kawaguchi Settlement) (Kyoto: Shibunkaku Shuppan, 1995), 43, 55; Hoare, "Japanese Treaty Ports," 43–44.

23. Hachiro Ebihara, *Nihon Oji Shinbun Zasshi Shi* (History of Western-language newspapers and magazines in Japan) (Tokyo: Taiseido, 1934), 73.

24. The *Japan Herald*, initially under British management, was founded in 1861 and continued to exist until the outbreak of World War I in September 1914, when the Japanese government ordered the paper to close down because its owner then was a German. The *Japan Mail* was founded in the 1870s. In 1918 it was absorbed by the *Japan Times* of Tokyo. See Ebihara, *Nihon Oji Shinbun Zasshi Shi*, 18–20, 81, 210–12.

25. Many daily newspapers printed special weekly mail editions, containing a digest of local news, for consumption in foreign countries. The British Library has maintained copies of these mail editions of the *Japan Mail* and the *Kobe Chronicle*. The microfilms are maintained by major Japanese libraries. The relevant newspaper clippings from Taylor's scrapbook are reproduced in chapter four of Brady, "The Japanese Reaction to Mormonism." See also Nichols, "History of the Japan Mission." Both Brady and Nichols, however, erroneously call the *Japan Advertiser* the *Yokohama Advertiser*, because the latter is how Taylor called it.

26. The arrival of the Mormon missionaries was also anticipated by the Japanese press. See, for example, "Morumonshu no Nihon Fukyo," *Kyogaku Hochi*, July 23, 1901, 1, which cited an American newspaper for the information.

27. As quoted in Taylor, Journal, August 13, 1901. We do not know what else was said in the article, but Taylor thought of it as "a beginning of the ill feeling which we found had been created by the efforts of wicked men who claimed to be members of Christianity."

28. As reported in the August 27 issue of the *Yamato Shinbun*. Knapp is reported to have heard Grant say on the ship that he would take a Japanese woman as a plural wife. Of course, this cannot possibly be true, calling into question the credibility of the very story that Knapp and Grant traveled together across the Pacific.

29. Grant, Journal, August 12–18. However, the August 20 issue of the *Japan Times* suggests that the *Japan Advertiser* apparently argued against allowing the Mormon missionaries to preach in Japan.

30. After the publication of the *Japan Herald* and the *Japan Mail* ceased, however, the *Japan Advertiser* became a very influential English language newspaper in Japan. Ebihara, *Nihon Oji Shinbun Zasshi Shi*, 151, 204; Hoare, "Japanese Treaty Ports," appendix.

31. According to Preston Nibley, a Church historian, this address was prepared by James E. Talmage. See Murray L. Nichols to Shinji Takagi, July 1996, in author's possession.

32. Grant, Journal, August 12–18.

33. J. H. Brooke owned the paper from 1870 to 1902 and edited it from 1893 to 1902. Hoare, "Japanese Treaty Ports," 339.

34. "Mr. Grant's Explanation," *Japan Mail*, September 6, 1901; "The Mormon Controversy," *Japan Mail*, September 7, 1901.

35. Brinkley was owner and editor from 1881 to 1912. Hoare, "Japanese Treaty Ports," 337. The *Mail*'s rivals accused Brinkley of being in Japanese pay, to which he admitted only that the Japanese government had a number of subscriptions to the *Mail*. According to Hoare, "Japanese Ports," 337–38, the

paper did tend to give the Japanese view, though it could be critical of the Japanese when British interests were concerned. The views expressed in the *Mail* on the Mormon missionaries, however, should not be taken to reflect the views of the Japanese government, which at least initially did not have any position on the matter.

36. Hoare, "Japanese Treaty Ports," 327.

37. *Japan Mail*, August 17, 1901; *Japan Herald*, August 17, 1901; "The Mormons," *Japan Times*, August 20, 1901, 2. The *Japan Times* was founded in 1897 by a group of prominent Japanese in Tokyo. In 1918 it absorbed the financially troubled *Japan Mail* and, for a time, changed its name to the *Japan Times and Mail*. See Ebihara, *Nihon Oji Shinbun Zasshi Shi*, 165–69.

38. Kobe was opened as a foreign settlement in 1868, some nine years after the opening of Yokohama. In 1901, it had about one thousand foreign residents, in contrast to over two thousand in Yokohama. Ebihara, *Nihon Oji Shinbun Zasshi Shi*, 77. It should be noted that these figures exclude Chinese residents. With Chinese included, the population of foreign residents was about five thousand in Yokohama and two thousand in Kobe. Hoare, "Japanese Treaty Ports," 47.

39. The *Kobe Chronicle*, founded by Robert Young in 1890, was renamed the *Japan Chronicle* later in 1901 and remained as one of the most influential foreign language newspapers in Japan throughout the pre-WWII period. The editorial office later moved to Tokyo. It is said that, in the early 20th century, it had the largest circulation of any English language newspaper in Japan, followed by the *Japan Herald*. See Ebihara, *Nihon Oji Shinbun Zasshi Shi*, 149, 203–4.

40. "Mormon Missions," *Kobe Chronicle*, weekly edition, August 21, 1901, 226.

41. Ebihara, *Nihon Oji Shinbun Zasshi Shi*, 204.

42. Hoare, "Japanese Treaty Ports," 340.

43. Hoare, "Japanese Treaty Ports," 339.

44. After the fact, towards the end of the year, the missionaries were told in a letter from the First Presidency to avoid newspaper controversy. See Ronald W. Walker, "Strangers in a Strange Land: Heber J. Grant and the Opening of the Japan Mission," *Journal of Mormon History* 13 (1986–87): 29.

45. The August 15 issue of the *Japan Herald* states that it had "a few days ago" chronicled the arrival of Apostle Heber J. Grant.

46. During the period under investigation, the *Yorozu Choho* did not publish an article of its own on the Mormon missionaries. On August 21 and 22, however, it quoted on its front pages the thrust of the editorials published in the *Jiji Shinpo*, the *Japan Times*, the *Osaka Asahi Shinbun*, and the *Mainichi*

Shinbun on Mormonism, thus acknowledging the width with which the arrival of the Mormon missionaries was known in Japanese society.

47. Hideo Ono, *Nihon Shinbun Hattatsu Shi* (Development history of Japanese newspapers) (Tokyo: Itsuki Shobo, 1982), 252–53.

48. Ono, *Nihon Shinbun Hattatsu Shi*, 226–40. In 1936 the *Jiji Shinpo* was merged with the *Tokyo Nichinichi Shinbun*, which was then under the ownership of the *Osaka Mainichi Shinbun*.

49. There were wire services by the late 1880s, providing national and international news to local newspapers. Tsushinshashi Kankokai, *Tsushinsha Shi* (History of news services) (Tokyo: Tsushinshashi Kankokai, 1958), 21–23.

50. This number includes the English-language *Japan Times*, the *Kokumin Shinbun*, and the *Shakai Shinpo*, in addition to the twelve Japanese-language newspapers listed in the appendix. Brady, "The Japanese Reaction to Mormonism," chapter 5, provides, without much commentary or analysis, a chronological listing of Mormon-related articles and editorials in seven Tokyo-based newspapers. It should be cautioned that Brady's translation is less than accurate, particularly when fine nuances, subtleties, and sarcasms are involved or when meaning must be understood within a particular social and historical context. Some translated texts are even outright misinterpretations or mistranslations (for example, the important *Mainichi* editorial of August 21, 1901, on pages 130–31).

51. Its name was changed to the *Chugai Nippo* in January 1902. See Ruikotsu Matani, *Ningen Ruikotsu* (Ruikotsu the man) (Kyoto: Chugai Nipposha, 1968), 202–5. Currently, the *Chugai Nippo* is published three times a week, with a circulation ranging between eighty and one hundred thousand. It is entirely devoted to reporting news of religious significance.

52. Goro Takahashi (1856–1935), a nationally recognized Christian scholar who was a member of the joint Protestant committee that translated the Bible into Japanese in the 1870s and 1880s, befriended the missionaries in late 1901 and offered to write a book to help the Church. His book, *Morumonkyo to Morumonkyoto* (Mormonism and the Mormons), was published in August 1902. In this process, at the request of Heber J. Grant, he translated the Articles of Faith and other Church tracts. His relationship with the Church, however, did not last long. Takagi and McIntyre, *Nihon Matsujitsu Seito Shi*, 57–62.

53. The expression *Batsujitsu Seito* was also used by the Tokyo *Mainichi Shinbun* in its front-page three-part article published on September 5, 7–8. During the post–World War II period, the same configuration of Chinese characters has been pronounced in the Church as *Matsujitsu Seito*.

54. Taylor, Journal, August 13, 1901.

55. See "Our Elders in Japan," *Deseret Evening News*, September 5, 1901, 4.

56. The *Hochi Shinbun*, the *Niroku Shinpo*, and the *Yomiuri Shinbun* (all of Tokyo) reported the event on August 19; the *Chukyo Shinpo* (Nagoya), the *Kyogaku Hochi* and the *Osaka Asahi* on August 21; the *Kyushu Nippo* (Fukuoka) and the *Moji Shinpo* on August 22; and the *Ryukyu Shinpo* on September 1.

57. Ono, *Nihon Shinbun Hattatsu Shi*, 257. The *Mainichi Shinbun* changed its name to the *Tokyo Mainichi Shinbun* in 1906.

58. Tamio Takemura, *Haisho Undo* (The antiprostitution movement) (Tokyo: Chuo Koronsha, 1982), 4–5. For instance, licensed prostitution was abolished in Britain in 1886.

59. Takemura, *Haisho Undo*, 2–7.

60. Takemura, *Haisho Undo*, 19–21; Kaneko Yoshimi, *Baisho no Shakaishi* (Social history of prostitution) (Tokyo: Yuzankaku, 1984), 45–47.

61. There were important legal developments as well. In February 1900, the Supreme Court ruled in a landmark case that a prostitute was not bound by any contract that required her to work to pay off her debt. The case involved an indentured prostitute in Hakodate, Hokkaido, by the name of Futa Sakai, who had borrowed money from the owner of a brothel and agreed to work for him for thirty months. She, however, did not like the work and desired to quit. Although the rulings of both the District Court and the appeal court were against Futa, the Supreme Court overruled, stating that, although the financial contract was valid, the labor contract was void as it violated the Prostitute Liberalization Law of 1872. On October 2, 1900, in response to the Supreme Court ruling, the Ministry of Home Affairs established a formal procedure stipulating that (1) no one under the age of eighteen could be a prostitute, (2) one must be registered at the police to be a prostitute, (3) cancellation of the registration could be done either in writing or verbally, and (4) the cancellation could not be challenged by anyone. Takemura, *Haisho Undo*, 22–23; Yoshimi, *Baisho no Shakaishi*, 103–4.

62. Yoshimi, *Baisho no Shakaishi*, 93.

63. Takemura, *Haisho Undo*, 21–24; "Joroshu ni Yoseru Fumi" (A letter addressed to prostitutes), *Toki no Koe*, August 1, 1900, 1.

64. The newspapers included the *Jiji* (August 6), the *Mainichi* (August 7), and the *Tokyo Asahi* (August 8). Takemura, *Haisho Undo*, 24; Yoshimi, *Baisho no Shakaishi*, 101–2.

65. The *Yamato Shinbun* was generally believed to be a nationalistic paper. Nishida, *Meiji Jidai no Shinbun to Zasshi*, 238–40.

66. An interesting sidelight in this context is that the Mormon quartet included not just one but two polygamists. Despite Grant's claim (made in the August 16 issue of the *Jiji Shinpo*) that the other two married elders were monogamists, Louis Kelsch, too, was in fact a polygamist. Kelsch, born in 1856

in Bavaria, Germany, was raised as a Catholic, emigrated to Nebraska in 1866 at the age of ten, and joined the Church while visiting Salt Lake City in 1876. He served missions for the Church in several areas, including the Southern States, the Northwestern States, the Eastern States, England, and Germany. When he was called to Japan, he was the president of the Northern States Mission. It was while he was serving in that capacity that he was asked by Lorenzo Snow to live the law of plural marriage, and with the permission of his first wife, Rosalia Atwood, he married Mary Lyerla. Dorothy K. Zitting and Barbara O. Kelsch, *The Life Story of Ludwig Koelsch (Louis A. Kelsch), 1856–1917* (Salt Lake City: By the family), 47.

67. *Kyogaku Hochi,* October 10, 1901. The whole text of the petition was reprinted in the October 25 issue.

68. *Jiji Shinpo,* March 29, 1907, 8.

69. See E. D. Thomas, "Netsuretsunaru Morumonkyo no Kyori" (The ardent doctrines of Mormonism), *Seiko* 20 (May 1911): 585–92.

70. Hirobumi Ito was born in the Choshu domain (now Yamaguchi Prefecture) and was sent clandestinely by the Choshu clan (one of the major forces opposing the Tokugawa shogunate) to study in England. Following the Meiji Restoration, he was appointed to various government positions, including junior councilor (in charge of foreign affairs), director of the Tax Division, vice-minister and then minister of public works, and minister of home affairs, before becoming the first prime minister under the modern cabinet system in 1885. He would again serve as prime minister three more times, finally resigning from the position in June 1901, shortly before the Mormon missionaries arrived. In 1906, Ito became the first Japanese resident general in Korea and, in 1907, he forced the Korean emperor to abdicate and established a full Japanese protectorate over Korea that paved the way for eventual annexation. Following his resignation as resident general in 1909, he was assassinated in Harbin, Manchuria, by a Korean nationalist.

Ito was largely responsible for establishing modern political institutions in Japan, most notably the Constitution of the Empire of Japan (the so-called Meiji Constitution), which was promulgated on February 11, 1889. He also helped draft the Peerage Act of July 1884, in which five hereditary titles for the nobility were established on the basis of the European system, namely, prince *(koshaku)*, marquis *(koshaku,* with a different character for *ko)*, count *(hakushaku)*, viscount *(shishaku)*, and baron *(danshaku)*. In this system, individuals with non-aristocratic backgrounds could be awarded hereditary titles for distinguished service to the nation. Ito himself (who was of the low-ranking samurai background) was appointed count in 1884, was promoted to the rank of marquis in 1895, and eventually rose to the highest rank of prince in 1907.

71. Angus Munn Cannon was born in Liverpool, England, on May 17, 1834. He was the business manager and later director and vice-president of the *Deseret News*. In the Church, he presided over the Salt Lake Stake from 1876 to 1904, when the stake was divided into the Salt Lake, Liberty, Pioneer, and Ensign stakes. He was then called as the patriarch of the new Salt Lake Stake and served in that capacity until his death on June 7, 1915. See Donald Q. Cannon, "Angus M. Cannon: Pioneer, President, Patriarch," in *Supporting Saints: Life Stories of Nineteenth-Century Mormons*, ed. Donald Q. Cannon and David J. Whittaker (Provo, Utah: Religious Studies Center, Brigham Young University, 1985) 369–401; and Andrew Jenson, *Latter-day Saint Biographical Encyclopedia: A Compilation of Biographical Sketches of Prominent Men and Women in The Church of Jesus Christ of Latter-day Saints*, 4 vols. (Salt Lake City: Andrew Jenson History, 1901–36), 1:292-95.

72. On the very first leg of its journey through the United States and several European countries, the Iwakura Mission became stranded by snow and stayed in Salt Lake City from February 4, 1872, to February 21, 1872. Charles Lanman, *The Japanese in America* (New York: University Publishing, 1872), 8, 23–24.

In the April 6, 1901, issue of the *Deseret Evening News*, we find the following statement of Angus M. Cannon:

> I have known Count [sic] Ito, now Prime Minister Ito, for a good many years. I met him first in the spring of 1871 [sic] at Ogden and traveled with him over the Union Pacific as far as Omaha. . . . The conductor knew me, and Count [sic] Ito on learning that there was a newspaper man on the train, expressed a desire to see him. I was introduced to him by the conductor and we soon found ourselves in an interesting conversation. . . .
>
> [He] was a bright, earnest and interesting character who absorbed information as a sponge does water. His people and their advancement seemed to be his particular pride and ambition. . . .
>
> [He] exhibited a lively interest in the 'Mormon' people, the origin of their faith and the struggles through which they had passed. He asked me for a detailed statement of their history. I gave it to him and he listened most attentively during the two days and a half that we were fellow travellers and expressed a desire to learn more of them. After we separated, I wrote home to my brother, President George Q. Cannon . . . to forward him a full list of books containing the principles of 'Mormonism.'

I heard nothing further of Count [sic] Ito until, I think, in 1873 [sic] when I met him again, this time in Salt Lake City. I recognized him at once and his recognition of me was just as prompt. With him were a number of Japanese gentlemen and one of our own officials from Washington. The latter marvelled at the familiarity that Ito showed concerning our faith and people, adding that his knowledge seemed much more extensive in this particular than that of most Americans. Ito had now been promoted to the position of head of the board of public works, a very important office in Japan. I met him a third time in Ogden, later. He was then homeward bound from Washington, having been entrusted with important dispatches to the emperor.... He gave me the most urgent kind of an invitation to visit him in his own home should I ever have occasion to go to Japan. ("Opening of a Mission in Japan," *Deseret Evening News,* April 6, 1901, 9)

73. Yoshimi, *Baisho no Shakaishi,* 52.

74. "Ito Ko no Danwa (Saying of Marquis Ito)," *Fujin Shinpo* 20 (September 15, 1896): 30–31.

75. Quoted in *Deseret Evening News,* August 13, 1901, 2. *Mikado* is an English word for the Japanese emperor.

76. Some newspapers, such as the August 17 issue of the *Tokyo Asahi,* had the heading "A Mormon Elder Shakes Hands with Marquis Ito." It should be noted, however, that the Japanese verb "shake" in its infinitive form, as it typically appears in a newspaper heading, may indicate a future intention, not necessarily an accomplished fact.

77. Elder Grant was in Tokyo on August 20, August 21, August 27, September 2, and September 3. If it took place at all, the meeting between Grant and Ito could not have been held much later. From September 6 to September 15, Grant made a tour of Japan, travelling through Lake Biwa, Suruga Bay, Kanazawa, Toyama, Naoetsu, and Karuizawa. On Ito's part, he left for the United States on September 18 to meet President Theodore Roosevelt (who had just assumed office at the death of President William McKinley Jr.) and to receive an honorary doctorate from Yale University (in its bicentennial commemoration on October 23). He then made a tour of Europe and did not return to Japan until February of the following year. See Minoru Toyoda, *Shodai Sori Ito Hirobumi* (Hirobumi Ito, the first prime minister), 2 vols. (Tokyo: Kodansha, 1987), 2:256–64.

As to the whereabouts of Ito in August, although he was spending his summer in the northern Japan Sea coast, he was in his villa in Oiso on the Pacific coast on August 8 and August 25 (according to the daily reports published in the *Tokyo Nichinichi Shinbun,* which was controlled by the ruling Choshu faction of the government with Ito at the top). This means that Ito was in Tokyo at least twice during August 8–25. But as Grant was not successful in meeting the people he had the letters of introduction to on August 21, the only possible day on which he could have seen Ito was August 22, if the meeting took place at all. Nishida, *Meiji Jidai no Shinbun to Zasshi,* 167.

78. The man Akimoto must be Masanori Akimoto, a member of the 1894 entering class at Keio Gijuku (an elite private academy in Tokyo), who was the manager of Japanese laborers at the LDS Church–owned Utah-Idaho Sugar Company. See Eric Walz to Shinji Takagi, December 11, 1998, in author's possession. Keio Gijuku began its college division in 1890, with fifty-nine students in literature, economics, and law, offering three years of instruction. It is not surprising at all that a person of that background knew some prominent government figures. Fukuzawa Kenkyu Center, *Keio Gijuku Nyushacho* (Registration book of entering students at Keio Gijuku) (Tokyo: Keio Gijuku, 1986), 4:345; and Keio Gijuku, *Keio Gijuku Hyakunenshi* (Centennial history of Keio Gijuku), 3 vols. (Tokyo: Keio Gijuku, 1960), 2:52. Particularly in Idaho, the Utah-Idaho Sugar Company employed immigrant workers, including Japanese, because "thinning" beets to create living space was "stoop labor," which most American farmers would not perform. Leonard J. Arrington, *Beet Sugar in the West: A History of the Utah-Idaho Sugar Company, 1891–1966* (Seattle: University of Washington Press, 1966), 23, 71–73.

79. "Constitution of the Empire of Japan, 1889," in *Japan: An Illustrated Encyclopedia,* 2 vols. (Tokyo: Kodansha, 1993), 1:232–35.

80. The dates on which these newspapers picked up this position were August 20 for *Chugoku, Hinode,* and *Osaka Mainichi;* August 21 for *Moji Shinpo;* August 22 for *Kyushu Shinbun;* and August 23 for *Yonezawa Shinbun.*

81. Japan Mission, Historical records and minutes, August 27, 1901, Archives Division, Historical Department, The Church of Jesus Christ of Latter-day Saints, Salt Lake City.

82. Japan Mission, Historical records and minutes, September 2–3, 1901.

83. Some of the newspapers dealing with this issue were the *Kobe Yushin,* the *Kyochu Nippo,* the *Kyushu Nichinichi,* the *Yamanashi Nichinichi,* the *Hinode,* and the *Yonezawa Shinbun.*

84. Taylor, Journal, September 6, 1901; Grant, Journal, September 6, 1901.

85. Taylor, Journal, September 20–21, 1901; Japan Mission, Historical records and minutes, September 17, 20–21, 1901.

86. "Monthly Communications," *Chuo Koron* 16 (October 1901): 70. The dates of the missionaries' actions were inaccurately reported by the press.

87. Taylor, Journal, October 5, 1901.

88. Among the national magazines, the article published in the September 5 issue of the *Taiyo* argued against allowing the Mormons to preach in Japan, while the editorial in the September issue of the *Chuo Koron* supported the prerogative of the Mormons to do so, saying that there were some Shinto and Buddhist sects that should be banned first. The editorial then went on to say that, compared with the dubious character of these sects, Mormonism was even "respectable." Gakujin Tatsuyama, "Morumonshu Kitaru (Mormonism Has Come)," *Taiyo* 7 (September 5, 1901): 57–58; "Morumonshu (Mormonism)," *Chuo Koron* 16 (September 1901): 64.

89. Nishida, *Meiji Jidai no Shinbun to Zasshi*, 157; Hideo Ono, *Shinbun no Rekishi* (History of newspapers), enlarged ed. (Tokyo: Tokyodo Shuppan, 1970), 50. The separate names were kept until 1940, when the *Asahi Shinbun* became the common name for both *Asahi* papers.

90. The process towards a corporate form of management was completed when they legally became joint stock companies in 1918 (in the case of the *Mainichi*) and 1919 (the *Asahi*).

91. In 1900, Hara left the company to join the political party founded by Hirobumi Ito. He later served in the cabinets of three prime ministers (including Ito) and as prime minister from 1918 to 1921, when he was assassinated.

92. At that time, the *Osaka Asahi* and the *Yorozu Choho* (of Tokyo) were called the two giants, representing Western and Eastern Japan, respectively, each claiming about 120,000 subscribers. See Ono, *Shinbun no Rekishi*, 66–67, 76; and Ono, *Nihon Shinbun Hattatsu Shi*, 316.

93. Okano was one of three leading English-language reporters. Nishida, *Meiji Jidai no Shinbun to Zasshi*, 240. One of the other two was Eigo Fukai, of the *Kokumin Shinbun*, who later became governor of the Bank of Japan. According to the calling card pasted in Alma O. Taylor's scrapbook, Okano had apparently been educated in the United States, with an LL.B., a Litt.B., and a doctorate in public speech.

94. Nishida, *Meiji Jidai no Shinbun to Zasshi*, 241.

95. Nishida, *Meiji Jidai no Shinbun to Zasshi*, 176, 237; Ono, *Shinbun no Rekishi*, 64–65. The *Niroku Shinpo* was originally founded in 1893 but went out of circulation in 1895. It was started again in 1900 and began to compete with the *Yorozu Choho* for the same type of readers. By 1903 it surpassed the *Yorozu Choho* in the number of readers.

96. Alma O. Taylor, Scrapbook, 1901–24, Church Archives. It also shows that, on the previous day, the missionaries had met another reporter, Rihei Onishi of the *Jiji Shinpo*.

97. Grant, Journal, September 3, 1901.

98. In principle, Japanese newspaper editorials are unsigned.

99. Okano's generous attitude toward the Mormons, however, was made fun of by the author of the article published in *Taiyo* 7 (September 5, 1901): 57–58.

100. At the end of 1896, there were eighty-seven respectable newspapers in Japan outside of Tokyo, Osaka, Kyoto, and Okinawa. Nishida, *Meiji Jidai no Shinbun to Zasshi*, 251.

101. The two magazines were the *Chuo Koron* and the *Taiyo*.

102. Goro Takahashi, "Morumonkyo to Ramakyo (Mormonism and Lamaism)," *Taiyo* 7 (October 5, 1901): 21–25. See Taylor, Journal, August 25, 1901, for an offer of a speaking engagement in a large public hall in Tokyo. On Goro Takahashi's involvement with the Church, see note 52.

103. In his journal entry on August 18, 1901, Taylor spoke of "a majority" of the visitors the missionaries received as "fraudulent and absolutely devoid of desire to assist us," while the "expressions of friendship" came from "their pockets rather than their hearts." See Nichols, "History of the Japan Mission," 17–19; and Takagi and McIntyre, *Nihon Matsujitsu Seito Shi*, 53–65.

8

Two Meiji Scholars Introduce the Mormons to Japan

Frederick R. Brady

By the time Elder Heber J. Grant and his three companions—Louis A. Kelsch, Horace S. Ensign, and Alma O. Taylor—arrived in Yokohama to begin their missionary labors in August 1901, other Christian denominations had been proselytizing actively in Japan for over thirty years. The entire Bible had been translated into Japanese nearly fifteen years earlier, and a native clergy had arisen. Influential, though few in number, the Christians, both native and foreign, were firmly entrenched in Japan, and they were curious about and apprehensive of Mormonism.

The press soon learned of the arrival of the Mormon missionaries, and Elder Grant found himself the center of much attention.[1] His notoriety increased when the landlord of a foreign-owned boardinghouse denied Elder Grant and his companions rooms because Elder Grant was a polygamist.[2] The incident was reported in several English and Japanese newspapers, and at about this time reporters from two leading papers, the *Jiji Shimpō* and *Niroku Shinpō*, interviewed Elder Grant directly. Both interviews were highly informative and relatively free of bias, but they, like the articles in the other newspapers, focused primarily on polygamy.[3]

Many of these articles and letters in newspapers exhibited great animosity toward the Latter-day Saints, mainly because of their practice of polygamy. To lay to rest some of the rumors about himself and the Church and to actively begin his labors, Elder Grant met with the editors of several English-language newspapers, leaving calling cards he had printed in Japanese that bore his portrait. One of Elder Grant's major initial activities in Japan was replying to letters and editorials about the Church.

Although Elder Grant and the other missionaries could write the letters and rebuttals to newspapers about the slanderous articles by themselves in English, they needed a teacher to help them with the Japanese language. Unfortunately, many qualified teachers were also missionaries of other churches and were hostile toward Mormonism. Finally the Latter-day Saint elders found two Christian Japanese gentlemen who willingly gave them assistance, and the elders eventually learned the language well enough to produce their own literature, creating a foundation for the Church in Japan. One of these teachers was Takahashi Gorō.

Takahashi Gorō

Takahashi Gorō was a teacher and a scholar of renown who had participated in the translation of the Bible into Japanese.[4] Impressed with a magazine article in which Takahashi defended the Latter-day Saints, Elder Grant invited him to dinner, and a friendship resulted. Takahashi spoke fluent English, and during his weekly dinners with the elders he learned a great deal about the history and doctrines of the Church. He offered to write a book about the Church, finance its publication from his own pocket, and receive his reimbursement from its sales. Elder Grant was very enthusiastic, and he lent Takahashi a number of books and photographs to use in his research.[5]

Takahashi's book, *Morumonkyō to Morumon kyōto* (Mormonism and Mormons), was published in August 1902.[6] A thick tome, it is filled with philosophizing about polygamy and speculation about the origins of the American Indians. It might have sold better without this padding; the poor sales were to prove disillusioning. But the basic material about the history and teachings of the Church, illustrated with photographs, is excellent, and the viewpoint of the entire work is one of an admiring observer. Interestingly, the first translation of the Articles of Faith into Japanese is found in the book, the modern version of which differs only slightly from Takahashi's version in some of the articles.[7] Another strong point is the fine translation of Joseph Smith's personal account of the First Vision.

Sadly, Takahashi had a falling out with the missionaries in late 1903, several months after Elder Grant had been released and had returned to America. The circumstances were tragic, and to relate them we must backtrack to March 1902.

Shortly before leaving to attend the Church's general conference in Salt Lake City in spring 1902, Elder Grant baptized two Japanese converts. The first, Nakazawa Hajime, was a Shintō priest who spoke no English.[8] Nakazawa began to be disaffected when Elder Grant refused to lend him money to start a new vocation.[9] Finally, Nakazawa was caught attempting to burglarize the mission headquarters. The elders excommunicated him on the spot and turned him over to the police. Hearing news of the arrest and witnessing the associated small sensation, Takahashi wrote a disgruntled letter to President Horace S. Ensign, Grant's successor. Following are excerpts from the letter Takahashi wrote President Ensign, which Elder Alma O. Taylor inserted in his personal journal.

> My dear Rev. Mr. Ensign,—
>
> I am very sorry to learn that Nakazawa has become a thief on account of his poverty. You know the fact better than any other in the world. I heartily sympathize with him. . . . Everybody knows that Nakazawa lost his lucrative profession for sympathizing with "Mormonism." You cannot forget it, as no one can. But Mr. Grant quite cold-bloodedly, has left him destitute of help. . . . Mr. Grant's sudden change of his proceedings and his non-fulfillment of his promises have contributed more than any other to check your progress, or rather to annihilate your prospects. . . . The public has forgotten you, and my book has sold only <u>a few copies</u>. . . .
>
> In short, some persons are now very angry with you for this unhappy issue of one of your "brothers," and ready to assail you to crush your prospects trumpeting your cold-bloodedness in respect to Mr. N. Of course, I shall and will endeavor to defend you, the consequence is to be much feared. I believe you remember what I have often spoken about Nakazawa's future. I was right to my great grief. I cannot write any more. Adieu!
>
> Yours truly
> Takahashi Goro

Elder Taylor then added the following commentary in his journal:

> The purpose for inserting this letter here is to record the sentiments of a soured friend. This man Takahashi's name, appears many times in this journal of my mission to Japan. He was our closest and most daring advocate just as long as the phantomistic idea he had formed concerning the wealth and position he would obtain by befriending and writing about us, lasted. In my opinion he is a man who loves foreigners so long as he can make a fat living off them and turns traitor . . . as soon as he finds they cannot be duped neither by his flattering speeches nor by his threats. His remarks concerning Bro. Grant's cold-bloodedness and non-fulfillment of promises are a reflection upon his own dishonesty and breach of promise.[10]

Elder Taylor was saddened, but apparently not surprised, by what he saw as Takahashi's duplicity. The rest of this journal entry indicates Elder Taylor was used to such treatment, though he deeply regretted it. It is also obvious from this incident why he did not ask for Takahashi's help when the Japanese translation of the Book of Mormon began in 1904.

Still the missionaries lent and sold *Morumonkyō* as a proselytizing tool, which they had hoped would be the first book about Mormonism ever published in Japanese. If so, that was not the case.

Uchida Yū

In January 1902, eight months before Takahashi's book was published, a writer named Uchida Yū had published a booklet entitled *Morumon shū* (The Mormon sect).[11] There is almost no information available about the author, but he was probably a young scholar and perhaps a Christian.[12]

Uchida's book is brief and to the point, but a wealth of misinformation suggests careless scholarship and prejudiced sources. In contrast to Takahashi, he never cites a source, but occasionally refers in passing to "accounts by Joseph Smith's enemies" and "Smith's own history." Despite continually asserting his objectivity, Uchida expresses frank distaste for certain aspects of the Church in some instances and guarded admiration in others. Still, in spite of its flaws, *Morumon shū* is an adequate introduction to the religion, sufficient to arouse curiosity and raise questions.

While we know Takahashi spent many hours conversing with and getting background information from Elder Grant, the extent of Uchida's contact with the Mormon missionaries is unclear. He never mentions meeting the elders, but he does note the death of President Lorenzo Snow in October 1901, and it is likely he learned about it from Elder Grant. On their part, the missionaries experienced a steady stream of callers, many of whom seemed to want only to practice their English.[13] If Uchida were among these callers, he would not have stood out. Also, his clumsy renderings of Book of Mormon and American names show that he must not have spoken long with the elders, if at all.

The matter of terminology shows another great difference between the scholarship of Takahashi and Uchida and the extent of their different degrees of contact with Mormon missionaries. Uchida's translations of Mormon terms are at great variance with the terms used by the Church in Japan today; some of Uchida's translations are from the Protestant lexicon and others are merely poor translations of his own. In contrast, Takahashi's translations show that he had discussed the meanings with Elder Grant before giving interpretations. Takahashi seems even to have coined a few new words. In helping the Saints in Japan develop a lexicon of their own, he provided the Church a great service; in fact, most of his terms are still used by the Church in Japan.

Joseph Smith and Polygamy

Although there are many important similarities and differences between the two books *Morumonkyō to Morumon kyōto* and *Morumon shū*, it is in their treatment of two major subjects—the character of Joseph Smith and the Church's practice of polygamy—that they show most clearly the differences between the two authors' viewpoints.

In Uchida's opinion, polygamy and Joseph Smith's character cannot be considered separately. His book begins with a denunciation of polygamy, and he plainly saw Joseph Smith as an undisciplined, irresponsible charlatan, and country boor whose natural abilities were obscured by a taste for adultery. Of polygamy he says:

> If a man hears the word "Mormonism" he immediately associates it with polygamy. . . . However, at present, due to legal prohibitions against polygamy in the United States, where Mormonism arose, and

> also because of society's condemnation of polygamy as an immoral practice, the Mormon Church abolished the doctrine sanctioning polygamy ten years ago. Nevertheless, while appearing outwardly to conform, we see that the Mormons are in fact continuing to adhere to this evil practice.
>
> Polygamy is a barbaric custom.... Even so, ... strange religious customs still exist in ... uncultured lands. But Mormonism has appeared in an enlightened society, in ... America! ...
>
> Since the American government abolished polygamy, the Mormons have ceased to preach it publicly as a doctrine; still, even now it is practiced privately. Of course the Mormon scriptures prohibit it too, but it originated when Smith received a so-called revelation about it on July 12, 1843, in Nauvoo. Smith from the first had affections for many women besides his legal wife Emma, but when that fact began to be openly and loudly criticized in public, Smith said he had received a revelation stating that polygamy was a divine mystery approved by God, and he ignored the rage of his wife and the reviling of society. But it was not until 1852 that polygamy was announced publicly....
>
> ... within the sect there are those who oppose polygamy and have formed a new, monogamous faction within Mormonism....
>
> There is no other single reason for the Mormons' having been ostracized.[14]

Such an attitude may seem hypocritical to those familiar with the ancient practice of concubinage in Japan, but Uchida is speaking for those Japanese who had accepted traditional Christian morality as their standard. Almost since the opening of their country, the Japanese had felt that a certain amount of Westernization (often confused with civilization) was necessary to gain acceptance among the industrialized Western nations. Internal and external pressures had forced a number of political and social reforms, and forward-thinking Japanese—many of whom were greatly influenced by Christianity—were ready to repudiate anything looked at with disapproval by the Christian nations. This is the view finally taken by the *Jiji Shimpō* and the *Niroku Shinpō* articles concerning polygamy and Mormonism, though these newspapers had at first treated Elder Grant with great kindness.[15]

Uchida also took an antagonistic view of most of Joseph Smith's deeds, believing and passing on various rumors and exaggerations:

His parents were so poor that they were subjected to suspicions of being stupid, lawless, and given to thieving. Of course, one need not hesitate to state that Smith's lack of education was due to his disadvantaged childhood. According to accounts by his enemies, he was given by nature to idle fancies and was, though deluded, a good person; and when we refer to Smith's own history of his life we find that this is true. . . .

Smith was from among the illiterate masses and was not a polished speaker. Whenever he was cornered during a discussion it was his custom to assume a dignified attitude, open his mouth in the manner of a holy prophet of God, and expound a didactic conclusion convincing to the simple-minded. He also managed all of the church's internal and external affairs, suppressing any internal discord, through the use of these revelations. . . .

Because Smith was an uneducated prophet with no self-control nor morals, because these flaws became known to some people, and because among the Saints some influential members were loudly criticizing him, some gradually began to forsake him, and even his inner circle of associates started to show evidence of a coming rift. At the same time, the brethren of the church's rank and file were being persecuted by the Gentiles and there was a movement in Missouri to throw the Saints out of the state. Being anxious about the sect's prospects during this time, . . . Smith's faction set up a secret clique called the Danites in October 1838. Their sworn purpose was to protect Smith and his doctrine from enemies and to make him governor of the state, then president of the United States, and finally ruler of all the world. . . .

In this way Smith was using his sect at Nauvoo as the gateway to power, . . . and thus the seeds of his evil and immoral actions began to blossom and bear fruit.[16]

Takahashi did not believe Joseph Smith was a prophet either, but he did believe in his sincerity. Takahashi, unlike Uchida, did not believe that polygamy was a relic of barbarism, and he took the Latter-day Saints at their word when they said they would not preach it in Japan.

Polygamy is the characteristic by which Mormonism is known throughout the world, but Mormonism is not alone in the practice. In Buddhism, too, polygamy—or, rather, concubinage—is allowed under some circumstances. And India is a polygamous country.

> Tibet is a polygamous country. Concubinage is practiced in China. Is not concubinage practiced in Japan? . . .
>
> . . . Over ten years ago, President [Wilford] Woodruff, in accordance with federal law, abolished plural marriage. Are the Mormons going to preach it in Japan? Though suffering cowardly slander, they have determined not to preach it, in keeping with Smith's spirit of submitting to governmental authority. Some continue to loudly attack the Mormons concerning this matter of polygamy, but they are wasting their arrows without a target.[17]

Because of polygamy's long history and considerable prevalence throughout the world, including Japan, Takahashi saw no reason why the Mormons should not be allowed to practice it. But he is sidestepping an issue: does popularity alone make concubinage or polygamy right? The adversaries of the Church might have replied that Elder Grant was indeed preaching polygamy in Japan, because that was how they saw his futile attempts to explain the practice when it was attacked in the newspapers.[18]

Takahashi included in his book a brief summary of the doctrine of plural marriage as it appears in Doctrine and Covenants 132, but this summary does not do the subject justice. When one considers his excellent translations in full of the Articles of Faith and the account of the First Vision, his treatment of the plural marriage revelation is a keen disappointment.

Takahashi also makes fewer judgmental comments about Joseph Smith and his character than Uchida does. Takahashi frankly admired and obviously considered Joseph Smith a great man, continually giving Joseph the benefit of the doubt. In his introduction to his translation of the First Vision, he reminds the reader that Joseph Smith was "only an artless youth," asks how "such a one [could] sinisterly aspire to take advantage of the confusion of society and deceive the whole world," and then says with emphasis, "*However much we want to call Smith an impostor and a deceiver, it is yet too early to make such a statement.*"[19] Takahashi emphasizes this point further on:

> It is claimed that Peter, James and John appeared to Smith and Cowdery in June of 1829 and ordained them to . . . the priesthood of Melchizedek. Earlier, John the Baptist had ordained them to the priesthood of Aaron. . . . Though Smith did not belong to any church, it

is claimed that—like Saint Paul of old, who received the apostolic witness directly from Christ—Smith was given the power of the highest priesthood directly from this ancient group. Of course, this is hard for an outsider to accept. But if it is true that Christ appeared to Paul, is it unreasonable for Peter, John and others to have appeared to Smith?[20]

Though Elder Grant had reported happily on the upcoming publication of Takahashi's book at the April 1902 general conference, *Morumonkyō* was not able to do as much good as had been hoped. Uchida's book probably did not do much harm, either—Japan was a hard mission for Christian missionaries of all denominations.[21] Polygamy then continued to be the major reason for Japan's cold reception of Mormonism. Regardless, the Latter-day Saint missionaries continued to protest the accusation that they were preaching polygamy:

> We here forcefully reaffirm that no missionary, officer or member of the Church of Jesus Christ of Latter-day Saints in Japan is permitted to practice polygamy, nor is authority given to preach this doctrine to the inhabitants of any part of the Empire. Enemies of our religion who claim in writing or speech that the Mormon Church is anywhere in the world preaching, urging or allowing its members to practice plural marriage are guilty of falsehood.[22]

The elders eventually learned Japanese well enough to begin producing their own literature. Despite the biased and inaccurate press the Church initially received, the missionary work certainly did not cease there. Eighty-eight missionaries labored in twenty-nine different locations, mostly in the regions of Tokyo, Sapporo, and Osaka, and 166 baptisms were performed from 1902 to 1924.[23]

On July 31, 1924, Heber J. Grant—by that time Church President—closed the Japan Mission. It would not be reopened for twenty-four years. If statistics are a measure of success, the low number of baptisms during nearly a quarter century may seem to indicate that the mission was a failure, but the opposite is true. Many impressive accomplishments in this early period established the foundation for the growth of the Church after World War II. Among them are the following, showing that success is not always measured in numbers.

- An Apostle of the Lord dedicated Japan for the preaching of the gospel.

- The Book of Mormon was translated into Japanese and specially bound copies were presented to the Imperial Family and top government officials.
- A hymnbook, a history of the Church, a biography of Joseph Smith, and other literature were translated and published.
- Some Japanese members remained faithful during the war, including several who emigrated to Hawaii to establish a Japanese branch of the Church there and to perform temple ordinances.
- Missionaries in Japan gained priceless experience, benefitting them, the Church, and their communities. A few returned to Japan later as mission leaders.
- Hundreds of English-language books about Japan and East Asia collected by missionaries, particularly Alma O. Taylor and Elbert D. Thomas, later became the nucleus of the East Asian collection at the University of Utah's Marriott Library.
- Church leaders as a whole gained some understanding of Japan, making them better prepared to re-establish the Church there in 1948.
- The Church's own Japanese lexicon was largely established, making language study and translation work for post–World War II missionaries much easier.

Postwar Japan was a different nation, humbled by the horrors of war and more receptive to the message brought by new missionaries who built on a foundation laid by others earlier in the century. Tens of thousands of Japanese have been baptized. Chapels, stake centers, and temples are found throughout the nation, and Japan is even supplying leaders to the Church in general. Now, more than a century after Elder Grant's first efforts, we can say confidently that he and his companions put the Church in Japan on the road to success.

An earlier version of this article appeared as Frederick R. Brady, "Two Meiji Scholars Introduce the Mormons to Japan," BYU Studies 23, no. 2 (1983): 167–78.

Notes

1. See Shinji Takagi, "Mormons in the Press: Reactions to the 1901 Opening of the Japan Mission," *BYU Studies* 40, no. 1 (2001): 141–75, reprinted herein.

2. *The Japan Times*, August 22, 1901, 3; F. Staniland to the Editor, *The Japan Weekly Mail*, August 31, 1901, 226; *Hōchi Shinbun*, August 19, 1901, 3; *Yomiuri Shinbun*, August 19, 1901. These letters are translated by and quoted in Frederick R. Brady, "The Japanese Reaction to Mormonism and the Translation of Mormon Scripture into Japanese" (master's thesis, Sophia University International College, 1979), 94, 97–98, 126–27.

3. See Brady, "Japanese Reaction to Mormonism," chapter 5.

4. Otis Cary, *A History of Christianity in Japan: Protestant Missions*, 2 vols. (Tokyo: Charles E. Tuttle, 1976), 1:149.

5. Heber J. Grant, in *Seventy-Second Annual Conference of The Church of Jesus Christ of Latter-day Saints* (Salt Lake City: The Church of Jesus Christ of Latter-day Saints, 1902), 47. See also Murray L. Nichols, "History of the Japan Mission of The Church of Jesus Christ of Latter-day Saints, 1901–1924" (master's thesis, Brigham Young University, 1957), 19, 34.

6. Takahashi Gorō, *Morumonkyō to Morumon kyōto* (Mormonism and Mormons) (Tokyo: by the author, 1902). A copy is in L. Tom Perry Special Collections, Harold B. Lee Library, Brigham Young University, Provo, Utah. The missionaries called the book "Mormons and Mormonism." For a translation of significant portions, see Brady, "Japanese Reaction to Mormonism," chapter 7.

7. Takahashi, *Morumonkyō to Morumon kyōto*, 17–22.

8. Nichols, "History of the Japan Mission," 25–26.

9. Heber J. Grant, in *Seventy-Third Annual Conference of The Church of Jesus Christ of Latter-day Saints* (Salt Lake City: The Church of Jesus Christ of Latter-day Saints, 1903), 13.

10. Alma O. Taylor, "Journals, 1901–1946," December 17–20, 1903, L. Tom Perry Special Collections, Harold B. Lee Library, Brigham Young University, Provo, Utah. See also, Reid L. Neilson, "*The Japanese Missionary Journals of Elder Alma O. Taylor, 1901–10*" (master's thesis, Brigham Young University, 2001; BYU Studies and Joseph Fielding Smith Institute for Latter-day Saint History, 2001).

11. Uchida Yū Akira, *Morumon shū* (The Mormon sect) (Tokyo: Bunmeidō, 1902). For a translation of significant portions, see Brady, "Japanese Reaction to Mormonism," chapter 6.

12. An Uchida Akira wrote a book entitled *Jidai no dōryoku* (Efforts of an era) in 1938. I identify him with Uchida Yū because it was and is common for Japanese writers to use pseudonyms, and scholars prefer Chinese-sounding

names, which are often adapted from their given names. The character for *Yū* is the same as one of the characters in *Akira*.

13. Nichols, "History of the Japan Mission," 17.

14. Uchida, *Morumon shū*, 1–3, 68–69, 91–92. For translations, see Brady, "Japanese Reaction to Mormonism," 140–41, 158–59, 161.

15. Brady, "Japanese Reaction to Mormonism," 126–28.

16. Uchida, *Morumon shū*, 9–10, 21–22, 26, 28. See Brady, "Japanese Reaction to Mormonism," 142, 145, 147–48.

17. Takahashi, *Morumonkyō to Morumon kyōto,* 221, 233–34. See Brady, "Japanese Reaction to Mormonism," 178–79.

18. Brady, "Japanese Reaction to Mormonism," 109–10.

19. Takahashi, *Morumonkyō to Morumon kyōto,* 33. See Brady, "Japanese Reaction to Mormonism," 168; emphasis in original.

20. Takahashi, *Morumonkyō to Morumon kyōto,* 172–73. See Brady, "Japanese Reaction to Mormonism," 172.

21. Heber J. Grant, in *Seventy-Second Annual Conference of The Church of Jesus Christ of Latter-day Saints* (Salt Lake City: The Church of Jesus Christ of Latter-day Saints, 1902), 45–49.

22. Alma O. Taylor, "The Mormon Church and Polygamy," appendix to John W. Stoker, trans., *Matsujitsu Seito Iesu Kirisuto Kyōkai Ryakushi* (*A Brief history of The Church of Jesus Christ of Latter-day Saints*), by Edward H. Anderson (Tokyo: Japan L.D.S. Mission, 1907), 24–25. See Brady, "Japanese Reaction to Mormonism," 116.

23. Nichols, "History of the Japan Mission," appendixes C and E.

9

Languages of the Lord: The Japanese Translations of the Book of Mormon

Van C. Gessel

Some years ago, in an introductory note to my translation of the novel *The Samurai* by the Japanese Christian writer Endō Shūsaku, I wrote:

> The process of dismantling a work of foreign literature brick by brick and rebuilding it on one's native soil is seldom a thoroughly satisfying experience. At times the foundation will not conform to the unfamiliar terrain; occasionally it is only that the sun-porch looks somewhat ludicrous in a region of incessant rains. In an essay many years back, Mr. Endō very properly referred to literary translation as a task of "transformation," for a piece of literature that is forcibly uprooted from its natural environment and thrust into strange surroundings will of necessity go through some painful but necessary changes.[1]

The careful dismantling of a text, not to mention the rebuilding of it, becomes an even more daunting task when the text is a sacred document regarded as the word and will of the Lord and as the key to conversion. Over the course of the twentieth century, the entire Book of Mormon has been translated into Japanese three times. The history of the translation process is in a sense a microcosmic view of the progress of the Church in Japan, replicating the shift from foreign to native administration of Church business. The first translation was done by a young American missionary who stood at the side of Heber J. Grant when Japan was dedicated for the preaching of the gospel in 1901. After the calamities of World War II, a small but dedicated group of Japanese individuals joined the Church, and the first of their number to be baptized was also charged with producing a second translation of the sacred text. Finally, as the Japanese Church grew in membership and became fully organized, a native committee was commissioned by the First Presidency in the mid-1980s to create yet a third translation.

The First Translation

The story of the first translation of the Book of Mormon into Japanese is so extraordinary that I must try to sketch its rough outlines. That initial translation, started in 1904 and completed five years later, was done by Alma O. Taylor (illus. 9-1), a remarkable young American missionary who, when he received the call to undertake the translation, prayed

> for the assistance of the Holy Spirit & gift of interpretation & translation that I may be successful in writing for the Japanese in their own tongue the great truths & powerful testimonies of the Book of Mormon. While my heart throbs with gratitude unspeakable for the honor conferred upon me yet every time I contemplate the magnitude and importance . . . of . . . the work before me and the responsibility it places upon me, I fear & tremble from head to foot and sense a weakness such as I have never before known. O God, remember thy young servant. Magnify him in his new calling. Cause that his mind shall be lit up by the direct inspiration of Heaven that the task which now lies before him might be successfully accomplished by him in the time which Thou hast alloted and make Thine alloted time not too far distant. O Almighty God, forget not the way in which Thou didst support & bless Thy servant Joseph Smith in his weakness and didst make it possible for him to bring forth to the

Illus. 9-1. Alma O. Taylor, taken in Tokyo, Japan, ca. 1906, by S. Yeghi.

Courtesy Church Archives, The Church of Jesus Christ of Latter-day Saints

world the most glorious & authentic sacred record the world has, . . . and, in this time, when that sacred record is to be written in a language made up of strange characters & expressions like unto the . . . strangeness of the Egyptian writings & language found on the Gold Plates, again open the windows of heaven and pour forth upon Thy young servant, Alma, the gift of tongues & translation to such an extent that the purity of the Book of Mormon may in no wise be lost, the clearness in no wise obscured, and the spirit and testimony that always accompanies it in no wise impaired.[2]

Initially, Horace S. Ensign, who succeeded Heber J. Grant as the president of the Japan Mission, asked all his elders to work on different sections of the translation in hopes that they could be easily stitched together to produce a complete rendering. Soon, however, it became evident that not all were equally blessed with the gift of tongues and that a smooth translation would primarily have to be the work of one author. So on July 16, 1904, Elder Taylor was given the special labor of working on the book until it was completed. By late August, he was already reading from his own translation of 1 Nephi 13 in a sacrament meeting.

Heartened by a letter he received from the First Presidency in which the leaders expressed both their gratitude for his success in learning the difficult language and their full support and confidence in his capabilities, Taylor moved efficiently forward in his labors. He wrote in Roman letters to speed the process. In his journal he occasionally noted his struggles to find appropriate words to translate the doctrinal concepts in the text. He seemed to encounter his first great difficulty in the twelfth and thirteenth chapters of Alma, where Alma teaches Zeezrom about spiritual death, the mortal probation, the plan of redemption, and the nature of the priesthood. Those portions, he noted, contained "many expressions in English the equivalents of which if indeed there are any in Japanese I am as yet unfamiliar with."[3]

Taylor had worked through his translation as far as the book of Alma by summer 1905, when he received word that President Ensign was to be released and that Taylor himself would be called as the new mission president. This news frustrated Taylor, for he realized that he would lose the ability to focus his time on the translation. Within a month he had extended a call to Elder Frederick A. Caine (illus. 9-2) to be mission secretary, including assisting him in copying his Roman letters into kanji (illus. 9-3). Caine would prove an invaluable companion throughout the rest of the process; in 1906 he was called to read through the first draft of the completed translation, providing suggestions and criticisms and comparing the English version with the translation to catch any omissions or careless renderings. In October 1907, Caine was released as mission secretary so he could devote all his time to this labor. Once the translation was completed, Taylor wrote in his journal:

Illus. 9-2. Frederick A. Caine. Beginning in summer 1905, Elder Caine assisted Japan Mission President Alma O. Taylor in translating the Book of Mormon into Japanese.

> The faithful assistance given by Elder Caine to the work since he was first called to take part July 30, 1905 is fully appreciated by me and for his care and devotion to this translation I have and do now again commend him to the Lord as one who has done his duty well. His suggestions have been of great value and his untiring work has not been inferior to my own.... I thank [the Lord] forever for the faithful, untireing, and most valuable aid he has given to the work through Elder Fred A. Caine. Elder Caine is a Latter-day Saint after my own heart and his associations with me in the work of translation—he has acted mostly as critic, scribe and councelor [sic]—has endeared him to me with a bond of the closest affection.[4]

Because the project of translation took five years, it was inevitable that Taylor would want to review and update his earlier translations as he progressed in the language. In March 1906, he mused:

> When I began the translation I did not know as much about the language as I do now therefore I am aware of many places in the first of this translation which I can improve myself. I have enjoyed good

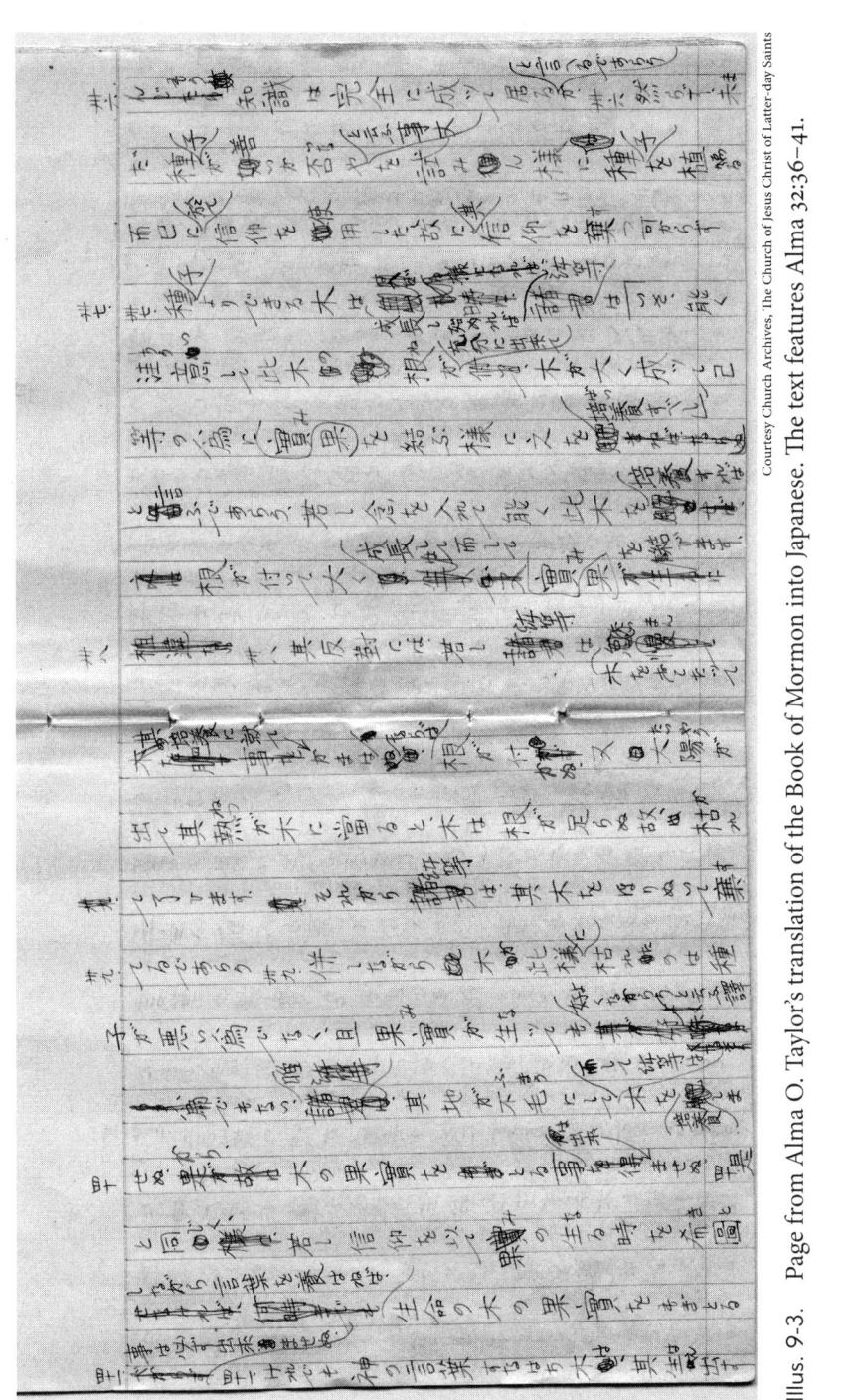

Illus. 9-3. Page from Alma O. Taylor's translation of the Book of Mormon into Japanese. The text features Alma 32:36–41.

health since beginning the translation and have had nothing but joy and satisfaction in the work, being worried only about making mistakes. It is my earnest prayer that the way will be opened up for the entire translation to be carefully and well corrected and revised.[5]

This dedicated enterprise took its toll on Taylor. As he went about the work of revision, he wrote in his journal: "In the evening I did nothing but sit and think. My eyes are getting weak and I have to be careful how I use them at night."[6] However, the focus of all his physical and spiritual energies on the work of translation had a profoundly positive effect on Taylor. In a letter written to the First Presidency on January 29, 1906, he commented:

> I fast and pray that the way will be opened for this work to go on uninterruptedly till the translation is thoroughly looked over and put into pure and intelligible Japanese and made free from all errors in meaning so that it will be acceptable to God and accompanied by the Holy Spirit, becoming thereby the same powerful witness for God and Jesus Christ that it is in English.
>
> It is hard for me to express just the feelings that I have in regard to the translation of this sacred record. The work has been, and is, a source of great joy to me. I have learned to love the book more and more and I have received testimony upon testimony of its divinity—the translation has been almost an inspiration to me, so far as teaching me the worth of the record is concerned. Occasionally I read from the translation that I have made to the saints and they have each time been edified by the clearness and superiority of the principles taught. I would feel very sad indeed if the work on the translation should have to experience a lull from any cause whatever.[7]

Only a few weeks earlier, he wrote to Elder George Reynolds of the First Council of the Seventy to report:

> You who have had so much study and work in connection with this sacred book can realize more than others the great joy and inspiration I am receiving as I continue with the translation which has now been under way for two years and which will require at least that much more time before it is ready to be printed. God has been a faithful friend to me in this labor and I have not prayed to Him in vain about many, at first, perplexing questions which have arisen.[8]

After a series of consultations about the translation with various Japanese, including individuals who were not members of the Church, Taylor received a suggestion that his translation into the contemporary colloquial language was ill suited for a text believed by its adherents to be a sacred book of revelation straight from God. He was encouraged by his native informants to have his translation rewritten into the more formal literary language. Taylor had hoped to avoid this more difficult form of the language,[9] but the inclination of his fellow missionaries was that the literary style was preferable. He finally concurred, though no doubt he was saddened to think that so much of his own work would have to be changed.

Several Japanese were approached and hired to write the stylistic transformation, and a good portion of the book was refashioned. But perhaps because he was less confident in his own ability to critique the more difficult grammatical usages in the literary language, Taylor decided he should have the revised translation examined by a man of solid literary reputation. He ended up calling on two of the most important figures in the development of modern Japanese literature: Tsubouchi Shōyō, a critic, novelist, playwright, and translator of the complete plays of Shakespeare; and Natsume Sōseki, the first truly world-class novelist to emerge in twentieth-century Japan. Neither Shōyō nor Sōseki had the time or the interest to become involved in the project,[10] but Sōseki introduced Taylor to one of his bright young disciples, Ikuta Chōkō, who was more than willing to undertake the revisions. Before he was fully confident in Ikuta's abilities, though, Taylor had him practice translating and then showed the work to Shōyō, who gave it high marks. Thereafter, Taylor entrusted the entire work to Ikuta and often sat in conversation with him over points of interpretation.[11]

As the work of rewriting progressed, Taylor was delighted with the result, and his confidence in Ikuta mounted. In August 1908 he recorded:

> It looks good to see the translation in its completed garb and the feelings that pass through my heart when I look upon this translation feeling satisfied that it is well done, are undiscribable. The joy is just a taste of what I hope it will be when the whole labor is finished.... Mr. Ikuta is a gentleman. He is quick and frank in acknowledging his errors. He gives respectful ear to my side of the questions discussed and thus we get along well and rapidly.[12]

The types of stylistic differences that resulted from Ikuta's rewrite can in part be demonstrated by comparing Taylor's original manuscript version of the first verse of the Book of Mormon to the published translation.[13] The first passage is from Taylor's own revision of his work in the colloquial, dated May 30, 1906:

> Watakushi Niifuai wa yoi ryōshin yori umarete waga chichi no moromoro no gakumon o tashō oshierareteorimasu. Shikashite watakushi wa isshō no aida nangi o takusan nametakeredomo, itsumo tenshu ni yoku megumi o uke, mata kami no megumi to sono okugi o yoku shitte iru yue ni, wagashōgai no aida kakishirusō to itashimasu.

The published version in a more literary mode reads:

> Ware Niifuai wa yoki ryōshin yori umarekereba, subete waga chichi no gakumon wa tashō oshierarenu. Shikashite ware wa shōgai amata no kannan o nameshikadomo tsuneni tenshu yori atsuki megumi o kōmuri, mata kami no megumi to sono ōgi to o fukaku shireru yue, mizukara isshō no uchi ni naseshi waza o kakishirusan to su.[14]

Taylor completed the final revisions and rewrites of the translation on June 10, 1909. On that day he wrote in his journal:

> This labor has received my best efforts and the great majority of my time.... Hence, today the finishing of the translation which includes all the references makes this day of great importance and one long to be remembered as the day looked forward to and striven hard for mid toils, prayers and fasting for almost five years. God has blessed me abundantly and sustained me, physically, mentally and spiritually so that I was able to lay down the pen of translation today in health and strength of body and mind and with a grateful heart for the countless blessings of heaven bestowed upon me and the work. Of course there still remains a question or two regarding some parts of the latest translations which will have to be decided before this part can go into the printer's hands but such things as dotting i s and crossing t s will not cease till the last proof sheet is approved.[15]

Three months later, when he laid down his pen after correcting the final proof sheets, Taylor wrote:

> This then, so far as my work is concerned, is the grand finale. My feelings of joy, my gratitude, my satisfaction at being permitted to attain this day and see the successful close of this colossal labor cannot

be described. It is a day I have hoped, prayed and walked [sic] hard for, and I must acknowledge that the work has been so arduous, and confining, requiring the consentration of all my physical and mental power for such long stretches at a time, that in taking a retrospective view of the last 5 years and 9 months, I consider my physical and mental endurance almost a miracle—at any rate a direct answer to fervant appeals to God for strength to hold out to the end. And if the Lord sees fit to recognize the fruit of this labor performed in weakness as worthy of his benediction, and commissions the Holy Spirit to companion the Japanese Book of Mormon in its travels in Japan or wherever it goes, then will my most earnest and ultimate hope in regard to the work be realized, and all my toils and anxiety become my ever-joyful memories. I praise the Lord with all my might mind and strength. . . . The Lord also has raised up in time of need sufficient Japanese help thus making it possible to eliminate most if not all the grammatical and rethorical [sic] blunders in my manuscript.[16]

The first thousand of the five thousand copies ordered from the printer were delivered to the mission office on October 11, 1909. Arrangements were made to have copies specially bound in "deep cardinal red and deep violet morocco" with cover lettering in gold and silver for presentation to the Meiji Emperor and his Empress, along with limited edition copies for the Crown Prince and Princess and various government officials. By Taylor's own reckoning,

> The number of critics of my work is five—Elder Caine and four natives. The number of scribes who labored on the translation is eight—Elder Caine and seven natives. In making the translation and reviews, I read the English text verse by verse five times and after writing the Romanji manuscript in my own hand, I read the translation twice in Romanji and seven times after it was copied in the ideographs. It has been read seven times by the critics. None of these include proof readings. Four manuscripts, one in Romanji and three in the native characters, have been required.[17]

Less than three months after the book was published, Elders Taylor and Caine were released from their missions. Looking today at the translation they produced, and even factoring in the many layers of assistance provided them, it is sobering and inspiring to see what two young Americans were able to accomplish in making the Book of Mormon available for the first time in the Japanese language.

The Second Translation

The second pioneer translator was the first native Japanese to undertake a rendering of the sacred book. Brother Satō Tatsui was baptized only eleven months after the Japanese unconditional surrender in World War II. He received the Melchizedek Priesthood and was ordained to the office of elder by Elder Matthew Cowley, who told Satō in his blessing that he would spend his life translating and interpreting for his people. Not long after that blessing, Satō undertook the work of retranslating the Book of Mormon text while simultaneously translating the complete Doctrine and Covenants and the Pearl of Great Price for the first time into Japanese. His labors spanned the tenure of three mission presidents and included some brief but direct interaction regarding doctrinal questions with President Joseph Fielding Smith. Brother Satō's Book of Mormon translation was published on May 30, 1957.

One of the unique characteristics of the translation lies in the motivation behind creating new translations within a mere forty or fifty years of one another. Most of the new translations of the text into the major languages of the world have been inspired by a desire to correct the wording of a previous translation in order to make it more doctrinally correct. While one cannot overlook the likelihood that such was also part of the motivation in Japan, it appears that the biggest motivation for the revision was concerns over dramatic changes that had come to the Japanese language, not concerns over doctrinal accuracy.

Brother Satō was undoubtedly one of the humblest of geniuses ever to tackle a project such as the Book of Mormon translation. Perhaps it was an expression of his own unassuming nature that his translation of the eighth Article of Faith literally means "We believe the Bible to be the word of God as far as it is translated correctly; we also believe the Book of Mormon (in English) to be the word of God."[18] Concerning the reasons motivating the second translation, Satō stated:

> When we began to translate this amended version of the Book of Mormon, President Clissold asked that we "translate it into simple Japanese so that many people will be able to understand the Gospel." It was not because of imperfections in the earlier Book of Mormon translation that a new rendition was planned. As I retranslated the book, I frequently opened the older translation. It made me realize

how truly superb that translation is. But more than forty years have elapsed since that translation was published in 1909, and social conditions in Japan have changed dramatically in that interval. In the postwar period in particular, a multitude of changes have come in Japanese education and culture. I used a special method in translating the book. I produced the main passages in colloquial language, while revelations and the words of the Lord are translated in the formal written style. But my intention was to stay as close as possible to the style of the earlier translation.[19]

As Brother Satō suggested, the written Japanese language has changed dramatically over the past century. It is safe to say that a twenty-year-old, educated Japanese in the twenty-first century would have a very difficult time understanding Taylor's earlier translation. It would be akin to asking a young American student to gain profound insights from an unannotated text of *Beowulf.*

Brother Satō recorded the challenges that faced him as he evaluated the first translation. The older literary language into which Ikuta revised Taylor's translation was no longer taught as one of the critical core subjects in Japanese schools in the postwar period. Governmental regulations reduced the use of kanji and modernized the use of the phonetic syllabary, significantly lowering the number of kanji in published texts. To give some notion of how extensive the changes needed to be to accommodate postwar readers, Brother Satō calculated that the total number of kanji—including numerous repetitions of the same characters—that he eliminated from Taylor's translation came to 41,000.[20] Some of the most noteworthy changes in religious vocabulary that Brother Satō introduced into the translation are summarized in example 1 in my appendix to this chapter, which also includes, for comparative purposes, the corresponding vocabulary choice from the 1995 translation.[21]

The Third Translation

When I arrived in Japan in 1970, young American missionaries were already calling for yet another translation of the Book of Mormon because they were having a hard time understanding some of the classical verb forms and vocabulary employed in the Satō version. Not much weight should normally be given to linguistic judgments passed by nineteen- to twenty-one-year-old American missionaries who largely learned Japanese by mimicking what they heard on the street. But the fact is that with each passing generation of Japanese, familiarity with the older forms of the language decreases. Contemporary writers in Japan use fewer kanji as they write. Consequently, it is fair to say that the Satō translation seems a little quaint and dated to the younger generation in Japan and is, in fact, in some ways less accessible than the standard colloquial Japanese translation of the Bible in current usage.

By the mid-1980s, these linguistic changes and other factors were of sufficient concern that Church leaders authorized a committee of translators to produce yet another version to replace the Satō version, which was considered by some to be "too classic."[22] The First Presidency charged the committee not only to make the language of the scripture more comprehensible but also to put the emphasis on literal accuracy to preserve the doctrinal purity being taught by the book. To cite just two key changes, the term used for "charity" was changed from a simple *ai* (a generic sort of love) to *jiai* (a more compassionate kind of love), and "agency" was transformed from *jiyū ishi* (free will) to *sentaku no jiyū* (freedom of choice).[23] A very helpful "Guide to the Scriptures" was created for this edition, providing explanations of many terms and concepts unique to Latter-day Saint doctrine. The creation of this essential guide is but one indication that it is a daunting, often frustrating task to find suitable words to explain Christian concepts in a country where only 1 percent of the population is Christian.

The most recent translation is more accessible and has had a profound impact upon its readers. A Japanese high school student "said he used to read the old translation of the Book of Mormon, but had trouble understanding it and gaining a testimony. However, when he got a copy of the new translation, he read and re-read it, understood it and could visualize the scenes described in the book." Eugene M. Kitamura, Asia North Area director of temporal affairs and supervisor of the translation committee that produced the book, commented that this young man

> said at this time he got a testimony that the book was true. . . . And I have heard that kind of testimony from many others of the younger generation. They have received many blessings from this updated scripture. . . . The new translation of the Book of Mormon is easier for investigators to read and understand.[24]

Translation Nuances

What intrigues me most as I compare the three Book of Mormon translations into Japanese is the ways they are similar in their essential explication of the gospel in a non-Christian language and also the ways in which they are different. I will examine several examples from the translations to highlight how slippery words can be, regardless of how well we think we understand them. It is categorically not my intention to criticize or belittle any of these translators; having done a bit of secular translation myself, I have personal knowledge of how difficult the task is. My goal is to suggest that each of these translations, in its own way, is a work of inspired brilliance, reflecting the language and religious climate of its era and serving as the best possible means of conveying the teachings found in the ancient American record to the people of Japan. Such faults or shortcomings that might exist in the choice of words or interpretations can, I am persuaded, be laid at the feet of contemporary circumstances, and I do believe the Spirit has the capability to speak through imperfect words with perfect, persuasive clarity.

The changes that have developed in the Japanese language are problematic for a number of reasons, one of which is that levels of respect in the language play such a significant role in distinguishing the status of the narrator in relation to the reader. There are literally hundreds of examples where all three translators of the Japanese Book of Mormon have wrestled with this issue and made some thorny stylistic decisions. The most obvious example, encountered repeatedly by the Japanese Saints, is the translation of the sacrament prayers. In example 2 in the appendix, I have produced a line-by-line comparison of the three different translations. In the first two translations, every verb used to address God is in a deeply humble form, and not a single pronoun is used to address or refer to the Father. The most recent translation moves away from this style. In its revision of the sacrament prayers, God is twice referred to as *anata* (informal "you"). The usage of *anata* is complex and fluid over the centuries, but according to one of the most authoritative dictionaries of the Japanese language, "At present, 'anata' is used with peers and inferiors; in addition, it is the pronoun most commonly used by wives to address their husbands."[25] Small wonder, then, that a few Japanese members were startled by the introduction of this pronoun into the sacrament prayer.[26]

One key scriptural passage that leaped out at me as I began comparing the translations was Mosiah 3:19, "For the natural man is an enemy to God." This is an interesting example of the first and third translations being in agreement, while the second differs with them. The translation for "natural man" in Taylor's version is *umarenagara no sei*, literally meaning "the nature with which one is born; one's inherent nature." The 1995 translation varies only in changing *sei* to *hito*, literally making it "a person in the state he was born."[27] It is interesting that Satō chose to be much more interpretive in his rendition of this verse. He translates "natural man" as *nikuyoku ni shitagau hito*, literally a "person who follows the lusts of the flesh." It is difficult to argue with his interpretation, but it is likewise difficult to imagine how his version could be retranslated back into English and end up as "natural." And yet, there is something comfortably attractive about the way Satō comes right out and defines what the phrase means to him. I might point out here that the Greek term for "natural" in Paul's sermon on the natural man in 1 Corinthians is *psuchikos*, defined as "the sensuous nature with its subjection to appetite and passion,"[28] which affirms the accuracy of Satō's rendition.

When attempting to communicate in a culture that does not acknowledge a supreme deity, a kinship connection between God and man, or a life after death, simple concepts such as damnation can be challenging to convey. All three translations render "damned" (for example, Alma 14:21 when Alma and Amulek's persecutors revile them and cry, "How shall we look when we are damned?") as "when we receive 'punishment after death' *(shigo no batsu)*." In other locations where "damned" appears in English, the same sorts of circumlocutions are employed, including one in Mosiah 3:35, "therefore they have drunk damnation to their own souls," where Satō resorts to "cannot be saved in either body or spirit" *(mi mo rei mo sukuwarezaru nari)*.

These circumlocutions lead to yet another fascinating translation conundrum. Taylor recognized the problem as he translated. In a letter of April 15, 1908, addressed to the First Presidency, Taylor wrote:

> Your kind letter answering my questions on the Book of Mormon has been carefully read. All of your suggestions are perfectly clear. With but one exception I am very happy over them. The exception is on the rendition of the word "soul." In the first place the Japanese Bible

(because of the limitations made by the language) is no criterion on any difficult question like this. There is no word in Japanese for "soul" which could possibly be stretched to include both body and spirit. It must be straight "spirit" or "heart" or "body." The Japanese Bible always uses the words meaning "spirit" or "heart." In the great majority of cases these words may do for our "soul" but, for example, in II Nephi 9:13. The word "spirit" as well as the word " body" are used in their true, distinct meaning while "soul" refers to the two united. There, I may change "soul" to "being" or "person," but, so said, there is a decided weakness, as the same word in Japanese also means "thing."[29]

Part of 2 Nephi 9:13 reads, "The spirit and the body is restored to itself again, and all men become incorruptible, and immortal, and they are living souls." As Taylor indicates, this scripture seems to teach precisely what is taught in D&C 88:15, that when the spirit and the body are restored to one another, the result is "living souls." For "living souls," Taylor gives *sude ni ikeru hito,* or "already living persons." None of his successors have yet come up with a persuasive solution to the problem. Satō provides *ikeru hito,* basically the same notion of a "living person"; and the committee offers *ikeru mono,* returning to the word *(mono)* Taylor ultimately decided to avoid that refers both to "person" and "thing." To underscore the insoluble challenge here, let me cite the two Japanese translations of D&C 88. Satō's says, *ningen wa rei to tai to yori naru* (literally, man is made up of a spirit and a body); the current translation reads, *rei to karada ga hito o nasu* (the spirit and the body comprise man).

Similarly, a response from members of the First Presidency to some of Taylor's translation questions points out the difficulties of rendering the subtle nuances of Latter-day Saint doctrine into the language of a non-Christian nation. On December 12, 1908, a letter signed by John R. Winder and Anthon H. Lund commented:

> You desire to know whether, in translating "Holy Ghost", "Holy Spirit", "Spirit of the Lord", &c., you should render the same meaning to each and all of them as though they were interchangeable, or whether you should undertake to give each its distinct meaning.
>
> We take it that you will experience no difficulty in conveying the true meaning of "Holy Ghost", but can readily perceive that you may

experience difficulty in translating "Holy Spirit" and "Spirit of the Lord", as both are not always used to precisely express the same idea. As for instance, in our own literature and language, "Church of God" and "Kingdom of God" are ofttimes used interchangeably, whereas in reality they are two distinct things and, strictly speaking, cannot be used correctly to express the same thing, but notwithstanding this the general reader is not confused because of the seeming inaccuracy. This will doubtless be the case, in some instances, in your translation of "Holy Spirit" and "Spirit of the Lord", with no harmful effect however; but at the same time it will be for you to do the very best you can according to your own judgment and the light in you when translating these words, so as to convey as near as possible the correct meaning.[30]

This difficulty in translating is evident elsewhere in the scriptures. In Alma 19:6, when Ammon is describing the spiritual transformation that is occurring within King Lamoni, the English translation from the plates reads: "Yea, he knew that this [meaning 'the light of everlasting life'] had overcome his natural frame, and he was carried away with God." We have already touched on the problem of translating "natural"; my interest here is in the phrase "carried away with God." I do not pretend to know precisely what this means; but the translator must make a decision regarding meaning. Taylor says that because of the light, "His body became weak, and his spirit communed with God" (*kore ga tame sono shintai yowarite sono reikon no kami to aitsūzuru*). Satō offers: "His body became weak, and he was led away by God" (*kore ga tame ni sono shintai ga yowatte ō wa kami ni tsurerarete itta*). And the current translation suggests that the light "won out over the king's body, and through God the king lost consciousness" (*kore ga ō no nikutai ni uchikatte, ō ga kami ni yotte ishiki o ushinatte ita*).

There are a number of references in the Book of Mormon, particularly in Alma, which describe the "holy order of God." For instance, Alma 5:54 describes the "brethren, who humble themselves and do walk after the holy order of God, wherewith they have been brought into this church." Taylor translates the latter portion as: "They obeyed the law of the holy priesthood and entered into this church" (*karera wa kiyoki shinken no hō o mamorite kono kyōkai ni iritari*). Satō essentially concurs, writing that they "followed the path designated by the holy priesthood and were brought into this church" (*kiyoi shinken ga sadamete iru michi ni shitagatte kono kyōkai ni irerare*). In the committee's revision, these brethren "were led to this church through the holy rank of God" (*kami no seinaru kurai ni yotte kono kyōkai ni michibikare*), with "rank" instead of "priesthood" used in the sense of "order."

Words such as "temporal" are variously rendered by the translators as *gense* (the present world) or *nikutai*, which is used in the phrase *nikutai no shi* (temporal death; literally, the death of the body). I find myself not fully satisfied with some of the translations. One of these is the rendering of Alma 38:12: "See that ye bridle all your passions, that ye may be filled with love."[31] Taylor's version provides: "In order that you may be filled with love, control all of your lusts" (*ai o motte mitasaruru yō, issai no yoku o osaeyo*). Satō says: "Control all of your lusts and be filled with love" (*issai no yoku o osaete ai ni michiyo*). The committee version offers: "Make sure that you restrain all of your violent emotions and are filled with love" (*mata, gekijō o subete sei shi, ai de mitasareru yō ni shinasai*). Notice that two translators use *yoku* (lusts or passions), while the third uses *gekijō*, which can mean "passions" but has the primary sense of "violent emotions." The notion of restraint is twice rendered as *osaeru*, which literally means "to push down" and can go so far as to mean "put a stop to," though that nuance is not essential. The verb the committee recently used, *seisuru*, seems most successful at suggesting some kind of control that does not totally wipe out the object being controlled. Taylor seems to do the best job of providing the critical link between bridling of passions and being filled with love, providing a "so that" phrase to create a sense of cause and effect. The two subsequent translations seem to lose that connection.

It is interesting to ponder how difficult it is to identify suitable translations for some of the most fundamental principles of the gospel. We can thank earlier missionaries of other denominations for coming up with the Japanese word *tsumi* to translate "sin." But we could have a very long and inconclusive discussion about the nuances of the term *tsumi* in the Japanese context. By and large, *tsumi* is a violation of the laws of society. Since Japanese religions are devoid of the notion of accountability to a supreme being who is our father and creator, it is a stretch to assume that the term is automatically interpreted by a typical

Japanese as the violation of the spiritual contract between man and God. Instead, *tsumi* connotes an action contrary to the accepted social order; it can often be an offense against one's peers, and even when it is an act of rebellion against a superior power, that power is the laws of the land or a feudal master or political ruler. In the indigenous Shintō religion, *tsumi* is a physical defilement removed through washing or confinement. The term could be translated more correctly as "crime"; in fact, the Japanese title of Dostoevsky's novel *Crime and Punishment* is *Tsumi to Batsu*.

Similar problems attend the attempt to describe violations of the law of chastity in Japanese. I confess I have nothing but painful memories of my attempts to teach this law many decades ago as a missionary. The lesson plan directed us to have our investigators read from the Ten Commandments: "Thou shalt not commit adultery." In the current Japanese translation of the Bible (1966), that reads: *Kan'in shite wa naranai*. Using the word *kan'in* with a Japanese born since World War II would be roughly equivalent to teaching the seventh commandment in English as: "Thou shalt avoid all concupiscence." It is not a turn of phrase that trips easily off the Japanese tongue. In fact, because of all the homonyms in the Japanese language, a young person in particular hearing this phrase might believe she was being told: "You must never become a government official," (*kan'in*) or even "Avoid using the governmental seal" (*kan'in*). I exaggerate slightly, but I can assure you that the vast majority of those to whom I taught that discussion had no clue what I was talking about. The archaic term *kan'in* (roughly meaning "illicit indecency," but written with obscure characters) is also employed throughout all three Japanese translations of the Book of Mormon.

There are some real problems attending decisions that make Christianity seem even more foreign to the Japanese by suggesting that the religion itself is and will always be alien. Though I must reemphasize that there are perhaps equal dangers in trying to approximate gospel terminology in a foreign language in ways that confuse them with indigenous concepts. An example of this is the gospel term "baptism." The originally coined Japanese term was *senrei* (literally, the ordinance of washing). The Protestant translations of the Bible from the late nineteenth and early twentieth centuries, however, rejected that term, perhaps because it was too firmly associated with the Catholic practice of baptism by sprinkling. Instead these translations phoneticized the English term and produced the foreign-looking and foreign-sounding term *baputesuma*.

Taylor seems to have sensed that using the Catholic or Protestant terms for the washing ordinance would not be a proper approximation for the revealed doctrine of immersion. So he used the term *shinrei* in his Book of Mormon translation, since it means an "ordinance of immersion." The two later translations, however, return to the use of *baputesuma*.

Semantics

Alma Taylor was not the first religious translator to encounter difficulties rendering Christian terms into Japanese. The first Catholic missionary, Francis Xavier, who arrived in Japan in 1549 and promptly declared the Japanese "the best race yet discovered," also experienced similar struggles.[32] Once the initial words of greeting and praise had passed his lips, Xavier encountered increasing difficulty being understood by his hosts. From the outset, the name of "God" has posed difficulties. Xavier quickly discovered that the Judeo-Christian concept of God has no comfortable equivalent—or even clumsy counterpart—in the history of Japanese spiritual experience. The Japanese term *kami*, commonly translated as *gods*, refers to a spiritual essence that is an equal-opportunity inhabiter of man and beast, wind and rain, tree and flower, the living and the dead. It makes no distinctions of rank between the realm of man and the realm of nature and does not allow for the notion of a supreme being who has created man as his own offspring, placing him "a little lower than the angels," (Psalms 8:5) and giving him dominion over all the earth. As a Catholic missionary in Endō Shūsaku's novel *The Samurai* declares:

> The Japanese basically lack a sensitivity to anything that is absolute, to anything that transcends the human level, to the existence of anything beyond the realm of Nature: what we would call the supernatural.... They abhor the idea of making clear distinctions between man and God. To them, even if there should be something greater than man, it is something which man himself can one day become.... Within the realm of Nature their sensibilities are remarkably delicate and subtle, but those sensibilities are unable to grasp anything

on a higher plane. That is why the Japanese cannot conceive of our God, who dwells on a separate plane from man.³³

Consequently, Xavier, wise enough to try to meet the Japanese at their level of spiritual understanding and then move forward from there, consulted a number of friendly Buddhist priests for help in finding an appropriate Japanese name to describe his concept of God. What they gave him was the closest equivalent of which they could conceive: the Buddhist deity *Dainichi*, the "Great Sun Buddha" who is the mystical cosmic illuminator of the universe. Once Xavier realized his dilemma, however, he turned on his Buddhist informants, declared their deities devils, and thereafter resorted to using the Latin term *Deus* to describe what he was trying to teach. Sadly, the Japanese rendition *Deusu* was too easy to toy with, and the Buddhists in retaliation began calling the God of Catholicism *Daiuso*, meaning "the Great Lie."³⁴ Subsequent Catholic missionaries in Japan opted for the term coined by the Jesuit priest Matteo Ricci in the China mission, *Tenshu* (literally, the Lord of Heaven). *Tenshu* is in fact the word that Alma Taylor decided to use to translate each appearance of "Lord" in the Book of Mormon.

Of this choice, Taylor wrote in a letter to fellow missionary John W. Stoker, dated August 20, 1906:

> I have been thinking very seriously of adopting in the Book of Mormon translation the [Catholic Church's] translation of "Lord" which is tenshu. . . . It seems to me that this word gives better the meaning of our word "Lord" than the simple shu which is used in referring to earthly lords. There are no capital letters in Japanese to draw the distinction, so I have, in the revision of my translation, caused tenshu to be written in all cases except such as "Lord of Hosts" where I say bangun no shu. But in such expressions as "The Lord my Redeemer" (waga aganainushi naru tenshu), the "tenshu" certainly appeals to me as just the proper thing.³⁵

By the postwar period when Brother Satō began his translation, *tenshu* had become virtually synonymous with the Catholic Church, which was known as *Tenshukyō*. Consequently, Satō and the later translators followed the lead of the Protestants in using the simple *shu* (Lord or lord).

The ultimate compromise in finding a word for God, adopted universally among Christians in Japan including all three editions of the

Book of Mormon, has been to add an honorific ending to the indigenous Japanese term *kami (kami-sama)* giving us something that might, with a great stretch of the imagination, be rendered "the honorable gods that dwell in all manifestations of natural phenomena." It can be challenging to talk about the finer points of theology when one struggles with how to name even the central object of worship.

The task of trying to render the Christian lexicon in Japanese is cleverly and somewhat frighteningly examined in a story written in 1922 by Akutagawa Ryūnosuke, modern Japan's greatest short story writer. The story is called "Kamigami no bishō" (The smile of the gods), and it consists primarily of a debate between a Catholic priest laboring in Japan in the early sixteenth century and an old man who represents the native gods of the land. At one point in the story, when the old immortal has argued that the foreigner's religion cannot succeed in Japan, the priest insists that Christianity is thriving in Japan, and that each day more of the locals are converted. The Japanese god, however, has a quick and facile answer to that objection: "I imagine any number of them will convert. If we're talking merely about conversion, a majority of the natives of this land have converted to the teachings of Siddartha [Buddha]. But our power is not the power to destroy. It is the power to transform *(tsukurikaeru chikara)*."

The native Japanese god (basically a Shintō deity) expresses no concern over the fact that the overwhelming majority of Japanese have converted to Buddhism. He argues that the Japanese have a wonderfully fluid syncretic ability to pick and choose what they want from foreign ideas, almost as if a system of belief can be created by making selections from a religious smorgasbord. It may be true, he concedes, that the Japanese profess belief in the Buddhist deity *Dainichi*. But when the Japanese sleep at night and dream of *Dainichi*, he insists, the figure they actually see in their dreams is not some masculine foreign image, but in fact the face and form of *Amaterasu*, the Shintō sun goddess. It is this marvelously fluid ability to absorb, transform, and Japanize anything that comes into the country from abroad that both amazes and distresses me.

The role of the translator, in any age and for any purpose, is a complex and challenging one. When the work being translated is a sacred text, the difficulties multiply. Such a translator must be a linguistic expert in two languages, a deft and careful doctrinal arbitrator, a creative circumlocutionist, a cautious and thorough editor, and a sensitive listener to the tutorials of the Spirit that will expand his or her natural capacities. It is a thankless task, unless of course one takes into consideration the largely unspoken gratitude of tens of thousands of Japanese who have, despite any possible "weakness in writing" (Ether 12:23), discovered that the Spirit is able to penetrate linguistic walls and convey the message of the book with even greater clarity than any word could express. As one who has translated, I am filled with admiration, respect, and gratitude for all who dedicated themselves, body, mind, and spirit, to the arduous task of transforming that "most perfect book" into "a marvelous work and a wonder" in Japanese.

Appendix

Example 1:
Some Significant Vocabulary Differences in the Three Translations

	Taylor	**Satō**	**Committee**
1 Nephi 2:17 (Holy Spirit)	seirei (holy ghost)	kiyoki "mitama" (pure "spirit")	sei naru mitama (holy spirit)
1 Nephi 10:9 (baptize)	shinrei (ordinance of immersion)	baputesuma	baputesuma
2 Nephi 3:4 (fruit of my loins)	koshi no mi (fruit of loins)	shison (descendants)	koshi kara deta mono (that which emerged from loins)
2 Nephi 6:2 (his holy order)	Kami no seihan (God's holy regiment)	Kami no shinken (God's priesthood)	Kami no sei naru kurai (God's holy ranks)

2 Nephi 18:19 (familiar spirits)	kuchiyose (spirit medium)	shitashii rei o motsu mono (one with a recognized spirit)	reibai (spirit medium)
Mosiah 3:10 (natural man)	umarenagara no sei (the nature to which one is born)	nikuyoku ni shitagau hito (one who follows fleshly lusts)	umarenagara no hito (a person in the state to which born)
Mosiah 23:14 (minister)	bokushi (pastor)	kyōkai no shidōsha (church leader)	oshiemichibiku mono (one who teaches and leads)
Alma 9:28 (damnation of their souls)	shigo no batsu (punishment after death)	mi mo rei mo eien ni Kami no mae yori tachikirareru batsu (punishment through which both body and spirit are cut off from the presence of God)	batsu no sadame (determination of punishment)
Alma 30:22 (there shall be no Christ)	Kirisuto wa aru bekarazu (Christ shall not exist)	Kirisuto wa kitaritamawanai (Christ will not come)	naze Kirisuto wa arawareru hazu ga nai (there is no reason why Christ should appear)
Alma 40:12 (paradise)	rakuen (garden of bliss)	Paradaisu	Paradaisu

3 Nephi 11:34 (damned)	shigo no batsu o uku beshi (shall received punishment after death)	sukuwarezu (shall not be saved)	batsu no sadame (determination of punishment)
3 Nephi 18:1 (wine)	budōshu (wine)	budōeki (grape liquid)	budōshu (wine)
Mormon 7:7 (which are one God)	hitotsu no shinkai naru santai (a trinity made up of one godhead)	hitotsu no shinkai o nashitamou (forming one godhead)	hitotsu no Kami de aru (which are one God)

Example 2:
Translations of Sacrament Prayers on Bread
Taylor's Translation:

Eien no tempu naru Kami yo,
Warera Onko Iesu Kirisuto no mina ni yorite
    negaitatematsuraku wa,
Subete kono pan o azukari kurau hitobito ga,
Onko no karada no kinen ni kore o kurau koto
    o uru yō,
Mata tsuneni Onko no mitama o onorera to
    tomo ni arashimen tame,
Onko no mina o amanji ukete
Tsuneni Onko o kinen shi,
Sono kudashitamaishi imashime o mamoru o
    Nanji ni seiyaku suru koto o uru yō,
Kono pan o karera no kokoro no tame ni
    iwaikiyometamawan koto o
Amen.

Literal English Meaning of Taylor's Translation:
O God, the Eternal Father,
That which we ask in the name of Thy Son
Jesus Christ,
Is that all people who receive and eat this bread
So that they may eat it in remembrance of Thy body,
And in order that the Spirit of Thy Son may
always be with them,
Willingly taking upon them the name of Thy Son
Always remembering Thy Son,
So that they may take upon themselves a covenant with Thee to obey
    His commandments,
We pray Thou wilt bless and sanctify this
bread for the benefit of their hearts.
Amen.

Satō's Translation:
Eien no chichi naru Kami yo, Warera Onko Iesu Kirisuto no mina ni yorite negaitatematsuru, Koko ni kono pan o itadaku subete no hitobito ga, Onko no karada no kinen ni kore o itadaku yō, Mata yorokobite Onko no mina o uke, Onko o tsuneni wasurezu, Mata sono kudashitamaeru imashime o mamoru koto o Eien no chichi naru Kami no onmae ni shōmei shi, Kakushite Onko no "Mitama" tsuneni ichidō to tomo ni mashimasu yō, Kono pan o iwaikiyometamae. Amen.

Literal English Meaning of Satō's Translation:
O God, the Eternal Father, We humbly ask Thee in the name of Thy Son, Jesus Christ, That all of the people who partake here of this bread So that they may partake of it in remembrance of the body of Thy Son, And gladly receive the name of Thy Son, Never forgetting Him, And that they will keep the commandments which He has given them, They witness before Thee, O God the Eternal Father, So that they will always have the "Spirit" of Thy Son with them, We implore thee to bless and sanctify this bread. Amen.

Current Translation:

Eien no chichi naru Kami yo, Watashitachi wa Onko Iesu Kirisuto no mina ni yotte Anata ni negaimotomemasu. Kono pan wo itadaku subete no hitobito ga, Onko no karada no kinen ni kore o itadakeru yō ni, mata, susunde Onko no mina o uke, Itsumo Onko o oboe, Onko ga ataete kudasatta imashime o mamoru koto o Eien no chichi naru Kami yo, anata ni shōmei shite, Itsumo Onko no mitama o ukerareru yō ni, Kono pan o shukufuku shi, kiyomete kudasai. Amen.

Literal English Meaning of Current Translation:

O God, the Eternal Father, We ask You in the name of Thy Son, Jesus Christ, That all of the people who partake of this bread, So that they may partake of it in remembrance of the body of Thy Son, And willingly taken upon them the name of Thy Son, Always remembering Thy Son, To keep the commandments which Thy Son has given them, They witness unto You, O God the Eternal Father, So that they may always receive Thy Son's spirit, Please bless and sanctify this bread. Amen.

This paper was presented at "A Centennial Celebration: The LDS Church in Japan, 1901–2001," October 13, 2001, Brigham Young University, Provo, Utah.

Notes

1. Van C. Gessel, translator's note, in Shūsaku Endō, *The Samurai*, trans. Van C. Gessel (New York: Harper and Row/Kodansha International, 1982), 5.
2. Alma O. Taylor, "Journals, 1901–1946," July 16, 1904, L. Tom Perry Special Collections, Harold B. Lee Library, Brigham Young University, Provo, Utah. Taylor's original spellings are retained here and in all later quotations. See also Reid L. Neilson, "The Japanese Missionary Journals of Elder O. Taylor, 1901–10" (master's thesis, Brigham Young University, 2001; BYU Studies and Joseph Fielding Smith Institute for Latter-day Saint History, 2001).
3. Taylor, Journals, April 28, 1905.
4. Taylor, Journals, June 10 and September 30, 1909.
5. Taylor, Journals, March 21, 1906.
6. Taylor, Journals, August 4, 1906.
7. Alma O. Taylor to Joseph F. Smith, John R. Winder, and Anthon H. Lund, January 29, 1906, Japan Mission Letterpress Copybooks, 1901–23, Church Archives, The Church of Jesus Christ of Latter-day Saints, Salt Lake City.

8. Alma O. Taylor to George Reynolds, January 6, 1906, Japan Mission Letterpress Copybooks, 1901–23, Church Archives.

9. In Taylor, Journals, entry dated August 15, 1907, Taylor reviewed the arguments for and against the use of the literary language, commenting, "The classical is more difficult than the colloquial therefore it was my hope to avoid it."

10. Though there is no way to determine the reasons for Sōseki's refusal to become involved, it is interesting to speculate on whether the negative experiences he had had with overbearing Christians on his sea voyage to London in 1900, as well as the unpleasant experience of being coerced into reading the Bible by some British ladies at a tea party in 1902, might have made Sōseki less receptive to Taylor's petition. See Van C. Gessel, *Three Modern Novelists: Sōseki, Tanizaki, Kawabata* (Tokyo: Kodansha International, 1993), 39–42, 47–8.

11. See Taylor, Journals, August 17, 1908, September 15, 1908, and February 17, 1909.

12. Taylor, Journals, August 18 and 27, 1908.

13. For the benefit of readers who do not know Japanese, I should point out that the differences between the more colloquial draft translation by Taylor and the final published version in the literary style manifest themselves in such items as the use of pronouns (Taylor, for instance, has Nephi refer to himself as *watakushi*, the colloquial form of "I," whereas the published version uses the literary pronoun *ware*); verb endings (Taylor says *umarete*, the contemporary verb form of "to be born," while the literary version uses the more complex and outdated *umarekereba*; in Taylor's version, having been "favored" by the Lord is translated as *megumi o uke*, while the literary form provides a humbler verb in *megumi o kōmuri*; Taylor uses a colloquial humble form *oshierareteorimasu*, literally "I was taught," while the older verb form in the published version is *oshierarenu*); and other subtleties of rhetorical usage that cannot easily be translated into English. These subtle differences are, however, apparent to Japanese readers.

14. Alma O. Taylor, Japanese Book of Mormon Translation Papers, Church Archives. Compare Taylor's notebook version with a reprint of the published version, *Morumon Kei* (Tokyo: Jūichibō Insatsusha, 1950), 2. It is also instructive to compare both these renditions with Frederick A. Caine, Notebooks, January 20, 1904, Church Archives. See p. 253. The version attempted by Elder Fred A. Caine, reads:

> Ware, Nephi wa yoki ryōshin ni umareta yue ni waga chichi no subete no chishiki/gakumon ni tsuite zuibun oswarimashita [*sic*]. Shikashite waga isshō no aida ōku no kurushimi o ukemashita ni mo

kakawarazu itsu de mo shu ni ōi ni megumarete jitsu ni Kami no zen naru koto oyobi fushigi naru koto ni tsuku ōki na chishiki o motsu kara isshō no aida no waga waza no kiroku o kakimasu.

15. Taylor, Journals, June 10, 1909.

16. Taylor, Journals, September 30, 1909.

17. Taylor, Journals, "The History of the Japanese Translation of the Book of Mormon," manuscript, n.p., n.d., 2.

18. *Kōka naru shinjū* (The Pearl of Great Price), trans. Satō Tatsui (Tokyo: The Church of Jesus Christ of Latter-day Saints, 1970), 95.

19. Quoted in "'Morumon Sho no hensen," part 11 of "Shashin de miru Nihon kyōkai 100-nenshi," *Liahona* 3 (September 2001): 15.

20. Satō Tatsui, "Shin'yaku Morumon Kei ni tsuite," *Seito-No-Michi* (October 1957): 5.

21. Satō, "Shin'yaku Morumon Kei ni tsuite," *Seito-No-Michi* (December 1957): 10–11; (January 1958): 13–14; (February 1958): 13. "The missionaries were able to go into the homes of investigators and tell them the story of Joseph Smith, give or sell them a copy of the Book of Mormon, and invite them to be baptized. . . . Convert baptisms jumped from 129 in 1956 to 616 in 1957." R. Lanier Britsch, *From the East: The History of the Latter-day Saints in Asia, 1851–1996* (Salt Lake City: Deseret Book, 1998), 105.

22. See the brief discussion in Britsch, *From the East*, 156–57.

23. Quoted in "Morumon Sho no hensen," 15.

24. Greg Hill, "New Translation Brings 'New Day,'" *Church News*, published by *Deseret News*, January 25, 1997, 6.

25. *Kokugo Daijiten* (Tokyo: Shōgakkan, 1981), s.v. "anata."

26. And what are we to make, for instance, of the contrast between the familiar *anata* to refer to God and the honorific *onko* to refer to the Son? "*Anata no onko*" (literally "your Son," but using the familiar "your" and the honorific "Son") simply does not work in Japanese. An interesting study of (1) linguistic problems, (2) extra-linguistic problems, and (3) other problems caused by Hebraisms in the English Book of Mormon with reference to the first two translations may be found in Numano Jiro, "The Japanese Translation of the Book of Mormon: A Study in the Theory and Practice of Translation" (master's thesis, Brigham Young University, 1976).

27. We could ponder the implications of this translation in light of our understanding of original sin, but there is, I think, a risk of misunderstanding. The verse seems to indicate that we are enemies to God in the state in which we are born, but other verses indicate that we must become like a little child.

28. Crosswalk.com, "King James Version New Testament Greek Lexicon,"

s.v. "psuchikos," http://bible1.crosswalk.com/Lexicons/NewTestamentGreek/. The online dictionary is based on the Bible Dictionary of Thayer and Smith.

29. Alma O. Taylor to First Presidency, April 15, 1908, Japan Mission Letterpress Copybooks, 1901–23, Church Archives.

30. John R. Winder and Anthon H. Lund to Alma O. Taylor, December 12, 1908, Japan Mission Incoming Letters, 1903–21, Church Archives.

31. I am grateful to Wade Fillmore for drawing my attention to the translations of this verse.

32. Michael Cooper, ed., *They Came to Japan: An Anthology of European Reports on Japan, 1543–1640* (Berkeley: University of California Press, 1965), 60.

33. Endō, *Samurai*, 162.

34. Summarized in Neil S. Fujita, *Japan's Encounter with Christianity: The Catholic Mission in Pre-Modern Japan* (New York: Paulist Press, 1991), 28ff.

35. Alma O. Taylor to John W. Stoker, August 20, 1906, Japan Mission Letterpress Copybooks, 1901–23, Church Archives.

10

The Closing of the Early Japan Mission

R. Lanier Britsch

On June 13, 1924, Hilton A. Robertson, president of the Japan Mission, received a telegram from Latter-day Saint Church headquarters in Salt Lake City; the note contained 12,000 yen but no explanation.[1] Nevertheless, Robertson and his missionaries had a good idea why the money had been sent. For several years, rumors had circulated among them concerning the possible closing of the mission. Even during a missionary conference the month before, President Robertson had "touched upon the possibilities of the Japan Mission closing and said that under present conditions, with the current thot [sic] as it is, it is impossible for the Missionaries to spend their best efforts in the work." He also told the missionaries that "he hoped to learn in the very near future the fate of the Mission."[2]

President Robertson had been corresponding with the First Presidency regarding this matter. On January 31, 1924, after he had consulted with all his missionaries to find how they evaluated conditions in their areas, Robertson sent the First Presidency a very carefully written five-page appraisal of the condition of the mission. Robertson's letter had indicated that all the missionaries felt "the same amount of labor with some other people would bring better results." Church President Heber J. Grant and his counselors considered this when they replied to President Robertson on February 20. The only concern that appears to have kept them from closing the mission was "whether we have done our duty in warning the Japanese nation."[3] The First Presidency gave several indications that they were seriously considering closing the mission. The words "if the work continues" were used in one instance, and elsewhere they wrote they had "doubted as to the wisdom of continuing the mission." The most direct reference to closing the mission was written as follows:

> When we stop to think that over twenty years of hard labor have been performed in Japan, it certainly looks as though the Lord would justify us if we saw fit to close that mission, when we read the words: "I feel perfectly safe in saying that we haven't over five or six real Saints in the mission who are willing and ready to help carry on the work."[4] The Lord has said in Section 18 of the Doctrine and Covenants:
>
> "And if it so be that you should labor all your days in crying repentance unto this people, and bring, save it be one soul unto me, how great shall be your joy with him in the kingdom of my Father!"
>
> We do not wish to lose one soul in Japan, but if the same amount of labor in some other country was performed the chances are we would have many times as many converts.[5]

By May 1924, the missionaries in Osaka, Sapporo, Sendai, and Tokyo found attendance at scheduled meetings dropping weekly. Furthermore, some of the elders were insulted by irate Japanese who were aroused by the Americans' recent passage of the exclusion laws, which prevented Japanese immigrating to the United States. Notes telling the missionaries to go home had been left on their doors. To the missionaries' surprise, on Sunday, June 15, a Tokyo newspaper "contained a short telegram message stating that the Mormon missionaries would be immediately withdrawn from Japan."[6]

A telegram from Salt Lake City with the same message arrived at the mission office on Thursday, June 26, 1924. It was dated June 9 and read[7]:

> Have decided to withdraw all missionaries from Japan temporarily. Cabling you twelve thousand Yen for that purpose. If more needed cable us. Arrange return immediately. Heber J. Grant.[8]

Now as Church President, Heber J. Grant, who had opened the Japan Mission in 1901, made the decision to temporarily close it in 1924.

The Decision to Close the Mission

From 1920, the Japan Mission had been on trial. There is no question that from this time on, Church leaders in Salt Lake City were harboring

Closing of the Early Japan Mission   265

grave doubts concerning the value of continuing the mission. During the administration of President Joseph H. Stimpson (1915–21, illus. 10-1), some missionaries received reports that Church authorities were thinking about closing the mission. When Elder David O. McKay went to Japan as part of a world mission tour in 1920, his assignment was to assess the situation and decide whether the mission should remain open.

Elder McKay arrived in Japan on December 20, 1920. During his month-long stay, he visited all the conferences (illus. 10-2) of the mission (except Sapporo due to a blizzard). He spent considerable time asking questions and seeking to learn more about the Japanese people. At the end of his visit he concluded that the mission was worth continuing and that enough missionaries must be assigned to do it right. "It is like trying to run a sixty horsepower machine with a one horsepower motor and that out of repair," said Elder McKay.[9] He decided that the mission would do better if there were several married couples appointed and distributed to each of the conferences.[10] These couples were to have six or eight missionaries working under them, and they were to act as guardians and counselors for their missionaries. This idea began to be implemented during the coming months but never became fully operational. In June 1921, Hilton A. Robertson and his wife, Hazel, arrived in Tokyo, and in November 1922, three more couples arrived in the mission. At the end of the year there were twenty missionaries in the field—only three more than in 1921, which had previously been the year with the most missionaries.[11]

In addition to the plan for more missionaries, Elder McKay made suggestions for improving the work of individual missionaries. He stressed the need to turn every conversation into a gospel discussion. Missionaries were also directed to always carry tracts and other literature. They were to spend more time teaching the gospel in public places such as markets, and to continue holding street meetings. Assessing the missionaries' current efforts, Elder McKay wrote the following to the missionaries:

> As far as the Truth is concerned, the Japanese people are in darkness, though we believe that hundreds of thousands of them are groping blindly for the light. The light is now in their midst, but "the darkness comprehendeth it not." And

Illus. 10-1. Japan missionaries, ca. 1921. Standing (*left to right*): Unidentified person, Irwin T. Hicken (?), Howard Jensen, Myrl L. Bodily, Lowring A. Whitaker. Sitting (*left to right*): Deloss W. Holley, Joseph S. Payne, Mary E. Stimpson, three Stimpson children, President Joseph H. Stimpson, Owen McGary, unidentified person.

Courtesy Church Archives, The Church of Jesus Christ of Latter-day Saints

Illus. 10-2. Japan Mission special conference, January 1921. Standing (*left to right*): Irwin T. Hicken, Deloss W. Holley, Howard Jensen, Joseph S. Payne, Lowring A. Whitaker. Sitting (*left to right*): President Joseph H. Stimpson, Mary E. Stimpson, David O. McKay, Hugh J. Cannon, Myrl L. Bodily, and Owen McGary.

Juvenile Instructor 56 (March 1921): 122

we wonder whether we are not, perhaps unintentionally and unconsciously, hiding our light under a bushel, or at least to hold it aloft, so that all who see us must have their attention directed toward it.[12]

Apparently he did not feel that the missionaries had been working hard enough. They were told to work at least as hard as if they were working for a salary.

Elder McKay's last official act was to release Stimpson as mission president. The Stimpsons (illus. 10-3) left Japan on February 11, 1921. In March 1921, Lloyd O. Ivie, a former missionary to Japan, and his new bride, Nora, arrived in Japan to assume the reins of leadership. Ivie continued in the spirit of the reforms started by Elder McKay. For a brief moment, total numbers of missionaries, Book of Mormon sales, and baptisms increased, but by the end of 1922, the old pattern had returned. In January 1922, the Kōfu conference was closed after fourteen consecutive years of missionary presence. This left only three

Courtesy Church Archives, The Church of Jesus Christ of Latter-day Saints

Illus. 10-3. Stimpson family, in Japan, ca. 1921, dressed in traditional Japanese kimonos. Joseph H. Stimpson served as president of the Japan Mission from 1915 to 1921.

Closing of the Early Japan Mission   269

conferences in the mission. Unfortunately, after the arrival of couples, the leaders in Salt Lake City did not continue to send the numbers of missionaries that had been suggested by Elder McKay. Enthusiasm among the missionaries subsequently dropped.

Elder Hilton A. Robertson succeeded President Ivie as mission president in 1923. The period of his leadership was short-lived. During the mission's final years, missionary activity varied little throughout the mission. The missionaries spent most mornings studying, teaching English at local schools, and taking care of various tasks such as letter writing, picture taking, and shopping. Active proselytizing did not usually begin until afternoon. Evenings were filled with teaching English classes, holding Mutual Improvement Association, teaching gospel lessons, and visiting friends and investigators. On Sunday, three meetings were usually held. Sunday School was the largest, attended by large numbers of children (illus. 10-4). The missionaries hoped these children would be a successful avenue of approach to their parents. Sacrament meetings were usually attended by only a few members and investigators. The third meeting was an evening preaching meeting.

Attendance patterns in the individual branches of the mission were not promising. Just before Kōfu was closed, there were only two or three Church members and about the same number of investigators attending sacrament meeting. The elders claimed these figures

Courtesy John W. Welch

Illus. 10-4. Elders with Japanese Sunday School children in Tokyo, ca. 1920s.

were encouraging.[13] However, this claim was in spite of the fact that thirty baptized members were still living in Kōfu[14] and ten years earlier, between five and eight members attended church regularly.[15] The situation in Osaka was slightly more encouraging. On seven Sundays picked at random during 1923 and 1924, an average of about twelve individuals attended sacrament meeting (including missionaries), about thirty-seven attended Sunday School, and about twenty-five attended the evening preaching meeting.[16]

In 1924 the elders in Sapporo reported a regular attendance of between twenty-five and fifty people at Sunday School and about eight to ten people at sacrament meeting.[17] Sendai, formed in 1923, was a much newer area, and had met with little success. Even though Tokyo had twenty more potential members than any other area, the attendance figures were more erratic than in other branches. Average attendance there was only eight individuals attending sacrament meeting. Tithe paying was reportedly very poor throughout the mission. In summary, the statistics for the mission were far from impressive. In June of that year, the decision was made to pull all missionaries from Japan.

In a letter dated June 10, 1924, the First Presidency stated that they were not "particularly alarmed over the situation in Japan." They believed that the current problems would soon subside. The reason for closing the mission was because "from the standpoint of converts," success had been "so limited that, at least for the present, under existing circumstances, it will be better to withdraw."[18]

Were the Latter-day Saints unusual in their lack of success, or was their record similar to that of missionary groups from other religions? I believe the Latter-day Saints were no less successful than other missionaries, though it is difficult to accumulate the statistics to prove this statement. However, the ratio of effectiveness was about proportional to the number of man-years put in by any missionary group. During the first thirteen years of the Protestant missions, only ten converts were baptized, although political conditions were much different then (see chapter 1). By 1882 there were 145 Protestant missionaries and 4,987 members.[19] Many of the missionaries had been there for ten years or more. By figuring in terms of man-years put in, the Latter-day Saint missionaries actually gained converts a little faster than did the Protestants.

Few missions of the Church have been closed, especially after being in operation for so many years. There are some slight similarities between the closing of the Japan Mission and the earlier mission closures in the Society Islands (1852–92), Tonga (1897–1907), and other places. However, most of the circumstances that caused this temporary defeat were peculiar to the Japan Mission.

The official announcement of the First Presidency stated that the mission was being closed because of "existing conditions in Japan and because of the almost negligible results of missionary effort in that country."[20] It should be explained what the "conditions" in Japan were and why the results were "almost negligible." The problems and contributing difficulties the Church faced in Japan fit broadly into three categories. First, a number of problems were constant during the entire length of the mission: difficulties with language, proselytizing approach, cultural differences, a small missionary force, the long tenure of service, and failure to attract many converts. Second, there were a number of external hindrances that arose during the last several years of the mission. Among these were the great Tokyo earthquake of 1923, international problems (such as the Japanese exclusion laws that were passed in the United States), the Church's failure to acquire any real property, and the near-closing of the Tonga Mission at approximately the same time. Third, to these definable historic facts can be added the general psychological distress or defeatism that plagued missionaries in Japan and Church leaders in Salt Lake City. Another intangible factor that must certainly be considered is the dimension of inspiration that guided the First Presidency.

Ongoing Problems in the Japan Mission Contributing to the Closing

The Japanese language was recognized by every Latter-day Saint missionary as the main difficulty in the quest for baptisms. As a missionary in Japan, Heber J. Grant complained that he constantly fell asleep while studying the language. He also reportedly quipped that "he learned the Japanese language but the people couldn't understand their own language when he spoke it."[21] Years after the mission was closed, Hilton A. Robertson said he felt that many Latter-day Saints had wrongly condemned the Japanese for not accepting the gospel more readily. He placed partial blame on the poor language abilities of the missionaries. They simply did not communicate well.[22]

However, it is incorrect to conclude that none of the missionaries mastered the language. A number of elders accomplished remarkable tasks, such as translating the Book of Mormon, Anderson's *Brief History of the Church,* Talmage's *Articles of Faith,* and other materials. But the fact remains that mastery of the language took years, not months, and frequently the ability to communicate came concurrently with waning enthusiasm for the work and a missionary's personal desire to return home.

Spoken language mastery was important, but missionaries recognized from the beginning that potential converts needed printed information to study. The earliest missionaries expected that translated materials would bring in converts more rapidly. Unfortunately, after years of diligent effort and a number of good publications, there was no evidence that tracts and books helped the conversion rate at all.

An important aspect of the language and translation problem was transculturization, or the adaptation of terms from one culture to another. Special terminology has developed since the founding of the Church that sets Latter-day Saints apart from other religious organizations. Words as basic as "God" and "Savior" carry different meanings for Latter-day Saints than for other groups. The early missionaries to Japan soon learned that finding the proper vocabulary to convey their special message was difficult. The case of Elder John W. Stoker's translation of the *Brief History of the Church* illustrates this problem well. In writing the First Presidency of the Church after the book had been published, Alma O. Taylor said,

> Being a book in which nearly all of our "Mormon" terms are used, it seemed that we would never get through with all the problems that came up, for no words in common use even approached an equivalent for the English meaning as we interpret it; hence, study, inquiry, and experiment had to follow . . . but these words . . . are not necessarily beyond the grasp of the reading circle . . . for new words are only a new combination of old words.[23]

Selecting good material for translation and publication was another challenge. Several poor choices were made, along with some wise ones. It must be added, however, that generally efforts were made to fit tracts to the needs of the people. An intelligent, early effort to accommodate preaching to local needs was a pamphlet titled "The True and Living God." In its entirety this tract contained a very simple, step-by-step analysis of the Latter-day Saint concept of God.[24]

The problem of relying on traditional published materials was compounded by the fact that the Japanese did not share with Christians the same patterns of logic, belief in scriptures, or ideas about God. This is to be expected in a non-Christian part of the world. Missionaries with keen insight—such as Alma O. Taylor, Elbert D. Thomas, H. Grant Ivins, and Joseph H. Stimpson—recognized this problem and worked to overcome it. Taylor wrote concerning this difficulty after his arrival home:

> I remember being asked to address an audience in Salt Lake City, before I went to Japan, on the subject, "Why I am a Latter-day Saint." After stating that my birth and bringing up in the Church were the first and foundation reasons for being a Latter-day Saint, I proceeded to quote scriptures to show that "Mormonism" was true. I am not ashamed of that speech, but I often smile when I think of the effect, or rather the lack of effect, such a speech would have on an audience in Japan, where we have to give reason for our faith independent of The Bible and the scriptures.[25]

Taylor continued this line of reasoning by suggesting that many Church members placed too much reliance upon the testimonies of the ancient Apostles and disciples of Christ. He said, "In Japan the elders have to preach God and Jesus Christ, not in the name of Paul, John, Peter, Nephi, Samuel, Joseph Smith, or any other prophet, but in their own names and through the testimony of their own works."[26] He felt missionaries succeeded "best by earnestly and prayerfully seeking the evidences which God has amply provided in his own creations and dealings, and by using these evidences under the direction of the Holy Spirit."[27]

Missionaries tried to put a positive spin on language difference by using it to approach Japanese. English language classes were used to attract prospective investigators throughout the mission. Some members were introduced to the Church through this means, but the missionaries frequently felt that this approach was a waste of time—their students were often interested only in the English language and not in religion. President Grant became disgusted with the attitude of many Japanese who attended Latter-day Saint services. One of Grant's counselors, speaking for the president, wrote to President Robertson saying,

> President Grant's experience in Japan teaches him that the average Japanese who comes to our meetings comes to see what he can get out of it. There is one little illustration of a man who learned French, German and English by belonging to three different churches and he was only too anxious to become a member of our church, providing we would employ him as interpreter and translator.[28]

Even though the language classes had drawbacks, they continued until the end of the mission. In fact, the language classes were the main approach missionaries used during the period from 1921 to 1924, particularly the married couples who were serving in the mission at that time.[29]

Other missionary techniques were also unsuccessful. Street meetings were a regular means of preaching the gospel. Large crowds were usually easy to attract. Passers-by were courteous and willingly accepted tracts, announcements about meetings, and other literature. But successfully communicating the ideas of the Church to a constantly fluctuating audience was a difficult task. Missionaries distributed thousands of tracts, but these tracts did not lead to many serious inquiries.

To further encourage missionary contacts, special gospel lessons were devised for the Japanese members. Newsletters and periodicals were also circulated among the members, and hymnbooks were published in Japanese. Additionally, the Mutual Improvement Association was organized in an attempt to attract and retain young people. These efforts accomplished some good, but the barriers of language and culture seemed to be insurmountable no matter which of the approaches was used.

Cultural differences affected every facet of missionary work, not only the approach. Another important cultural point to consider is the difference in religious intensity between the Church and Japan. Historically, the Japanese have not been outwardly religious. Although exceptions exist, Japanese religions are generally classified as "perfunctory, weak, and indifferent."[30] In contrast, it is evident that most Latter-day Saint groups could be classified as "lively, intense, and strong." The Church may not have met Japanese expectations of how a religion should function. This difference in religious intensity is a probable explanation for some of the lack of Latter-day Saint missionary success with the Japanese people.

Another Japanese trait is that of familism, or family-centeredness. This cultural trait was especially strong in Japan during the early mission period. The family group has traditionally been the individual's means of establishing his or her identity. Efforts, whether economic, social, or religious, have usually been made by family members in behalf of the whole family organization. Fathers have ruled the Japanese home, and sons have respected the desires of their fathers, as have wives and daughters. Marriages have been intended to be as compatible as possible, but they have been arranged for the benefit of the extended families as well as the parties involved. Occupations have frequently been family occupations. These traditions, and others like them, tended to discourage affiliation by individual Japanese with an alien institution such as a Christian or Western religion. In essence, missionaries had the difficult task of replacing the family or becoming the primary socio-religious group. It was through constant association with the missionaries that converts, at least those who remained active in the Church, became acculturated to and comfortable with the new social group to which they belonged.

In these situations, the missionaries had to determine how to influence people sufficiently that they would be willing to leave the secure environment of their natal family (which could be enlarged to include the entire Japanese national family) and take a chance with the Mormon family. Several of the most faithful converts were women who worked as cooks in the mission headquarters and thus became part of the Mormon family, so to speak, and were able to establish a new identity. When the conservative nature of the Japanese family and society is considered, the number of converts during the years of the early mission, 174, seems quite remarkable.

While Japan's unfamiliar culture and language caused problems for missionary work, the internal structure of the mission exacerbated those problems. One internal problem was that of a small missionary force. At no time were there more than twenty missionaries, and on several occasions there were as few as four. It is implicit that the leaders of the Church felt ambivalent toward Japan. It was almost as though they had a policy of succeeding first and sending missionaries later. Requests for more missionaries to Japan were frequent from the various mission presidents, but the requests were seldom granted.

The lack of missionaries was recognized as a very real detriment to the work. President Stimpson struggled with this handicap and sought the help of Elder David O. McKay, then of the Quorum of the Twelve Apostles, to overcome it. In March 1920, President Stimpson wrote a letter of invitation to Elder McKay, asking him to return to Tokyo for an international Sunday School convention that fall; he also included in his letter statistics concerning the progress of the mission. To that date, sixty baptisms had been performed during his tenure as president, sixteen children had been blessed, thirty-seven men had been ordained to the Aaronic Priesthood, and the total membership was 124. At that time there were only eight missionaries in the field. He pleaded with Elder McKay to use whatever influence he could to have six more missionaries sent to Japan. Three new elders did arrive in May 1920, the first to come in two-and-a-half years, but they merely replaced several others who were released. There were only two elders working in each conference, and Sendai had been closed for lack of missionaries. Stimpson wrote: "We have so few missionaries here in the mission at the present time that the devil has to look elsewhere for a workshop."[31] It is apparent that the missionary force was so small that they made virtually no impression upon the Japanese nation.

Another problem that was related to that of a small missionary force was the problem of long tenure of service. From the days of Heber J. Grant to the end of the mission, time served in the Japan mission field was longer than for other missions of the Church. A survey of Manuscript History of the Church reveals average mission length was three years and three months. President Alma O. Taylor stayed longest of all—eight years and five months.

Parents, sweethearts, and ward members sometimes wrote to the presiding Brethren, asking why some elder had been left in Japan for so long. The missionaries themselves were usually less concerned because they knew that it was necessary to remain long enough to conquer the language and to do some good. But the pressure from home did have an effect on the work in Japan. Alma O. Taylor once wrote an article in the *Improvement Era* in which he tried to explain why such lengthy stays were necessary.[32] Still the parents and friends at home had a hard time understanding the situation.

Pressing External Problems Contributing to the Closing

The last years of the mission were plagued with difficulties outside the control of the missionaries. The first of these was the great Tokyo earthquake of September 1, 1923. About 130,000 people died as a result of fires, falling debris, and riots and disorders. Several missionaries, including the Robertsons, were in Tokyo at the time of the disaster and were very fortunate to escape bodily harm or death. Fortunately, throughout the entire disaster, Robertson reported, not one member of the Church was injured nor were any of the missionaries. The mission home lost some tile from the roof and plaster from the wall, but aside from those minor damages the place fared very well.[33]

The earthquake halted proselytizing in Tokyo for several months. The missionaries filled their days by helping members repair their homes or relocate. Back in the states, newspapers circulated gloomy reports and in one instance incorrectly reported the death of President Robertson.[34] Not until September 11 did the friends and relatives of the missionaries know that they were safe.[35]

The earthquake had a lasting effect on the mission in at least one way. It encouraged the leaders at home to more seriously reassess the position of the Church in Japan. The parents of the missionaries also felt the distance from their sons and daughters to be greater than ever before. Family members of missionaries were concerned by scriptural passages telling of earthquakes occurring as warnings to wicked peoples. After his release, Robertson concurred in this reasoning. He said, "We are told in the Doctrine and Covenants that after the testimony of the servants of God, earthquakes, pestilence, and disease, etc., will follow, and I bear testimony to you folks, . . . that those things have taken place in that land."[36] The question at that point was simply what to do next, and it was not answered immediately.

The earthquake disrupted missionary work, but the most serious tension between missionaries and the Japanese was caused by the American passing of the Japanese Exclusion Act in 1924. These laws prevented Japanese from immigrating to the United States. Racial discrimination against Chinese and Japanese living on the West Coast of the United States certainly contributed to the passage of these laws. A long series of state and national issues concerning the immigration of "Orientals" into the United States and subsequent issues relating to their possession of land had begun in 1882. This was culminated by the enactment by Congress of a new immigration law, the second Johnson Act, which contained a section forbidding admittance to the United States of "aliens ineligible for citizenship."[37] Because the Chinese and Japanese were the only aliens not eligible for citizenship, the law was a direct insult to Japan and was accepted by the Japanese as such.

The situation became very tense for the missionaries after this law was passed. Americans were temporarily not welcome in Japan. On one occasion, shortly after the Exclusion Act went into effect, President Robertson found two posters tacked to his door saying, "Bei-jin Haiseki" or "American go home!"

Alma O. Taylor had been prophetic in his assessment of the situation. As early as October 1920, Taylor wrote the following to President Stimpson:

> You are perhaps anxious about the present agitation and ill feelings over the pending legislation in California against the Japanese. I can see no way out of the situation as the people of California have more support from the rest of the U. S. than ever before. Something should be done now to prevent the constant recurrence of the question. Before the settlement the feeling in Japan among the populous will perhaps run high against the Americans.[38]

Taylor's fear was accurate. Christian missionary groups felt the negative effects of the law. A *Salt Lake Telegram* article printed June 18, 1924, noted that the Reverend Dr. Paul B. Waterhouse had asserted, "The passage of the exclusion act has made Christian missionary work in Japan almost impossible." The law went into effect on July 1, 1924, only days after the fateful telegram to close the mission had been delivered. It was sent June 9, 1924, and arrived June 26, 1924. The final decision, however, probably had been made not too long before then.

July 1 was observed throughout Japan as a "day of humiliation," and Tokyo blazed with posters that read "Hate Everything American." The largest of sixteen protests lasted continuously from one in the afternoon until ten in the evening, with an audience ranging from 5,000 to 12,000.[39]

Several other external items may have contributed to the willingness of the First Presidency to close the Japan-based operation. One was that the Church had not acquired any real property, so it was possible to leave easily. Another development that may have had some bearing was the consideration being given to closing the Tonga Mission around the same time. The mission president in Tonga made a valiant plea for the continuance of his mission. There were over a thousand Saints in Tonga. Nevertheless the Tonga mission came very close to being shut down during summer 1924.[40] Such thinking seems to reflect a willingness in Salt Lake City to assess missions and determine their worth. The Japan Mission was found wanting.

Intangible Factors Contributing to the Closing

As a result of the difficulties mentioned above, the rate of conversions to the Church was very slow—so slow, in fact, that the missionaries never had a chance to become elated with their success. This was reflected upon both missionaries and converts alike. The missionaries did not learn to expect rapid success, and members and prospective members did not feel that they were a part of a successful operation. The old saying that nothing succeeds like success was, without question, true in the case of the Japan Mission. The overall psychology was not one of winning.

Closely related to the above reasoning was the concern of psychological failure. This was a cumulative matter. The sad concomitant was that the missionaries felt that they were not a part of a going concern, and this was reflected in their attitude toward the work. Since the mission was first opened, President Grant had questioned its validity. A feeling of questioning the possible success of the mission had also been in the mind of President Lorenzo Snow when he first called Grant to Japan. On June 26, 1901, President Snow told Elder Grant, "Noah preached 120 years, he was a grand man, he did his duty but failed. . . . As to these brethren who will shortly leave for Japan the Lord has not revealed to me that they will succeed, but He has shown me that it is their duty to go."[41] This attitude may have helped President Grant finally decide to close the mission. The Mormons had been doing their duty for twenty-three years with few results.

There is still one further ingredient that many Latter-day Saints would suggest as an essential reason for President Grant's decision to close the mission: inspiration or direction from the Lord. When the missionaries from Japan arrived in Salt Lake City on August 22, 1924, President Grant greeted them saying, "Thank God you are home because I know what is in store for the people of that land and we are glad you are safely home."[42] President Robertson made a statement many years later that was similar in spirit to President Grant's greeting. "I think that the mission was closed for a purpose in 1924 when we returned home. . . . Later on we find that the other denominations throughout the world [that] were proselytizing in Japan were forced to close their missions and return to America at great loss and sacrifice."[43]

Conclusion

When the telegram arrived on June 26, 1924, instructing the missionaries in Japan to return home, they promptly set about making the necessary arrangements for closing the mission. Arrangements were immediately made for Elder and Sister W. Lamont Glover to sail home because Sister Glover's health was failing. They sailed on July 8 aboard the *Shinyo Maru*. On July 16, 1924, Elder Elwood L. Christensen baptized Morita Yosaku in Tokyo; Morita would be the last Latter-day Saint convert in Japan for over fourteen years. During the first three weeks of July, elders and sisters arrived at Tokyo from their various locations. Most of the last month or so was spent visiting members, selling and giving away mission-owned goods, shipping books, and other activities. Then on July 24, Elders William E. Davies and Milton B. Taylor, along with Elder and Sister F. Wallace Browning, boarded the SS *President Cleveland* and sailed for the United States.

All meetings after June 29 were cancelled except sacrament meeting, which was held until the last Sunday before departure. Only two to four Japanese Mormons attended during that time. Finally, on August 2, President and Sister Robertson went to Osaka to encourage the Saints there to "live up to their duties." They boarded the SS *President Pierce* in Kobe, and all the remaining missionaries—Elder and Sister Elwood Christensen, and Elders Rulon Esplin, Vinal G. Mauss, Lewis H. Moore, and Ernest B. Woodward—boarded the same ship in Yokohama. They sailed from Japan on August 7, 1924. Thus, the early mission of The Church of Jesus Christ of Latter-day Saints to Japan was closed.[44]

Considering the number of problems the mission had faced through the years, the disruptions of the final two years, and the psychological distress suffered by the missionaries, it is easy to understand the decision of the First Presidency and the Quorum of the Twelve to close the mission. It was true that the results of their missionary effort had been "almost negligible," especially when compared to other fields of labor. Nevertheless, the mission did produce some lasting contributions—translation work in particular—and a few converts who remained faithful through the years until the work recommenced following World War II.

An earlier version of this article appeared as R. Lanier Britsch, "The Closing of the Early Japan Mission," BYU Studies *15, no. 2 (1975): 171–90.*

Notes

1. Japan Mission General Minutes, June 13, 1924, Church Archives, The Church of Jesus Christ of Latter-day Saints, Salt Lake City.

2. Japan Mission General Minutes, May 14, 1924.

3. Heber J. Grant to Hilton A. Robertson, Heber J. Grant Letterpress Copybook, February 22, 1924, 156, Church Archives. Because current Latter-day Saint archival policy limits the access and use of materials, particularly those of the presidents of the Church, I have been unable to verify some of my footnote citations to which I had earlier access.

4. In the same letter, the First Presidency mentioned that Lloyd O. Ivie, the previous mission president, estimated that there were "only five or six real converts to the Gospel in that mission."

5. Heber J. Grant to Hilton A. Robertson, Grant Letterpress Copybook, February 20, 1924, 154.

6. Japan Mission Journals, June 15, 1924. The Latter-day Saint missionaries in Japan were not aware that a formal public announcement concerning the closing of the mission had been made in the Church's *Deseret Evening News* on June 12, 1924. So it is not surprising that international news wire services had picked up this information by June 15.

7. The First Presidency was a little upset that this telegram did not arrive sooner than the money. They conjectured that the Church's cable address "Quickmere" was not registered in Tokyo, which would have accounted for the

failure of the telegram to reach the mission immediately. Grant to Robertson, Grant Letterpress Copybook, July 12, 1924, 969.

8. Manuscript History of the Japan Mission, n.d., Church Archives. See also Heber J. Grant to Hilton A. Robertson, Grant Letterpress Copybook, June 9, 1924, 752.

9. "Missionary Annual Reports," December 31, 1921, 191, Church Archives.

10. Joseph H. Stimpson to Alma O. Taylor, January 19, 1921, Stimpson Papers, L. Tom Perry Special Collections, Brigam Young University, Provo, Utah.

11. Mission Financial and Statistical Reports, Japan, 1921, 1922, 1923, Church Archives.

12. David O. McKay and Hugh J. Cannon to the Elders of the Japan Mission, Tokyo, Japan, January 23, 1921, Stimpson Papers.

13. Japan Mission District Records, Kofu Conference, April 1921 through January 1922, Church Archives.

14. Record of Members, Japan Mission, Form E, microfilm, Church Archives.

15. Lloyd O. Ivie, Missionary Journal, November 5, 1911, Perry Special Collections.

16. Japan Mission District Records, Osaka Conference, 1923, 1924, Church Archives.

17. Japan Mission General Minutes, August 14, 1924.

18. Heber J. Grant, Charles W. Penrose, and Anthony W. Ivins to Hilton A. Robertson, Grant Letterpress Copybook, June 10, 1924.

19. See Kenneth Scott Latourette, *A History of the Expansion of Christianity* 7 vols. (New York: Harper and Brothers, 1944), 6:385–90.

20. "Japanese Mission of Church Closed," *Deseret Evening News,* June 12, 1924, 6. The official text of the announcement also stated the closing was temporary.

21. Hilton A. Robertson, in *One-Hundred-Seventeenth Annual Conference of The Church of Jesus Christ of Latter-day Saints* (Salt Lake City: The Church of Jesus Christ of Latter-day Saints, 1947), 53.

22. Robertson, in *One-Hundred-Seventeenth Annual Conference*, 53.

23. Alma O. Taylor to the First Presidency, September 3, 1907, Japan Mission Letterpress Copybook, Copybook C, 153, Church Archives.

24. Alma O. Taylor, "Journals, 1901–1946," June 15, 1903, Perry Special Collections.

25. Alma O. Taylor, "Japan, the Ideal Mission Field," *Improvement Era* 13 (June 1910): 780.

26. Taylor, "Ideal Mission Field," 781.

27. Taylor, "Ideal Mission Field," 780.

28. Letter to Hilton A. Robertson, Grant Letterpress Copybook, February 22, 1924, 155.

29. Hilton A. Robertson, interview by author, typescript, Provo, Utah, August 1, 1967.

30. Joachim Wach, *The Comparative Study of Religions* (New York: Columbia University Press, 1958), 125.

31. Joseph H. Stimpson to David O. McKay, March 18, 1920, Stimpson Papers. See also David O. McKay to Joseph H. Stimpson, June 10, 1920, Stimpson Papers.

32. Alma O. Taylor, "About Japan and the Japan Mission," *Improvement Era* 10 (November 1906): 6.

33. Hilton A. Robertson, in *Ninety-Fifth Semi-Annual Conference of The Church of Jesus Christ of Latter-day Saints* (Salt Lake City: The Church of Jesus Christ of Latter-day Saints, 1924), 123–24.

34. Unidentified article found in scrapbook of Hilton A. Robertson.

35. "Official List of American Dead," *Deseret Evening News,* September 11, 1923, 1.

36. Robertson, in *Ninety-Fifth Semi-Annual Conference,* 123.

37. See Edwin O. Reischauer, *The United States and Japan* (New York: Viking, 1963), 16–17.

38. Alma O. Taylor to Joseph H. Stimpson, October 17, 1920, Stimpson Papers.

39. Sidney L. Gulick, "American-Japanese Relations: The Logic of the Exclusionists," *The Annals of the American Academy of Social and Political Sciences* (November 1924): 181.

40. R. Lanier Britsch, "Mormon Intruders in Tonga: The Passport Act of 1922," in Davis Bitton, ed., *Mormons, Scripture, and the Ancient World: Studies in Honor of John L. Sorenson* (Provo, Utah: Foundation for Ancient Research and Mormon Studies), 121–48.

41. Gordon A. Madsen, comp., *A Japanese Journal* (n.p., 1970), 12.

42. Japan Mission Journals, August 22, 1924.

43. Robertson, in *One-Hundred-Seventeenth Annual Conference,* 53.

44. Manuscript History of the Japan Mission, August 7, 1924.

11

Members without a Church: Latter-day Saints in Japan from 1924 to 1945

Chris Conkling

What happens to faithful Latter-day Saints who are almost totally isolated from the Church for over twenty years? We gain insights into this type of situation by studying The Church of Jesus Christ of Latter-day Saints in Japan.

After twenty-three years of proselytizing, the Church withdrew its missionaries, leadership, and organizational structure from Japan in 1924 and did not reopen its Japan Mission until 1948 (although member soldiers had been meeting with the Saints since 1945). The 137 Latter-day Saints in Japan—about two dozen of whom were active members—were left almost entirely on their own.[1] This small band of Japanese members was concentrated in four cities: Kōfu (where the missionaries had been withdrawn in 1922), Tokyo, Osaka, and Sapporo.

Many of these Saints felt hurt, isolated, or abandoned by the Church. They reacted to their situation in a variety of ways. Some worked to build the Church despite frustration and lack of external support. Some never attended Church meetings during the interim but came back once the Church again sent representatives to Japan. Others, perhaps longing for a more intimate and simpler organization, worshipped privately during the bleakest times. However, even private worship waned as the temporary closure stretched on for years.

Before Church President Heber J. Grant closed the mission and its headquarters, Japan Mission President Hilton A. Robertson visited several of the active members to tell them that the closing could be temporary. Other than providing reassurances, he and his missionaries were unable to prepare the members for the trials that loomed in the future. Perhaps feeling that Japan had not yet born fruit in developing enough mature and well-trained leaders, Church leaders in Salt Lake City instructed Robertson to prohibit Japanese brethren from exercising their priesthood. The Japanese Saints could not hold sacrament meetings or officiate in other priesthood ordinances. They were, however, encouraged to gather for Mutual Improvement Association (MIA) meetings.[2] Within a decade, war would be raging across the world, and the Saints in Japan would find themselves even more spiritually alone. Sister Kumagai Tamano of Sapporo said, "Zen to kuraku natta yōna kimochi" ("I felt like all had become darkness").[3]

The Nara Era, 1924–33

The departure of American leadership and missionaries left a gaping hole in the fabric of Church organization in Japan. For a time the efforts of individual members who sought to act as spiritual shepherds in Japan partially filled the hole. The first of these, Brother Nara Fujiya, was born on May 10, 1898, in Akita Prefecture (province). At the age of twelve, he was befriended by Latter-day Saint elders in Sapporo. He moved to Tokyo and was baptized by mission president Joseph H. Stimpson in 1915. Thereafter, he began working for the Japanese National Railway in Kōfu, where he attended the local branch and advanced in the Aaronic Priesthood.[4] In 1919, Nara returned to Tokyo to further his education. While remaining a faithful member of the Church, he graduated from two Japanese universities and was ordained an elder in 1923. He also served as mission secretary under Presidents Joseph H. Stimpson and Lloyd O. Ivie. On April 6, 1924, he married Yoshimizu Motoko.[5]

After the mission closed in August 1924, Nara and some fellow Saints gathered in Tokyo to establish the Japan MIA. They also discussed publishing a periodical to unify and uplift the native membership. That November, Nara's group circulated the names and addresses of all members of the Japan MIA.[6] Later, they began publishing and distributing *Shuro* (The palm) (illus. 11-1), named for the palm leaves strewn on the way as Christ entered Jerusalem. They planned to publish ten issues per year, sixty-five copies of each issue, and to send copies to all known Japanese Saints as well as to interested members in Hawaii and on the U.S. mainland.

Through extant *Shuro* issues, we can gain insights into the hearts and minds of participating Japanese Saints. The premier issue appeared on January 1, 1925.[7] In his first article, "About the Beginning," Nara described the emotional pain and spiritual void caused by the mission's closing. However, he also expressed that the MIA was like a path to the light in the current darkness and that he hoped *Shuro* would strengthen his fellow Japanese brothers and sisters.[8] In subsequent issues, other Saints followed suit. They submitted editorials, correspondence, scripture study notes, personal news, short stories, poems, and serialized articles. Many of their submissions were filled with raw emotion. For example, in "Deep Feelings," Brother Fujiwara Takeo of Sapporo admitted that he looked for anything to bolster his faith. *Shuro* was a source of strength and sometimes moved him to tears.[9] One former Latter-day Saint even expressed how happy his family had become attending a different Christian congregation. Some, like the editorial assistants Sister Mochizuki Reiko and Brother Yamaide Torao, expressed their feelings through poetry. I have included a rough translation of one of Brother Yamaide's poems, "If One's Alone," because it provides modern readers with insight into the longing and despair that some Saints felt.

Courtesy Perry Special Collections, HBLL, BYU

Illus. 11-1. Japanese Saints published *Shuro* for three or four years beginning in 1925. As can be seen, it was published in Japanese only, handwritten and mimeographed without page numbers. Many issues are available at the L. Tom Perry Special Collections, Harold B. Lee Library, BYU.

If One's Alone

by Yamaide Torao

If one's sad and lonely
And looks at the sunset,
And hears the faint
    temple bells ringing

If one hears the distant temple bells
It touches his heart,
He will pray with a sad heart

His card is a hateful spade,
But, sorrowfully,
It's just a game he is playing with his fortune-telling cards

When I see the hearts of all the
    noisy people
I see sadness.
I'm opposed to flowers, and yet,
    Spring will come anyway

If one's alone,
My heart is sad

Despite the thin fog
I can still see you, disappearing

If one's alone,
The night is sad
O miserable heart!
What a pity,
The light is disappearing

If one's alone,
I try to pray
My heart is hollow
I can still see your
Dear fleeting form[10]

Hitori i nareba
(tanka to shokyoku)

Hitori i no kokoro sabishi mo
Yōzareba
Mido no kane to
    kasokeku hibiku

Tōdera no kane no ne kikeba
Shimijimi to
Susamishi kokoro mo ino
ran tosu

Zō chō tefu su-pei-do no fuda wa
Kanashikari
Uranai no asobi nite
arishikado

Uchi sawagu hito ra no
    kokoro
Sabishi mite
Hana ni somukishi haru
    wo ayumeri

Hitori i nareba
Kokoro sabishiya

Usu moya no uchi ni
Natsumishi kimi no
Sugata kie yuku

Hitori i nareba
Yoru wa sabishiya
Urabureshiku kokoro
Aware kanashiya
Hikari kie e yuku

Hitori i nareba
Inoran to suredo
Utsuro no kokoro
Itoshiya kimi no
Sugata nomi ukabu

Despite initial exuberance over *Shuro*, the publication efforts gradually decreased, and Nara became the periodical's major benefactor as well as editor. The plight of *Shuro* seems to represent Church activity as a whole during these years. Brother Nara and others published it ten times in 1925, but only four times in 1926, and in December of that year they decided that it should only be a seasonal publication. After 1926 only the winter 1928 issue is available, but there is mention of *Shuro*'s being published through fall 1929.[11] Presumably, publishing ceased altogether at about that time.[12]

During the early era under Nara's guidance, Church members gathered periodically to keep in contact with each other and with Church leaders in Utah. For instance, Sister Kumagai held weekly meetings in Sapporo, but eventually gave up when attendance became too sporadic. Still, she invited all her friends, including Church members, to her home at Christmastime and other special occasions. Moreover, Saints corresponded with friends in Hawaii and other U.S. states through *Shuro* and through personal letters. Help also came from America. Concerned for the Saints' well-being, the First Presidency asked Alma O. Taylor (third president of the Japan Mission, 1905–10) to write to the Japanese Saints.[13] In February 1926, Taylor began corresponding with Brother Nara in Tokyo, Brother Katsura in Osaka, and Sister Kumagai in Sapporo.[14] On behalf of the Japanese Saints, Nara responded and implored Taylor to ask the First Presidency to reopen the Japan Mission and to provide a Church meetingplace.[15]

Furthermore, President Grant asked Franklin S. Harris, President of Brigham Young University, to formally organize the MIA in Japan and to visit the Japanese Saints during the 1926 Pan Pacific Congress of Arts and Sciences held in Japan. President Harris met with the Saints in Tokyo, Osaka, and Sapporo, and organized an MIA presidency in each city. He then appointed Brother Nara to preside over the MIA in Japan.[16] President Harris was touched by the kindness of the Japanese and their feelings of abandonment caused by the withdrawal of the Church. "I was busy with official things till 9 P.M.," he recorded after meeting with a few individuals, "so my meetings with them began at that hour and continued till 12:00. They clung onto me as if I were the only old friend they had." A few days later he recorded:

As we passed through Sapporo last night at nine there were four members of the church there to meet me. One of them had come 200 miles to see me. . . . As we only remained at the station a few minutes the saints asked to ride a few stations with me, so we went into the dining car and they stayed with me till one A.M. when they got off. They were so tremendously hungry for someone from Utah and there were so many things they wanted to ask about—a fine lot they are.[17]

While in Sapporo, President Harris invited two young members, Sada Saburō and Fujiwara Takeo, to move to America and attend BYU. Only Brother Fujiwara accepted the invitation and later completed a degree at BYU (illus. 11-2). Harris's visit rejuvenated some of the Japanese Saints and helped them realize Church leaders had not forgotten them.

Throughout 1927, members held monthly meetings in Tokyo, Osaka, and Sapporo. Some met to study the Book of Mormon while others gathered to sing and chat or to go mountain climbing. Between six and nine members gathered at each meeting in Tokyo—higher numbers than the last few weeks before the mission was closed.[18]

Improvement Era 36 (Sept. 1933): 655

Illus. 11-2. Fujiwara Takeo in BYU graduation hat.

Support from the Saints in the United States continued in a variety of ways. For instance, in July 1927 Sister Nachie Tsuneko (called Tsune Nachie in Hawaii) returned from Hawaii and met with her former Latter-day Saint friends. For the previous five years she had been living in Laie, Hawaii, actively performing missionary and temple work on her own. Nine people attended both her welcome home and her farewell parties in 1927. During these meetings she told the Japanese Saints about temple work and encouraged them to remain faithful.[19]

Another example of support from the United States came from Brother Fujiwara Takeo, who was then studying at BYU in Provo, Utah. He contacted the First Presidency on behalf of the Japanese Saints and expressed their desire for the Church organization to be established again in Japan. On December 2, 1927—thanks to the efforts of Fujiwara, Elbert D. Thomas (former president of the Japan Mission), and Alma O. Taylor—the First Presidency appointed Nara Fujiya, by letter, as Presiding Elder over Japan.[20]

In addition to Nara's appointment, Church leaders removed previous restrictions so that priesthood holders in Japan could prepare to again exercise their authority. However, Nara was cautioned against proselytizing or ordaining members to priesthood offices without the approval of the First Presidency.[21] Taylor communicated all this to Nara and reported to President Grant that Nara had humbly accepted his calling but was concerned that it might take him some time to fully translate and understand all the forwarded directives.[22] Not surprisingly, when Nara received a booklet of fifty pages in English with detailed instructions on the priesthood, he may have felt overwhelmed and somewhat confused by his new responsibilities. Nevertheless, under his leadership, members continued to hold regular MIA meetings through the end of 1927.[23]

The following winter, Nara and his team published an issue of *Shuro* that reproduced letters from Church President Grant, BYU President Franklin S. Harris, and Brother Fujiwara. The issue also contained news from the Saints in Kōfu for the first time since 1924. Earlier, Nara had sent his friend, a Mr. Kubota, who was not a Latter-day Saint, to Kōfu to tell the members there that they could organize the MIA and again hold meetings.[24]

Despite this resurgence in Church activity, all but the most stalwart members seemed to fade away. For a time, Nara tried to shepherd his scattered sheep, but the details are unclear. We do know that the Tokyo Saints held a Christmas party in December 1928 and published two additional issues of *Shuro*,[25] but Church activity in Japan between 1929 and 1933 remains a mystery due to a lack of record keeping and limited communication between the Japanese Saints and Church leadership in Utah. To further complicate matters, the railroad company transferred Nara to Manchuria in January 1934.

Of Nara's calling as Presiding Elder, Alma Taylor wrote the First Presidency some years later, "Nothing came of this assignment. . . . Elder Nara dried up and blew away to Manchuria before any preaching activities got going."[26] Taylor's assessment may be a little harsh, considering that Nara had taken upon himself the responsibility of publishing *Shuro*, initiating MIA activities, and communicating with Church leadership. However, it is true that within twenty months of Nara's calling as Presiding Elder, Church headquarters' knowledge of all activities in Japan, and most of the activities themselves, completely ceased. The records are blank until the end of 1933, and after that time Nara was in Manchuria and out of the picture until the end of World War II. Years later, Nara described his feelings of failure: "Although I was given the honorable mission with the keys of authority as a holder of the Melchizedek priesthood, I could not perform it fully. This was indeed regrettable, and for this I only ask God for forgiveness."[27]

The Fujiwara Era, 1934–36

On July 7, 1934, six months after Nara moved to Manchuria, President Grant released Nara and set apart Brother Fujiwara Takeo as Presiding Elder over Japan. Fujiwara was born in Hokkaidō in 1905 and was baptized on May 10, 1924, just before the mission closed. Three years later he accepted President Harris's invitation to study at BYU, earning his master's degree in history in 1934. During his seven-year stint in America, Fujiwara became fluent in English and proved to be a faithful member. He wrote an article for the *Improvement Era* and supported himself as a lecturer and an entertainer, giving jujitsu and dance demonstrations in native costume (illus. 11-3). Following his setting apart in the United States, he departed for Japan. He also began receiving $35 a month from Church leaders for travel and communication expenses.[28]

Unlike Nara who had been surprised by his appointment, given instructions in a foreign language, and sustained and set apart "by mail," Fujiwara had been set apart in person by the First Presidency, had lived in Utah, had received leadership training, and had seen how the Church could function in favorable circumstances. In retrospect, the degrees of success of both men seem to be based heavily upon the preparation and support they received from Church headquarters.

Although Nara's "light" gradually dimmed through the years because of lack of institutional support, Fujiwara's "new bulb" lit so brightly that it burnt itself out in a flash. From September 1934 until a sickness in summer 1935, Fujiwara worked diligently to restore the faith and activity levels of the members. Brother Watanabe Yoshijirō (formerly of the Osaka MIA Presidency but at that time living in Tokyo) and his daughter Tazuko were Elder Fujiwara's greatest supporters. Within his first two months as Presiding Elder, Fujiwara visited the Saints in Sapporo, Osaka, Tokyo, and Kōfu. Sadly, his welcome home party in Sapporo was canceled when no one attended. His reception in Osaka was better—seven members attended a Church meeting held at Brother Katsura Tsuruichi's house. In Osaka, Fujiwara learned that Nara had not reinstated the brethren's priesthood functions; however, MIA meetings were being held every month or two.²⁹ In November the Presiding Elder met with six Saints in Kōfu: five members of the Yoneyama family and Sister Watanabe Tazuko. These Saints complained that they had been excluded, with the exception of Mr. Kubota's visit in 1927, from Church communication since the mission had closed in 1924.

Brother Fujiwara worked hard to locate and reactivate the Saints. Using the names and addresses from the *Shuro* mailing list, he sent out greeting cards and invitations for Church meetings and parties. For example, he invited thirty-three Saints to the 1934 Tokyo Christmas party, but only seven attended.³⁰ By the following spring he began to make some progress. He located six Sapporo members and organized a branch there. He also noted that nine members were attending sacrament meeting in Kōfu that April and that the Saints in Osaka had

Improvement Era 36 (Sept. 1933): 655
Illus. 11-3. Fujiwara Takeo in native costume as he traveled about to support himself giving lectures and demonstrations of Japanese culure.

held their first sacrament and testimony meeting in over ten years that same month. In May 1935, he baptized two of Sister Mochizuki Reiko's children—the first Latter-day Saint baptisms in Japan since the mission closed. "I am very happy to have two new members within a year of my mission in Japan. May the Lord continue his favor and blessings upon me," he wrote to the First Presidency.[31]

That May, Elder Fujiwara and the Saints published the first—and last—issue of *Hattatsu* (The progress),[32] (illus. 11-4) a magazine fashioned after *Shuro* but published in both Japanese and English. He hoped its publication would help interested Saints in Hawaii and the U.S. mainland keep abreast of mission developments in Japan. *Hattatsu* offered mission history and contemporary news as well as letters between Japanese Saints and friends overseas. A published letter from Brother Tomigoro Takagi (who had studied in America) to then-Senator Elbert D. Thomas and Alma O. Taylor pleaded, "with my ardent desire for PEACE of the whole human kind on the earth I do earnestly point out that NOW is the best and finest chance for restoration of the Japan Mission of the Church."[33]

Illus. 11-4. Unlike *Shuro*, *Hattatsu* had a professional typeset look and was printed in both English and Japanese, aimed at a Japanese, Hawaiian, and Utah audience.

Courtesy Perry Special Collections, HBLL, BYU

Special Situation in Kōfu

If we are to understand how the mission closing may have affected the lives of Japanese Saints, then the Yoneyama family of Kōfu might be our best-documented example. Yoneyama Renji and his wife were baptized in 1908, the first married couple to join the Church in Japan. Although Kōfu had once been a thriving branch, members gradually lost interest, few joined the Church, and the elders left the area in 1922. Between 1922 and 1934, the only partial contact the Kōfu Saints had with the Church was the visit in 1927 by Nara's friend, Mr. Kubota, who was not actually a Church member.[34]

Elder Fujiwara visited the Kōfu Saints in November 1934 and asked Brother Yoneyama Renji to serve as branch president, a call he initially refused and then later accepted. In an official report to Alma O. Taylor, Fujiwara wrote, "We understood that Brother R. Yoneyama (father) blamed the conduct of the church for the closing of the mission and seemed to have stood against the church and changed to his old Buddhist religion." He further noted that Brother Yoneyama's son Morizō had written and informed him that his family had canceled the Latter-day Saint Christmas party they had planned to hold in their home because "there will be no earnest and faithful saints who do come to a church meeting." Not surprisingly, Fujiwara postponed Yoneyama's appointment.[35]

However, by the time Fujiwara and Taylor again exchanged letters, the Presiding Elder's views had softened. The Yoneyama family suffered tremendously through the sickness of several of its members and the later death of their young son Kenji. Fujiwara, Watanabe Yoshijirō, and his daughter Watanabe Tazuko hurried to Kōfu to help comfort the family and to pray for their recovery.[36] Although he still encouraged Elder Fujiwara to postpone Yoneyama's advancement in the priesthood, Taylor showed increased compassion for the plight of the struggling Japanese Saints.

> If Ren Yoneyama has definitely joined the Buddhist Church, he should probably be dropped from the rolls of our church, however, we do not recommend any hasty action in these matters. We must remember that the saints were, as you say, left without organization, leadership, church building, church literature, etc. and it is a wonder that any of them kept the faith. We too are proud of their loyalty.[37]

In April 1935, Elder Fujiwara presided over an emotional meeting—the first Kōfu sacrament meeting held in over twelve years. He then called Yoneyama Renji as branch president. In a report to Taylor, Elder Fujiwara tried to put President Yoneyama's earlier behavior in context. He had not lost faith in the Church, but he had become embittered at the organization that he felt had abandoned his devoted and faithful family in 1922 and again in 1924 with the closing of the mission. Brother Fujiwara continued:

> We must pity, indeed, on the lonesomeness of his heart without the church, its leaders, its meetings—in fact, there was nothing of the church affairs except the members were drifted in the wandering path. He was, I understand, one of the most faithful saints who the Japan Mission had ever had . . . [his is the only family] all of whom (but last girl) joined the church.
>
> He is rather frank, honest, and faithful. That is perhaps a reason why he blamed the sudden action of the church in the withdrawal of the missionary activities from Japan, especially from Kōfu before the closing of the mission. Since then the saints in Kōfu were left alone without any instruction and some of them did not know why it was withdrawn. . . . So we cannot after all blame Brother Ren Yoneyama who is, I am sure, far better than the average saint in Japan. If we will excommunicate him, we must excommunicate most of the members in Japan.[38]

Although Taylor and Fujiwara corresponded regularly about the Church in Japan, Taylor continued to facilitate communication between Elder Fujiwara and the First Presidency.[39] Fujiwara summarized the feeling of many former Saints in a letter to Taylor.

> If we investigate the Saints in Japan, we will find no saints who can be said to be really faithful and real members of the church of Christ. Many of them will say that they are not interested in religion any longer, for religion does not give them anything spiritually and, of course, nothing materially. So they say they are in changing their mind, "Shinkyō no henka" . . . I always send them cards . . . but only five or six Saints have ever answered my greetings.[40]

While some members responded to Fujiwara's persistence, others were somewhat annoyed by it. He described one member's family who were "very ignorant or funny, as they told us wrong places of this brother's business and they told us just wrong things."[41]

Just as the situation of the Church in Japan was beginning to improve, Fujiwara became seriously ill and was confined to his bed for two weeks. Thanks to Sister Watanabe Tazuko's care, he recovered.

However, his illness returned in August 1935. He then moved home to Hokkaidō to be with his family in hopes of recovery. From his hospital bed he dictated letters to Taylor apologizing for not accomplishing more. He finally passed away from pleurisy (and possibly tuberculosis) on January 27, 1936. Taylor later received a letter from Fujiwara's father. "With words of regret upon his lips that he had done so little for the church, uttering words of deep gratitude to all who had helped him . . . he went to what he calls heaven. Not knowing much about his religion, it is all very strange to me," he wrote.[42] Saddened by the news, Taylor reported the death of Japan's Presiding Elder to the First Presidency in March 1936. Taylor asked, "Now what is to be done about a successor to Elder Fujiwara? . . . We wish that you do not abandon the work in Japan, but that you continue it, in that connection I suggest you send someone from America or designate some desireable Japanese to carry on. Please let us know."[43]

We know very little about what happened in Japan over the ten years following Fujiwara's passing. After World War II, Nara, describing this period, remarked, "Mattaku sono ju nen wa ankoku no jidai de atta" ("Those ten years were the absolute dark ages").[44] A few Saints in each city were meeting somewhat regularly before Fujiwara's death, so these meetings may have continued for a few years. Sister Kumagai still held her meetings, and at least one member, Brother Ono, came for a while.[45] Although some Saints may have exchanged cards and letters for a time after 1936, any formal Church activities likely came to an end with the outbreak of World War II. During the war, playing or singing foreign hymns and even using Japanese forms of English words was forbidden.[46]

The Hawaiian Era, 1936–50

As Europe was plunged into World War II and the Japanese army was overrunning Asia, President Grant (who had opened the Japan Mission in 1901 as an Apostle and closed it in 1924 as Church President) determined to work among the Japanese in Hawaii. In 1935 he traveled to Hawaii to organize the Oahu Stake, and, while there, met several Japanese converts. His experience in Hawaii confirmed his ideas, shared by his counselor J. Reuben Clark Jr., that Hawaii would play a major role in the Church's expansion into Asia.[47] President Clark later wrote:

> It would seem not improbable that Hawaii is the most favorable place for the Church to make its next effort to preach the Gospel to the Japanese people; and it would further appear that a strong colony of Japanese Saints in Hawaii could operate from there into their homeland in a way that might bring many Japanese to a knowledge not only of Christianity, but of the restored Gospel. There are evidences that the fields are ripening; if so, they will be ready sooner or later for the harvest to begin.[48]

In November 1936, the First Presidency called Hilton A. Robertson to reestablish missionary work among the Japanese, but this time in Hawaii. The Japan Mission became known as the Japanese Mission.

The Robertsons arrived in Honolulu in February 1937 and resumed their earlier missionary work. That first Sunday in Hawaii, the Robertsons met with thirty-five Japanese Saints. Present in the group were Sister Nachie Tsuneko (Tsune Nachie), who had been living in Laie doing temple work since 1923, and Brother Katsunuma Tomizo, who was possibly the first Japanese member of the Church.[49] Preston D. Evans, Roy W. Spear, and Melvyn A. Weenig were the first three missionaries called to the Japanese Mission in Hawaii. At the close of 1937, the mission had already seen four convert baptisms. Missionary work among the Japanese was expanded to the other Hawaiian Islands, and baptisms steadily increased. When the aged Sister Nachie died in December 1938, President Robertson stated that the Lord had left her on earth until he had twenty-five missionaries to replace her[50] (illus. 11-5).

In early 1939, President Robertson returned to Japan for one month to evaluate the condition of the Japanese Saints in his former mission. With only inaccurate addresses, he began searching for Sister Suzuki Nami, who had once worked in the mission home. Miraculously, he met a young girl near a public bath who announced to him that Suzuki was her mother. She then took him to Sister Suzuki's home, where they had a sweet reunion. After receiving several addresses from her, Robertson located and met with some of the Saints in Tokyo, Sapporo, and Osaka. He assured them that they had not been forgotten and that missionaries would return to Japan in the future. He also baptized eight people, including two of Suzuki's daughters and Brother Katsura Tsuruichi's daughter. Brother Watanabe Yoshijirō confirmed her.[51] One evidence

Illus. 11-5. Friends and Relatives of Nachie Tsune gather at her grave. Sister Nachie spent the last fifteen years of her life (1923–38) living in Laie, Hawaii, doing temple work during the Church's absence from Japan.

of the amazing faithfulness of these new Japanese converts in Hawaii was their tithe-paying record in excess of 90 percent.[52]

In 1940, President Robertson was succeeded by Jay C. Jensen, who had served in Japan from 1908 to 1910 and as a missionary in Kōfu in 1910 had confirmed Yoneyama Morizō.[53] In 1942, Edward L. Clissold, first counselor in the Oahu Stake presidency, replaced President Jensen and also served concurrently as president of the Hawaii Temple. President Clissold changed the name of the mission to the Central Pacific Mission, because the term "Japanese" had acquired such a negative connotation during World War II. In 1944, Melvyn A. Weenig was called to preside over the Central Pacific Mission.[54] By the end of 1945, membership had reached 484.[55] Due to the number of young Latter-day Saint men serving in the military, the number of missionaries had dropped significantly. But, after the end of the war, dozens of missionaries were sent to the mission, several of whom were later transferred to Japan itself in 1948.

Between Fujiwara's death in 1936 and the end of the war, the only contacts between Saints in Japan and the United States were Hilton A. Robertson's visit in 1939, another visit by future mission president Jay C. Jensen in 1939,[56] and some radio addresses broadcast to Japan in Japanese by former mission president and then current U.S. Senator Elbert D. Thomas.

Conclusion

Japanese Latter-day Saints in Japan from 1924 to 1945 reacted to the closing of the Japan Mission in a variety of ways. Some members wanted and needed official Church support to keep them strong. As a Brother Nakagawa Kōji admitted to Fujiwara at a Christmas party in 1934, "We are generally less faithful, and could not continue our faith with some reasons. But we are still 'Mormons.'"[57] Others remained close to the gospel without Church structure. For example, although there is no record that Sister Tai Fude (Sister Nachie Tsuneko's sister) attended any meetings, when Fujiwara and Watanabe Tazuko visited her home in 1935, they found her studying the Book of Mormon with her son and his wife.[58] Sister Kumagai Tamano and others held Church-type meetings, whether or not members came. Others, who felt abandoned, returned to their old lifestyles and were indifferent to Fujiwara's reactivation efforts. Still others, like the Yoneyama family, felt as if God had neglected them but overcame their hurt feelings when the Church sought them out.[59]

As we contemplate what it means to be a faithful member of The Church of Jesus Christ of Latter-day Saints, we can gain insight by considering this history of baptized members who were stripped of all external programs, encouragement, buildings, facilities, and monetary support for over two decades, as well as priesthood ordinances for almost a decade. Such circumstances are testing grounds for communication, devotion, and endurance—a crucial value of both Latter-day Saint and Japanese culture.

An earlier version of this article appeared as J. Christopher Conkling, "Members without a Church: Japanese Mormons in Japan from 1924 to 1948," BYU Studies 15, no. 2 (1975): 191–214.

Notes

1. Yukiko Konno, "Fujiya Nara: Twice a Pioneer," *Ensign* 23 (April 1993): 31. Hilton A. Robertson, last president of the original Japan Mission, reported that of the 137 members, about a dozen still considered themselves Latter-day Saints by 1924. See Hilton A. Robertson, *Ninety-fifth Semi-Annual Conference of The Church of Jesus Christ of Latter-day Saints* (Salt Lake City: The Church of Jesus Christ of Latter-day Saints, 1924), 123. Other sources show up to 174 total baptisms through 1924 and upwards of two to three dozen Saints remaining in various stages of activity. For more informaton on the closing of the Japan Mission, see R. Lanier Britsch, "The Closing of the Early Japan Mission," *BYU Studies* 15, no. 2 (1975): 171–90, reprinted herein.

2. Hilton A. Robertson, interview by author, November 13, 1973, Provo, Utah.

3. Kumagai Tamano, interview by Professor Katanuma Seiji, November 1973, Sapporo, Hokkaidō, Japan, translation by the author.

4. Shinji Takagi, "The Eagle and the Scattered Flock: Church Beginnings in Occupied Japan, 1945–48," unpublished paper, August 2001, 36; and Konno, "Fujiya Nara," 31.

5. Konno, "Fujiya Nara," 31; Nara Fujiya, interview by author, October 8, 1973, Provo, Utah.

6. Fujiwara Takeo, "Past Events in the Church," *Hattatsu* (May 1, 1935): 16, copy in L. Tom Perry Special Collections, Harold B. Lee Library, Brigham

Young University, Provo, Utah. This publication was "edited by Mochizuki Reiko, published by Fuiwara Takeo."

7. Thirteen different issues of *Shuro* published by the Japan Mutual Improvement Association, dating from January 1, 1925 to winter 1928, can be found in Perry Special Collections. These mimeographed, handwritten pamphlets do not contain page numbers, so we have numbered the pages by counting the front cover as page 1. I looked at these issues with the gracious help of Ashizawa Hiromi, Watanabe Masa, and Fujita Tetsuro.

8. Konno, "Fujiya Nara," 31; Nara Fujiya, "About the Beginning," *Shuro* 1 (January 1, 1925): [6].

9. Fujiwara Takeo, "Kangeki" (Deep Feelings), *Shuro* 4 (April 1925): [17].

10. Yamaide Torao, "Hitorii Naraba" (If One's Alone), *Shuro* 9 (November 1, 1925): [13–16].

11. Fujiwara, "Past Events in the Church," 16–18.

12. Fujiya Nara, "The Joy of This Publication," *LDS Messenger* (December 1949): 2.

13. Alma O. Taylor, "Correspondence," *Shuro* 2 (May 10, 1926): [18–20].

14. Alma O. Taylor, "Letters," *Hattatsu* (1935): [6–12].

15. Fujiwara, "Past Events in the Church," 16–18.

16. Takagi, "Eagle and the Scattered Flock," 35.

17. Franklin S. Harris to Estella Harris, October 22, 1926, Franklin S. Harris personal papers, Perry Special Collections.

18. Fujiwara, "Past Events in the Church," 16–19, reported an average attendance of two to four before the mission closed.

19. Fujiwara, "Past Events in the Church," 16–19.

20. Fujiwara, "Past Events in the Church," 16–19.

21. First Presidency to Fujiya Nara, *Shuro* (Winter 1928): [5–9]; Fujiwara Takeo, "Greetings from Elder Fujiwara to the Readers in Hawaii and America," *Hattatsu* (1935): [30].

22. Alma O. Taylor to First Presidency, March 31, 1928, in Japan Mission General Files, 1901–66, Church Archives, The Church of Jesus Christ of Latter-day Saints, Salt Lake City.

23. Fujiwara, "Past Events in the Church," 16–19.

24. "MIA News from Four Branches," *Shuro* 1 (Winter 1927): [21–24].

25. Fujiwara, "Past Events in the Church," 16–19.

26. Alma O. Taylor to President Heber J. Grant, March 14, 1936, Japan Mission General Files.

27. Fujiya Nara, "Nihon Dendōbu no Kaikō" (A Reflection on the Japanese Mission), *Seito-No-Michi* (Way of the Saints) (July 1958): 27–29, as quoted in Takagi, "Eagle and the Scattered Flock," 36.

28. Fujiwara Takeo to Alma O. Taylor, August 14, 1934; Japan Mission General Files.

29. Fujiwara, "Past Events in the Church," 16–19; Fujiwara Takeo, "Official Record of Church in Japan until December 31, 1934," 1–5, in Manuscript History, Church Archives.

30. Fujiwara, "Official Record . . . until December 31, 1934," 1–3.

31. Fujiwara Takeo, "Official Report . . . January 1–April 30, 1935," Japan Mission General Files, 1–11; Fujiwara Takeo, "Official Report . . . 3 August 1935," Japan Mission General Files, 14.

32. The word *hattatsu* had both secular and religious meanings as the Mutual Improvement Association in Japan was called *Sōgo Hattatsu Kyōkai*, *hattatsu* meaning improvement or progress. *Shuro*'s official publisher had always been listed as the Tokyo *Sōgo Hattatsu Kyōkai*. See *Shuro* cover, 1928, vol. 1, in Perry Special Collections.

33. "Letter from Takagi Tomigoro to Senator Thomas and Mr. Taylor," trans. Fujiwara Takeo in *Hattatsu* (1935): [27–28]. The political feelings of the Latter-day Saints during this period are important. Fujiwara's master's thesis almost foresaw the importance of the Pacific Rim—assuming peace between Japan and America—as he saw the centers of influence move steadily west from Greece to Rome to England to America and to Japan. Letters between former mission president Elbert D. Thomas, then in the U.S. Senate, former convert Kuriyama Chōjiro, who worked for the Japanese government in New York, and Takagi Tomigoro in Tokyo suggested the hope that Latter-day Saints could lessen the growing tensions between these two world powers. See this Takagi letter in *Hattatsu*, as well as Fujiwara Takeo, "The Political and Military Policies of the Tokugawa Shogunate" (master's thesis, Brigham Young University, 1934), vii–viii; and letter from Thomas to Kuriyama begging him to convince Japan not to officially withdraw from the United Nations; Thomas to Kuriyama, March 25, 1935, in Japan Mission General Files, Church Archives. See also the note about this topic in visit between Fujiwara and Takagi on February 19, 1935, that reopening the mission then would improve Japanese-American relations in Fujiwara, "Official Report . . . January 1 and April 30, 1935," 8–9. After the war, as a government official, Kuriyama quietly assisted Edward L. Clissold, then the Japan Mission president, in reestablishing the Church. See Edward L. Clissold letter, December 5, 1948, in Manuscript History, Church Archives; and Nichols, "History of the Japan Mission," 146–47.

34. Nara's wife later reported that Kubota was unscrupulous and stole donation money, Fujiwara, "Official Report . . . January 1 and April 30, 1935," 11.

35. Fujiwara, "Official Report . . . January 1 and April 30, 1935," 21–22.

36. Fujiwara, " Official Report . . . January 1 and April 30, 1935," 21–22; Fujiwara, "Official Report . . . 3 August 1935," 1–7.

37. Alma O. Taylor to Fujiwara Takeo, April 14, 1935, Church Archives.

38. Fujiwara, "Official Report . . . 3 August 1935," 1–6. Although we don't know what happened to the Yoneyamas or their attitude toward the Church, or the Church's attitude toward them during the next fourteen years, Edward L. Clissold, the first mission president after the reopening, felt that the Lord still had a work to perform through them. In trying to reestablish Kōfu as a branch in 1949, he had spent the day with a Brother Yajima searching for old members, especially a photographer named Yoneyama. Having failed, President Clissold offered a silent prayer, in a last desperate hope, just before they were to return to Tokyo. He was impressed to return to the military translation office he had just come from. When he asked if anyone knew a Mormon named Yoneyama, one man asked if they were the people who used the Book of Mormon. He then said he had seen a Book of Mormon many years ago in the house of a school teacher named Yoneyama. Within minutes they were in contact with Renji and Morizō. The Yoneyamas greatly helped in the reestablishment of the work thereafter. See Don W. Marsh, *The Light of the Sun* (n.p., n.d.), 47–48; Edward L. Clissold, interview by Christopher Conkling, November 8, 1973, Salt Lake City, Utah; Nara, interview.

39. See letters in Japan Mission General Files. Also included were several letters from Fujiwara to the First Presidency containing condolences at the deaths of Church leaders, congratulations at the times of general conferences, and reminders that there were still Saints in Japan who desired the reopening of the mission.

40. Fujiwara, "Official Report . . . 3 August 1935," 3–5.

41. Fujiwara, "Official Report . . . January 1 and April 30, 1935," 7.

42. "Presiding Church Member in Japan Is Dead," *Deseret News* (February 29, 1936): 7; Fujiwara, "Official Report . . . 3 August 1935," 3–5.

43. Taylor to Grant, March 14, 1936.

44. Fujiya Nara, "Brief Record of My Conversion," a handwritten record of Church events in his life, with him, 2; see also Nara, "Joy of This Publication," 2.

45. Kumagai, interview.

46. Common words such as "erebeetaa" for "elevator," and "auto" for "out" in baseball were strictly forbidden. See Seiji Katanuma, "The Church in Japan," *BYU Studies* 14, no. 1 (1973): 21–22.

47. R. Lanier Britsch, *From the East: The History of the Latter-day Saints in Asia, 1851–1996* (Salt Lake City: Deseret Book, 1998), 72–73.

48. J. Reuben Clark Jr., "The Outpost in Mid-Pacific," *Improvement Era* 38 (September 1935): 533.

49. See Shinji Takagi, "Tomizo and Tokujiro: The First Japanese Mormons," *BYU Studies* 39, no. 2 (2000): 73–106, reprinted herein.

50. Castle H. Murphy, "A Brief Resume of the Organization of the Missionary Work among the Chinese and Japanese in Hawaii," typescript, March 30, 1973, 5.

51. Form E Membership Records, Church Archives; Marsh, *Light of the Sun,* 24; Takagi, "Eagle and the Scattered Flock," 2.

52. Taken from the year-end totals in the Missionary Annual Reports, 1937–48, Church Archives.

53. Murray L. Nichols, "History of the Japan Mission of the Church of Jesus Christ of Latter-day Saints" (master's thesis, Brigham Young University, Provo, Utah, 1957), 138; Form E Membership Records, reel 1, p. 5.

54. Britsch, *From the East,* 77.

55. Taken from the year-end totals in the Missionary Annual Reports, 1937–48.

56. "Japanese Mission President Appointed," *Improvement Era* 43 (August 1940): 478.

57. Fujiwara, "Official Record . . . until December 31, 1934," 8.

58. Fujiwara, "Official Report . . . January 1 and April 30, 1935," 5.

59. Fujiwara, "Official Report . . . 3 August 1935," 3–5; Fujiwara, "Official Record . . . until December 31, 1934," 4–9.

12

The Reopening and Foundation Years

R. Lanier Britsch

When World War II finally ended on August 15, 1945, the Japanese nation was exhausted and prostrate before the Allied forces. The Allied forces instituted a military government to reshape the country. The Japanese people had been told that the American and other Allied troops would be harsh overlords, but this expectation proved to be untrue. The Allied forces, in turn, were surprised to find that the Japanese people, a people who had fought bitterly, even ferociously, were submissive and cooperative subjects of the Occupation government.

On October 4, 1945, the Supreme Commander for the Allied Powers (SCAP), a designation that was applied not only to General Douglas MacArthur but also to his Occupation government, repealed the Religious Bodies Law. By repealing this law, the government freed religion from state control. Two months later, on December 28, SCAP gave a directive that became the Religious Juridical Persons Law. The freedom of religion implied in this law was given legal validity when it was accepted as Article Twenty of the new Japanese constitution, which went into effect in May 1947.

An even more important step toward religious freedom was Emperor Hirohito's proclamation on January 1, 1946, that he was not a divine or quasi-divine person and that the Japanese people were not superior in any way to other races and peoples. "By this statement," writes Richard H. Drummond,

> the traditional spiritual basis of the Japanese government and society, the doctrine of the divinity of the emperor, which had been

developed with increasing explicitness for over half a century, was at one stroke demolished. For many Japanese the act was psychically more shattering than military defeat and surrender, and it left literally millions to reconstruct their spiritual foundations and standards of value.[1]

It was in this spiritual vacuum that dedicated Latter-day Saint servicemen first taught the restored gospel of Jesus Christ. The time was right for the growth of all Christian churches as well as for the emergence of many new religious movements that sprang from the Japanese people themselves. Protestants and Roman Catholics frequently refer to the period from 1945 to 1951—the years of the Occupation—as the "Christian boom." The Japanese were excited about most things American, and they were grateful to have religious freedom. After 1951, when the economic growth of the nation began to spiral upward and most Japanese became quite comfortable with their new postwar standard of living, interest in religion slackened, and the difficulty of converting Japanese became greater.

The Church, which had closed its early mission in Japan in 1924, saw fit to reestablish its presence there in 1948. The first five mission presidents who served during and following the Christian boom responded sensitively to changing economical, organizational, and spiritual needs to firmly plant the Church on Japanese soil.

The Presidency of Edward L. Clissold

In 1944, Edward L. Clissold (illus. 12-1) was a member of the Oahu Stake presidency and president of the Hawaii temple in Laie and of the Central Pacific Mission. He was also an active-duty naval officer who was sent to military government school at the University of Chicago to be trained as a government administrator. He expected to be assigned as a provincial governor in Japan when the war ended. As he had anticipated, Clissold was sent to Japan immediately after the conclusion of hostilities. But contrary to his expectations, he was assigned to work in the education and religion section of SCAP. During his two-month tour of duty in Japan, Clissold became thoroughly familiar with the officers within the section of SCAP that had the greatest influence on the development of religious affairs in postwar Japan. He also became

Courtesy Church Archives, The Church of Jesus Christ of Latter-day Saints

Illus. 12-1. Edward L. Clissold *(center)* with two unidentified men. Clissold served as Japan's first mission president upon the Church's official return after a twenty-four-year absence from the country.

acquainted with a number of Latter-day Saint servicemen and the operation of Church servicemen's groups. In addition, Clissold did what he could to find the remaining Japanese Latter-day Saints from the previous mission era. On October 30, 1945, he placed a small ad, written in Japanese, in a Tokyo newspaper that read, incorrectly translated, "URGENT NOTICE—I would like any member of the Church of Jesus Christ of Near-Day Saints (Mormon Church) to contact me as soon as possible. Daiichi Hotel, Room 548. Lt. Col. Edward Clissold."[2] Brother Nara Fujiya, who had helped shepherd the Japanese Saints from 1924 until 1933, responded to Brother Clissold's notice. As a result, a few other Japanese Saints were located and integrated into the activities of the Latter-day Saint servicemen.[3]

In February 1946, the Clissold family returned to Honolulu to resume their business and Church activities that had been curtailed by the war. Brother Clissold was soon called as both a stake high councilor and stake mission president.

In spring 1947, the First Presidency called Clissold and Melvyn A. Weenig, then the president of the Central Pacific Mission, to go to Japan to investigate the possibility of reopening the Japanese mission. Because the mission had been closed since 1924, however, the U.S. Department of War would allow only one representative of the Church to enter the country. Because Clissold had been in Japan recently and knew how to deal with the military government, he was selected to reopen the mission. He received word of this appointment and was set apart as mission president on October 22, 1947.

The First Presidency instructed President Clissold to preside over the members, to organize the Church, to establish a mission headquarters, and to make arrangements for missionaries to enter Japan. Clissold arrived in Japan on March 6, 1948. The next day, he was taken to a Japanese Sunday School that was directed by his friend Nara Fujiya and conducted by Tsukayama Kiyoshi. Forty-three people were in attendance. Brother Nara's little group was to become the nucleus of the Ogikubo Branch, which was organized later that year.

Clissold's first task as mission president was to search for living and office quarters, since missionaries were not permitted to enter Japan until provision had been made for their maintenance. In April he located a partly burned mansion in Azabu, Tokyo; this mansion had served as the residence of the Japanese minister of welfare during the war. Although it had taken a direct hit from an incendiary bomb, the walls of the ferro-concrete structure were still solid.[4] Through the help of many influential people, including even Prince Takamatsu, and after a series of extremely complex negotiations, he obtained permission to buy the property.[5] Clissold felt that there had been a divine reason for his previous appointment to the education and religion section of SCAP. Throughout his presidency, he had regular contact with many of the men he had worked with in his military assignment. Through these affiliations he found help that greatly facilitated the organization of the mission.[6]

Renovation of the mansion began in May (illus. 12-2), and by the twenty-second of that month President Clissold moved into the servants' quarters over the garage. Although Sister Clissold and other missionaries moved into the home in September, the remodeling work was not completed until November 25, 1948.[7] The building was in an

Reopening and Foundation Years 311

Courtesy Church Archives, The Church of Jesus Christ of Latter-day Saints

Illus. 12-2. Japanese Mission home during renovation, ca. 1948, Tokyo, Japan.

Courtesy Church Archives, The Church of Jesus Christ of Latter-day Saints

Illus. 12-3. Japanese Mission home after refurbishing, Tokyo, Japan. This building served as the mission home and office from 1948 until the late 1970s, when it was razed for construction of the Tokyo Japan Temple.

excellent part of the city and served the Church well as a mission home and office for almost thirty years (illus. 12-3). The fact that the Church bought property in Japan within the first month of the new mission shows that leaders intended to reestablish the mission permanently; no property had been acquired between 1901 and 1924.

The first group of missionaries arrived in Japan on June 26, 1948. They were allowed to enter Japan only after President Clissold had made arrangements for them to live with American Saints in the Occupation forces.[8] The first missionary, Harrison Theodore "Ted" Price, had been called to serve in late 1947. The other four were Paul C. Andrus; Wayne McDaniel; Koji Okauchi, who was a *nisei* (a second-generation American of Japanese ancestry); and Raymond C. Price, brother to Ted.[9] At least two of these men—Andrus and Ted Price—had fought against the Japanese in the Pacific theater during World War II. Now they were returning to teach the gospel of peace.

Between December 1947 and March 1948, these five elders were assigned to the Central Pacific Mission in Hawaii for Japanese language training under Paul V. Hyer. They not only studied Japanese but also tracted and taught the gospel with companions from the Central Pacific Mission. Their experience in Hawaii prepared them to teach the gospel so they would not enter the Japanese mission field as complete "greenies."[10] By the end of 1948, the mission force had grown to seventeen: President and Sister Clissold, thirteen elders (seven Caucasians and six nisei), and two sister missionaries (both nisei).

Even before the mission was officially reopened in March 1948, some Japanese had already converted to the Church. The first were Satō Tatsui and his wife, Chiyo, who were taught the gospel by servicemen Ray Hanks and C. Elliott Richards. Mel Arnold and Boyd K. Packer also became friends and gospel teachers of the Satōs. On July 7, 1946, the Satōs were baptized in a swimming pool at Kansaigakuin University. Elliott Richards baptized Brother Satō, and Boyd K. Packer baptized Chiyo.[11] Brother Satō organized a Sunday School in Nagoya in 1946 and conducted it almost single-handedly until missionaries were sent there in October 1948. He later became the official translator for the Church in Japan and eventually retranslated the Book of Mormon as well as produced translations of the Doctrine and Covenants, the Pearl of Great Price, and a number of other Church publications.[12]

One of the early assignments President Clissold gave the first group of elders was to find any Saints baptized during the former mission who were still alive. Some of the converts of the early mission, such as Brothers Nara, Shiraishi, and Takagi, as well as a few sisters, had already found the Church and were serving well in one or two small Sunday school groups. But by no means had all the previous members found the reestablished Church. Paul C. Andrus and his companion Ray Price found some Saints in the Yokohama area who had been out of touch with the Church since the late 1930s but who had nevertheless remained faithful. One of those was Sister Suzuki Nami. According to Elder Andrus,

> she remained faithful even though during the war and during the Japanese incident in Manchuria she lost two of her sons and one daughter....
>
> Her very nice home in Yokohama was bombed and burned and destroyed completely. When Ray Price and I found her we found she and her husband were living on two tatami straw mats. Each mat is six by three feet. Over these they had a corrugated iron lean-to. They cooked in there on a charcoal brazier, a hibachi, and they slept there. This was their property where they had had their restaurant, which had also been destroyed.[13]

In their search, the elders found a few other Japanese Saints, and along with new investigators and new converts they began to build not only a new church but also new lives from the rubble of war.

Certainly the circumstances of the reestablishment were better than those that had prevailed during the early mission. As the missionaries went to work proselytizing, they found the Japanese much more willing to listen to the message of the restored gospel than they had been before the war. The new elders had several advantages that the original missionaries in 1901 had not enjoyed. Among these were translated materials, such as a collection of hymns and a few tracts, to share with contacts. The most important item was, of course, the Japanese translation of the Book of Mormon. But more important to the missionary effort than the literature were the people, those Saints who remained faithful from the early mission, the members of the U.S. military who not only lived the gospel and taught it to their Japanese friends but also contributed time, money, and leadership to the newly established mission, and the nisei missionaries who spoke Japanese and acted as visual models that it was possible to be Japanese and Mormon.

The popularity of English classes also helped reestablish the Church in Japan. As had been true during the early mission, many Japanese were eager to learn the English language. President Clissold noted that he had almost daily requests for the elders and sisters to teach spoken English at schools from elementary to college level, as well as at clubs and businesses. The missionaries took advantage of many of these opportunities to teach, provided that the students were willing to be taught from Latter-day Saint materials. English classes became the foundation of the first Mutual Improvement Associations in Japan after the war.

By the end of 1948, President Clissold had organized a branch and four Sunday Schools—all separate from the servicemen's groups. At that time, he reported that nine hundred members and investigators were attending Latter-day Saint services every week. Twenty-two converts' names were entered on the Church records in 1948.[14]

When President Clissold submitted his year-end report to the Presiding Bishopric, he expressed confidence that the missionaries would bring many converts into the Church during the coming year. However, he stressed that the mission needed more translated Church literature and more missionaries. The missionaries could translate additional literature, but the personnel shortage could be alleviated only at Church headquarters. President Clissold repeatedly asked the First Presidency to supply ten missionaries each month, five Caucasians and five Japanese-speaking nisei. His plan was to put Japanese speakers together with the language learners; this would eliminate time lost in language study. The understanding was that eventually the Caucasian missionaries would be able to function well, but in the meantime the nisei could carry the load.

Considering the worldwide missionary demands of the Church, it was difficult for Church leaders to meet this request. Taking into account the dislocation, the political upheaval, the cultural transitions in the family system, and the newfound freedom of religion in Occupation Japan, 1948 through 1951 might have been the best possible years for the Church to rapidly expand.

Although President Clissold was not satisfied with the number of missionaries assigned to Japan, he used those he had to expand the proselytizing area to include Sapporo in the north and Osaka-Kobe in west-central Honshu. By the time he was released on August 31, 1949, elders and sisters were teaching the restored gospel in at least ten major cities, including Tokyo, the largest city in the world. That summer, Elder Matthew Cowley of the Quorum of the Twelve and his wife, Elva, arrived in Tokyo for a tour of the mission. Elder Cowley was then president of the Asian and Pacific missions of the Church. During his stay, he visited most of the Japanese branches and traveled as far west as Hiroshima. He prophetically promised "many Church buildings and even [Latter-day Saint] temples in this land."[15]

Clissold's eighteen-month term as mission president was short by late twentieth-century standards, but considering his previous service to the Church in Hawaii and his years away from home while in the military, his arrangements with the First Presidency were understandable. By the time he departed for home, he had accomplished the tasks assigned him. Vinal G. Mauss, who succeeded Clissold, gave his predecessor high praise when he said, "I don't see how any one man could accomplish what he did, in the time he was there in getting the facilities and the organization that was necessary."[16]

The Presidency of Vinal G. Mauss

Vinal G. Mauss, a businessman and mortician from Oakland, California, had served as a missionary to Japan during the last years of the early mission. When he arrived in Japan as mission president on August 20, 1949, he began his service that would last for more than four years. During his presidency, from 1949 to 1953, Church membership in Japan grew from 211 to more than 800. The number of districts expanded from one to five, and the number of branches grew from twelve Sunday Schools and one or two branches to twenty-five branches. The number of missionaries also expanded to a new high of eighty-four.

President Mauss's greatest contributions, however, were not in numerical growth but in enlargement of Church organization, work with Latter-day Saint servicemen's groups, expansion of proselytizing, training of local missionaries and leaders, and acquisition of property.

If President Clissold laid the foundation for the Japanese Mission, President Mauss can be credited with constructing the walls. With the added number of missionaries, Mauss asked all branch leaders to expand the Sunday Schools and to begin holding sacrament meetings. It was at that time that many of the Sunday Schools became branches. By the end of 1950, there were fifteen branches in Japan, presided over almost exclusively by missionaries.

In 1950 war broke out in Korea, and soon the Japanese Mission was feeling the effects of the fighting. The American military draft greatly diminished the supply of new Latter-day Saint missionaries. But because the missionary terms in Japan were for three years rather than two or two and one-half years, the number of missionaries did not drop as quickly or as low as in other missions before the cease-fire in 1953. Still, Mauss was diligent to keep the effects of the setback minimal. If baptism is a measure of success, Mauss's success was unprecedented in Japan. His missionaries baptized 184 people into the Church in 1950, ten more than the total number who had joined from 1901 to 1924 during the early history of the mission.

Another effect of the Korean War was the assignment by the U.S. military of thousands of servicemen to Korea, Japan (a major staging area), Guam, Okinawa, and the Philippines. Among these military personnel were hundreds of Latter-day Saints. On June 23, 1951, the First Presidency asked President Mauss to include in the Japanese Mission Guam, the Philippines, and Okinawa, as well as all other parts of East Asia where Latter-day Saint service personnel were stationed. They also asked him to visit the major cities and supervise the servicemen's groups and districts. The servicemen's organization was completely separate from the Japanese Mission organization but was also presided over by President Mauss.[17] By 1953 servicemen had seven groups and two districts in Japan. There were even larger numbers in Korea, as well as other groups elsewhere in East Asia and the Philippines.

In 1953, President Mauss's son Armand, who was serving as president of one of the servicemen's districts in Japan, compiled a manual of operations for servicemen's organizations. This manual, published and distributed widely among Latter-day Saint military personnel, unified recordkeeping and helped leaders understand not only how to keep records but also why priesthood ordinances such as baptisms, blessings, and ordinations should be cleared with the proper priesthood authority and be recorded.[18]

The service personnel supported the development of the Church in many ways, including giving financial support. When it became evident to President Mauss that the supply of American missionaries was going to be diminished, he decided to call local Japanese members on full-time missions. By the end of 1952, eleven young Japanese men and women were serving two-year missions, and by mid-1953 the number was up to twenty. Almost all of them were supported by money contributed by Latter-day Saint servicemen. Years later, President Mauss asserted that his most important contribution to the Church in Japan was the calling of local missionaries. Nearly all these local missionaries went on to become strong Church leaders.[19]

President Mauss recognized that some Japanese Saints were ready for greater leadership positions. In September 1951, before he was able to initiate missionary calls for local Saints, he decided to combine the four Tokyo branches into two. Only two foreign elders supervised the two new branch presidencies. The Tokyo First Branch was presided over by Takagi Tomigoro and his counselors, Shiraishi Genkichi and Imai Kazuo. The president of the Tokyo Second Branch was Nara Fujiya, and his counselors were Satō Tatsui, who had moved to Tokyo from Nagoya to work for the mission as a full-time translator, and Nakahigashi Mikio.[20]

The activity of the Japanese Saints was impressive. Many of the young Church members influenced their parents to stop drinking tea. Members were eager and willing to pay tithes and offerings. By 1951, Japan was definitely well on the way to economic recovery, and this fact was reflected in the well-being of the members and investigators.[21] There was little unemployment or need for welfare help. And at the end of 1952 there was 75 percent activity among priesthood holders and an average attendance of more than 50 percent at sacrament meetings.[22]

Despite positive activity in the Church, Japan began to experience a growing apathy toward religion. President Mauss noted, "There has developed that spirit of indifference which always seems to come when there is an abundance of material things."[23] The Latter-day Saints and other Christian groups observed this by-product of the country's new economic prosperity. The number of Latter-day Saint baptisms declined steadily from 214 in 1951 to 55 in 1955.[24] Economic prosperity was not the only cause of the decline in convert baptisms. Other problems—including Japanese customs, economics, obligations, duties, and religious relativity—became evident to the foreign missionaries during Mauss's administration. Only in 1956 did the mission begin to have greater success, but some of that success was actually achieved in Korea, which was a district of the mission.

President Mauss's final contribution as mission president was his purchase of land. Because real estate prices were rising, he decided to raise money to buy property for meeting places as rapidly as possible. Before his release, he succeeded in securing four fine homes to be used as chapels. President Mauss and the Saints also decided to raise money to build a chapel in Tokyo. Although they did not succeed in collecting enough to move ahead with the project, they did carry out fund-raising activities such as banquets and bazaars that welded the local Saints, the missionaries, and the military personnel together. After faithful service, President Mauss was released in October 1953.

Two More Years of Service for Hilton A. Robertson

Hilton A. Robertson, recently released as president of the Chinese Mission in California, replaced President Mauss. Robertson had previously served missions in Japan, where he was one of the last missionaries in the early mission, and in Hawaii, where he organized and presided over the Japanese-Central Pacific Mission from 1937 to 1940. When President David O. McKay set Robertson apart as mission president, he gave him unusually broad authority. He was to preside over not only the Japanese Mission but also the Chinese Mission. "Yours is now a distinct responsibility, a mighty one, in holding the Presidency of the Missions in the Orient, in Asia," said President McKay. He told Robertson to "organize these missions" and to "expand in excellency, in permanency." He specifically told President Robertson to take care of the small group of Chinese Saints in Hong Kong.[25]

When President Robertson arrived in Japan in late 1953, he found the demands of the mission and the servicemen's organization to be very time-consuming. In fact, he hardly had time to think about China or other areas such as Korea, Okinawa, the Philippines, and Guam. Missionary work in Japan alone proved challenging enough. President Robertson's missionaries did not convert many Japanese. The principal reason was the tremendous turnover in missionaries. Most of the local Japanese missionaries completed their terms during 1954 and early 1955, and they were not replaced with more natives. To compound problems, many of the foreign missionaries did not speak Japanese well enough to be effective.

But Church leaders in Salt Lake City, particularly President McKay, had a larger vision of the world and the missionary responsibility of the Church. In summer 1954, President McKay sent Elder Harold B. Lee of the Quorum of the Twelve to Japan and the Asian mainland to survey the progress of the mission and to study the possibilities for growth.

Elder Lee visited all five mission districts and the servicemen's districts in Japan. Elder Lee and President Robertson traveled together to Korea, where they visited with many servicemen and held several conferences. The five Latter-day Saint chaplains in Korea all strongly encouraged Elder Lee to send missionaries into Korea. Although Elder Lee was favorably impressed by their positive attitude, President Robertson was concerned about possible problems of health, housing, and food.[26] Elder Lee, President Robertson, and their wives then traveled to Okinawa, Hong Kong, the Philippines, and Guam (illus. 12-4). When Lee reported on his trip to Asia at the October 1954 general conference a week after he returned to Salt Lake City, he told the Church, "The signs of divinity are in the Far East. The work of the Almighty is increasing with a tremendous surge."[27]

One year later, Joseph Fielding Smith, then President of the Quorum of the Twelve, visited Asia. President Smith arrived in Tokyo on July 25, 1955, and two days later he met with the missionaries and servicemen at Karuizawa. There he proposed that the Japanese or Far East Mission should be divided into two missions. Japan, Korea, and Okinawa were subsequently grouped into the Northern Far East Mission, and Hong Kong, Taiwan, the Philippines, and Guam were grouped into the Southern Far East Mission.[28] At that time, the Latter-day Saint servicemen outnumbered the Asian members (1,600 servicemen in 34 groups compared to 1,050 Asian members in 25 branches), but the prospects among the Asians were recognized as excellent.

President Robertson's leadership was important in three other areas. First, he supported Satō Tatsui in his retranslation of the Book of Mormon—a project that Satō began while President Clissold was still

Illus. 12-4. Elder Harold B. Lee and his wife, Fern Lucinda Tanner Lee (*center*), at a Latter-day Saint Church service in Okinawa, 1954. Elder and Sister Lee, with President Hilton A. Robertson (president of the Japanese Mission) and his wife, visited the servicemen's districts in Okinawa, Hong Kong, the Philippines, and Guam.

Courtesy Church Archives, The Church of Jesus Christ of Latter-day Saints

in Japan—and in his translations of the Doctrine and Covenants and the Pearl of Great Price. Second, President Robertson acquired more property for the Church. He purchased at least three homes to use as chapels that doubled as living quarters for missionaries. He noted that wherever the Church had buildings, the work was "greatly facilitated."[29] Third, he strengthened the auxiliaries, including the MIA, the Sunday Schools, and the Relief Society. In 1954 he instituted the Primary. After years of faithful service, President Robertson's health began to decline, and he and his wife were honorably released in October 1955.[30]

The Lengthy Presidency of Paul Andrus

Paul C. Andrus and his wife, Frances, of Honolulu, were next called to lead the Northern Far East Mission. Similar to prior mission presidents there, both Paul and Frances had served previously in Japan, under Presidents Clissold and Mauss. The Andruses arrived in Japan on December 9, 1955, eleven days after the Robertsons sailed for home. The Andruses were thrilled at what they observed. Thirty-one-year-old President Andrus could see nothing but significant progress during the five years since his release from his first Japanese Mission. To him the future looked bright. He wrote:

> The growth and the progress of the Church in Japan seems striking indeed as I return after an absence of five years and compare our position now with our position at that time. Although the number of branches is approximately the same, they are organized and functioning much more completely; there are more good leaders serving in the branches; the Church owns more property, and meeting places in general have improved; our members generally have grown stronger in faith and in works as their experience has increased and their testimonies have congealed. The Japanese economy has made very good progress in the last five years, and the goods and services available to the missionaries have grown in number and improved in quality accordingly. The present position of the Church in Japan seems all the more marvelous when I recall that not quite eight years have elapsed since Pres. Edward L. Clissold, and subsequently the missionaries, arrived back in Japan to reopen the work.[31]

President Andrus's positive attitude sustained him during the six years he presided over the mission (1955–62). His term was marked by rapid growth on many fronts. The member population grew from just over one thousand to more than sixty-six hundred. The Church in Korea grew so rapidly that it was made a separate mission in 1962 (it had only sixty-five members in 1955). The missionary force also doubled, growing from 82 to 179 foreign missionaries.

Shortly after President Andrus arrived, he learned that there was no uniform teaching plan and that each companionship used whatever methods suited them best. During President Clissold's era, the missionaries had concluded that because the Japanese people were not Christian it would be necessary to teach them first about Christianity and then about the restored gospel. During President Mauss's time, the mission used the Anderson-Bankhead Plan.[32] Furthermore, missionaries were not instructed to invite investigators to be baptized; rather, they waited until baptism was requested. As a result, by the end of the Robertson administration the missionaries were baptizing only 0.7 converts a year per missionary. If baptisms were a measurement of success, something needed to change.

About this time, President Andrus received a copy of Willard Aston's book *Teaching the Gospel with Prayer and Testimony*. One of the basic principles taught in that volume was that one should teach the gospel, bear testimony, and then invite the investigator to be baptized. "At the end of 1956," said President Andrus, "I called together our leading elders and talked about this. We came up with a six-lesson teaching plan that was geared for the Japanese. We incorporated into it these principles. We announced the introduction of this plan and began using it in 1957."[33] This new uniform teaching plan helped his missionaries improve their former slow approach. They converted the Japanese directly to the restored gospel "and let them find out about so-called Christianity thereafter."[34] It brought great growth during the next five years.

The new uniform plan for teaching the gospel dovetailed perfectly with the publication of the standard works in Japanese. Brother Satō completed his retranslation of the Book of Mormon as well as his translations of the Doctrine and Covenants and the Pearl of Great Price in 1955. Because President Andrus had done a considerable amount of translation work during his first mission, he obtained permission from the First Presidency to organize a translation review committee in Japan to approve the translation of the standard works. The committee consisted of President Andrus, Satō Tatsui, Takagi Tomigoro, Ben Oniki, and Don Lundberg. For a number of months, they met every day for three or four hours until they completed the review and revision of the manuscripts. Sanseido Printing Company, a large dictionary firm, printed 10,000 copies of the Book of Mormon, which were delivered to the mission home a day or two before Christmas 1956. The Doctrine and Covenants and Pearl of Great Price came off the press about a year later.

The missionaries were then able to go into the homes of investigators, tell them the story of Joseph Smith, give or sell them a copy of the Book of Mormon, and invite them to be baptized. Before long the missionaries were baptizing people whom they had known for months or even years but whom they had failed to invite to join the Church. Convert baptisms jumped from 129 in 1956 to 616 in 1957. The average number of baptisms per missionary climbed to 5.8 per year.[35]

When Elder Delbert L. Stapley of the Quorum of the Twelve set apart President Andrus in Hawaii, he had charged him to prepare the Saints in Japan for the organization of a stake and to open missionary work in Korea and Okinawa. After President Andrus arrived in Japan, he surveyed the branches and decided that a stake would be only in the distant future unless he reorganized the existing branches and opened new ones. For instance, in 1955 there were two branches in Tokyo (a city of nine million people), one in Yokohama, one in Osaka, and so on. President Mauss had tried moving missionaries into smaller cities, hoping the people might be more receptive, but people in small towns were more fearful of change, so the missionaries had little success. Constrained by missionary numbers, President Andrus decided to relocate his missionaries to primarily large, metropolitan areas and close small, out-of-the-way branches. Soon the number of branches increased to five each in Tokyo and Osaka-Kobe, Japan, and Seoul, Korea. These branches later became the nuclei for stakes in all three cities.

President Andrus was able to make other important changes to prepare Japan and Korea for stakes. He determined to increase the number of native priesthood holders in the mission. By the end of 1955, there were only forty-one Japanese Melchizedek Priesthood holders. Many Japanese Church leaders did not understand the value of ordaining new members to the priesthood and sharing in Church leadership. Some mistakenly believed new converts needed to prove themselves for three to five years before receiving the priesthood. This may have been one reason that missionaries, not local priesthood holders, led most branches and districts. To remedy the situation, President Andrus set up a two-year program for advancement in the priesthood. By the time he was released in 1962, there were more than 350 Japanese and Korean Melchizedek Priesthood holders in the mission. This increase enabled mission leaders to call local men to almost all (75 to 80 percent) branch and district positions, which prepared them for future stake leadership. It also released many missionaries from administrative duties and allowed them to proselyte full time.[36]

In Okinawa the Lord opened the door to missionary work in a most unusual way. In 1955, Ralph Bird, a former missionary to Japan, was assigned a military post in Guam. From Guam, he received orders to go to Okinawa. His superiors there were surprised when he arrived. They had not been told to expect him, and they had nothing for him to do. They gave him time off while they evaluated his situation. President Andrus recalled of Bird:

> So, speaking Japanese, he was interested in the Okinawans. He walked out into the countryside and as he was walking along the road he came to a home and decided he would go in . . . and speak with the people to see if he could take a picture of their home. So he slid open the door and said, "Gomen kudasai." [Excuse me or pardon me.] He didn't realize that at this very moment Sister Nakamura was in her home on her knees praying that the Lord would lead her to the true church. And here Elder Bird came, opened the door, and said, "Gomen kudasai."
>
> So she came out and was very impressed that here was an American who could speak Japanese. So she asked, "How is it that you speak Japanese so well?" He said, "Well, I was a missionary for the Mormon Church in Japan." She said, "Wouldn't you come in and tell me about your church?" This is how they came together. He taught her and she was converted and baptized.[37]

Sister Nakamura Nobu, her teenaged daughter Ayako, and a woman named Tamanaha Kuniko were baptized into the Church in the East China Sea on Christmas Day 1955.

When President Andrus went to Okinawa looking for a place for the missionaries to stay, Sister Nakamura offered her home, a comfortable one by Okinawan standards. The first elders to Okinawa—Clarence LeRoy B. Anderson and Sam K. Shimabukuro (the latter served in the Second Quorum of the Seventy from 1992 to 1997)—traveled to Okinawa from Japan by boat and arrived there on April 17, 1956. They stayed at the Nakamura home for several months, and before long they had established a small branch and built a Quonset hut chapel.

In addition to his efforts to expand the mission, to prepare the Saints for stakes, and to improve proselytizing efforts, President Andrus also made Church materials beyond the standard works available in Japanese and Korean. He organized a staff of translators, typists, and printers and produced most of the priesthood and auxiliary manuals and handbooks. During this time the mission began publishing *Seito-No-Michi* (Way of the Saints), which developed into a fine monthly magazine that replaced an earlier Church magazine, *Messenger and the Grapevine*. In addition, the mission translated *Recreational Songs* into Japanese and published a new book of hymns. Although there was need for materials to be translated into Korean, the list of materials needing to be translated into Japanese was much longer.[38]

During the Andrus years, the number of branches in Japan and Okinawa grew from twenty-six to thirty-seven; the number of Korean branches climbed to seven. Chapels were sorely needed. To meet this need, President Andrus purchased twenty-three chapel sites. These properties, which were obtained at great expense and after considerable expenditure of time and effort, became the basis for a large building program during later years.[39]

The most important property purchase made during this time, and probably the most profitable in the history of the Church to that time, was the acquisition of a Yoyogi Street property in Omote Sando, Tokyo. When Elder Gordon B. Hinckley looked at the property, he was impressed with its potential but staggered by its price. Before he had a chance to reject the property, Andrus told him that the land President Mauss had purchased for $20,000 was now worth $500,000. Elder Hinckley immediately saw the possibility of gaining approval for purchase of this land. After prayerful consideration of the matter and a telephone discussion with Henry D. Moyle of the First Presidency,

Elder Hinckley recommended that the Church buy the property. President McKay approved,[40] and on June 3, 1960, Elder Hinckley and President Andrus completed the transaction.

Over the years, this Yoyogi Street property in Omote Sando served as the Central Branch meeting place as it appreciated in monetary value. Church leaders were undecided regarding its future, but one thing was clear: it was too valuable for a meetinghouse alone. At one point, the Church considered building a six-story structure that would house not only a chapel but also apartments, offices, a distribution center, translating facilities, missionary quarters and offices, and other functions.[41] Finally, after receiving escalating offers of $5 million then $13.5 million, the Church sold the property in 1973 for $24,150,943. Miraculously, the Church's net outlay was a mere $150,000. The principal and interest from the transaction became available to help with the acquisition of hundreds of other chapel sites throughout Japan in addition to other inspired expenditures.[42] By the time President Andrus and his wife were released, the Church's building program in Japan was expanding.

The Presidency of Dwayne N. Andersen

Dwayne N. Andersen, who had served as a missionary under President Mauss, returned to Japan as mission president in 1962, a time of transition. Korea had just become its own mission and the Church's Missionary Committee had recently introduced its first worldwide uniform proselytizing plan. President Andersen realized how much growth had occurred in his absence. There were nearly 7,000 Japanese members, seven times more than when he left Japan in 1953. He also observed that although only ten or twelve branches had been added, the branches were much larger and stronger than before. Church leaders in Japan and Utah were beginning to consider creating the first stake in Japan. Furthermore, the number of missionaries had grown from 66 in 1953 to exceed 180 in 1962.

The incredible growth impressed President Andersen but also created a new set of challenges for his administration. Much training and preparation was needed before a stake could be organized. The mission needed more modern chapels, better-trained priesthood leaders, and a core of solid families who had been sealed in the temple. "I felt that we shouldn't expand," said Andersen, "but should try to consolidate and build a strong foundation."[43]

By the time President Andersen arrived in Japan, the Church's Japanese building program was already underway. In May 1961, Elder Gordon B. Hinckley, supervisor over the Asian missions, noted the need for chapels.[44] He arranged for Wendell B. Mendenhall, chairman of the Church's Building Committee, to go to Japan and make arrangements to start a substantial building program.[45] Soon the First Presidency and Quorum of the Twelve approved construction of five new meetinghouses under the building (or labor) missionary program.

Following his arrival, President Andersen began calling labor missionaries. However, it was difficult to find Japanese members willing to work construction because of the traditional stigma against hand laborers. Many Church members were white-collar workers, students, or business people. Unaccustomed to working with their hands, they initially shied away from the building program. Their attitude changed when they saw American military officers, including colonels and captains, working side by side with young enlisted men. U.S. military personnel serving in the region also contributed thousands of dollars to the mission's building fund.[46]

The building missionary program eventually took off and continued into the late 1970s. During Andersen's administration, the Tokyo North, Tokyo West, Naha (Okinawa), and Gunma branch buildings were completed and dedicated. The Tokyo East and the Fukuoka branch buildings were completely remodeled. Four other buildings were under construction—the Abeno, Tokyo South, Yokohama, and Sapporo branches. The Church also purchased seven future meetinghouse sites.[47] The new chapels helped firmly establish the Church in Japan. The Saints took new pride in their membership, for they now had physical proof of the Church's stability and respectability. Moreover, the Japanese Saints were able to follow more completely the worship patterns of the global Church in the new buildings. The buildings were available for use throughout the week, and they had more classroom space as well as standard sacrament tables and pulpits. Many Japanese building missionaries, including Elder Kikuchi Yoshihiko (called to the First Quorum of the Seventy in 1977), developed into strong Church leaders.

In addition to building new meetinghouses, President Andersen sought to increase the quantity and quality of Japanese priesthood leadership. From the existing membership ranks, he handpicked and trained leadership prospects. President Andersen chose Watanabe Kan and Yamada Goro as counselors. Watanabe lived in Osaka, and Yamada lived near Tokyo. Whenever President Andersen traveled west and south, Watanabe accompanied him and served as his translator. During their travels, Andersen explained the Church's policies, procedures, and organizations. Whenever Andersen held conferences in Tokyo or cities in the north, Yamada accompanied him, received instructions, and acted as translator.[48] Many other leaders received similar training during Andersen's administration.

President Andersen also involved new converts in meaningful Church activity. His missionaries developed convert lessons that further introduced Church programs and the priesthood. Branch presidents were asked to interview and ordain all new male converts to the Aaronic Priesthood during their first month of membership. During Andersen's administration, the number of Japanese priesthood holders and the level of their devotion improved dramatically. For instance, 670 males were baptized during 1964 and the first six months of 1965, and 67 percent of this group received the Aaronic Priesthood. Furthermore, from 1962 to 1965, the number of Melchizedek Priesthood holders rose from 355 to 584.[49] President Andersen also instituted training programs in conjunction with quarterly district conferences. He held corresponding training for the sisters serving in the auxiliary organizations.

For devoted Latter-day Saints, few earthly acts have more significance than participation in temple ordinances. The young leaders in Japan were no exception. They wanted to receive their own temple endowments and be sealed eternally to their spouses and children. But until 1964, there was not a way for a group of Japanese Saints to attend the temple.

The stimulus to organize a temple excursion to Salt Lake City or to Hawaii came from Yamanaka Kenji, a longtime member and professional tour director. He calculated that thirty or forty branch and district officers could afford to go to Salt Lake City. However, in early 1964, President Andersen learned that Flying Tiger Airlines would be willing to transport about 160 passengers to Hawaii for $300 per seat. Mission leaders surveyed the Japanese Saints to see how many would be interested in participating during summer 1965, a year and a half away. One hundred and seventy Saints committed to the necessary financial and spiritual preparations. The mission subsequently sponsored fundraising projects, such as selling pearl tie tacks, and even recording a stereo record of Church music and Japanese songs.[50]

After the mission announced the excursion, complications arose. The U.S. Civil Aeronautics Board would not allow Flying Tiger Airlines to come into Japan to pick up passengers. So the Saints turned to Japan Air Lines (JAL). JAL was uncooperative until President Andersen pointed out that during 1964 the Church had purchased over $70,000 worth of airline tickets from them, making the Church their largest client. JAL officials finally agreed to charter a jetliner for $273 per person, round trip.[51]

In preparation for their first temple experience, the participating Saints read translated chapters on the significance and purpose of temple worship from N. B. Lundwall's *Temples of the Most High* and Wilson Anderson's *Endowment for the Faithful*. When necessary, the Saints repented and changed their lifestyles. The First Presidency asked President Andersen to send a Japanese member to Hawaii to translate the temple ceremony into Japanese. Satō Tatsui was selected and later played a leading role in the Japanese temple ceremony recording.[52]

In July 1965, after eighteen months of planning and preparation, 164 Japanese Saints, accompanied by President and Sister Andersen, boarded their aircraft and departed for Hawaii. As their plane approached Pearl Harbor, at least one of the participants wondered what kind of reception he would receive. When the plane landed, the Hawaiian Saints gave the Japanese Saints a wonderful welcome. They piled leis high on every Japanese neck and warmly greeted each guest. "But to my surprise," recalled the brother who had been worried, "they showed greater love and kindness than I had ever seen in my life. Now I have a clearer understanding of Godly love and brotherly love."[53]

Elder Hinckley joined the group in the temple and sealed several of the couples. Many of the visitors were overcome by emotion. Watanabe Kan remembered, "The spirit that was there was just indescribable and it burned so strong that those offering prayers were choked up for lengthy periods of time before continuing in the supplications to the Lord."[54] The Japanese Saints also participated in Oahu stake and ward services and training meetings. Japanese branch presidents trained with Hawaiian bishops; likewise, district presidents went with stake presidents, district councilors with high councilors, and so on. The leadership training was of immeasurable worth to the Japanese.[55] The 1965 temple trip was the first of many that followed. Charter groups went to Hawaii almost yearly until the building of the Tokyo Temple in 1980. A week after the first group returned from Hawaii, President Andersen was released and replaced by Adney Yoshio Komatsu.

The first five mission presidents of post–World War II Japan each had a distinctive and important role in making the Church permanent. President Clissold laid the foundation, President Mauss constructed the walls, and President Robertson continued the project. President Andrus populated the Japanese Church, and President Andersen educated the new members.

An earlier version of this article appeared as R. Lanier Britsch, "The Reopening and Foundation Years," and part of "Japan 1962–1978, To the Building of the Tokyo Temple," From the East: The History of the Latter-day Saints in Asia, 1851–1996 (Salt Lake City: Deseret Book, 1998), 80–124.

Notes

1. Richard Henry Drummond, *A History of Christianity in Japan* (Grand Rapids, Mich.: William B. Eerdmans, 1971), 273.

2. A photocopy of the original advertisement in author's possession.

3. See Yukiko Konno, "Fujiya Nara: Twice a Pioneer," *Ensign* 23 (April 1993): 31, 33.

4. See Paul C. Andrus, Oral history, interview by author, Honolulu, Hawaii, 1974, typescript, 5, Oral History Program, Church Archives, The Church of Jesus Christ of Latter-day Saints, Salt Lake City.

5. See Mission Financial and Statistical Records (hereafter cited as MFSR), Japanese Mission, 1948, Church Archives.

6. Edward L. Clissold, interview by Kenneth Barnum and J. Christopher Conkling, November 8, 1973, tape recording, in author's possession.

7. A large addition came later, and in the late 1970s the building was razed to make way for the Tokyo Japan Temple.

8. Paul V. Hyer, "Preparations for a Mission in Postwar Japan: Paul Hyer's 'Mini-Mission Training Center'" (unpublished paper, in author's possession); MFSR, Japanese Mission, 1948.

9. Elders Paul Andrus and Ted Price both later served as mission presidents in Japan, and Ray Price later served in the presidency of the Tokyo Temple.

10. Hyer, "Preparations for a Mission in Postwar Japan," 3.

11. See Lucile C. Tate, *Boyd K. Packer: A Watchman on the Tower* (Salt Lake City: Bookcraft, 1995), 64–66.

12. See Harrison T. Price, "A Cup of Tea," *Improvement Era* 65 (March 1962): 161, 184, 186; and Spencer J. Palmer, *The Church Encounters Asia* (Salt Lake City: Deseret Book, 1970), 65–69.

13. Andrus, Oral history, 7–8.

14. See MFSR, Japanese Mission, 1948.

15. Kan Watanabe, Kiyoshi Sakai, Shuichi Yaginuma, Mildred E. Handy, and Grace Vlam, "Japan: Land of the Rising Sun," *Ensign* 5 (August 1975): 41.

16. Vinal Grant Mauss, Oral history, interviews by R. Lanier Britsch, Provo, Utah, 1975, typescript, 15, James Moyle Oral History Program, Church Archives.

17. See Vinal G. Mauss, Oral history, 20–21.

18. See Armand L. Mauss, Oral history, interviews by William G. Hartley, 1974, typescript, James Moyle Oral History Program, Church Archives, 35.

19. Vinal G. Mauss, Oral history, 27–28.

20. See Manuscript History of Japanese Mission, September 30, 1951, Church Archives.

21. See MFSR, Japanese Mission, 1951, 1952.

22. MFSR, Japanese Mission, 1951.

23. MFSR, Japanese Mission, 1951.

24. MFSR, Japanese Mission, 1951–55.

25. See Hilton A. Robertson, Diary of Japanese Mission, 1954–55, copy in author's possession, 3.

26. Robertson, Diary of Japanese Mission, August 31, 1954, 100.

27. Harold B. Lee, "Report on the Orient," *Improvement Era* 57 (December 1954): 926.

28. See Joseph Fielding Smith, "Report From the Far East Missions," *Improvement Era* 58 (December 1955): 917.

29. MFSR, Japanese Mission, 1954.

30. For a fine tribute to the Robertsons, see Muriel Jenkins Heal, "'We Will Go': The Robertson Response," *Ensign* 12 (April 1982): 32–35.

31. MFSR, Japanese Mission, 1955.

32. Since 1830, when Joseph Smith's brother Samuel placed copies of the Book of Mormon in his bag and set out to spread the message of the Restoration, the methods used to teach the gospel have been many and varied. Until

the post–World War II era, there was not a unified system for teaching the gospel to investigators. Richard Lloyd Anderson and Reed Bankhead devised the first systematic, sequential method of explaining gospel concepts and moving contacts toward baptism. See Richard O. Cowan, *The Church in the Twentieth Century* (Salt Lake City: Bookcraft, 1985), 279–81.

33. Andrus, Oral history, 25.

34. Andrus, Oral history, 25.

35. The number of convert baptisms for the remaining years of Andrus's presidency was 735 in 1958, 596 in 1959, 896 in 1960, and 1,290 in 1961. There were 1,622 baptisms in 1962, but that number belonged to President Andersen as well as to President Andrus. See MFSR, Japanese Mission, for applicable years.

36. See Andrus, Oral history, 51.

37. Andrus, Oral history, 19.

38. Andrus, Oral history, 52.

39. See Andrus, Oral history, 50–51.

40. Gordon B. Hinckley, Journals, May 29–30, 1960, in possession of Gordon B. Hinckley.

41. See Ezra Taft Benson, "A World Message," *Improvement Era* 73 (June 1970): 97.

42. See Andrus, Oral history, 32.

43. Dwayne N. Andersen, oral history by R. Lanier Britsch, August 3 and 13, 1973, Provo, Utah, typescript, 50, Oral History Program, Church Archives.

44. Hinckley, Journals, May 20, 1961.

45. Hinckley, Journals, March 1962.

46. Anderson, Oral history, 38.

47. Andersen, Oral history, 47.

48. Anderson, Oral history, 32–33.

49. Andersen, Oral history, 45–47; see also MFSR, Japanese Mission, 1965.

50. Terry G. Nelson, "A History of the Church of Jesus Christ of Latter-day Saints in Japan from 1948 to 1980" (master's thesis, Brigham Young University, 1986), appendix B, 158–59.

51. Anderson, Oral history, 18, 19, 21.

52. Anderson, Oral history, 23, 28.

53. Nelson, "The Church in Japan from 1948 to 1980," 166.

54. Watanabe and others, "Japan: Land of the Rising Sun," 42.

55. Andersen, Oral history, 36; see also Palmer, *The Church Encounters Asia*, 78–83.

13

Memoirs of the Relief Society in Japan, 1951–1991

Yanagida Toshiko
Translated by Numano Jiro

*My poems are my tears,
as my eyes are moistened at once
in joy and in sorrow.*
—Yanagida Toshiko

Introduction

Yanagida Toshiko is a Latter-day Saint who was baptized long ago. She is a daughter of Takagi Tomigoro, who was baptized in 1915 and an important Church member in Japan before the mission closed in 1924. Her uncle Takahashi Nikichi joined the Church in 1908 and later brought his brother Tomigoro into the Church. Sister Yanagida was a Japanese pioneer in the post–World War II era, called as the first Relief Society president in Japan and serving in that office for many years. She has been a very modern woman, and her character is marked by a studious and flexible mind. She enjoys composing tanka *(a form of Japanese poetry)*. She also wrote an autobiography entitled Ashiato *(My footsteps)* and was the editor and chief writer of Seiki wo koete—Matsujitsu-Seito-Iesu-Kirisuto-Kyokai Dendo 100-nen no Ayumi (Beyond the century—a story of 100 years of the LDS Church in Japan). *The following article is my translation of her memoirs, written in commemoration of the Relief Society's sesquicentennial in 1991, that tell the story of the organization's development and her contributions to it.*

—Numano Jiro

Earliest Days

I feel as if I am looking back at my own life in the Church when I try to trace the history of the Relief Society in Japan. The two are closely intertwined. In August 1949, I traveled nine hours from Nagoya to the mission headquarters in Tokyo to be baptized by Elder Ted Price in the presence of my father who lived in Urawa, Saitama. Mission President Edward L. Clissold confirmed me. I returned to Nagoya by myself on the same day. There were no Latter-day Saint meetings held in Nagoya at that time. The closest area that had meetings was Narumi, a suburb of Nagoya, and I made the two-hour trek there every week. So I wrote a letter to Mission President Vinal G. Mauss, who filled the position in September 1949, asking permission to begin holding regular meetings in Nagoya. A Sunday School was then started there. Toward the end of April 1950, a new missionary came to the area, and he served as branch president. A couple of sister missionaries also arrived about the same time. In those days, the congregation of the Nagoya Branch consisted of my husband, Tohkichi (who was baptized September 30, 1950), me, and another young single sister, in addition to the missionaries.

The women of the branch, including any visitors, began to meet in the sister missionaries' apartment on Tuesday nights, on the initiative of newly arrived Sister Philomena Andrade.[1] She shared her ideas of tidying houses, arranging cupboards, cooking simple dishes, and answering questions about the gospel. Elder Wayne R. Herlin, the branch president, said, "Let's call it a women's meeting as we cannot organize anything officially." Thanks to Sister Andrade's attractive personality, five to six women, including high school students, gathered regularly. Cooking classes were the main attraction. Because missionaries were often transferred, this women's gathering was sometimes held at night and other times during the day to accommodate the missionaries' schedules. Since there were no chapels then, we sat in the missionaries' *tatami* (straw mat) room and cooked inexpensive beefsteaks, pancakes, cookies, cakes, and so forth using an oven I had brought from my home and placed on a portable stove. On rainy days though, I sometimes found only myself and two sister missionaries there. The food we cooked together was a blessing to my home in those days when Japan had not yet made an economic recovery from the war.

Once, canned food and used clothes were sent to us from the U.S. Relief Society as welfare supplies. We walked with the sister missionaries on a hot summer day to deliver the goods to families whose children were attending Sunday School. In those days, my children were the only children of Latter-day Saint parents, so my family was both very surprised and thrilled to receive the goods. Another time when goods were sent to us, we delivered an especially great number of supplies to a very poor family, but the father of the family sold the goods to buy more *sake* (alcohol). The missionaries and I keenly realized how challenging welfare work can be at times. The experience, I think, helped me understand the gospel very much. As I was a new member then, the conversation I had with Sister Andrade strengthened my testimony of the gospel and taught me about brotherly love.

The members and those interested in the Church met together often. The missionaries' residence or a member's house typically became a meeting place, since there were no chapels in those days. On cold days, we wore an overcoat to meetings; on hot summer days, we burned a mosquito-repellant stick. We had no air conditioning. Although the room we typically met in was narrow and inconvenient, it was a good environment to nurture love among those who came.

Bazaars held a very important position in Relief Society work in Japan. We asked a Church member in the occupation army to purchase chocolate, chewing gum, and so forth from the PX (post exchange) at a low price, and then we sold the items at the busiest quarters in Sakaemachi, Nagoya, holding a bazaar at the square where a TV tower now stands. We sold chocolates, in a box hung from our necks, at an important intersection for three days in 1950 and 1951. Shops nearby complained to us that the prices were too low, so we got their permission to continue selling by limiting the activity to only three days. At that time, one U.S. dollar corresponded to 360 yen. Japan was destitute of commodities, and so U.S. members of the Church and missionaries, who gave us much assistance, all looked rich in the eyes of the Japanese.

Missionaries served for three years then, and their clothes often wore out before they went home. Patching trousers, washing bedclothes, and beating cotton mattresses to soften them, all became tasks of the Relief Society. When members were few, the Relief Society president took this responsibility, but sometimes I did, too.

Called as Relief Society President

Edward L. Clissold presided over the mission in Japan from 1948 to 1949, and Vinal G. Mauss presided from 1949 to 1953. A very modest branch Relief Society first saw the light of day in Nagoya as early as 1951 with me, Sister Yanagida, as president, and Sister Adachi Yoshie and Sister Fumie Swenson as counselors (illus. 13-1). (There was no secretary at that time.)

Hilton A. Robertson served as the next mission president (1953–55). Following Robertson was Paul C. Andrus, who presided over the Northern Far East Mission for two terms or six years (1955–62). On February 26, 1961, during President Andrus's term, I was called to be Relief Society district president of the West Central District. Sister Suzuki Toshi was called as president of the Central District (1962), Sister Matsushita Shoko as president of the Hokkaidō District (1963), and Sister Miyara of the Okinawa District (1963). I was responsible for eleven branches—Nagoya, Kanazawa, Kyoto, Okamachi, Abeno, Nishinomiya, Sannomiya, Okayama, Hiroshima, Yanai, and Fukuoka—

Courtesy Yanagida Toshiko

Illus. 13-1. Branch Relief Society presidency in 1951 pictured with Relief Society sisters. Front row, second from left, Adachi Yoshie; third from left, Yanagida Toshiko; fourth from left, Fumie Swenson.

and was to attend each branch conference. In order for me to attend remote branches in Hiroshima, Yanai, and Fukuoka, I took a night train with the district president, then Suzuki Shozo. There was no *Shinkansen* (bullet train) at that time.

Three years later, on June 21, 1964, Mission President Dwayne N. Andersen (1962–65) called me to be the Relief Society president of the Northern Far East Mission. Sister Uenoyama Emiko was called to the Relief Society presidency of the West Central district. I called Sister Yaginuma Setsuko to be my counselor (the only one at that time), and Sister Tange to be secretary. These sisters resided in Nagoya, making it convenient to conduct regular business. Before this time, the mission president's wife served as the president of the Relief Society in the international missions, but the responsibility was being transferred to local members. I am not sure whether this shift occurred all over the world or just in Japan. With her duty of overseeing Relief Society, Sister Peggy Andersen had put a message in *Seito-No-Michi*, the Church's monthly magazine in Japan (illus. 13-2), but she turned over this task to me. My main responsibilities, however, were to attend district conferences of the four districts, to assist Relief Societies in the districts, and to make an annual financial report to the Relief Society General Presidency in Salt Lake City.

Illus. 13-2. *Seito-No-Michi* (Way of the Saints), the Church magazine in Japan in 1962.

During this era, Relief Society had a separate budget from the mission budget. Expenses for Relief Society—such as transportation fees, correspondence, and so forth—had to be borne by the organization itself. Revenue came from female Church members eighteen years and older, who, in principle, automatically became members of Relief Society. Each member paid thirty yen a year and was given a membership card. Of the thirty yen, twenty went to mission headquarters, five to the district, and five to the branch Relief Society fund. Branch Relief Societies raised additional money by holding bazaars, dinner parties, and other activities; the district Relief Society occasionally held bazaars, too. Because our budget was separate from that of the priesthood leadership, we saved money by using night trains and ferryboats to go to Hokkaidō and Okinawa when attending district conferences. At midnight, I would travel on a ferryboat from Aomori to Hokkaidō; when going to Okinawa, the train trip took twenty-seven hours from Nagoya to Kagoshima, then I had to wait for the ship and it took another twenty-five hours on a smaller ship to Naha, Okinawa. In those days, Okinawa was under U.S. occupation, so I carried my passport with me and had to get the required vaccinations before boarding the ship there. When I first visited Okinawa in 1964, I found cars driving on the right hand side of the road and discovered that money was in dollars and cents—I remember the bus fare was 3 cents.

When I traveled to these district conferences, members of the local Relief Societies were kind enough to let me stay at their homes. Visiting remote districts offered opportunities to become familiar with local leaders such as Sisters Hachimine Yoshiko, Miyara Toyoko, and Tohma Misao, who took me to see the remains of the war in Okinawa. Sister Andersen advised me to visit four branches—there were only four at that time—in Hokkaidō when I was there to attend district conference in late September 1964. I stayed at the Matsushitas' in Sapporo, at a Sister Takahashi's in Otaru, at the Ohkawaras' in Asahikawa, and at the Kawasakis' in Muroran, where I saw the sole Latter-day Saint chapel made of wood in Japan. Those homes were all heated, but I saw large electric fans that helped cool the temperature in the chapel's hall where district conference was held in Okinawa in November of the same year. There were two branches in Okinawa, Naha and Futenma. In Futenma, a half-cylindrical barrack disposed of by the U.S. Army was used as a meetinghouse and as the missionary quarters. Experiencing the reverse sequence of seasons during the trip to Okinawa this fall, I realized how long Japan is, even though it is a small country.

In addition to visiting district conferences and the various district Relief Societies, I also had to oversee the organization's finances. Because Relief Society had its own budget, I had to send an annual financial report to the general board. This was a perplexing job because it was difficult for many branches to understand how to complete the forms. I often had to correct some parts before totaling up reports from the districts. It took Sister Yaginuma and me a few days to check the reports with an abacus, then we filled in the mission form, took it to mission headquarters, checked it again with Sister Andersen, and finally submitted it to the general board. It took a lot of time to calculate and fill in the form, so I had to stay the night at the mission home. Although my children were all boys and my husband was busy with his work, I managed to leave home because my mother, who had joined the Church, was in good health and was willing to fill in for me at home. Still, leaving home for days (it took a week just to go to Okinawa) burdened family members, which bothered me a lot; this was the period of my life when I was worried about my home affairs.

Manuals

When the Church was experiencing a boom of international growth in the mid-twentieth century, there was a long gap before the Relief Society lessons were translated into other languages. Thus, we did not have any manuals and we depended wholly on sister missionaries for materials. Separate, mimeographed booklets were sent to us, subject by subject, during the era of President Andrus. There were five subjects: visiting teacher messages, theology, social science, literature, and work meeting. One year for the subject of social science we read a small book about Japanese history that had been written after the war. For the first time I learned of historical figures like Himiko, a famous queen of ancient Japan. I found a striking difference between the contents of this book, based on real historical material, and that of the history books written before the war, which had been built around legends surrounding the Japanese Imperial House. I became fascinated with history even though I had had little interest in it when I was young. Reading this small book awoke me to the wonders of history. So I appreciate very much the Church's program that offered various stimuli for progress.

From 1965 to 1966, teaching materials for Relief Society lessons began to appear in the *Seito-No-Michi*. This was very convenient for us. But occasionally they did not appear in the magazine, and we had to prepare the materials ourselves. The Relief Society's study year lasted eight months from October through May, which meant we had no materials to teach from during the remaining four months. We spent those four months doing what was called "work meeting."[2]

In preparing the manual for work meeting, we had to translate it into English and submit it to the general board for their approval. So I selected and edited portions of old mimeographed manuals that many sisters had shown lots of interest in. For the visiting teacher messages, we picked up those used during 1957–58; for theology, *Signs of the Times* by Joseph Fielding Smith; for social science, *First Presidency*, which was used from 1957 to 1958. For literature we selected the topic of Japanese poetry and learned its genres and history, reading from classical poetry collections such as *Man-yo-shu* and *Kokin-shu*, along with haiku and modern poetry. We also studied some Japanese literature. We created curriculum for work meeting by selecting subject matter from *Mochimono to Kurashikata* (Possessions and life), published by a commercial press, Fujin-no-tomo. Thus, we needed the understanding and approval of the general board for preparing our own textbooks of literature and work meeting. We asked Sister Takahashi Motoko, a graduate of Brigham Young University, for help. She was one of the members on the mission Relief Society board.

After getting approval from the general presidency, we arranged to print the manuals in time for the start of Relief Society lessons in October. During a hot summer in 1965 in Nagoya, Sister Yaginuma and I managed to find a printing shop that would produce our job at a low price. We asked them to print it quickly, and we proofread the text ourselves. The book was finished on schedule. We used the same manual again in 1972. It was a humble thing with cheap paper and binding, but it was a memorable item for us.

Rapid Growth

In 1968 when he was leaving Japan, Mission President Adney Y. Komatsu said, "To have sufficient growth, we need to divide the mission so that we can have more branches." Exactly as he said, the mission was divided into two with the arrival of Mission President Edward Y. Okazaki in Osaka one month after Mission President Walter R. Bills took President Komatsu's post in Tokyo. Residing in Nagoya, I was assigned to serve in Relief Society under President Okazaki and his wife, Chieko, in the Japan-Okinawa Mission. Since we were separated from the Relief Society of the Japan Mission, and having no part in their work, I do not know how they progressed after that. I do know, however, that Church leaders decided to sponsor a Mormon Pavilion at Expo '70 to be held in Osaka in 1970. We all worked hard in the local units and hoped the Church would experience growth. President Okazaki oversaw our work on the project. Just as we expected, missionary work advanced extensively after Expo '70.[3] I feel dazzled to see the growth of the Church as missions increased successively to reach ten in 1992, and stakes multiplied to twenty-two that same year. I sense the rush of the latter days as I witness the rapid increase in the number of temples in the world.

Unrealized Volunteer Work Plan

When the Tokyo Temple was completed in 1980, I was the Relief Society president of the Tokyo North Stake. The construction of the temple proceeded steadily, and the Relief Society was to do the final cleaning, behind the construction crew, before the building was to be opened to the public. Representing seven stake Relief Societies in Tokyo, I was given the responsibility to prepare for the cleaning from Tanaka Kenji, a Regional Representative (illus. 13-3). This involved mobilizing four hundred sisters in five days, dividing them into morning and

Courtesy Yanagida Toshiko

Illus. 13-3. Tanaka Kenji (1980) was the Regional Representative during the construction of the Tokyo Temple.

afternoon groups. While doing the scheduling, we were touched when sisters in remote areas, busy with raising children, willingly volunteered service despite the sacrifice involved.

On the day before the operation, we had a meeting in the temple for preliminary arrangements with Elder McFee from Salt Lake City, the staff of Kajima Construction Company, Regional Representative Tanaka, and the several ward Relief Society presidents. Elder McFee wanted the cleaning done according to the plan, just as the last cleaning of the previous ten temples in other countries had been done. However, the gentlemen from Kajima Construction said that such a cleaning was unnecessary, or rather would bring in dirt with so many people coming in and out. The Kajima representatives assured us they would deliver the temple only after a thorough cleaning. The discussion went on until evening, and finally the plan of volunteer clean up was dropped after Church leaders were satisfied with their inspections. We had to tell the sisters in various districts who were to come the next morning that the plan was cancelled. After 9:30 that night, we used what telephones we could find and quickly communicated this news to ward organizations. It was a night to be remembered because of the fuss. This incident impressed me with how Japanese construction companies handled things compared to those in other countries. At the same time, I privately felt the will of God behind it, supposing that sisters who offered service at any cost showed their testimony but were exempted from the sacrifice, just as Abraham of old was commanded to stop the sacrifice of Isaac.

Reminiscences

When I was traveling in America in 1991, I visited the Okazakis; the Andersens; former Mission President Mauss, then ninety-one years old, and his daughter Peggy; and the Andruses. All were in their declining years. Looking back upon the past, I remember how they were once young and energetic, so I worked in good spirit, even though I sometimes worried about problems. I am filled with a strong feeling of gratitude for the Lord's guidance as I remember those dear mission presidents and missionaries who taught us inexperienced members.

I am a witness to the current progress of the Church in Japan, and I am grateful for this. In this year of commemorating the Relief Society's sesquicentennial (1991), I cannot refrain from feeling happy and grateful for the present circumstances of the Relief Society in Japan after forty years of its history (illus. 13-4). Past events seem vast and obscure, as if in dreams. Now I feel obliged to the next generation for their unceasing service. I should say that we as women are responsible for fulfilling the Relief Society's motto "Charity Never Faileth," and our faith in the Lord leads us to his glory without fail.

This article is a translation of her memoirs, written in commemoration of the Relief Society's sesquicentennial in 1991.

Illus. 13-4. Sister Yanagida Toshiko in 2000.

Courtesy Yanagida Toshiko

Notes

1. In 1990, I happened to attend a reunion of missionaries from 1948 to 1954 in Salt Lake City. We were all very delighted to see each other. Sister Andrade (now Sister Clowson), who started the women's meeting, now white-haired, was actively engaged in running the reunion.

2. For a brief explanation of work meeting, also called work day, see Jill Mulvay Derr, Janath Russell Cannon, and Maureen Ursenbach Beecher, *Women of Covenant: The Story of Relief Society* (Salt Lake City: Deseret Book, 1992), 296–97.

3. For more information on Expo '70, see Terry G. Nelson, "The Church in Japan Comes of Age, 1968–1980," reprinted herein.

14

The Church in Japan Comes of Age, 1968–1980

Terry G. Nelson

While visiting Japan in 1967, President Hugh B. Brown of the First Presidency predicted, "This little corner of the garden of the Lord's will blossom and bloom and bear fruit. From this area will go messengers to kindred peoples in many parts of the world."[1] The coming decade proved to be a remarkable time for The Church of Jesus Christ of Latter-day Saints in Japan. Within a few years, the Church would have four missions instead of one, a new stake, and the benefit of exposure at the Osaka World's Fair in 1970. The Church in Japan was moving from adolescence to adulthood and from obscurity to prominence.

The Mission Divided

From the introduction of the gospel in Japan by Elder Heber J. Grant in 1901 until summer 1968, there was only one mission in Japan. The mission, first named the Japan Mission, was initially open from 1901 to 1924. Japanese missionary work was later resumed in 1937, this time in Hawaii by President Hilton A. Robertson. The mission was then called the Japanese Mission in Hawaii. In 1943 its name was changed to the Central Pacific Mission. When President Edward L. Clissold reopened the work in Japan in 1948, the mission was known as the Japanese Mission. The name was again changed in 1955, this time to the Northern Far East Mission, when the Southern Far East Mission was created. The mission name changes were usually also accompanied by boundary changes. This last time, interestingly, the boundaries became so large that the transfer from Naha, Okinawa Branch, in the south end of the mission to the branch at Asahigawa, Hokkaidō, in the north was the longest transfer within a mission boundary anywhere in the world.[2]

Rumors of a mission split began in 1968 when Elder Gordon B. Hinckley, then the area supervisor, requested that the Church secure a home for Edward Y. Okazaki and his family in either Osaka or Kobe. Okazaki had already been called as the president of the second mission in Japan, which was still formally unannounced. That fall, Walter R. Bills succeeded Adney Y. Komatsu as president of the Northern Far East Mission, and Church leaders held a short mission division ceremony at the Tokyo mission home. They cut a map of Japan in half at the Japanese Alps in central Japan; the actual division of the mission occurred September 1, 1968. The area covering the northern half of Japan was renamed the Japan Mission, presided over by Walter Bills, and the southern half of the mission was named the Japan-Okinawa Mission, presided over by Edward Okazaki.

The Japan Mission

Because the Japan Mission, headquartered in Tokyo, contained most of the local leadership and established Church programs, it initially grew much faster than its sister mission to the south. Soon after his appointment, President Bills opened three new branches, and the following year he opened nine additional cities for proselytizing. According to Bills, the most successful program in bringing people into the Church in the Japan Mission was referred to as the Book of Mormon placement program. President David O. McKay had promised, "For every Book of Mormon placed in the land of Japan, there will eventually be a baptism."[3] Bills had complete faith that conversions would result if the missionaries could get the Book of Mormon into Japanese hands. Thus in 1969 the Japan Mission began to more actively distribute copies of the Book of Mormon. Bills encouraged his missionaries to carry the Book of Mormon everywhere, and they soon found that their unusual black books featuring Japanese characters, a gold angel Moroni, and red pages attracted attention. Over the next two years, the Japan Mission distributed over 208,000 volumes; Bills believed that about 60 percent of the baptisms during his presidency could be attributed to the Book of Mormon placement program.[4]

In addition to overseeing missionary work, Bills was responsible for training leaders within the mission. After evaluating available branch leadership in the Japan Mission, Bills decided to train native Tokyo leaders for future stake leadership. He invited branch presidents, elders quorum presidents, district presidents, and other leaders to attend regular training meetings at the mission home. He also gathered Church handbooks, manuals, and other materials and had them translated into Japanese. These meetings, held over the course of a year, were instrumental in preparing local leadership for the eventual organization of the Tokyo Stake in 1972.[5] Church leaders also established all the auxiliary programs in Japan, including the Primary in 1968.

Preparations for Expo '70

One of the most significant events in Asian Latter-day Saint history was the Church's involvement in the Osaka World's Fair of 1970, often called Expo '70. During 1968 Church leaders decided to sponsor and build a fair pavilion. Plans were made for Elder Ezra Taft Benson, then a member of the Quorum of the Twelve, to make the formal announcement during an open house at the Tokyo mission home. In preparation for the announcement, Bills invited prominent members of the Japanese government and business community. He assigned missionaries and several members to deliver open house invitations to local dignitaries. But when Bills suggested they invite members of the Japanese Diet (parliament), many local members were concerned.

After resolving their concerns through fasting and prayer, the mission presidency and several members called upon Diet members and delivered open house invitations to them. The open house was held at the mission home on November 13, and many of those invited came. Elder Benson spoke and officially announced the plans of the Church to build a pavilion on the grounds of the World's Fair.[6] The evening was a great success and a fitting prelude to the remarkable influence the Mormon Pavilion was destined to have at Expo '70 for the advancement of the Church in Japan.

The Japan-Okinawa Mission

The newly formed Japan-Okinawa Mission, covering roughly the southern half of Japan, was initially not as successful as the northern

Japan Mission. In the first month after the old mission was divided, there were only nineteen baptisms in the new mission, and there were never more than thirty per month in that first year. The Japan-Okinawa mission also lagged behind the northern mission in other ways: initially there was no mission home, so leaders had to rent space in a Kobe office; the mission had only two chapels (the Japan Mission had seven); and much of the experienced Japanese leadership lived in the Japan Mission.

From humble beginnings, the Okazakis led the Japan-Okinawa Mission to great heights during its two-year existence. President Edward Y. Okazaki, a convert to the Church, had grown up on the Hawaiian island of Maui, and he was the second mission president of Japanese ancestry. By the end of 1969, sixteen new branches had been opened and baptisms had grown from nineteen in January to seventy-three in December. By his release in 1971, President Okazaki had achieved his long-time goal of a "One for One" baptism rate: each missionary baptized one convert per month, or about two hundred baptisms total.[7]

Like the Japan Mission, the Japan-Okinawa Mission was involved in preparations for the World's Fair in Osaka in 1970. Since Osaka was within its boundaries, the Japan-Okinawa Mission was named the host mission for the Expo '70 Mormon Pavilion. One of the Church's most ambitious projects in preparation for the pavilion was the refilming of *Man's Search for Happiness*, which portrays man's journey through life and eternity. The film had been made five years earlier for the Church's pavilion at the New York World's Fair in 1965. Because of its success, leaders decided to make a Japanese version with a Japanese cast. President Okazaki consulted with filming crews from BYU and helped convince General Authorities to film the movie on location in Japan instead of in San Francisco.[8]

A film crew from BYU's motion picture studio was sent to Japan for several weeks of filming. Ogasawara Hiroshi, a well-known Japanese movie and television star, was chosen for the lead role based on his acting ability, personable appearance, and previous film roles.[9] During the Expo, the finished film was shown continually in two theaters at the pavilion and introduced the gospel to millions of Japanese. Missionaries also used it later in their teaching. Clearly, the film played an important part in the Church's growth in Japan.

In spring 1969, the Church held a groundbreaking ceremony for the site of its Expo pavilion. Distinguished guests included Elder Ezra Taft Benson, a member of the Quorum of the Twelve; Ishizaka Taizō, president of Expo '70; Chuma Kauru, mayor of Osaka City; and Satō Gisen, governor of Osaka Prefecture. Elder Benson told the large audience that "our Church is a world Church and our message is a world message." He also stated that the pavilion would give the Church "an opportunity to tell its history, organization, and doctrine and to 'let you see our program in action.'"[10] Governor Satō, in his official remarks, said, "I heard that the theme of the Mormon Pavilion will be Man's Search for Happiness. In these modern times where materialistic values are abundant, you will show us a higher means of civilization through dignity and spirituality."[11] Mayor Chuma similarly stated,

> There has never been a time when people seek for peaceful minds and pure hearts as we do presently. Now spaceships and mechanical objects are flying freely through space. On the other hand, people hunger for humanity and something spiritual. This is due to the fact that people are suffering with solitude. In that sense we feel strongly that we have a necessity for spiritual culture. The Mormon Church's objective through their unique exhibits is to help people think about the purpose of life. I give my blessings to the success of this Pavilion.[12]

The Japanese Language Training Mission

In February 1969, the Church shortened the term of all its proselytizing missions to two years; foreign missions without formal language training had previously been for two and one-half years but were now reduced to only two years as well. To help its missionaries compensate for their shorter opportunity to learn a foreign language, the Church expanded its language-training program and opened two additional language-training centers at Ricks College in Idaho and at Brigham Young University–Hawaii. The Idaho center taught Danish, Dutch, Finnish, Norwegian, and Swedish, while the Hawaiian center taught Chinese, Japanese, Korean, Samoan, Tahitian, and Tongan.[13] Missionaries were expected to study their mission language for two months before leaving for their assigned field of labor. Those called to serve in Japan were also introduced to Japanese people, culture, and food at the center in Hawaii. In many ways the Language Training Mission (LTM) served as a cultural shock absorber to help the missionaries prepare for adjustment to life in Japan. The first group of missionaries trained at the Hawaiian LTM arrived in Japan in April 1969. They came with basic Japanese language training and familiarity with the missionary discussions. Unlike their predecessors, who were expected to learn the language and missionary skills on their own, these new missionaries were able to be more effective from the beginning. The missionaries were a great help in preparing for Expo '70.

The Mormon Pavilion

The Church's participation in Expo '70 was incredibly successful. The Mormon Pavilion, as it was called, was located near the main east gate, just off the moving sidewalk, and it was one of only two religiously oriented venues.[14] Elder Bernard P. Brockbank, Assistant to the Quorum of the Twelve, was appointed director of the pavilion. He had previously directed the Church's pavilions at the New York World's Fair, the HemisFair in San Antonio, Texas, and the Montreal, Canada Fair. Sensing the uniqueness of the Osaka fair, Elder Brockbank observed, "This is the first time we have had an exhibit of this type in a country where the people don't have a Christian background. We feel this is our opportunity to take the message of a living Jesus Christ and the living God that Jesus Christ prayed to and worshiped to these people."[15]

The Mormon Pavilion was dedicated on March 13, 1970, two days before the doors were opened to the crowds of Expo '70. In attendance were President Hugh B. Brown, First Counselor in the First Presidency, Elders Ezra Taft Benson and Gordon B. Hinckley of the Twelve, and Elder Brockbank. Nearly five hundred people crowded into the relatively small pavilion to witness the dedication. Following remarks by Elders Benson, Hinckley, and Brockbank, President Brown offered the dedicatory prayer.

The pavilion's success exceeded Church leaders' highest expectations. Of the approximately sixty-five million people who attended the Expo during its six-month life (March 15 to September 15), over 10 percent, or 6,658,532, visited the Mormon Pavilion.[16] Many signed the guest register and expressed interest in learning more about the Church. A highlight of the event was the visit paid by the Crown Prince of Japan, who was the honorary president of Expo '70. President Okazaki guided the Prince through the pavilion and shared the gospel message with him. Missionaries from President Okazaki's mission were assigned as guides in the pavilion.[17]

Although mission leaders feared that baptisms in the Japan-Okinawa Mission would drop during the Expo because of the number of missionary hours being spent at the pavilion, the number of baptisms actually climbed.[18] This was likely due to the favorable impression visitors received at the exhibition; many, in fact, commented upon the spirit of their missionary guides. Elder Brockbank said:

> Our most impressive exhibit was the spirit of the dedicated, loving, inspired missionaries. The missionaries radiated a great love for the Oriental people and the Oriental people had great respect for the missionaries. One Japanese gentleman said to me, "I can hardly believe that such fine, clean young people would leave their homes, pay their own way, and learn a new language. They must truly love us."[19]

The Church's heightened visibility during the Expo had far-reaching implications. Millions of Japanese became aware of the Church's existence and saw it as a respectable organization, which helped to improve the Church's image in Japan. Nearly fifty thousand copies of the Book of Mormon were given away, and the referrals that resulted from the Church's presentation led to thousands of baptisms. In 1970, for example, baptisms in Japan totaled 779, doubling the 1969 totals. The Church had received a boost that would influence its acceptance and growth for many years.

Two days after the dedication of the Mormon Pavilion at Expo '70, Church leaders created the first stake in Asia, the Tokyo Stake, which comprised six wards. For years leaders had been grooming local members for stake leadership positions. During his presidency, Paul Andrus, president of the Northern Far East Mission (1955–62), had concentrated his efforts on building the membership in the Tokyo-Yokoyama area, and President Bills had conducted several leadership training seminars. The long-awaited day came on March 15, 1970. Nearly a thousand members crowded into the Tokyo North Branch building to witness the proceedings. Elders Benson and Hinckley presided and spoke at the three-hour meeting, explaining to the Japanese members the blessings and responsibilities of stake membership. Tanaka Kenji was called as president of the Tokyo Stake; his counselors were Kikuchi Yoshihiko and Sagara Kenichi. It was a momentous occasion and a milestone for the Church in Asia.

Two Missions Become Four

At the same conference, the visiting Brethren announced that the two existing missions in Japan would be divided to form four. The Japan Mission would be divided to create the Japan Mission and the Japan East Mission, and the Japan-Okinawa Mission would become the Japan Central Mission and the Japan West Mission. What had been only one mission in Japan as recently as September 1968 was now four. Bills and Okazaki retained their callings over the Japan and Japan Central Missions, respectively, while two new presidents were called to preside over the Japan East and Japan West Missions.

Russell Horiuchi, a geography professor at BYU, was called to preside over the Japan East Mission. The headquarters for this mission were in Sapporo, and the mission boundaries included Hokkaidō and the northern quarter of Honshu. Previously, missionaries had not heavily proselyted in northern Japan because they focused on the densely populated areas of central Japan, such as Tokyo, Osaka, Yokohama, and Kobe. Consequently, there were few members, branches, and church buildings in the mission. From March 1970 on, the Church began to spread its efforts to the less densely populated areas in the extreme northern and southwestern regions of the country. As expected, the work in the Japan East and Japan West Missions initially went forward slowly.[20]

Watanabe Kan's call as president of the newly formed Japan West Mission came as a surprise to some present at the conference: he would be the first native-born Japanese mission president. The Church had reached another milestone in Japan.

The First Area Conference

The first area conference in Japan was announced in 1975 and it caused a flurry of activity among the Japanese Saints. Over the next several months, the Saints invited members of other faiths and less-active

Latter-day Saints to attend the upcoming conference. Leaders held special meetings to increase spirituality,[21] and the Saints were encouraged to be more diligent in family prayer, family home evening, and scripture reading. The Saints also helped make financial arrangements for those who lived far away from the conference site, especially the Okinawan Saints, to be able to attend the conference. These island Saints had other possible hindrances besides finances. One member recalled, "All of us prayed and fasted fervently that the typhoons would not come, because if they did we could not take the boat to Tokyo. Our Father answered our prayers."[22]

The conference was held in the Budōkan, a large cultural arts center in Tokyo, and it ran for three days. General Authorities in attendance included Presidents Spencer W. Kimball and Marion G. Romney of the First Presidency; and Elders Ezra Taft Benson, Gordon B. Hinckley, and Marvin J. Ashton of the Twelve. Friday, the first day of the conference, was set aside for a Japanese cultural program performed by local Saints. It included a drum dance, a fan dance, and a history of the Church in Japan.[23] Members, including adults and youth, spent Saturday attending three general sessions. Sunday's schedule included two general sessions and an early morning priesthood session. Approximately twelve thousand Saints attended the three-day conference, about half the total Church membership in Japan.[24]

The highlight of the conference was President Kimball's announcement that the Church planned to build a temple in Japan. Cherie Campbell, an eyewitness to the conference, described the reaction of those present:

> The few young people who understood English grasped their chests and held their breath waiting for the translation to affirm what they had heard.
>
> A few of the older Saints had been listening to the prophet's address with their eyes closed. When they heard the translation of the prophet's announcement, they slowly opened their eyes, and then as if suddenly realizing what they had heard was true, folded their arms, bowed their heads and cried.[25]

One of the local leaders, Kikuchi Yoshihiko, held up an architect's rendering of the proposed temple for all to see. This was an inspiring moment. Formerly, only Japanese members who could afford a trip to

Hawaii could enjoy the blessings of the temple. Japanese Saints had waited and prayed many years for a temple in their own land.

Two years after the area conference in Tokyo, Kikuchi Yoshihiko was sustained to the First Quorum of the Seventy, the first native-born Japanese to be called as a General Authority, marking yet another milestone in growth and maturity.

The Japanese Missionary Training Center

"We shall find, I believe with all my heart," prophesied Elder Charles W. Penrose in 1902, "that the opening of the Japanese mission will prove the key to the entrance of the Gospel in the Orient. We will find that an influence will go out from Japan into other oriental nations."[26] Since the time of that prophecy, Church authorities and Saints have looked forward to the day when Japan would provide all of its own native missionaries and serve as a center for sending missionaries to other Asian nations. An important step in this direction occurred in December 1978 when Church leaders created the Japanese Missionary Training Center (JMTC) at the Tokyo South mission home. The JMTC had a humble beginning: the center's first missionaries were three Japanese natives who received three days of missionary training.[27] In May 1979, Kelly Crabb from the Provo Missionary Training Center arrived in Japan to formally establish the JMTC. Inoue Ryuichi was called as the program's coordinator, and he helped train thirteen missionaries that month. That July, Suzuki Shozo, former president of the Japan East Mission, was called as the director of the JMTC. By October 1980, Japanese missionaries were being trained there for ten days before starting to proselyte.[28]

The Tokyo Temple

The culminating event of the first thirty years of the Church in Japan after World War II was the construction and dedication of the Tokyo Temple. Not only was this the first Latter-day Saint temple in Japan, it was the first temple built in Asia and in a non-Christian nation. Its completion was an answer to the prayers of thousands of faithful Japanese and other Asian Saints. The Tokyo Temple also ushered in a new era. For the first time, the Japanese were offered local access to all the ordinances of the gospel, including baptisms for the dead, endowments, eternal marriages, and sealings. With the completion of the temple, the 115,000 Church members in Japan, Korea, the Philippines, Taiwan, and Hong Kong could more readily enjoy the blessings of the house of the Lord.

Church leaders decided to build the Tokyo Temple on the one-half acre site of the original Tokyo mission home; it had been purchased and renovated by Edward Clissold in 1948 when he reopened the mission. Located in the center of Tokyo, the site is surrounded by foreign embassies and is directly across the street from the beautiful Arisugawa Memorial Park. The park's large trees, lush green shrubbery, graceful bridges, and winding walkways provide a picturesque setting (illus. 14-1). The location was also convenient, being only five minutes from the Hiroo subway station. It was necessary to demolish the mission home to prepare for the temple, and many missionaries and members felt a twinge of sadness about losing a building so full of memories, but they were thrilled that a temple would soon be in their midst.

With the site selected, leaders began planning in earnest. Church architect Emil B. Fetzer was assisted by Wallace G. McPhie, director of Temples and Special Projects for the Church Building Department, and also by Nagata Sado, the resident engineer for the temple. They learned that Japanese construction requirements were much more stringent than in most countries because of earthquakes and typhoons. In addition, technicalities and some neighborhood resistance to building a Christian temple delayed construction. To meet these challenges, the Church hired the highly respected Kajima Construction Company to head the building project, and work began in April 1978. Twenty-two months and three thousand hours of work later, the temple was completed. It has walls that are made of concrete and steel and faced with fine, white stone, and it has steel-reinforced concrete pilings that extend sixty feet into the bedrock below to protect it in the event of an earthquake.[29]

Brother Nagata, the resident engineer, was the only member of the Church who actually worked on the temple. Despite this, the workers seemed to take great pride and care in the construction. Brother Fetzer observed:

Illus. 14-1. Tokyo Japan Temple, dedicated 1980.

Courtesy R. Lanier Britsch

They seemed to sense they were laboring on the House of the Lord and approached their task prayerfully. For example "When they started to assemble the massive steel beams framing the temple, which were required to meet earthquake standards, the workmen gathered in a group and offered a prayer that they would be able to do the work in the best possible manner and that no one would be injured as the section beams were put in place. In the years of construction not a single injury was sustained."[30]

The workers were also careful to obey the Word of Wisdom while on the temple grounds, and not to work on Sundays during the construction, which was unusual since the day is typically seen as just another workday.[31]

The Tokyo Temple was opened to dignitaries September 13–15, 1980. An open house for the general public was held between September 15 and October 18, and about forty-eight thousand people toured the temple. The large number of important visitors was encouraging to Dwayne Andersen, the newly called temple president. Before this he said "the Church has not been recognized by the VIPs in any number. This time many of them came. There were presidents of universities, churches, banks, actors, famous writers, baseball players, publishers and the head of the Tokyo Police department, largest in the world."[32]

The influence of the temple upon the Japanese was evident throughout the month-long open house. As the long lines of visitors silently walked through the building, a spirit of great reverence and respect prevailed. It was not uncommon to see Church members and those of other faiths alike shedding tears as they contemplated the significance of the rooms through which they passed. Many even seemed hesitant to leave the temple as they finished the tour.[33] President Andersen related an incident that occurred in one of the sealing rooms:

> One young lady came with her non-member father, and as they stood in the sealing room, she told him that was where she would be married. They discussed the fact that as a non-member the father would not be able to attend the wedding. Then the father decided to take the missionary lessons. Two weeks later, he was baptized.[34]

President Spencer W. Kimball dedicated the Tokyo temple on October 27, 1980 (illus. 14-2). Many General Authorities traveled from Utah with President and Sister Camilla Kimball to be in attendance.

They included President Marion G. Romney and Elders Ezra Taft Benson, Mark E. Petersen and Gordon B. Hinckley of the Twelve. Also in attendance were Marion D. Hanks, William Grant Bangerter, Adney Y. Komatsu, and Kikuchi Yoshihiko of the First Quorum of the Seventy. During the dedicatory services, President Kimball, President Romney, Elder Hinckley, and President Andersen spoke.[35]

After the speaking and singing, Presidents Kimball and Romney went outside and officiated in the cornerstone laying ceremony. Several items related to the history of the Church in Japan were placed in a time capsule. After the cornerstone was sealed into place, participants returned to the temple and President Kimball offered the dedicatory prayer. "We are jubilant this day, our Holy Father, and have hearts filled with praise to Thee that Thou hast permitted us to see the completion of this temple and to see this day for which we have so long hoped and toiled and prayed."[36] For those Japanese Saints who had worked and sacrificed for so many years, the dedication of the Tokyo temple was not just another temple dedication but the fulfillment of a dream and the reward for their diligence and patience. It also marked the beginning of a new era in the growth of the Church and the spread of the gospel to the Japanese.

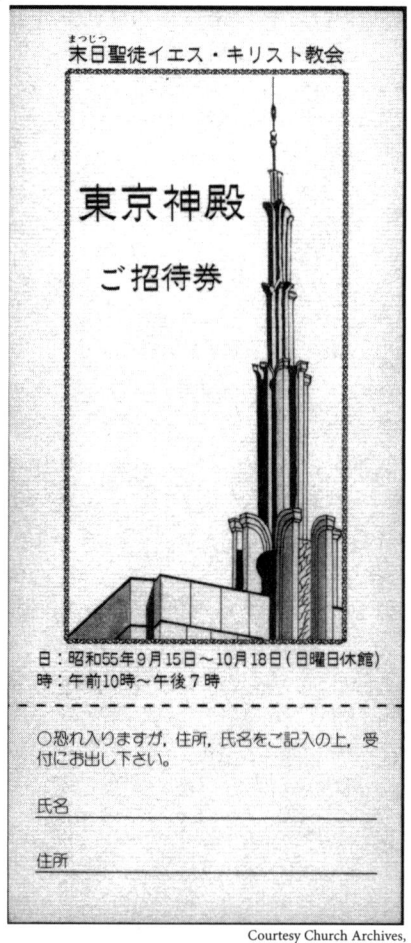

Courtesy Church Archives, The Church of Jesus Christ of Latter-day Saints

Illus. 14-2. Ticket to the dedication of the Tokyo Japan Temple. Church President Spencer W. Kimball dedicated the temple on October 27, 1980.

Conclusion

The late 1960s and the 1970s saw the Church in Japan grow to maturity. Major milestones included the pavilion at the Expo '70 World's Fair in Osaka, the creation of the first stake in Tokyo, the second division of the missions, the calling of the first native Japanese mission president, the calling of the first native Japanese General Authority, the first area conference in Japan, and the creation of the Japanese Missionary Training Center. However, the climax of that growth was the dedication of the Tokyo Temple in 1980. By the end of 1980, Japan had one of the top ten highest percentages of members in the world, members to population ratio with approximately 58,000 members.[37] President Heber J. Grant, who was Japan's first mission president, had prophesied, "I have an abiding faith that this is to be one of the most successful missions of the Church. The work will be slow at first but the harvest is to be something great and will astonish the world in the years to come. God has had His hand over this land."[38] Indeed, President Grant's prophesy is being fulfilled.

This paper was abridged from Terry G. Nelson, "A History of the Church of Jesus Christ of Latter-day Saints in Japan from 1948–1980" (master's thesis, Brigham Young University, 1986).

Notes

1. Hugh B. Brown, "Prophecies Regarding Japan by Hugh B. Brown," *BYU Studies* 10 (1970): 160.

2. Don W. Marsh, comp., *"The Light of the Sun": Japan and the Saints* (Tokyo: Japan Mission, The Church of Jesus Christ of Latter-day Saints, 1968), 68.

3. Walter R. Bills, Oral history, interview by Kenneth V. Barnum, 1973, transcript, 26, James Moyle Oral History Program, Church Archives, The Church of Jesus Christ of Latter-day Saints, Salt Lake City.

4. Bills, Oral history, 21.

5. Bills, Oral history, 6.

6. Japan Mission Manuscript History, November 13, 1968, Church Archives.

7. Edward Y. Okazaki to Terry G. Nelson, July 27, 1985, copy in possession of author.

8. Okazaki to Nelson, July 27, 1985.

9. "Church Movie Filmed in Japan For Pavilion at Expo '70," *Church News*, published by *Deseret News*, October 4, 1969, 4.

10. "Expo '70 Groundbreaking," *Church News*, May 17, 1969, 4.

11. "Expo '70 Groundbreaking," 4.

12. "Expo '70 Groundbreaking," 4.

13. "Language Program Expanded," *Church News*, January 18, 1969, 3.

14. The other religious venue was the Christian Ecumenical Pavilion. See Bernard P. Brockbank, "The Mormon Pavilion at Expo '70," *Improvement Era* 73 (December 1970): 120.

15. "Keys to Expo '70 Pavilion Given to Church," *Church News*, February 7, 1970, 3.

16. Brockbank, "Mormon Pavilion," 120.

17. Edward Y. Okazaki to author.

18. Brockbank, "Mormon Pavilion," 121.

19. Brockbank, "Mormon Pavilion," 120.

20. Kan Watanabe to Terry G. Nelson, July 8, 1985, copy in possession of author.

21. These special meetings, held months before the conference and leading up to the time of the conference, included topics such as testimonies of the importance of prayer, fasting, and other gospel principles that helped motivate the members to want to be in attendance. See Luanne Nelson, "Conference in Japan," *Ensign* 5 (October 1975): 88.

22. Nelson, "Conference in Japan," 89.

23. Nelson, "Conference in Japan," 89–90.

24. Nelson, "Conference in Japan," 88.

25. "Temple to Be Built in Tokyo," *Ensign* 5 (October 1975): 87.

26. Charles W. Penrose, in *72nd Annual Conference of The Church of Jesus Christ of Latter-day Saints* (Salt Lake City: The Church of Jesus Christ of Latter-day Saints, 1902), 52.

27. Ryuichi Inoue to Terry G. Nelson, June 28, 1985, copy in possession of author.

28. Inoue to Nelson.

29. "The First Temple in Asia," *Tambuli* (October 1980).

30. Carol Moses, "To Build a House of the Lord," *Tambuli* (October 1980): 14.

31. "First Temple in Asia," 60.

32. "48,000 Visit Tokyo Temple at Open House," *Church News*, October 25, 1980, 3.

33. "48,000 Visit Tokyo Temple," 3.
34. "48,000 Visit Tokyo Temple," 5.
35. Dell Van Orden, "Dedication of Temple Called Historic Event," *Church News,* November 8, 1980, 3.
36. "Dedication Prayer for Temple," *Church News,* November 8, 1980, 12.
37. *1983 Church Almanac* (Salt Lake City: Deseret News, 1982), 267.
38. Dell Van Orden, "'Tremendous' Future for Church in Japan," *Church News,* November 8, 1980, 10.

15

The Genealogical Society of Utah and Japan: A Personal Perspective

Greg Gubler

In 1842, during the construction of the Nauvoo Temple, the Prophet Joseph Smith instituted family history work because of revelations on baptism for the dead and other sealing ordinances. Over fifty years later, 1894, President Wilford Woodruff played a leading role in organizing the semi-independent Genealogical Society of Utah (GSU). Genealogical work within the Church received considerably more attention after President Joseph F. Smith's 1918 revelation on the redemption of the dead (D&C 138). As a result of the increased interest in genealogy, the Church absorbed the GSU as the Genealogical Society (GS) in 1944).[1]

Church leaders became convinced of the importance of records preservation after the devastation caused by World War II, and advances in microfilming made preservation more feasible. Soon after the war, Church officials authorized projects to microfilm ecclesiastical and governmental records throughout Europe. By the 1960s, the Church was using computer technology to process and compile its genealogical records. The Brethren announced the Three Generation Program in 1965 and the Four Generation Program in 1968. Still, there was an acute shortage of names ready for temple work. The 1970s were marked by a massive effort to acquire and preserve records worldwide, including those in Japan. President Spencer W. Kimball challenged members to submit names to the Church's Ancestral File and increase temple activity.

I first became interested in Japan as a young U.S. Marine stationed there (1961–63). After returning to the United States, I was called to serve in the Northern Far East Mission (1963–66). My love of the Japanese people and culture deepened during my missionary service; learning about Japan became my passion and eventually my profession. After completing my graduate work in East Asian history and teaching at the university level for a number of years, I was employed as a Senior Research Specialist for East Asia within the Church's genealogical departments (1976–82). As a result of my experiences there, I came to understand in the following ways the Church's efforts to acquire and preserve Japanese records as well as to promote family history work in Japan.

Japanese Genealogy and Record Keeping

By the 1960s, the Church's GS was well versed in Western genealogical sources. But as the Church expanded into Asia, local records and language barriers soon presented new challenges to its researchers. Japanese research was especially difficult due to multiple possible readings of Chinese characters. Furthermore, although the Japanese were traditionally interested in birth lineages and family history, that interest centered on Confucian ancestral veneration.

As birth lineage was considered among the most important qualifications for position and status, nobles carefully recorded their lineages during the Heian era (800–1185). A relationship to the Imperial line or one of the four powerful families—Fujiwara, Minamoto, Taira, and Tachibana—meant prestigious social status. Therefore, efforts were made to keep the lower classes ignorant of their lineage to prevent social mobility, which might have threatened the samurai and noble classes. In time, upper-class families created *kamon* (family crests), a practice that spread to the masses during the 1600s. Professional genealogists assisted upper-class families in compiling and recording their lineages, the majority of which were *nise keizu* (false genealogies) designed to legitimize class status.

During the Tokugawa era (1601–1868), family names were the privilege of the elite, and the bestowal of surnames to those below samurai rank was rare and meritorious. Fortunately, Buddhist priests in Japan had memorialized the deceased of all classes in *kakochō* (Buddhist death registers) for centuries. Commoners were also recorded in surveillance records originally conceived, ironically, as part of an inquisition against Christianity in the 1640s. Called *shumon-aratame-chō* (examination of religion registers), these records became the basis of a *ninbetsu-chō* (census system), normally conducted every three years after 1721. As the 250-plus feudal domains followed derivations of the census model, imposed by the Tokugawa shogunate, the coverage of records, when they exist, varies widely. Preservation is more problematic; there were few attempts made to collect and preserve the records after the fall of the Tokugawa.

The Japanese Meiji Restoration of 1868 was a social revolution that resulted in a nation of citizens on a more equal status than during the shogunate. Feudal distinctions were slowly abolished. The 1872 establishment of the *koseki* (household registration) system caused a scramble for surnames. Today, those who make an effort to acquire records and pursue their family histories beyond these relatively recent koseki face a hard reality: since most of the older records require paleographic reading skills and involve an understanding of local history, research can be extremely difficult even when records exist.[2]

Beginnings of Japanese Latter-day Saint Family History Work

Perhaps due to their traditions of ancestor veneration and generally strong feelings for their ancestors, genealogy resonated with some early Japanese members. Particularly noteworthy is the story of Nachie Tsune, who was baptized in 1905 while working at the mission home in Tokyo. Years later, after learning about family history and temple work, she decided to move to Hawaii, where she could redeem her kindred dead. She lived the remainder of her life near the Laie Hawaii Temple. In 1927 she returned temporarily to Japan and shared her feelings about temple work with local members. After collecting more family names, she returned to Hawaii. Former president of the Japan Mission Lloyd O. Ivie called Sister Nachi's temple service in Hawaii "the crowning achievement of the old mission" and concluded, "The mission was never closed, but transferred to the other side [of the veil],"[3] referring to the spirit world. Elder David O. McKay remarked at her passing, "a more faithful and dependable lady never lived."[4]

In 1948, Church leaders decided to reopen the Japan Mission under the leadership of President Edward L. Clissold. In order to make the entire Church curriculum—including basic family history—accessible to the Japanese Saints, leaders oversaw the translation of scriptures and manuals into Japanese. They also provided family history help through periodicals. For example, early articles such as "*Senzo e no sekinin wa*" (Responsibilities to our ancestors) and "*Shisha no kawari no baputesuma*" (Baptism for the dead) were featured in the Church's *Success Messenger*, and pictures of existing temples graced the magazine's covers.[5] Japanese Church members were also excited by the dedication of the Los Angeles California Temple in 1956 and the Hamilton New Zealand Temple two years later. A 1956 *LDS Messenger* article by President David O. McKay included a sample personal record and pedigree chart to fill out, complete with basic instructions on genealogical research.[6]

More advanced and Japan-specific family history guides soon became available. During the mission presidency of Paul C. Andrus (1955–62), Sister Joyce C. Worthen spent her entire mission developing *A Handbook for Genealogical Research in Japan* while serving as secretary to the newly formed Genealogical Committee of the Northern Far East Mission. With the help of local members, she wrote the text in transliterated romanization and resolved standards and procedural questions through correspondence with Archibald Bennett, general secretary of the GS in Salt Lake City.[7] This handbook was a significant achievement, and the work became the basis for future Japanese records submission and the further study of Japanese sources and research methodologies. Several years later, Church employee Watabe Masao wrote a series of chapters for Bennett for a manuscript titled "Our Ancestors." Watabe felt genealogical work would prosper in Japan since the "Japanese are people who worshiped their ancestors from ancient times."[8]

Sister Worthen's research helped increase Japanese interest in genealogy. Her research also prompted the GS to study the issues inherent in East Asian genealogy, specifically in Japan, Korea, and China. The 1958 dedication of the Hamilton New Zealand Temple also helped generate interest in Pacific genealogy. The resulting organization of an "Oriental Committee" in 1964 marked a departure from the Eurocentric approach favored by the GS's Research Division. That September, the Oriental Committee issued a basic names submissions manual for the Japanese Saints, which bore the influence of Sister Worthen's important efforts to determine lunar years, list adoptions, and denote jurisdictions. Furthermore, the GS hired Sister Nanjo Hiroko to process Japanese and Asian names.[9]

A special meeting of the Oriental Committee was held in conjunction with the April 1965 general conference. Among those at the meeting were Frank Smith of the Research Department, translator Satō Tatsui, former Mission President Edward Clissold, Elwin Jensen of Polynesian (now Oriental) Names Processing, William Cole, Henry Christiansen, and George Fudge, who later became managing director of the GS. The committee felt an urgent need to augment names processing from Japan. Satō (illus. 15-1) became involved with this project.[10]

Illus. 15-1. Satō Tatsui and his son Yasuo, ca. 1950. Satō Tatsui played a leading role in translating and acquiring Japanese materials.

In 1966 the Oriental Committee, by this time chaired by Elwin Jensen, hoped to send a knowledgeable Japanese member to Japan to draft a preliminary survey of Japanese records available for research. Jensen had in mind specific repositories such as the Asian collection at Tokyo University, the National Diet Library, Buddhist temples, koseki offices, and the *Momubushō-Shiryōkan* (Historical materials archives of the Ministry of Education). Satō was selected for the task, but some of the Church leaders felt the proposed fact-finding mission was premature. It was at this point that John Orton moved over from U.S. research to help with Asian acquisitions.[11]

During this period, Japanese members began expressing concern about names processing in Salt Lake City. Many had had family group sheets and other submissions rejected with little feedback since members had difficulty writing Japanese and the forms lacked proper instructions. They felt like only Church headquarters knew all the rules. In response, the Oriental Committee petitioned Elder Theodore M. Burton to require both Oriental characters and transliterated romanization on submissions "to avoid confusion in genealogical work."[12] Former Japan Mission President Lloyd O. Ivie tried to discourage Church leaders from "squeezing every [Japanese] researcher through the 'Romaji' spigot."[13] Finally, in June 1975, Church leaders resolved to drop romanization as a criterion for East Asian submissions because "many [researchers] simply could not do it."[14]

Dwayne N. Andersen succeeded Paul Andrus in 1962 as president of the Northern Far East Mission and was responsible for organizing temple excursions to Hawaii for Japanese Saints beginning in 1965. As the economy of Japan blossomed, more Japanese were able to go abroad and attend the temple. These official trips ended after the 1975 announcement that a temple was to be built in Tokyo, though some individuals and families continued to go to Hawaii. Certainly, the temple trips provided the impetus for the GS to try to acquire more records in Japan.

Great Hopes for Acquisitions in Japan

In 1965, John W. Orton added Asia to his assignments in the Research Department of the GS. Orton began his new assignment by determining the extent and preservation of certain types of Japanese records. He was particularly interested in koseki, and he wrote to the Japanese Bureau of Legal Affairs in 1966 for specific information on the records, including whether the bureau had any preservation program.[15] In 1967 the GS purchased five rolls of microfilm containing the genealogies of Japanese court nobles. Eventually, the Church's Japanese collection would approach 15,000 microfilm rolls by 2000, the equivalent of nearly 50,000 volumes of 300 pages each—impressive, but small in comparison with the Church's European and Mexican collections.[16]

Because of his expertise in Japanese language and culture, Satō's name was suggested for several other projects being undertaken by the GS. After returning from Hawaii, where Satō had translated the temple ceremony into Japanese, he worked part time at the GS with a project on Japanese names. In 1967 he married Hiranishi Tomoko, who was hired to handle Japanese submissions in Oriental Names Processing. Satō meanwhile continued translating various Church records into Japanese and helped on other projects.[17]

In May 1968, Satō accompanied Orton to Japan for a lengthy survey trip. They visited numerous koseki offices and had extensive discussions with archivists and government officials about the Japanese records and archival system. In addition, they visited Buddhist temples and became interested in Buddhist death registers and cemetery records. At each stop they took photos of various records and drafted a "researcher's record evaluation" report. The two men also met with Dr. Hayami Akira of Keiō University, Japan's foremost authority on the shumon-aratame-chō. This was a very productive trip in terms of surveying Japanese sources and repositories. Satō played a key role translating samples of various Japanese records and helping to produce a working paper titled "Genealogical Sources of Japan."[18]

The GS also asked Satō to draft a Japanese surname catalog. He used Dr. Ota Ryo's monumental survey of Japanese surnames and lineages as a basis and included both romanized and *kana* (syllabary) indexes for the various characters. This project required a herculean effort by Satō. He produced translations and research on the origins of surnames and an extensive list of Japanese research aids, repositories, and local history associations.[19] He also drafted a guide for the old script, an article on the use of kamon (family crests) in genealogical research, a study of the calendar system, and an explanation of *han* (domain) boundaries of the Tokugawa period, and he oversaw research and compilations on Japanese royalty and nobility.[20]

The GS, in its efforts to promote worldwide acquisitions and preservation, planned a World Conference on Records to be held in Salt Lake City in August 1969. Over 7,000 participants from forty-six nations attended sessions. Orton and Satō were involved in the planning process, and they handpicked scholars noted for their research on Japanese genealogy to participate in the event. For instance, Dr. Fujiki Norio, a noted geneticist, presented a paper titled "The Koseki as a Source for Genetic Studies." Dr. Yanase Toshiyuki of Kyushu University lectured on "The Koseki as a Source for the Scholar of Japan." Dr. Yoshida Masao of the National Diet Library provided an overview of the operation and collections at Japan's Library of Congress. Two American scholars, Dr. Ray A. Moore of Amherst University and Dr. Hiraga Noboru of the University of Washington, discussed "Family Records and Social History in Tokugawa Japan" and "The Extent and Preservation of Original Historical Records in Japan," respectively. The conference helped the GS build relationships with these and other scholars that have proven crucial over the years.[21]

Based on the success of the 1969 World Conference on Records and the development of influential relationships with scholars and officials in Japan, members of the GS were optimistic about future filming prospects in Japan. Orton determined to acquire copies of the koseki because of their historical significance; he was also concerned by reports of planned destruction of older koseki due to archival limitations in Japan. In February 1971, he and Satō again teamed up and initiated a comprehensive survey of koseki record offices to determine the policies of individual offices and the number of records involved.[22] Their survey proved essential in later estimating the scope and details of future acquisition projects.

Orton and Satō traveled again to Japan later that year and visited more archives, temples, and koseki offices. They also met with Dr. Hayami and perused his large collection of shumon-aratame-chō, visited cemeteries in Tokyo and Kyoto, and toured Shintō shrines to examine the genealogies of Shintō priests and view nearby tombstones. Their fact-finding report detailed further recommendations to the Records Selection Committee and suggested adding *keizu* (genealogies) from the Mombushō-Shiryōkan (Historical materials archives of the Ministry of Education) found in archives and collections, and Buddhist sources to 1900.[23]

Returning home, Orton tried to elicit Church support for a massive project to film registers throughout Japan. On his behalf, Theodore M. Burton, manager of the GS, asked the First Presidency in May 1971 for permission to film an estimated 12 to 14 million pre-1900 registers. This proposed project required thirteen and one-third camera years[24] and a large budget. The First Presidency gave tentative approval to proceed if the proposed acquisitions could be negotiated.[25]

Unfortunately, Church leaders' efforts to convince the Japanese Ministry of Justice to allow filming of the koseki continued throughout 1971 with little success. Edward Okazaki, a former mission president in Japan, appealed to Elder Ezra Taft Benson to have the Quorum of the Twelve discuss the critical task of microfilming koseki records in Japan. He felt the successful Mormon Pavilion at Expo '70 had greatly enhanced the Church's public image in Japan and "now was the time to act" to take advantage of "the opportunity to acquire a fantastic treasure in genealogy, especially at this crucial time."[26] President Koizumi Kotaro of the Sapporo Japan Mission suggested that the GS could block out sensitive personal information listed on the koseki and asked the Japanese Saints to unite in prayer.[27]

At the end of 1972, Orton asked for an employee to list records in Japan in preparation for a nine-month filming project that was under negotiation. One of the primary targets of this project was the Mombushō-Shiryōkan, where an estimated 5.3 million pages of genealogical records could be filmed, depending on exposures. The project awaited budget approval and final negotiations. Brother Amano Akira of Sendai was also hired to film kakochō from about a dozen Buddhist temples.[28] In April 1974, Elder Burton sent a memo to President Kimball titled "Genealogical Work in Japan" and mentioned that Orton and Amano had been "trying to work with officials of the Ministry of Justice since 1969." He expressed concern over the Japanese law that allows the withdrawn *joseki* (struck-out registers) to be destroyed after eighty years because of the shortage of shelf space. Even though the GS had offered to help the Japanese preserve their records, Elder Burton confessed they were getting nowhere with the Japanese bureaucracy.[29]

In 1974, Orton was named the new manager of Asia and Pacific Acquisitions in conjunction with the expansion of international acquisitions. Suzuki Kenji (illus. 15-2) was hired as field operations manager over Japanese Acquisitions to assist in the areas of cataloging and names processing. He was a key hire because of his superb ability to work with people and manage operations. Amano naturally came under his tutelage as the field representative in Japan.

"We were like pioneers, starting from the beginning,

Illus. 15-2. Suzuki Kenji, Japanese Specialist, Acquisitions Department, Genealogical Society of Utah, 1977.

Courtesy Greg Gubler

all amateurs feeling our way around," remembered Suzuki, who acted as group manager of Field Operations Service until 1978, when operations were moved from Salt Lake City to Tokyo.[30] During his tenure, he was able to help acquire microfilms of two major pre-1941 Japanese newspapers in Hawaii, investigate and list kakochō in Hawaii and Japanese immigrant records at the Bishop Museum and Hawaii Sugar Planters Association, and negotiate the filming of Japanese genealogies at several U.S. academic institutions and the Library of Congress. He also made annual trips to Japan to review operations and assist Brother Amano.

Looking back, this was one of the Church's most productive acquisition periods. Breakthroughs include the successful negotiations and filming projects at the Yamaguchi Prefectural Archives, the Miyagi Prefectural Archives, and the National Diet Library. Suzuki recalled that these efforts were blessed by the GS's presentation on the value of records preservation at the International Council of Archivists conference in 1975. Additionally, the GS was able to make contacts with several key Japanese archivists.[31] Amano continued working on acquisitions until 1978, when he was assigned to the newly opened Tokyo Service Center (TSC) to help process names.

Surviving quarterly project status reports demonstrate the group's efforts. By 1978 camera operators were filming at the Akita Prefectural Library, Kyushu University, Meiji University, the National Diet Library, and the Iwakuni City Library, to name a few. Amano also had hoped to introduce the GS's preservation program to Buddhist temple priests and expand the filming operations. Since there are over 80,000 Buddhist temples in Japan, this was only a beginning.[32] The surge of newly filmed materials impacted cataloging in Salt Lake City. The Asian operation was under the supervision of senior cataloger Basil Pei-nai Yang from 1974 until 1981. Three full-time and two part-time Japanese catalogers did most of the work. Fred Brady replaced Basil and led the Japanese cataloging team for the next fifteen years.

Priesthood Genealogy

In 1974 the Research Department became part of a new group called Priesthood Genealogy charged with bringing genealogy to the Church membership. At the same time, the GS was renamed the Genealogical

Department, though Acquisitions, under Ted Powell, was still known outside the Church as the GSU. The announcement of the Tokyo Temple in August 1975 created a sense of urgency both in acquiring and planning for names processing in Tokyo. Because of my background with both the Japanese and Chinese languages and my PhD in history, I was hired to join a group of research specialists under Frank Smith. I quickly realized I had much to learn because of my limited genealogy background. My boss, Smith, an Englishman known for his research ability, was very helpful. He hired Satō as my private tutor, allowing me to tap into Satō's vast knowledge and expertise about Japanese sources, names, and paleography.

Smith also petitioned management to let me make a trip to East Asia and acquire field experience. The Japanese portion of the trip lasted four weeks. Amano accompanied me for two weeks. He showed me Buddhist temples in Sendai and Hiroshima and introduced me to libraries and archives, including the National Diet Library, Hokkaidō University, Miyagi Prefectural Library, and Kyushu University. We made valuable contacts with Dr. Toshiyuki Yanase in Kyushu, Dr. Norio Fujiki in Fukui, Dr. Kiyoyuki Higuchi at Kokugakuin University, Brother Hosaka in the Tachikawa Koseki Office, Priest Kamomiya at Takehara on the Inland Sea, and members of the Japanese Ethnological Association.

While in Japan we also met with local Church leaders and members and heard their concerns about records processing in Salt Lake City. We sensed a resistance to the Church's new Priesthood Genealogy push. For example, President Kikuchi Yoshihiko of the Tokyo Stake explained that some of his members were "already exhausted" and many felt it was a "burden just to stay active." We also learned there was little genealogical "know how" among Church members and even resentment by some that Americans were dictating how Japanese should do their family history work. Fortunately, this last complaint was mollified by the subsequent announcement of the "service center" concept, which provided in-country access to queries and assistance.[33]

Our group, Priesthood Genealogy, was also engaged in preparing materials to assist members in their family history research. However, a dramatic policy change followed Presiding Bishop Vaughn J. Featherstone's April 1978 general conference address.

Bishop Featherstone observed the overabundance of Church-produced materials and stressed the need to simplify. The simplification program for Japan reduced submission requirements substantially, including rigid requirements to document and prove submitted genealogical work. However, without these controls, duplication chaos increased dramatically and simplification undermined the need for the division and for programs to teach members correct research and submissions procedures.

The Church also curtailed travel and other expenditures. For instance, although I had finished drafting *Nihon no koseki* (the Japanese household register) for publication in Japan, my final draft was subsequently abridged before publication.[34] Our group's even more ambitious project, "Tracing Your Ancestors to Japan: A Guide for Japanese Americans and Canadians," was shelved after over a year of exhaustive research. A basic guide to research designed for a Japanese audience did make it into the *Seito-No-Michi* (Way of the Saints) (the Church's magazine for Japan), but an exhaustive research series on Buddhist sources was cut.[35]

Soon, "controlled extraction" became a Church buzzword, and volunteers started replacing employees in Records Processing. In May 1978, Priesthood Genealogy was effectively organized into an extraction clearing house.[36] Extraction of original or microfilmed records was compared to a combine as opposed to the old method of hand-gleaning to produce names. The harvest of names was considerably greater and, with volunteers in stakes involved, considerably cheaper. Suzuki and I were asked to design a workable extraction program that would produce names for the Tokyo Temple and to draft a ten-year acquisitions plan. We completed these tasks by early 1982.

The Tokyo Service Center

In 1978, Church leaders announced the creation of service centers for the three new overseas temples under construction in Mexico City, São Paulo, and Tokyo. The Church hired Shiraishi Makoto, a computer expert, to manage the Tokyo Service Center (TSC). He recalled that he had to "start from scratch" but "felt thrilled when he gained a firm grasp of what he was to do over the next few years."[37] He was responsible for training staff to prepare for the opening of the Tokyo Temple.

Circumstances dictated that our institutional acquisitions efforts be given a lower priority.[38]

As with any new organization, not everything went smoothly at first. Suzuki, Shiraishi, and I recommended using a Japanese computer for names processing and indexing at the new TSC. However, because the Genealogical Department's American computer experts lacked the expertise to work with Chinese characters and kana syllabary, they recommended using romanization. Kikuchi Yoshihiko, a General Authority who was comfortable with English, supported Records Processing's decision. Within two years, however, TSC changed to Japanese computers due to complaints about romanization.[39] We also made progress in other areas. We completed a Japanese translation of *From You to Your Ancestors (Anata no senzo e)*, and at the suggestion of Katanuma Seiji we began developing materials to help members decipher Tokugawa era records.[40]

After four years of preparation, the Church's Second World Conference on Records was held in Salt Lake City in August 1980. Several employees on both sides of the Pacific were responsible for planning the Japanese sessions. The *Nihon Keizu Kyōkai* (Genealogical association of Japan) sent a delegation, led by Japan's most noted authority on names and crests, Dr. Niwa Motoji, to participate. Dr. Hirata Kin'itsu presented his extensive ancestral research relying on kakochō to reconstruct family lines to the twelfth century. I collaborated with Dr. Hirata on a presentation detailing sources beyond the koseki and also presented a paper on "Family History for Japanese Americans." Suzuki compiled a comprehensive listing on the Japanese collection of the GS. Several American scholars interested in genealogical sources and records of Japan as well as in Japanese society were also invited to present papers.[41] Over 10,000 people attended the conference. The event, covered by a number of American and Japanese newspapers, was a huge success for the Church, and it showcased the GS's preservation and genealogy programs.

Continued Extraction and Acquisition Efforts

Management of the Genealogical Department authorized a fact-finding committee on Japan in 1979, with myself as chair, to once again review acquisitions policies and records preservation in Japan.

Illus. 15-3.   Satō Tomoko and Greg Gubler, Genealogical Department, 1977.

As always, Suzuki and Shiraishi were of great assistance. Satō Tomoko (illus. 15-3) helped develop a pilot program to extract portions of the twenty-six-volume *Kansei chosu shokafu* (Collection of genealogies of the Kansei era). However, concerns about the structure of the record and multiple names resulted in shelving the project in favor of extraction of kakochō. Suzuki and Satō Tomoko also helped us develop an extraction manual and procedures for dealing with posthumous names.[42]

The Satōs left Salt Lake City for Tokyo the following summer on a temple mission. Elder Satō became a sealer and Sister Satō proved invaluable in name processing. The dedication of the Tokyo Temple by President Spencer W. Kimball in October 1980 was a glorious occasion for the Japanese Saints and their deceased ancestors. Following the Tokyo Temple dedication, the TSC was renamed the Genealogical Service Center (GSC) and combined with the Genealogical Society of Japan (GSJ). Due to increasing demands for name processing efforts, including an expensive film processing lab, records acquisition efforts in Japan were temporarily halted.[43]

In time we felt renewed pressure to provide materials for a records extraction project in Japan. As member volunteers had trouble with the handwriting in kakochō, we prepared a pilot program to extract the printed volumes of shumon-aratame-chō from Echizen (present-day Fukui Prefecture). In the process, I analyzed and mapped over a thousand sources and then drafted an extraction manual. Mitsuko Davies in the cataloging department was helpful in evaluating what sources should be extracted. After our manual was translated, it was approved and used in the first stake extraction program in Japan in 1983.[44]

Epilogue

Although I left the GS in 1982 for a faculty position at Brigham Young University–Hawaii, my association with Japanese genealogy and records did not end. For example, in 1983 I drafted a sample list of emigration records archived at the Diplomatic Records Office in Tokyo. I later discussed my research with a friend in Public Relations at BYU–Hawaii, and before I knew it I was reading in a small article in the *Ensign* that I had "discovered a bonanza of records."[45] By 1989 the GS was able to negotiate and buy most of the collection.

In 1985, Wayne Metcalf, manager of the Asia-Pacific Field Operations of the Genealogical Department, asked me to organize a records extraction program among Japanese members of the Honolulu Stake to see if kakochō and other records could be extracted despite paleography issues. I agreed and consequently helped train members for two years with the extraction manual I had previously developed for the GS Center in Tokyo. We also ordered specialized dictionaries to read *kuzushi-ji* (cursive style) and posthumous names. By 1989, when I was called to be the director of the Family History Center in Laie, Hawaii, thousands of Japanese names had been extracted and forwarded to Tokyo—thanks to the volunteer efforts of Japanese sisters.[46]

Genealogical work continues to move forward in Japan. By 1990 the total number of Japanese names submitted for family history research passed 300,000.[47] In the 1990s, the Church acquired small collections of genealogies and additional shumon-aratame-chō, and a large collection of *murakata-monjo* (village land and tax registers). Sadly, Buddhist temples have limited their archive access due to privacy issues. As for the koseki, "the trump card of Japanese family history research," it is now nearly impossible to negotiate the filming because of local sensitivities.[48]

On a brighter note, the Church in 2000 released a Japanese version of Personal Ancestral File software, which should accelerate family history research in Japan. Hopefully, increasing numbers of Japanese Saints will take advantage of the records and facilities in the Church's collections on both sides of the Pacific.

This paper was presented at "A Centennial Celebration: The LDS Church in Japan, 1901–2001," October 13, 2001, Brigham Young University, Provo, Utah.

Notes

1. The society still survives today as the incorporated records acquisitions program of the Church. The Church still uses the name "Genealogical Society of Utah."

2. For more information on the difficulties of Japanese records research, see Greg Gubler, "Looking East: The Realities of Genealogical Research in Japan," *Genealogical Journal* 8 (Spring 1979): 43–50.

3. President Lloyd O. Ivie, "Correspondence," Church Archives, The Church of Jesus Christ of Latter-day Saints, Salt Lake City.

4. Ivie, "Correspondence."

5. *Success Messenger* (monthly publication of the Japanese Mission) (1953–55).

6. David O. Mckay, *LDS Messenger* (September 1956).

7. "Correspondence, Northern Far East Mission," Church Archives.

8. Watabe Masao to Archibald F. Bennett, August 12, 1963, copy in possession of author.

9. Satō Tomiko, interview by author, May 15, 1979.

10. Minutes, Oriental Committee, April 1, 1965, Project Files, Asian, microfilm. Hereafter cited as PFA film.

11. Frank Smith to Theodore Burton, September 26, 1965, PFA film.

12. Elwin Jensen and the Oriental Committee to Theodore Burton, August 19, 1964, PFA film.

13. Lloyd O. Ivie to Frank Smith, June 12, 1967, PFA film.

14. Elwin Jensen, John Orton, and Ted Telford to Jimmy Parker, June 10, 1975, PFA film.

15. John W. Orton to Bureau of Legal Affairs, December 30, 1966, copy in possession of author.

16. See Suzuki Kenji, "The Japanese Collection of the Genealogical Society of Utah," *Proceedings of the 1980 World Conference on Records* 11, no. 814C (Salt

Lake City: Genealogical Department of the Church of Jesus Christ of Latter-day Saints), 1–15. Over 2 million reels for Europe, half a million for Mexico. Glen Harris, Acquisitions, Genealogical Society of Utah, August 15, 2001.

17. Satō Tomoko, interview by author, August 12, 2001, typescript, copy in possession of author.

18. In 1973 the GS published a more comprehensive paper on the same subject based on Satō's earlier work. *Major Genealogical Record Sources in Japan,* Research Paper Series, series J, no. 1 (Salt Lake City: Genealogical Society, 1973).

19. "Satō Tatsui Plays Important Role as Translator," *Genealogical Society Observer* 6 (August 1970): 1–2.

20. John Orton to Frank Smith, "Projects for Completion by Brother Sato," July 31, 1973, PFA film.

21. For detailed information on the 1969 conference, see Genealogical Society, Papers relating to the World Conference on Records, Church Archives. For papers and biographies of presenters, see Spencer J. Palmer, ed., *Studies in Asian Genealogy* (Provo, Utah: Brigham Young University Press, 1972).

22. Survey responses, February 18, 1971, Matsuyama City Office, copy in possession of the author.

23. John Orton to Records Selection Committee, September 15, 1971, copy in possession of author. See also John Orton to Delbert L. Roach, Chairman, Records Selection Committee, October 1, 1971, copy in possession of author.

24. Camera years refers to one camera operator working steadily for a full year on a project.

25. Genealogical Society, "Microfilming Projects, Japan, 1965–71," Church Archives.

26. Edward Okazaki to Ezra Taft Benson, [ca. 1971], PFA film.

27. Okazaki to Benson, [ca. 1971], PFA film.

28. John Orton to Delbert Roach, "Request for lister for Japan," October 12, 1971, PFA film.

29. Theodore M. Burton to Spencer W. Kimball, April 1, 1974, PFA film.

30. Suzuki Kenji, telephone conversation with author, September 23, 2001.

31. Suzuki Kenji, telephone conversation.

32. Genealogical Department, "Microfilming Projects, Japan, 1975–78," Church Archives.

33. "Trip Report to Japan and Korea, 1977," PFA film.

34. *Nihon no koseki,* Genealogical Research Papers, series J, no. 5 (Salt Lake City: Genealogical Department, 1978).

35. Greg Gubler, "Nihon keizu tankyō no yoran" (An overview of Japanese genealogy), *Seito-No-Michi* (Way of the Saints) 23 (January 1979): 15–18.

36. "Controlled extraction" volunteers performed their assigned projects under the tutelage of the extraction arm of Priesthood Genealogy. Once the program was authorized churchwide, the program was known simply as "extraction."

37. Genealogical Department, "Monthly Reports," 1978–79, copy in possession of author.

38. Shiraishi Makoto to author, fax, September 27, 2001, copy in possession of author.

39. Genealogical Department, "Monthly Reports," 1978–81, copy in possession of author. Additional information based on personal notes from conversations, 1978–82 journal entries.

40. Genealogical Department, "Monthly Reports," 1978–81.

41. "Preserving Our Heritage" (original conference program), copy in possession of author; *Proceedings of the World Conference on Records, 1980*, vol. 11 (Salt Lake City: Genealogical Department of The Church of Jesus Christ of Latter-day Saints, 1980).

42. Genealogical Department, "Monthly Reports," February 1978, copy in possession of author.

43. "Monthly Reports," December 1978; Satō Tomoko, interview.

44. Genealogical Department, "Monthly Reports," personal file copies, February–October 1982; Shiraishi Makoto to author, fax.

45. "LDS Scene," *Ensign* 14 (November 1984): 112.

46. Information based on personal notes and "Extraction Project Materials," Japanese Records Extraction Pilot Program, Honolulu Stake, 1985–90.

47. R. Lanier Britsch, *From the East: The History of the Latter-day Saints in Asia, 1851–1996* (Salt Lake City: Deseret Book, 1998), 151–52.

48. Masuda Setsuo to author, email, October 1, 2001.

16

A Geographical Study of the Acceptance of The Church of Jesus Christ of Latter-day Saints in Japanese Provincial Cities

Takemura Kazuo

Although Latter-day Saint missionary work in Japan did not enter full swing until after World War II, the number of members of The Church of Jesus Christ of Latter-day Saints (members of record) in Japan had at the time of this 1997 study reached approximately 110,000. This study sought to investigate regional variations in Church acceptance and the relationship of those variations with the regional religious climates. The present article examines these factors in the Yamagata and Toyama regions. Previously, little research has been published relating to Christian sects in Japan, and new religions in particular. Most sociological research on Christianity in Japan deals with the development of religious communities in particular areas. There is a strong likelihood that the addition of geographical research such as this study could illuminate both the current situation and the process through which religious acceptance occurs.[1]

Target Regions of the Study

The western side of the Shin-Etsu region of Japan is predominantly Pure Land Buddhist, while the eastern side is predominantly Zen Buddhist.[2] This tendency is especially pronounced in the Toyama Prefecture in the western part of the region and the Yamagata Prefecture in the east.[3] Field studies for these regions in the present article were conducted in four unit locations: in Yamagata and Yonezawa in the Yamagata Prefecture, and in Toyama and Uozu in the Toyama Prefecture, and the cities and towns encompassed by the regular commutes into these four areas for work or school. This comparative study of four cities in two prefectures may provide at least a suggestion concerning differences between eastern and western Japan in terms of the acceptance of Christianity.

Research Method

In the study, the number of Church members, the number of baptisms, and the history of mission areas were assessed. Research subjects included most of the members in the Church locations surveyed.[4] The members' territorial ties, attributes, and involvement with other religions were surveyed by means of interviews. Written questionnaire surveys[5] were conducted for members of junior high school age or older who attended sacrament meetings, and the distributed surveys were returned by mail. From a total of one hundred twenty surveys sent out, sixty-two (51.7 percent) were returned.[6] Because of extremely low numbers of converts, additional interviews were conducted with Church members, missionaries, and Church administrative personnel.[7]

Current State of Latter-day Saint Missionary Work in Japan

Contributing factors to post–World War II increases in Church membership may include the presence of second-generation members as well as more active proselytizing by Latter-day Saint missionaries compared to that of other sects. At the time of this study, the Church's direct missionary activities included door-to-door visits to local residents and street contacting in front of train stations or on city streets with heavy pedestrian traffic.[8] The Church also sponsored indirect proselytizing activities. These consisted of recreational activities and English conversation classes taught by foreign missionaries. Church units conducted missionary activities appropriate for the region in which they were located.[9] Therefore, the influence of regional characteristics on the difficulty of proselytizing was thought to be significant in the present research.[10]

Because nearly all missionaries traveled on foot or bicycle, the potential geographical range for missionary work was essentially limited to the neighborhood of the Church building and the surrounding area (table 1). Potential candidates for proselytizing were therefore

Table 1: Summary of Latter-day Saint Wards and Branches

Units	Building Location	Type of Facility	Members	Full-time Missionaries	Date Established
Yonezawa	Rinsenji, Yonezawa-shi	formerly a privately owned building	74	2 elders	1975: branch established; 1996: moved to present location
Toyama	Kurehatomita-machi, Toyama-shi	Church meeting-house	206	4 elders, 2 sisters	1972: branch established; 1991: moved to present location
Kureha			104		1993: split from Toyama branch
Uozu	Ekimae Shinmachi, Uozu-shi	second floor of privately owned building	60	2 elders	1991: split from Toyama branch

Based on 1997 data. Compiled by interview survey. Yamagata units not surveyed.

essentially limited to residents of the city in which the Church building was located and those who commuted to that area for work or school.

The Church in Yamagata Prefecture

The largest concentration of Latter-day Saints in the first study area—Yamagata Prefecture—was in Yamagata city. Of Buddhist religious sects in Yamagata city, Sōtō Zen Buddhism was predominant, accounting for 31.3 percent of the total Buddhist population, followed by True Pure Land Buddhism, with 21.2 percent, and Pure Land Buddhism, with 14.0 percent (table 2).[11] Sōtō Zen became somewhat more predominant in the area encompassed by the work and school

Table 2: Summary of Religions in Target Regions of the Study

Region	Predominant Buddhist Sect	Temple Percentage in Population (%)	Temple/Shrine Percentage in Population (%)	Catholic Members as Percentage of Population (%)	United Church of Christ in Japan Members as Percentage of Population (%)	Church of Jesus Christ of Latter-day Saints Members as Percentage of Population (%)
Yamagata City	Sōtō Zen/True	0.72	1.21	1.75	0.55	
(Commuting Range)	Pure Land/	0.91	1.57	0.96	0.42	
Yonezawa City	Pure Land/ Tendai/Shingon	1.26	1.87	1.46	1.26	(0.41)
Commuting Range	Sōtō Zen/ Shingon	1.34	2.25	0.78	0.67	
Toyama City	True Pure Land	1.04	2.05	1.36	0.99	(0.52)
Commuting Range		1.29	3.18	0.85	0.60	
Uozu City	True Pure Land	1.27	3.27	2.78	0.39	(0.58)
Commuting Range		1.31	3.84	1.60	0.28	

Predominant Buddhist sect determined by the modified Weaver's method. "Temple/shrine percentage in population" is the total population divided by the total number of temples and shrines. "Members of the Catholic Church/United Church of Christ in Japan/Church of Jesus Christ of Latter-day Saints as a percentage of the total population" is the number of Church members living in the region divided by the total population. The percentage of members of The Church of Jesus Christ of Latter-day Saints was calculated using the number of members as of 1994. The number of members in the Yamagata units could not be surveyed. The total populations for these regions are according to the 1991 national census report. (Compiled according to Yamagata Prefectural Administration Department, *Yamagata Prefectural Register of Official Religious Institutions*; Toyama Prefectural Administration Department, *Toyama Prefectural Register of Official Religious Institutions*; and Shinbunsha, *1994 Religion Almanac*.

commute to Yamagata city,[12] and application of the modified Weaver's method to identify prevalent sects showed five Buddhist sects, consisting of Sōtō Zen, True Pure Land, Pure Land, Tendai, and Shingon. On the questionnaires, many Church members reported being uncertain as to the Buddhist sect with which their family had traditionally been affiliated. Several members said they had been traditionally affiliated with the Sōtō Zen, True Pure Land, and Nichiren sects.

Most members in the Yamagata Branch were native residents of Yamagata city or regular commuters to the city. Its complement of six missionaries conducted street contacting in front of Yamagata Station and made door-to-door visits throughout the entire urban area of Yamagata city. Proselytizing in the city center was generally difficult, but people were more willing to listen in the surrounding area, particularly in the eastern part. The missionaries were giving new emphasis to twice-weekly English conversation classes, and large numbers of new members had emerged from these classrooms. Contacts were also made through barbeque parties held every two months and talent shows, volleyball games, and other activities conducted on the alternate months.

Nine out of fourteen members in the Yamagata region cited "the guidance of the Holy Ghost" as their reason for joining the Church from among options given in the survey questionnaire.

The second region studied in Yamagata Prefecture was Yonezawa city. In the region around the city, the prevalent Buddhist sect was the same as in the region around Yamagata city. The Sōtō Zen sect accounted for 45.2 percent of the total Buddhist population. This was followed by Shingon, with 27.4 percent, and True Pure Land, with 8.9 percent. Applying the modified Weaver's method to determine prevalent sects in the areas from which individuals commuted to Yonezawa city for work and school showed only two sects, Sōtō Zen and Shingon. Yet Pure Land Buddhist sects were common for the parents of Latter-day Saint converts in the region, with four out of eight respondents indicating True Pure Land and one indicating Pure Land. This was a small sample, but the result was interesting for Yonezawa, with its predominance of Sōtō Zen followers.

Latter-day Saint missionaries conducted door-to-door visits all over Yonezawa city but did not use street contacting. More people in this area were receptive to the message when it was presented during door-to-door visits. This tendency was strong due to the large number of college students in the area surrounding the Yamagata University Engineering Department.[13] English conversation classes were held in Yonezawa three times a week, but participants numbered only about five to eight people. Tennis was reportedly popular as a sport for Church proselytizing activities, and the number of musical concerts had decreased.

The number of Church members in the unit had fluctuated at around seventy since 1993. The highest number of baptisms in the city in a single year during the previous decade had been six, occurring in both 1988 and 1992 (table 3). Sacrament meeting attendance[14] was high, at 25 percent or more each year (table 4). It is possible, however, that sacrament meeting attendance was high because the work and school commuting range for this area was small and many of the Church members resided within Yonezawa city so they could more easily travel to branch meetings.

A final statistical difference between Yamagata city and Yonezawa city is that the percentage of members in Yonezawa citing "the guidance of the Holy Ghost" as their reason for joining the Church was higher than for members in Yamagata.

The Church in Toyama Prefecture

The Yamagata Prefecture in the eastern part of the Shin-Etsu region represented a different religious distribution than is present in the Toyama Prefecture on the western side of the region. In Toyama Prefecture, the True Pure Land sect was predominant, accounting for 64.2 percent of the Buddhist population, followed by Sōtō Zen, with 19.0 percent. The True Pure Land and Sōtō Zen sects existed in virtually these same ratios throughout Toyama city's work and school commuting area. Survey responses from Latter-day Saints in the Toyama region reflected the religious distribution of the prefecture. An overwhelming majority of baptized members in the Toyama Branch identified the True Pure Land and Pure Land sects as the Buddhist sects with which their families had traditionally been affiliated, and a few still supported a Buddhist temple.

Table 3: Baptisms per Branch of The Church of Jesus Christ of Latter-day Saints

Year	Toyama	Kureha	Uozu	Yonezawa
1990				5
1991				3
1992			1	6
1993		4	4	5
1994		2	6	3
1995	4	2	3	1
1996	3	3	3	2
1997	1 as of September	1 as of September	0 as of September	0 as of August

Numbers for empty spaces were either uncertain or unobtainable. Compiled by interviews and questionnaire survey. Yamagata units not surveyed.

Table 4: Sacrament Meeting Attendance Rates for Wards and Branches of The Church of Jesus Christ of Latter-day Saints

Year	Toyama	Kureha	Uozu	Yonezawa
1993		47%	35%	25%
1994		40%	40%	29%
1995	25%	39%	34%	26%
1996	24%	37%	30%	25%
1997		38%	25%	26%

Sacrament meeting attendance rate was found by calculating the annual average number in attendance at sacrament meeting divided by the number of members for that year. Numbers for empty spaces were either uncertain or unobtainable. The reason for the decline in numbers in the Uozu Branch after 1996 may be that its boundaries then came to include the area west of Nishikubiki County in Niigata Prefecture, and attendance may be higher for members who live within the city limits, as in the Yonezawa branch. Compiled by interviews and questionnaire survey. Yamagata units not surveyed.

The Toyama Branch was divided into the Toyama and Kureha branches in 1993 as a result of an increase in Church membership, but meetings for both branches were held in the same building. Proselytizing by the missionaries was conducted with no distinction between branch districts. Door-to-door visits were conducted in the urban area of Toyama city. Street contacting was conducted in the area around Toyama Station and in the Sōgawa business district. The difficulty of proselytizing was about the same everywhere in the city. Indirect proselytizing activities included beach volleyball, softball, and basketball; missionary work had reportedly shifted toward these kinds of Church activities and away from door-to-door visits and street contacting. English conversation class was held only once a week, with about fifteen people in attendance.

The number of Church members in the Toyama and Kureha branches reached 315 as of 1996. However, the number of annual baptisms had been in the single digits most years. Sacrament meeting attendance was high, particularly in the Kureha Branch, with an annual attendance rate of about 40 percent. Member retention levels were also quite high.

In contrast with the members in the Yamagata Prefecture, the percentage of Church members in Toyama Prefecture who cited "the guidance of the Holy Ghost" as their reason for becoming a member was low.

Uozu city was the second region in the Toyama Prefecture surveyed in the study. In Uozu, the True Pure Land sect accounts for 67.2 percent of Buddhist adherents, followed by the Pure Land sect, at 12.5 percent. Since many of the Church members had parents who were still living, they supported the True Pure Land sect as a matter of formality, holding Buddhist-style funeral rites and burials.[15] Only three survey responses were received from Church members who were converted in the Uozu Branch, and thus no accurate or comprehensive understanding of member composition is possible.

The Uozu Branch of the Church was divided from the Toyama Branch in 1991. In 1996 its boundaries were expanded to include part of Niigata Prefecture. Missionaries serving in the Uozu Branch area did not street contact, but they did make door-to-door visits over a wide area. A considerable number of Church members were baptized after encountering the missionaries while commuting to Toyama city for work or school. English conversation class was held twice a week, but there were few participants. No instances had been reported of Church activities and English conversation classes being specifically linked with conversion in Uozu city.

There were sixty Uozu Branch members in 1997, ten of whom were living in Niigata Prefecture. The number of baptisms in 1994 was six, which was large considering the population within the branch boundaries. Sacrament meeting attendance had been at 30 percent or more annually, but had since decreased, falling to 25 percent in 1997. There was little inflow or outflow of Church members, and their places of residence were scattered throughout the branch boundaries.

It is interesting that no members in the Church units in surrounding cities of the prefecture cited "the guidance of the Holy Ghost" as their reason for joining the Church.

Comparative Study of Missionary Work and Acceptance of the Church in the Yamagata and Toyama Regions

Folk Religion and Acceptance of the Church. Folk religions in these regions of Japan consist of the concurrent practice of Buddhism, Shintō, and personal religious beliefs. In the Japanese view, Buddhist ceremonies are often connected with the stages of adulthood, death, and life after death, and most funerals and memorial services are performed at Buddhist temples. Beliefs about redemption and sin in folk religion are largely based on Buddhist interpretations, which vary according to the particular Buddhist sect. The manner in which Buddhism developed through the assimilation of complex ancient folk beliefs cannot be overlooked, but the particular Buddhist sect of each region appears to have some influence on the religious views of all the people living there. One's parishioner sect may have an unconscious influence on his or her basic religious awareness as one experiences funerals and other ceremonies for family members.

The Buddhist sect affiliation for the parents of Latter-day Saints in the Yamagata and Toyama regions shows a high ratio of Pure Land Buddhism, which includes both True Pure Land and Pure Land sects (table 5).[16] For members who identified their families' Buddhist

Table 5: Traditional Buddhist Parishioner Sect for Members of The Church of Jesus Christ of Latter-day Saints

Sect	Number of Respondents	Percent of Total (%)
True Pure Land	18	49
Pure Land	8	22
Shingon	5	13
Zen	1	3
Sōtō Zen	3	8
Nichiren	2	5
Total	37	100

Includes only respondents who identified their sect on the questionnaire survey.

parishioner sect on the survey, 71 percent reported Pure Land, with True Pure Land alone accounting for 49 percent. Of the twenty-three persons who identified their own previous parishioner sect and who had been Church members for ten years or more, seventeen identified Pure Land, of which eleven were True Pure Land.[17]

When parishioners of the True Pure Land sect accept Christian sects such as the Church, a good deal of overlap may occur between True Pure Land and Christianity in their basic religious awareness. Research on similarities in religious ideas between True Pure Land and Christianity has been conducted both in and out of Japan since Karl Barth identified ideological commonalities between them as salvation religions.[18] The main similarities can be summarized according to the following three items:

1. Christianity and the True Pure Land sect both consider moral sin to be the root cause of mankind's fallen condition. Other Buddhist sects consider the cause to be physical life, aging, disease, and death.

2. Christianity and the True Pure Land sect both believe in salvation by faith, whereby mankind is freed from its fallen state by an "Absolute Being."[19] Other Buddhists sects claim salvation through individual efforts.

3. According to both Christianity and True Pure Land, mankind's redemption is completed in the next life. Other Buddhist sects maintain that redemption is possible while in this life.

These similarities also exist for The Church of Jesus Christ of Latter-day Saints as a Christian denomination.[20]

Regional Variation in Missionary Work and Acceptance. In regions with a predominant distribution of True Pure Land temples, the task of spreading the Church is not necessarily easy. Church officials in the Hokuriku area, a True Pure Land region, for example, often reported that missionary work there was difficult. Researchers from other religions concurred.[21] When Church members were surveyed about whether they experienced opposition from their families when they were baptized, results showed that nine out of eighteen True Pure Land respondents experienced opposition, one out of five Shingon respondents experienced opposition, and none of the three Sōtō Zen respondents experienced opposition.[22] Baptism numbers tended to be higher in Zen-dominant regions and regions without a clear predominant sect. While a straightforward comparison of baptism numbers by Takemura[23] for branches in Sanjō, a region with variety of Buddhist sects, and Matsumoto, a Sōtō Zen dominant area, is not possible because the numbers were obtained before 1994, those earlier numbers exceed the yearly baptism numbers for the Toyama, Kureha, and Uozu Branches (see table 3),[24] which are located in predominantly True Pure Land regions. Baptisms in the Toyama Prefecture have increased since 1994 in comparison to the Yonezawa Branch, which is in a predominantly Sōtō Zen region. However, the Church in Yamagata, for which a detailed survey of these numbers was not possible, had reportedly seen a large number of years in which there were ten or more baptisms. According to these survey results, it was difficult for the Church to enter predominantly True Pure Land regions, while entry was comparatively easy into regions with a large Sōtō Zen distribution and into regions that have a number of different sects.

At the same time, sacrament meeting attendance, as a measure for retention levels, could be considered high for the Pure Land–dominant branches in the study—Toyama, Kureha, and Uozu (see table 4). Takemura also showed the same elevated retention level for members of the Church in other predominantly True Pure Land regions.[25] The reason that member retention levels were high in predominantly True Pure Land or Pure Land regions seems to be that, given the large degree of overlap between the True Pure Land sect and Christianity in members' core religious consciousness, once people accepted The Church of Jesus Christ of Latter-day Saints, they practiced their faith enthusiastically. Since there are also polytheistic aspects in the Church's doctrine that teach that members can attain godhood in the presence of Heavenly Father after death, these similarities cannot be explained in simple terms.

Regional variation between western and eastern Shin-Etsu was also evident in the numbers of survey responses that indicated "the guidance of the Holy Ghost" as the reason given by local residents for joining the Church (table 6). The percentage of respondents who indicated having converted as a result of "the guidance of the Holy Ghost" was high in Yamagata city, in contrast with a low percentage in Toyama city. Differences in the folk religion may be related to differences in the way people accept the Church. It seems that one reason for the low percentage of people who converted through personal religious experience in the Toyama region may be the fact that many similarities in religious ideology exist between Christianity and the True Pure Land sect, which forms the folk religion of the region, and so more members there were baptized after having accepted Church doctrine on an intellectual basis.

Comprehensive View of Missionary Work and Acceptance of the Gospel

Has the process whereby local residents attend Church meetings, receive baptism, and join the Church changed over time? Questionnaire results show that from the 1960s to the 1980s, missionaries' proselytizing efforts and English conversation study made up the overwhelming majority of opportunities that led individuals to first investigate the Church. Converts' reasons for deciding to be baptized (table 7) included, "because the missionaries were admirable, engaging individuals," "through the guidance of the Holy Ghost," and "because I knew that the gospel taught by the missionaries was true." But beginning with

Table 6: Member Converts' Reasons for Being Baptized (according to unit in which they were baptized)

Reasons for Being Baptized	Number of Respondents			
	Toyama Units (19)	Uozu Branch (3)	Yamagata Ward (14)	Yonezawa Branch (8)
Read the Book of Mormon and was convinced of its truth	7	1	6	1
Believed the gospel as preached by the missionaries	8	2	8	5
Felt persuaded after talking with members (other than missionaries)	5	0	2	0
Through the guidance of the Holy Ghost	4	0	9	6
Because the missionaries were admirable, engaging individuals	9	1	8	4
Because the members were admirable, engaging individuals	4	0	3	0
Sensed the appeal of the members' community	2	0	2	0
Decided to marry and build a happy household in an atmosphere of religious faith	2	0	2	1
Family were members; influenced by them	1	0	2	1
Other reasons	6	1	8	2

Includes responses from questionnaire respondents only. Multiple responses to questions were allowed. Numbers in parentheses are numbers of respondents. "Toyama Units" includes Toyama and Kureha Branches.

Table 7: Change in Reasons for Being Baptized for Member Converts to The Church of Jesus Christ of Latter-day Saints (1997 survey)

Reasons for Being Baptized	Number of Respondents			
	1960s	1970s	1980s	1990s
Because the missionaries were admirable, engaging individuals	0	9	11	4
Through the guidance of the Holy Ghost	1	5	11	5
Believed the gospel as preached by the missionaries	1	6	10	8
Read the Book of Mormon and was convinced of its truth	1	3	8	7
Because the members were admirable, engaging individuals	0	4	4	3
Felt persuaded after talking with members (other than missionaries)	0	1	3	2
Sensed the appeal of the members' community	1	2	2	2
Family were members; influenced by them	0	2	1	0
Decided to marry and build a happy household in an atmosphere of religious faith	0	2	1	4
Other reasons	0	1	8	6

Includes responses to questionnaire surveys conducted in the Yamagata Ward, Yonezawa Branch, Toyama Ward, and Uozu Branch in 1997. Includes multiple responses. Respondents numbered sixty-two. Years indicate the time each member was baptized.

increases in Church membership in the 1990s, there was an increase in cases in which people were baptized through the efforts of members or after having sensed the appeal of the member community. This may indicate a trend toward diversification and decentralization in opportunities for introduction to the Church and reasons for receiving baptism.

Survey Results

This study revealed the following results.

First, Church members' reasons for first coming to Church prior to conversion and their reasons for deciding to be baptized are diversifying in pace with the changing times. Until the 1980s, proselytizing was centered around the efforts of the missionaries. With increases in Church membership by the 1990s, the ratio of instances in which people joined the Church through the efforts of members or after being attracted by the mutual amicability of the members began to rise.

Second, the ratio of True Pure Land and Pure Land sects as the traditional parishioner sect of the family was high for Latter-day Saints. This tendency is seen in the Church units of Toyama Prefecture, which is a True Pure Land region, as well as in the Church units of Yamagata Prefecture, which is a Zen Buddhist region.

Third, the Yamagata and Yonezawa regions, which had a predominant distribution of Sōtō Zen temples, had more cases in which members joined the Church as a result of a religious experience. In the Toyama region, which had a predominant distribution of True Pure Land temples, fewer people joined the Church as a result of a religious experience. More people in the region may have joined the Church after accepting its doctrine on an intellectual basis. This regional variation stems from the folk religions of the regions.

Fourth, most geographical variations in acceptance and retention were shown to be related to regional folk religions. In the Toyama area, with its significant distribution of Pure Land sect temples, proselytizing was difficult but sacrament meeting attendance levels there were high, which may indicate high convert retention rates. Missionary work was comparatively easy in regions such as Yamagata that had a significant distribution of Sōtō Zen Buddhist temples and in regions with a numerous array of Buddhist sects, but member retention levels in Yamagata were low. The study does not indicate that local residents fully understand Buddhist doctrines, but rather that the residents' views concerning life, death, redemption, and other aspects of fundamental religious awareness are influenced to varying degrees by the doctrines. We must wait for further research to determine whether these results indicate east-to-west regional variation in the way Christianity is received in Japan.

Fifth, no significant trends are apparent in the attributes of Church members from surveys in Yamagata and Toyama Prefectures.

This paper was presented at "A Symposium Commemorating 100th year of the Japan Mission of the LDS Church," Shinagawa Hoken Center, Tokyo, Japan, 2001.

Notes

1. The works that do deal with Christian sects from a geographical perspective include, for example, Tokuhisa's study concerning acceptance of Protestant Churches in Shibukawa City, Gunma Prefecture, during the early Meiji period. Tokuhisa Tamao, "Bunkaichirigaku no Kadai" (Issues in cultural geography), in *Gendai Chirigaku e no Kadai* (Issues in modern geography), ed. Kobayashi Nozomi, Tokuhisa Tamao, and Kobayashi Tooru (Tokyo: Gakubunsha, 1989), 212–35.

2. While Shintō, Shugendō (syncretic mountain asceticism), and popular beliefs are all parts of regional folk religion, the present article will focus only on the relevance of Buddhism, leaving the treatment of these other influences on regional folk religion as a topic for future consideration.

3. The number of True Pure Land religious institutions in Toyama Prefecture accounts for 71 percent of the total number of Buddhist-type religious institutions. The percentage of Christians in the population for Toyama Prefecture is the lowest in the nation, at 0.24 percent. The number of Zen religious institutions in Yamagata Prefecture represents a majority of the total number of Buddhist-type religious institutions there.

4. There were few elderly respondents, but no significant imbalances are evident in the ratio of men to women, occupation, education, or other member attributes.

5. Questionnaire forms contained forty-two questions, with thirty-one in multiple-choice format (some response alternatives had a fill-in-the-blank column) and eleven in fill-in-the-blank format. Question items consisted mainly

of "reason for joining the Church," "religion/religious views/parishioner sect/parishioner shrine before joining the Church," "hometown," "address (house number omitted)/age/occupation/school(s) attended/family composition at the time you joined the Church," "present address (house number omitted)/age/occupation/school(s) attended/family composition," and similar items.

6. The numbers of questionnaire forms distributed and recovered for each Church unit are as follows: Yamagata Ward (50 sent, 15 returned), Yonezawa Branch (17 sent, 11 returned), Toyama Ward (42 sent, 31 returned), Uozu Branch (11 sent, 5 returned). The same trends are more clearly shown by Takemura, "Geographical Examination of the Propagation of the Church," with responses obtained from 157 people.

7. On-site surveys in The Church of Jesus Christ of Latter-day Saints were conducted in August 1997 for the Yamagata Ward and Yonezawa Branch of the Church, and in September of the same year for the Toyama and Kureha Branches as well as the Uozu Branch.

8. The number of missionaries for the Church in Japan, according to the Ministry of Cultural Affairs, *Shūkyō Nenkan* (The religion almanac, 1998 edition), ed. Bunkachō (Tokyo: Gyōsei, 1998) was 994, consisting of 741 missionaries from overseas and 253 missionaries from Japan. Concerning the missionaries of the Church, see Takemura Kazuo, "Nihon Chihōtoshi niokeru Matsujitsuseito Iesu Kirisuto Kyōkai" (The Church of Jesus Christ of Latter-day Saints in Japanese provincial cities), Editing Committee for Essays in Honor of Yoshiaki Numa, PhD on his 70th Birthday, in *Shūkyō to Shakaiseikatsu no Shosō* (Religion and social life aspects) (Tokyo: Ryūbunkan, 1998), 143–69.

9. For example, door-to-door visits might be considered more effective in an area with comparatively little pedestrian traffic in front of main train stations, such as in Yonezawa City or Uozu City.

10. Overall, the difficulty of proselytizing was considered to vary according to the region rather than according to missionary strategy. Even if individual abilities differed from missionary to missionary, the effectiveness of proselytizing was equalized for each Church unit by the fact that each unit's group of missionaries changed every four to six months.

11. The composition ratios of distinct sects for the number of Buddhist religious institutions and the temple population ratios/temple shrine population ratios in the areas covered in the present article were calculated using the *1988 Yamagata Prefectural Register of Official Religious Institutions* and the *1972 Toyama Prefectural Register of Official Religious Institutions*.

12. The 1991 census report was used in deciding the range of the work and school commute in this article. Municipalities were included if 25 percent or

more of the total number of regular residents fifteen years of age or older who attended work or school commuted to another city. Further selection included those towns that surrounded municipalities that are primary and secondary commuting destinations for half or more of the commuters to other cities.

13. College students tended to listen to the missionaries' message more than regular residents, but they did not necessarily join the Church in greater numbers. Among questionnaire respondents, only one out of eight people in the Yonezawa Branch was a college student when baptized.

14. The sacrament meeting attendance rate in the present article consists of the annual average number of people attending sacrament meeting divided by the annual number of Church members for that unit.

15. Some young Church members who have become independent and have their own households do not keep a Buddhist altar, even if there is room for one to be built in their living space. A single member among the Kinoshita and Fujii members said, "I plan to marry, but I don't intend to keep a Buddhist altar in my new house."

16. The nationwide relative strength of Buddhist sects in the numbers of Buddhist followers in Ministry of Cultural Affairs, *1994 Religion Almanac,* indicates Pure Land at 30.1 percent, with True Pure Land accounting for 19.9 percent thereof. As for the number of religious institutions, 39.3 percent are Pure Land, with True Pure Land making up 27.8 percent of those.

17. This same tendency was seen in surveys by Takemura, "Geographical Examination of the Propagation of the Church," centered around the Shin-Etsu region. Among eighty-three respondents who identified their Buddhist parishioner sect, thirty-nine claimed True Pure Land (47 percent), and eight claimed Pure Land (10 percent). For practicing members of ten years or more, twenty-seven out of fifty-five respondents claimed True Pure Land (49 percent) and eight claimed Pure Land (15 percent).

18. See Nanzan Institute for Religion and Culture, *Jodokyō to Kirisutokyō* (Pure Land Buddhism and Christianity), ed. Nanzan Bunka Kenkyūjo (Tokyo: Shunjūsha, 1990).

19. In one example of a survey interview with a Church member, Mr. M., a Church member in his thirties who was originally a True Pure Land parishioner, reported that he had been in the habit of praying to "Nyorai-sama" since he was a child, and that an important factor in his joining the Church was that he already had a basic belief in an absolute being, such as Amida Nyorai or God. He says that the religious discussion given to him by missionaries when he was a high school student seemed very convincing. At the same time, autobiographical accounts of religionists and theologians mention ideological commonalities between Christianity and the True Pure Land sect. See Kamegaya

Ryuun, *Bukkyō kara Kirisuto e* (From Buddhism to Christianity) (Tokyo: Fukuinkan Shoten, 1957) and Takao Toshikazu, *Jidenteki Seishoron* (Autobiographical bibliology) (Tokyo: Kashiwa Shoten, 1994).

20. Latter-day Saints in the Uozu Branch reported that while there was some overlap between True Pure Land ancestor worship and reverence for ancestors in the Church, from their perspective the doctrine of the True Pure Land sect generally reflected only an external form that did not provide a satisfactory basis for faith.

21. Takano Tomoharu, "Tenrikyō no Denpa to Kiseishūkyōdan tono Kankei" (Transmission of Tenrikyō and its relation to preexisting religious groups), *Tenri Daigaku Gakuhō* (Tenri University review) 26 (February 1958): 21–40; and Takano Tomoharu, introduction to "Nihon Shūkyō Bunpu no Kenkyū (jo)" (Study of the distribution of religion in Japan), *Tenri Daigaku Gakuhō* 65 (February 1970): 1–19, discuss regional acceptance of Tenrikyō, particularly in relation to True Pure Land among preexisting religions in the region. Iwahana Michiaki, *Dewasanzan Shinkō no Rekishichirigakuteki Kenkyū* (Historico-geographical study of Dewa Sanzan) (Tokyo: Meicho Shuppan, 1992), discusses the relation between Buddhist sects and private religion but points out that almost no spread of the Dewa Sanzan faith has occurred in the Hokuriku True Pure Land belt.

On the other hand, it can also be gathered from documents of "hidden" Christians from the Sengoku period that the True Pure Land sect historically was antagonistic toward the Christian religious group but was also considered to be a significant target for Christian proselytization as conversion was possible through debate. Mitara Takaaki, "Kirishitan no Shinshū Rikai nitsuite" (Christian understanding of True Pure Land Buddhism), *Shūkyō Kenkyū* (Journal of religious studies) 315 (March 1998), 186–87.

22. According to Takemura, "Geographical Examination of the Propagation of the Church," members who experienced family opposition to their baptism numbered twenty-one out of thirty-nine True Pure Land respondents, and two out of eight Pure Land respondents. Out of eighteen parishioners of Zen sects including Sōtō Zen, none experienced family opposition.

23. Takemura, "Geographical Examination of the Propagation of the Church."

24. Per annum baptism statistics for the Sanjō branch according to Takemura, "Geographical Examination of the Propagation of the Church," show eight in 1990, nine in 1991, eleven in 1992, eight in 1993, and one as of October 1994.

25. Takemura, "Geographical Examination of the Propagation of the Church."

17

Japanese Members of the LDS Church: A Qualitative View

John P. Hoffmann and Charlie V. Morgan

In 1998 I (the senior author) was invited to Japan to serve as a visiting faculty member in the Department of Behavioral Sciences at Hokkaidō University in Sapporo. I had never been outside of North America and did not speak any language except English, yet I couldn't miss the opportunity to embark on an adventure to a place that I found both mysterious and inviting. My wife also shared my enthusiasm, so she and our young children accompanied me. Our hosts from the university found a house for us to rent in a small town outside of Sapporo, and we proceeded to acclimate ourselves to the cold weather and the large amount of snow (we arrived in March, a time when winter had finished dumping several feet of snow on northern Japan). With the help of some new acquaintances, we also located the local Latter-day Saint branch. Although it was a bit daunting to consider attending church meetings that were conducted in Japanese, there was little choice if we wished to remain active members. As far as we could determine, the closest English-speaking ward was many miles away. So on the Sunday following our arrival, after learning how to negotiate the train system, we gathered our small family and traveled several rail stops to another small town that housed the local branch building.

The small building that contained the branch was old, cold, and held the slight scent of spoiled vegetables tinged with a hint of disinfectant. But the Saints there greeted us warmly. Still anticipating the awkward verbal exchanges that might occur if I attempted to utter a few phrases of jagged Japanese, I breathed a sigh of relief when my family and I encountered two American missionaries. The first, Elder Winget, was a large lad from northern Montana; the second, Elder Oshima, was a Japanese-American who hailed from San Diego, California.[1] Also in attendance was a Brazilian student, Brother Avellar, who spoke excellent English. All three of these men provided much needed translation services as we struggled to pay attention to our new surroundings.

Although the branch was small, with only about twenty-five to thirty adults attending sacrament and other church meetings, we noticed few ostensible differences between the meetings we attended in the United States and those in this branch in Japan (which may not be representative of others in the country). One amusing difference, however, involved the exchanges that often took place between those giving sacrament talks and those listening. Several members thought it appropriate to offer editorial comments about talks or to interrupt the speaker to ask questions. At times, the speaker would directly address a member of the audience. The branch members appeared to perceive all this as entirely appropriate, even though I had never seen such exchanges in more than ten years of attending Latter-day Saint services in the U.S.

As a social scientist, it was easy to be aware of not only the modest differences between church services in Japan and those in the United States, but also, more important, the striking similarities. While these similarities seem to represent the success of the Church's correlation program and the Japanese expertise in bureaucratic efficiency, it appeared, however, that our Japanese brothers and sisters had actually internalized many of the norms, practices, and mannerisms that define Mormonism. The only exception to these similarities was the way in which the sacrament area—a small, austere room with simple folding chairs facing a pulpit and a kerosene heater resting in one corner—was quickly transformed from one to two rooms by placing a portable wall down its middle. Priesthood met in one room and Relief Society met in the other. Space issues aside, I was curious about these similarities. As my new missionary friends translated the conversations, talks, and lessons for me, I heard standard rhetoric about the Church and its teachings.

Knowing a little of Japanese culture, especially some of the nuances that make Japanese Christianity a small sapling with shallow roots,[2] I wondered what social and cultural factors might attract or dissuade the potential Japanese member. Although a mission had existed in Hokkaidō for several decades, I learned that almost all the adult members of this small branch were converts, some of them the sole members of their families.* What had the Japanese Saints' parents and siblings thought when they learned that their loved one had joined a foreign religion? Were familial lines frayed or torn by their decision to be baptized, oftentimes giving up widespread Japanese habits such as smoking, or drinking alcohol and tea?

Studies in the sociology of religion instruct us that joining a new religious group is based primarily on the family or friendship ties that one has with members of the group.[3] Yet given the Japanese Saints' well-ingrained hesitancy to discuss personal matters, especially matters as close to the heart as one's religious beliefs, I found it unlikely that interpersonal connections could explain much about why these visibly strong members had joined a strange, foreign religion. Observing their faithfulness to the Church and its tenets, I wondered what types of familial, behavioral, and cultural conflicts the Japanese Saints had to endure to become and to remain active, faithful members.

Over the next few days, I combed the library holdings of the university to see what I could learn about the Church and the Japanese Saints. Although I found substantial information about the history and demographics of the Church in Japan,[4] there was little systematic research about the people and their lives inside and outside the Church.[5] So I remained curious about the members and undertook a research project to learn more about these fascinating, faith-bearing people, how their lives shaped the Church, and how they were shaped by their membership.

Overview of the Qualitative Project

After obtaining a small amount of financial support from Hokkaidō University, my hosts met with the branch president, Aizawa Seiji, to request permission to interview branch members about various issues relating to their membership in the Church and their lives in general. He agreed but asked that we also contact the mission president and the stake president to secure their permission. After acquiring their permission, we distributed brief questionnaires in Japanese to all active adult members of the branch.[6] The questionnaires requested basic demographic information (for example, age, sex, education, and occupation), as well as information about their church membership (for example, length of time in the Church; types of callings; missionary service; and any relatives who were also members).

With the assistance of colleagues at Hokkaidō University who have expertise on Japanese culture and religion, I developed a series of open-ended questions from which to structure intensive interviews about a number of topics.[7] The interview topics were divided into two broad areas: prebaptism and postbaptism. The prebaptism topics included respondents' first contacts with the Church, exposure to missionaries, experiences with English classes, reactions to scriptures and doctrine, and interaction with friends and family members who had previously joined the Church. The questionnaire also inquired about their thoughts as they considered their decision to join the Church and the reactions of those outside the Church, including relatives and coworkers, to their decision. The postbaptism topics included members' perceptions of Church practices and doctrine, relationships with members and nonmembers, and how they reconciled being a member of the Church with being a member of Japanese society.

Two graduate students from Hokkaidō University—both of whom spoke Japanese and English—were thoroughly trained to interview members of the branch. With the help of a colleague at Hokkaidō University, we set up the interviews to take place in a private location, where the persons interviewed were tape-recorded for later transcription. The interviews lasted between one and one and a half hours each. Twenty-two out of the twenty-eight active adult members of the branch completed interviews. The completed tapes were then shipped to the United States, where translators whose native language was Japanese were employed to translate and transcribe the tapes. Since completing interviews with the branch members, we have also interviewed two dozen returned missionaries who served in the Sapporo area about their experiences with members and those of other faiths.[8]

Aims of the Present Study

Since there is little systematic information on Japanese members, the present study is largely exploratory. Obviously, our interviews yielded large amounts of qualitative data, far too much to present in a brief report. We thus opted to focus on the issue of church-temporal conflicts and conciliations. Although there are Latter-day Saint practices and values that clearly appeal to many conventional Japanese people, such as revering ancestors, striving for perfection, and abiding by patriarchal household structures, there are also norms, codes, and behaviors that are inconsistent with many contemporary Japanese cultural styles.[9]

Besides the common reservations—some of which border on distaste—that many Japanese people have toward Western religions,[10] the dietary and behavioral restrictions in the Church and the time commitments that pull members away from culturally encouraged commitments (such as workplace and school activities) are potential sources of strain and disruption in their lives. Many members must also address family pressures, especially during the early stages of their membership. It is not necessarily that family members see the person as abandoning conventional Japanese religions; rather, they are seen as deserting their heritage—of becoming someone who is no longer fully Japanese. Yet, as we shall see, these cultural shifts are usually negotiated to the satisfaction of members and nonmembers alike. It is these cultural inconsistencies, conciliations, and negotiated solutions that are the primary focus of this chapter.

The Members

During several months of qualitative observation, about three-quarters of the twenty-two branch members who participated in meetings were female, about one-quarter male.[11] Although the branch records may have indicated a higher percentage of male members than are represented in this study, many were inactive or semi-active, often due to work commitments. The participants' ages ranged from nineteen to sixty-six, with a mean age of forty-two. Similar to general education statistics in Japan, all had graduated from high school yet fewer than 20 percent had graduated from college.[12] Most were married with, on average, more than two children. A majority were in either professional and management occupations or homemakers.

The participants' church membership experiences varied substantially. The average length of membership was about eighteen years, with a range of two years to forty-five. Almost half of the participants were currently in Church leadership positions. Only about one-quarter had served missions. Most participants had other family members who were also members, but only two participants were second-generation members. Reported total lifetime attendance at a Latter-day Saint temple ranged from zero to thirty-one times, with an average of about nine. Although this may seem to indicate a lack of temple attendance, the closest temple at the time of the study was Tokyo, which involved a lengthy and expensive trip. Some of the long-term members reported attending the temple in Laie, Hawaii, before the Tokyo Temple was built.

Negotiating Membership in the Church

Family Opposition and Conciliation. When asked about their decision to join the Church, most branch members gave standard responses that included perceiving the truth about missionary messages. Moreover, several had family members or friends who were already members, so they knew something about missionary activities and the basic principles of the Church. A majority, however, were not familiar with the Church before they had met the missionaries. Unlike standard sociological explanations that emphasize the influence of family and friendship networks on conversion to a religious tradition,[13] more than two-thirds of those interviewed were introduced to the Church through missionary contacts, typically when the missionaries were tracting or teaching English classes. Friends or family members introduced the remaining participants to the Church. In three cases, the husband and wife participated jointly in the missionary lessons that led to baptism. In almost all our interviews, however, the prospective member faced at least some opposition from other family members. For example, Tanabe Teruo, a thirty-year-old man who had been a member of the Church for about ten years, reported that after he had been taking the missionary lessons in preparation for baptism: "My mother opposed me joining the church, so I returned the Book of Mormon to the missionaries. I told them I couldn't be a member and I couldn't see them any more, but they still taught me the lessons." Similarly, Aizawa Seiji, a fifty-eight-year-old man who had been a member for more than thirty years and was at the time of the interview the branch president, recalled that after making a decision about baptism: "I wrote to my mother to tell her what I decided. She was very upset, saying that we have our religion handed down from our ancestors and that we don't need an American religion."

There were also clear gender differences in the reported reactions of family members. Although husbands sometimes objected to their wives joining the Church, the women's parents appeared less likely to oppose baptism than the men's parents. Tanaka Emiko, a forty-two-year-old woman who had been a member for only two years, reported that after her baptism:

> I knew I had to tell my mother. After I got baptized I felt very spiritual for a month and I went to see my mother and I brought the Book of Mormon. [Feeling some trepidation] . . . I gave the Book of Mormon to my mother and told her that I became a member, she said, "That's great." She also said, "You are still young, so do your best." I was very surprised.

Tanaka was a bit older than most of the other branch members at the time she converted, so it is likely that the age at baptism is another factor.

Some members we interviewed mentioned that they were old enough, usually at least twenty years old, at the time of their baptism to make their own decisions, thus any objections raised by their parents were not seen as obstacles. Yet, at least among the female participants, even the younger members claimed surprisingly little opposition from parents. When we asked Honda Yuki, a thirty-year-old woman who had converted when she was eighteen years old, about her parents' reaction to her baptism, she responded:

> I might be good at persuasion. They didn't oppose my decision. They might not have known how serious the decision was. I didn't have any objection from my parents on what I wanted to do if I didn't cause any problems. When I became twenty years old, my father said to me that I changed. He was glad that I obeyed the Word of Wisdom and that I had more savings than my sister . . . even though my income was less than my sister's. He complimented me on it.

The Church, even though it was often perceived as a foreign institution, was viewed by many of the parents of the female members as a stabilizing force and as a source of moral guidance. Since drinking, smoking, and even sexual experimentation were seen as normative by many Japanese youth, parents often searched for ways to help their children refrain from such activities. The Church's strict behavioral proscriptions were thus appealing to parents whose children were members.

In contrast to the female interviewees, it appeared at first glance that for many male participants parental opposition persisted at least until the time of baptism, so we asked them whether their parents had ended up accepting their membership in the Church. Tanabe Teruo said that after he had taken the missionary discussions (against his mother's wishes) and decided to be baptized, his mother acquiesced.

> The reason why my mother gave me permission was because I had changed since I met the missionaries. I changed a lot. The missionaries visited my house and they were good people so she thought what they believed wasn't bad. And also I changed in a better way. [He stopped drinking and smoking and thought he had developed a calmer demeanor.]

Members also discovered ways to reconcile their decision to join the Church with their parents' initial opposition. Branch President Aizawa, for instance, stated that after he decided to be baptized: "I said to myself that I was not going to treat my parents badly because of what I believed and that I was not going to abandon them and that what I decided was not a problem!"

It is important to keep in mind, however, that only one of the male branch members we contacted was the eldest son in his family. Moreover, most of the opposition came from mothers; fathers tended to have little to say about their sons joining the Church. Research on the Japanese family has discussed at length the traditional responsibilities of the eldest son to care for his family and the strong attachment that often exists between sons and mothers.[14] It is likely that the fact that only one of the adult male members of the branch was an eldest son is reflective of the strong opposition that such a person might face if he wished to convert. When asked about her husband's interest in the Church, Miyada Yuko, a thirty-five-year-old homemaker who had joined the Church seven years earlier, replied:

> My husband doesn't belong to any religions, but [as the eldest son] he has a responsibility to take care of ritual things for the ancestors of the Miyadas. He said to me that as his wife, it might not be appropriate that I become Christian. However, his parents don't care about it. When I go to the Tokyo Temple, I always ask his parents to tend my children. They are quite cooperative.

One wonders, though, how her in-laws would react if their eldest son wished to join the Church. We suspect they would care deeply and may even become uncooperative.

Culture, Commitments, and Church Membership. Although overcoming parental opposition, especially for the women, was surprisingly smooth for the branch members, reconciling Church membership with their roles in Japanese society proved slightly more difficult. Drinking alcohol and tea and smoking cigarettes are common practices in Japan. The social pressure to drink is well known, especially after the workday has ended and workers, primarily males, congregate in clubs to relax after a long day.[15] Those who do not participate in these activities are often at a disadvantage in terms of their work relationships and perceived ability to work harmoniously with their group. There is also similar pressure to drink tea or alcohol at family functions.

A preliminary review of our interviews with returned missionaries suggests that Word of Wisdom issues are probably the most difficult hurdle to surmount for prospective members and are a key source of inactivity. Yet the members we interviewed were remarkably adept at fitting their new Latter-day Saint lifestyles and commitments with their previous Japanese identities. Some branch members engaged us in frank discussions about the problems that result from following Latter-day Saint codes of behavior, but many had experienced only a few difficulties as they sought to refrain from behaviors that violate the Word of Wisdom.

To see these contrasting experiences, listen to two participants answer questions about how they handled workplace pressures to drink alcohol. Miyazaki Toshio, a fifty-five-year-old "salaryman," answered a question about his workplace in this manner:

> There are many times that I am asked to do things like drinking alcohol at work. Of course, I have to decline these offerings. That makes my co-workers wonder and ask me what is going on. I just

say that I am a Christian. Once in a while, people get mad at me, asking why I won't drink their alcohol, but that is what I decided, so I don't drink. . . . Sometimes they make fun of me, saying, "You are something! You even want to come to our second party right after the main party even though you don't drink alcohol! If I were you, I wouldn't go. It's foolish!"

However, his decision to attend work parties was probably anything but foolish. Refusing to attend these parties can be a clear sign that a worker considers himself outside the group, possibly opening himself up for ostracism.[16]

By way of contrast, Tanabe Teruo, when asked if he had any problems with the Word of Wisdom, responded:

Well, I don't have big problems but when I was a high school student I smoked and drank, so when I meet my friends from high school who smoke and drink, I feel tempted a little bit. However, it is not hard to be with them. My friends and co-workers know I don't drink so they don't force me to drink.

It might be rather simple for Tanabe to swear off drinking with his colleagues, however, because he works for an American company that is based in Utah. So most of his co-workers, some of whom are also Latter-day Saints, are very familiar with the Church's behavioral proscriptions.

As with their family reactions to decisions about baptism, there were obvious gender differences in how participants negotiated Word of Wisdom requirements with cultural pressures to drink and smoke. The women, in particular the homemakers in the branch, did not face the same workplace pressures as the men, and even decisions concerning tea did not seem difficult. Tanabe Miko, a young wife and mother who had grown up in the Church, admitted little pressure to share her co-workers' fondness for tea when she worked outside the home. The interviewer asked, "Did they ask you why you didn't drink coffee and tea?" She responded, "When they asked me, I told them I was a member. So if I [told] them at first, I [didn't] have any problems." Tanabe may have been able to resist any ostensible pressure because she had been raised in the Church and, presumably, had never developed a taste for coffee or tea. But even the women who had not grown up in the Church reported few problems resisting any temptation or pressure to drink tea or coffee. Abe Reiko, a thirty-six-year-old woman who converted as a teenager, said that when co-workers asked her about drinking tea, she responded:

> "I told them I don't drink tea and alcohol."
>
> "Did you tell them at the start?"
>
> "Yes, I told them so they understood it. I brought [herbal or wheat] tea that I could drink and they didn't give me tea. Some people asked if they could have my tea. So I didn't have any problems with that. There was also a welcome party for new people and there was alcohol, but I told them I couldn't have alcohol in a casual way. I always asked to have soft drinks. It may depend on personalities, but I tried not to give bad feedback or be too offensive when they asked me to have some alcohol."

Family pressures were slightly more troublesome for some of the branch members. Social gatherings—which are often held on Sundays, the traditional "day-off" in Japan—are typically a time for drinking alcohol. Some family members who did not belong to the Church were bothered when their relatives would not imbibe with them or gather for family activities on Sunday. Uchida Akiko, a forty-eight-year-old woman, explained, "They [my family] may think it is inconvenient because we can't go out on Sundays and we can't drink. So they may think we are troublesome."

This type of response, however, was not as common as we had anticipated. Most branch members made the decision to refrain from alcohol, tea, and coffee with strong determination, and there were few obstacles they could not overcome. However, for most this was not an immediate result of baptism but rather a lengthy process of socialization into the Church, of identifying as a member, and of admitting membership to nonmembers:

> [When I joined the Church my] friends asked why I stopped drinking coffee. They thought I was strange. Some friends said that they couldn't be friends any more. Because I didn't drink and smoke, they had a prejudice against my change. [At] first, I couldn't say that I couldn't have tea, but eventually I was able to say that I don't drink tea. They responded to me, "All right." I thought it was not so diffi-

cult to say no. Later, I found that I was used to that kind of situation. It was not a matter of my friends but myself.[17]

Clearly, conversion to a new religious tradition requires a shift in one's identity and the realization that changes come from within—what some term a commitment process—before they may be manifest to others outside the tradition.[18]

Another cultural negotiation and conciliation that must be addressed by those who join the Church involves Japanese religious traditions, despite the fact that Japan has been termed a highly secularized society. The country has low attendance at religious services and theological or spiritual beliefs are highly diversified.[19] Institutionalized religions are not widely supported by Japanese, especially since many of the traditional social service and community integration functions that Western religious institutions provide are offered mainly by government and quasi-governmental organizations and by employers.[20]

Institutional affiliations and practices are uncommon because most Japanese take a highly syncretic approach to religion and spirituality. Various traditions are blended into an amalgam of practices and beliefs, most of which stem from selected aspects of Buddhism, Shintōism, Confucianism, and Taoism.[21] The influence of these religions has existed for centuries, although recent decades have seen an infusion of Christian traditions that are vaguely related to such traditions in the West.[22] One needs only to stroll through any Japanese city and notice the Christian wedding chapels to realize the putative effect of Christian ritual on contemporary Japanese society. Yet many dimensions of Japanese religion remain at the level of ritual, with a general lack of a concomitant set of coherent beliefs. A tradition of adherence to ritual in the absence of a specific set of beliefs has created a system of cultural norms and proscriptions about what distinguishes Japanese religious behavior from other forms of religious behavior. Normative Japanese religious behavior includes, for example, Buddhist funerals and Shintō weddings; veneration of ancestors through Buddhist altars—known as *butsudan*—in the homes; and the annual pilgrimage to the shrine in one's hometown at the New Year's festival. These traditions are such an important part of Japanese culture that joining a Western religion and possibly abandoning traditional rituals is likened to shedding one's Japanese identity.

The branch members we interviewed took a rather temperate view of Japanese religious rituals. In general they recognized the tradition-laden aspects of these rituals and did not see them strictly as religious behavior that was at odds with their Latter-day Saint beliefs and practices. Although the members did not have butsudan or *kamidana* (a Shintō household altar) in their homes, many continued to participate, at least halfheartedly, in Buddhist and Shintō rituals with their family and friends who did not belong to the Church. Only rarely did their fellow Latter-day Saints frown upon this type of participation. When asked about her family's Buddhist background, Nakajima Miyoko, a thirty-seven-year-old woman who had been a member for seven years, replied,

> "Buddhists [don't] teach their religion so seriously. I wonder what a Buddhist priest does. I sometimes hear a good talk in a meeting like [a] funeral, but they need to teach people more often about how to live their daily lives. Then, I think Japanese people will become more religious. To me, Christianity, Buddhism, or any religion is okay as long as they teach good things."

> "Is your mother Buddhist?"

> "Yes. . . . She is a smoker. It is difficult to invite our own family members to church. We have to be a good example to them."

> "Was the funeral for your father Buddhist style?"

> "Yes."

> "What do you do about your faith?"

> "I respect any way of doing something since our beliefs are similar with other religions. I follow their rituals. I follow every custom."

There is a sense in these responses of the Japanese predilection to syncretize religious and other cultural traditions. Often, members reported how similar their Latter-day Saint beliefs were to the ethical beliefs they had inherited from Japanese religious traditions. Some were able to use these presumed similarities to reconcile their new responsibilities as Latter-day Saints with cultural practices that seemed at odds with traditional Latter-day Saint practices. A stark example of this conciliation process was found in one interview we conducted. Kimura Yuriko, a thirty-five-year-old woman who had been a member for twelve years, had this to say when asked to compare the beliefs and practices of Japanese religions and the Church:

> As I converted, I was at first perplexed, thinking what I would do when my parents died. I fortunately have an older sister who could take care of the funeral. I didn't want to, but I helped anyway because I thought it might be important to keep harmony with other relatives. Then, I noticed that Buddhist teachings and the Christian teachings are the same. I have a religion and others have another religion, but when it comes to thinking about God, we are one. I think all religions are related and have to be respected. So, when I go to the [Buddhist] graveyard with my children, we pray as we do in our church, and when we are with other people, we pray in our mind with them. I don't have any sense of incongruity any more. I respect the Japanese religion as being actively alive in our customs, which were formed in Japanese history. I can't say that believing other religions is useless because we are the true church or that our church is the same [as] other religions.

There is a strong sense of cognitive conciliation in this statement. By bringing the potentially disparate concepts of God closer together,[23] emphasizing the similarities rather than the differences among religious traditions, and linking Japanese religions with historically entrenched customs, Kimura has found a comfortable position as a member of a Western religion in traditional Japanese society; she is at ease participating in Latter-day Saint rituals as well as Buddhist-inspired customs.

Others discussed their participation in rituals and festivals, but they clearly recognized them as part of Japanese culture and tradition rather than strictly religious observations. Similar to the beliefs of young Asian-American Latter-day Saints interviewed by Jessie L. Embry,[24] branch members in Japan also recognized the need to maintain ties to Japanese traditions. There was a commonly reported distinction, moreover, between Latter-day Saint rituals that symbolized reverence of deity and Japanese traditions that served as recreational activities.

When asked whether her family attends Shintō festivals, Suzuki Keiko, a forty-seven-year-old woman said:

> "We go. I like the stands. I think we can enjoy our culture."
> "Do you go to the Shrine on New Year's Eve?"

"I used to, but not lately. It is too cold. I think it's a member's choice. I'm flexible. It's a tradition. I think it is for fun. . . . Our church says not to be deceived, but I tend to be drawn to the traditional activities. I like to buy *Omikuji* [printed fortunes]. Various fortunes are [said] to have a bad influence on us. God says we have to overcome things by our own effort. So, fortune telling contradicts our beliefs."

"There are some people who really like fortune telling."

"I think it is okay to enjoy it as a game. Faith is hope and love. We shouldn't look back."

Although families may enjoy these activities as recreational pursuits, we were also curious about younger people for whom participation in some traditional Japanese activities may serve a more important social function. Thus, we asked Hidaka Michiru, a twenty-one-year-old single woman, about participating in festivals and attending shrines with friends and family:

"[Do you go to] the first sunrise of the New Year?"

"I haven't gone. I have gone to a Shrine festival. I've even purchased an *Omikuji*. I don't believe in it, but did it for fun. We celebrate the New Year as you do. But, one time one of my friends asked why I celebrate the New Year even though we believe in another religion. I said I wanted to eat traditional food. I think the New Year is not a religious festival; rather it is a Japanese custom."

"Haven't your friends invited you to go visit the Shrine on the New Year?"

"Sometimes. But, I usually worked during my high school years, so I didn't have any time. I also visited my grandmother's place for the New Year. I usually spend time with my family."

"Then, you didn't need to give religious reasons for not going with your friends because you were working."

"Right. Besides, since they know I am Christian, they don't invite me anyway. Some friends say that I don't need to pray at the Shrine, so why don't I go? But, I didn't go because I had something to do."

"Then, would you go if you had time?"

"Probably. But, it is not that I will go because I believe, but that I just want to spend time with my friends for fun. Also, it is always crowded."

"Have you attended [a] wedding or funeral, which might have involved religious beliefs?"

"I . . . attended a funeral before. I think it is a matter of believing or not, so if I loyally believe my religion and light incense at the funeral, it is okay."

Hidaka had been raised in the Church, yet was clearly aware of and wished to remain a part of Japanese culture. Although it took a bit more cognitive negotiation for most converts in the branch to reach this point, almost all said that participation in rituals based on Japanese religions was mainly a cultural vehicle for remaining Japanese even while they maintained a strong allegiance to the Church. A useful distinction is to view Japanese religious traditions, such as Buddhist funerals and New Year's festivals, as part of Japan's "civil religion"[25] that is separate from religious rituals that are sanctioned by one's denomination. Similar to activities in the United States that involve New Year's celebrations, Thanksgiving Day parades, and Memorial Day observance, Japan has its own set of activities that foster a patriotic spirit. In the United States, we find members of many denominations—even non-Christians—participating in these "civil religious" activities, so it should not be surprising that Japanese Latter-day Saints are also drawn to traditional activities, even if they are linked to specific Japanese religions.

Discussion

In this chapter we have tried to provide a small taste of what it is like to be both Japanese and Latter-day Saint. Since there are several inconsistencies between Latter-day Saint beliefs and practices and Japanese culture, we expected that branch members would report many more problems both before and after they had joined the Church. It came as somewhat of a surprise, therefore, that the way they navigated their way through these presumed inconsistencies took place in a relatively calm sea. Although our interviews provided only a superficial glimpse of their experiences, thoughts, and beliefs, perhaps the Japanese tradition of cultural integration and religious syncretism helped ease the path for many. The fact that there are many religions practiced in Japan, including several that have either been directly imported or indirectly adapted to fit Japanese culture,[26] permits at least a grudging acceptance from parents and friends when loved ones join the Church. Moreover, the Japanese emphasis on ritual over belief and the way that many Latter-day Saints continued to participate in Japanese traditions even after they had been members for many years showed their friends and family that it was possible to be a member of an American religion and still remain Japanese. Linking these rituals to traditions rather than religious beliefs also helped the members reconcile their church obligations with their continued participation in these rituals. Hence, members could remain both fully Latter-day Saint and fully Japanese.

For the parents of the young women, in particular, the Church's behavioral proscriptions may have been appealing as they anticipated the movement of their children toward adulthood, a period of life with many freedoms and responsibilities. For the men, the road to familial acceptance became smoother once they familiarized their parents with the Church. According to the members at least, their parents no longer saw the Church as a negative influence once they became familiar with it. Rather, the Church was seen as a calming force and a moral guide, something that Japan's traditional religions may not clearly provide to the average person. It is not an exaggeration to claim that some parents, even those who had little interest in the Church, came to admire the effect that membership had on their children.

Perhaps even more surprising than the relatively uncomplicated conciliation of family relations and Church membership was the manner in which the branch members accepted and internalized the behavioral mandates of the Church. Although some of the members reported moderate family or workplace pressure to smoke cigarettes or to drink alcohol, coffee, or tea, they were highly proficient at counteracting this pressure. Some simply responded to the pressure by claiming that, as Christians, they were not allowed to use these substances. Others provided more intricate explanations but with the same effect. Once co-workers, friends, and family understood that the members had made a firm decision about these behaviors, there was little additional discussion. Even though there was some teasing by co-workers, the members had the fortitude to resist pressures and maintain their behavioral standards.

Of course, we must admit that the branch members we interviewed would clearly be considered strong members. Hence their recollection of how they negotiated and reconciled membership in the Church with their Japanese identities represents one extreme in a continuum of members' experiences. As indicated by our preliminary review of the interviews with returned missionaries, Word of Wisdom problems and lifestyle inconsistencies put up barriers to membership for those who may have had some interest in the Church and for those who had become inactive. The members we interviewed have successfully hurdled these barriers, so they provide only one part of the picture. Unfortunately we have no data from investigators or inactive members with which to compare the strong members' experiences. Nevertheless, we suspect, but cannot confirm, that there are a host of intra- and interpersonal factors that distinguish Japanese members from other Japanese people. For studies of Japanese Latter-day Saints to become more sophisticated and informative, it is necessary that researchers interview investigators who do not join the Church and members who are no longer active to determine their perceptions of the cultural inconsistencies that exist between Japanese society and the Church as well as the potential success of negotiating solutions to these inconsistencies.

This paper was presented at "A Centennial Celebration: The LDS Church in Japan, 1901–2001," October 13, 2001, Brigham Young University, Provo, Utah.

Notes

1. Due to confidentiality agreements, all names, including missionaries' names, have been changed.

2. Joseph M. Kitagawa, *On Understanding Japanese Religion* (Princeton: Princeton University Press, 1987), 283; Mark R. Mullins, *Christianity Made in Japan: A Study of Indigenous Movements* (Honolulu: University of Hawaii Press, 1998), 156–58.

3. Rodney Stark and Roger Finke, *Acts of Faith: Explaining the Human Side of Religion* (Berkeley: University of California Press, 2000), 116–25.

4. See R. Lanier Britsch, *From the East: The History of the Latter-day Saints in Asia, 1851–1996* (Salt Lake City: Deseret Book, 1998), 114–69; and Terry G.

Nelson, "A History of the Church of Jesus Christ of Latter-day Saints in Japan from 1948 to 1980" (master's thesis, Brigham Young University, 1986).

5. Notable exceptions include Tomoko Aizawa, "The LDS Church as a New Religious Movement in Japan" (master's thesis, Brigham Young University, 1995); Sachiko Sugiyama, "Japanese Folk Religion and Mormonism," *Journal of Religious Studies* 313 (1998): 93–118; Jiro Numano, "Mormonism in Modern Japan," *Dialogue: A Journal of Mormon Thought* 29 (Spring 1996): 223–35; Seiji Katanuma, "The Church in Japan," *BYU Studies* 14 (Autumn 1973): 16–28; and Jessie L. Embry, *Asian American Mormons: Bridging Cultures* (Provo, Utah: Charles Redd Center for Western Studies, Brigham Young University, 1999), 47–72.

6. Although the number of adult members on the Church rolls numbered more than a hundred, on average only about twenty-five to twenty-eight adult members regularly attended meetings over a four-month period of observation.

7. Given the lack of sociological research on Latter-day Saints in Japan and my deficiencies with the language, open-ended interviews provided the best means for beginning to understand members' lives and for formulating inductive conceptual schema to comprehend the social and cultural qualities of Church membership in Japan. See John Lofland and Lyn H. Lofland, *Analyzing Social Settings: A Guide to Qualitative Observation and Analysis*, 3d ed. (Belmont, Calif.: Wadsworth Publishing, 1995), 179–203.

8. With one exception, we address only the Japanese branch member interviews in this paper. All the completed transcriptions were entered into the qualitative analysis program N5 for coding and cross-referencing. The program allows a variety of analyses, primarily in the form of thematic cross-tabulations and vector or matrix representations. Lyn Richards, *Using N5 in Qualitative Research* (Bundoora, Victoria, Australia: QSR International, 2000), 35–64.

9. Numano, "Mormonism in Modern Japan," 230–32.

10. Mullins, *Christianity Made in Japan*, 3.

11. Aizawa, *LDS Church as a New Religious Movement*, 77, found a similar distribution.

12. Statistics Bureau & Statistics Center, Management and Coordination Agency, *Employment Status Survey* (Tokyo, 1998), 156.

13. Stark and Finke, *Acts of Faith*, 116–25.

14. Ochiai Emiko, *The Japanese Family System in Transition: A Sociological Analysis of Family Change in Postwar Japan* (Tokyo: LTCB International Library Foundation, 1996), 158–60.

15. Akihito Hagihara, Kimio Tarumi, and Koichi Nobutomo, "Work Stressors, Drinking with Colleagues After Work, and Job Satisfaction among

White-Collar Workers in Japan," *Substance Use & Misuse* 35 (2000): 737–56; Sepp Linhart, "Sakariba: Zone of 'Evaporation' Between Work and Home?" in *Interpreting Japanese Society: Anthropological Approaches*, ed. Joy Hendry, 2d ed. (London: Routledge, 1998), 237–38.

16. Linhart, "Sakariba," 237.

17. Matsuoka Kinuyo, forty-two-year-old woman.

18. Lewis R. Rambo, *Understanding Religious Conversion* (New Haven: Yale University Press, 1993), 124–41; Stark and Finke, *Acts of Faith*, 103–4.

19. Alan S. Miller, "Why Japanese Religions Look Different: The Social Role of Religious Organizations in Japan," *Review of Religious Research* 39 (1998): 360–70; Mark R. Mullins, "The Changing Role of Religion and Social Action Groups in Japanese Society," in *Religion, Mobilization, and Social Action*, ed. Anson Shupe and Bronislaw Misztal (Westport, Conn.: Praeger, 1998), 115–16.

20. Miller, "Why Japanese Religions Look Different," 362–64.

21. Alan S. Miller, "Predicting Nonconventional Religious Affiliation in Tokyo: A Control Theory Application," *Social Forces* 71 (December 1992): 400; Alan S. Miller, "A Rational Choice Model of Religious Behavior in Japan," *Journal for the Scientific Study of Religion* 34 (1995): 235.

22. Mullins, *Christianity Made In Japan*, 116–18.

23. Compare with Spencer J. Palmer, Roger R. Keller, Dong Sull Choi, and James A. Toronto, *Religions of the World: A Latter-day Saint View* (Provo, Utah: Brigham Young University Press, 1997), 49–71.

24. Embry, *Asian American Mormons*, 47–62.

25. K. Peter Takayama, "Revitalization Movement of Modern Japanese Civil Religion," *Sociological Analysis* 48 (1988): 328–41.

26. Mullins, *Christianity Made in Japan*, 95–128.

18

Japanese and American Mormons in Utah: Bridging Cultures

Jessie L. Embry

In 1979, Watabe Masakazu was in the bishopric of a Brigham Young University (BYU) student ward I attended. He spoke English without an accent and understood American and Mormon culture so well I assumed he was a third- or fourth-generation Japanese-American Latter-day Saint. Not until 1994, when he was interviewed as part of the LDS Asian American Oral History Project conducted by the Charles Redd Center for Western Studies, did I learn that he immigrated to the United States from Japan because his father wanted him to attend BYU. Watabe always planned to return to Japan to help the Church grow there, but instead he completed a PhD in California and accepted a position at BYU.

Watabe, like other Japanese Saints who have come to the United States, has learned to combine Japanese, American, and Mormon cultures. To varying degrees, these Japanese have learned to adapt to life in Utah despite language and cultural differences.

Immigrants have always been part of the Utah experience. During the nineteenth century, European converts to the Church accepted their religious leaders' requests to "gather" to Utah. The newcomers learned the English language as well as both American and Mormon traditions. They intermarried and within two generations were assimilated into a melting pot of culture.

During the twentieth century, however, Church leaders encouraged new members to stay in their home countries and build up the Church there. Still, while gathering to Utah is discouraged, individuals continue to come to be near other members of the Church. So many

Chinese immigrated to the United States in the 1990s, for example, that one scholar exclaimed it was easier to find Chinese members to serve in Church positions in California or Salt Lake City than it was in Taiwan or Hong Kong.[1]

Asian Latter-day Saint converts are a twentieth-century occurrence. While most Japanese Saints remain in their home country, some come to Utah. Determining how many have immigrated is difficult since Church membership records are closed to researchers and do not list national origin or race. Understanding the Japanese Latter-day Saint experience is also arduous since few have written their stories. This paper is based on oral history interviews conducted by the Redd Center, a research center at BYU. These interviews with twenty-three randomly selected Japanese Latter-day Saint immigrants in Utah are part of the LDS Ethnic American Oral History Project, which includes African American, Native American, Hispanic American, Polynesian American, and other Asian American interviewees.

As the oral history program director at the Redd Center, I wanted to hire interviewers who would understand the cultures of the interviewees. Although funding limitations required that the interviews be conducted in English, I wanted interviewers who understood the people's language and cultural norms. The ideal interviewers would have been natives of the particular ethnic or cultural group they were interviewing, but since that was not always possible, I ended up hiring Americans who had served Latter-day Saint missions to Asian countries. Matt Eyre, a BYU student, conducted all the Japanese interviews in Utah County.

Findings from this small sample of oral history interviews of Japanese Mormons in Utah revealed a wealth of personal information. Interviewees discussed their experiences within the Utah Mormon culture, their struggles with the English language, and their decisions to attend Church meetings in English or Japanese.

Joining the Church

In the oral history interviews, the Japanese Saints discussed their conversions to the Church, their immigration to the United States, and their relationships with Utahns. Most were interested in the United States and wanted to learn English even before their conversion. As

Tsuchida Michiru explained, "Even before I joined the Church, I was interested in learning English. I also had a special feeling towards America. In my heart America was a dream country for me."[2] Some took English classes from the American missionaries, learning about the Church and developing a close relationship with the young Americans. Watanabe Masumi remembered, "I had an interest in English. I had friends in America because they were missionaries. They said, 'Come to America.'"[3]

Generally speaking, many of the interviewees were in their twenties and interested in attending college in the United States. Some attended BYU, but due to strict academic and language entrance requirements, others went to neighboring Utah Valley State College (UVSC).

On an individual level, Uchida Norikazu wanted to study bionics, a field not taught at Japanese universities.[4] Kawasaki Kinuyo and her mother came to Provo because her mother wanted her to learn English. She attended UVSC and felt comfortable using her second language. "Speaking, writing, and reading English is so much easier for me than expressing myself in Japanese."[5] Kimura Kumiko wanted to study English. It was too expensive to go to England, "so I chose America. . . . BYU was cheap and also safe."[6]

Unlike the other interviewees, Watabe Masakazu never felt an affinity for Americans nor did he wish to attend BYU. He felt that the only Japanese who came to the United States "were the ones that didn't make it in the Japanese educational system. I wasn't about to give myself that kind of stigma." But even after Watabe was accepted at a Japanese national university, his father asked him to attend BYU. After prayer and thought, Watabe obeyed his father and agreed to attend the Church-run university.[7]

Watabe's dislike for BYU changed when he arrived: "I felt like this was my home and my family." He was now surrounded by members of his faith who shared his values. "These were the values that I've always been nurtured with. . . . I felt really good, and I felt at home."[8]

In Watabe's case, the respect for family found in both Latter-day Saint and Confucian beliefs matched, so he did not experience a conflict. Other Japanese Saints whose parents were not members of the Church faced split loyalties. While both their cultural and Latter-day Saint beliefs emphasized the importance of family and reverence for ancestors, many parents opposed the change in religion. Without the parents' blessing, even an adult is often reluctant to change religions. In Japanese culture, relationships are considered to be more important than what society might deem as right or wrong. According to Watabe, unlike Koreans, most Japanese do not recognize the similar values between Latter-day Saint and Confucian beliefs because the Church is perceived to be only an American Christian religion.[9]

Although most interviewees joined the Church in Japan and then came to Utah, several were not Latter-day Saints when they came to the United States. They were taking English classes at BYU, because it was less expensive than other universities, when they were introduced to the Church. Nishigaki Yukie was living in Seattle near a cousin, but "it was too expensive to live by myself." She started attending an English class in Washington offered by Latter-day Saint missionaries. They suggested that she go to Provo and attend BYU because it was more affordable.[10]

Those who were Church members came to Utah to be near the organization's headquarters. Miyagi Haruo came to Utah because he wanted to provide an example of a successful Japanese in America.[11] Nakanishi Yuko, also a member from Japan, was impressed with the size of the Church in Utah. There are "a lot of temples and churches. I am always going to church or the temple. . . . It always feels good."[12] Other interviewees referred to the nineteenth-century concept that Utah was a chosen place, a Zion. Watabe Masao, Masakazu's father, moved to Provo because "so far this is Zion, where family members had gathered. All my family is here in this state of Zion."[13]

Life in Utah

Once in Utah, this small sample of interviewees varied in how they perceived their acceptance. Watabe Masakazu was excited to be around people who shared his values. From time to time "I do hear some insensitive comments about not just Japanese but other races."[14] However, Watabe had seen similar treatment of *gaijin* (foreigners), especially toward American missionaries when he was in Japan. As a young Latter-day Saint boy, he "was very embarrassed because everybody in town seemed to be talking behind my back, saying, 'That little Masakazu knows a Caucasian.'"[15]

Ogasahara Hiroko found BYU to be "a Caucasian world, a white society. They do not really see the different people."[16] Yanagida Kaori conceded, "To be honest, I always feel like an outsider. People are nice in the church, but they never become a friend.... There's a circle of people, and I'm always outside the circle. But that doesn't mean that they kick me out, but it's just different." She disliked people who "treat me like I don't speak the language and that means I can't do anything."[17] Integrating into any foreign culture can be challenging, and for some people it is more difficult than for others.

Language was also a concern for Tsuchida Michiru. She did not agree with Yanagida but acknowledged that some of her friends were "totally offended by the way Americans treat them." She continued,

> I know that it wouldn't be the same for American people to talk with me.... It must be hard and boring in some way. I suppose they don't think I can feel like they do. I have fun like they do [and] I have a mouth to speak like they do. I feel pretty accepted in the community, but being a minority makes me feel like I am a little kid.[18]

Nishigaki Yukie agreed that she felt left out "not because I'm Japanese, but I think it's because of my English."[19]

All the interviewees expressed similar concerns about language. Miyahira Akiko saw cultural differences reflected through language, explaining, "The jokes are different.... It is hard for me to get into the conversation or get the jokes."[20] Even Watabe Masakazu insisted, "English is my second language. Some of the things that I could do with the native language, I may not be able to do that well with the second language."[21]

Seiko Higgins, a Japanese immigrant, attended BYU–Hawaii in the 1950s, and she felt frustrated by the lack of nuance in English. "There is no politeness in English like in Japanese. When I saw the president of the school coming toward me, I said, 'Good morning.' To me that was not enough. I would [want to] say, 'Good morning, sir.'" Higgins felt that unlike the Japanese language, English does not have the capabilities to express varying degrees of respect and esteem for people. She wanted to compliment people "working on the roadside or a stranger working hard and sweating," but felt English lacked words to express those feelings. She continued, "You say in English, 'You don't go to school?' We would say, 'Yes, I don't go to school.' But you say, 'No, I don't go to school.' That was really hard for me."[22]

Kurogi Minako, born in Japan in 1967, also said language was her major limitation. She attended Ricks College (now BYU–Idaho), served an English-speaking mission from 1989 to 1990, and was living in Orem, Utah, in 1995. She still felt that she could not "speak English fluently. Sometimes it makes it hard to communicate with people. If I knew how to express my feelings and ideas in fluent English, I can live in the United States without any problems."[23]

Other interviewees found people in Provo who confused Asian people. Nakanishi Yuko was amazed that some did not know the difference between Chinese and Korean and assumed they spoke the same language.[24] Kawasaki Kinuyo agreed, "I am accepted as an Asian. It is funny because a lot of the people think that Chinese, Korean, and Japanese are all the same."[25]

Asian Wards and Branches in Utah

Because of language and cultural difficulties, some Japanese immigrants attended Asian wards and branches. In Salt Lake City, there were enough Japanese to have a separate group, which was originally formed in 1952 as part of an ethnic regional mission. The *Church News* proudly announced two years later that "an eight-course Japanese dinner recently marked the inauguration" of the missionary efforts with Japanese people in Utah. Six Japanese Americans had already been baptized, and one recent convert was translating at cottage meetings.[26]

To serve these individuals and as a way of offering more leadership experience to newer Church members, the regional mission first organized the Japanese Dai-Ichi Sunday School. Historical records are often incomplete for wards and branches during this period, but a few minutes have survived for the Dai-Ichi Sunday School and Branch. In 1952 a secretary recorded in both Japanese and English who taught classes and gave talks.[27] The group also sponsored social and devotional activities. It started holding evening activities during the week in October 1955, averaging thirty-five members and investigators each week.[28] The next year the mission assigned fifteen missionaries to the Sunday School, most having served missions in Hawaii or Japan. They approached their missionary service by offering classes in leather crafts, Japanese gardening, and English tutoring. As a result of their efforts, an average of forty-five people attended Sunday School each week.[29]

The Sunday School continued to grow, and on April 10, 1962, Elders Spencer W. Kimball and Mark E. Petersen organized a branch. Members sustained Ralph Noboru Shino as the branch president. The first worship services were on Sunday, April 15, 1962, in the regional mission offices. Two weeks later members met in the Salt Lake Nineteenth Ward chapel.

The Dai-Ichi Branch sponsored fundraising activities, as did other Latter-day Saint congregations in the 1960s. For example, in 1963 the branch sold soap as a welfare project. But the fundraisers also had cultural twists. The branch Relief Society and other members catered sukiyaki and teriyaki chicken dinners to religious and civic groups. Each year the branch held a fundraising dinner and invited the community. On April 10, 1963, 325 people from throughout the Salt Lake Valley paid $2.50 per ticket to sample Japanese specialties. The next year, on April 27, 1968, 450 to 500 people attended. This annual fundraising dinner was still being held in the 1990s.

The branch also sponsored Halloween and Christmas parties, an annual campout at Bear Lake in northern Utah, and beginning in 1964, a New Year's dinner. The branch's manuscript history explained, "By tradition, New Year's marks a period of special celebration and festivity for the Japanese, and we, therefore, have adopted this tradition of holding an annual potluck." A month later the branch members completed building a large wooden *torii* (a Japanese gateway) and installed it as an entrance way into the cultural hall.[30]

While a torii is a symbol of Shintoism, the Japanese Saints viewed it as a cultural symbol and attached no religious significance to it. When Watabe Masakazu was the president of a student Japanese club at BYU, the club obtained a torii, possibly the one from the Salt Lake City congregation, for a festival. In the 1990s the Dai-Ichi Branch still used a torii for its celebrations.[31]

The branch Relief Society sisters were taught lessons from two teachers, one speaking in English and one in Japanese. Secretaries usually wrote in English, but sometimes they kept the minutes in Japanese. In 1986 the branch published a newsletter in both English and Japanese that listed speakers and ward activities and included special articles.

In Salt Lake City, branch members provided a bridge between Japanese Latter-day Saints and Japanese of other faiths. For example, at the first fundraising dinner in 1963, members of the Salt Lake Buddhist Women's Association provided entertainment. In 1969 the branch loaned its torii to the Japanese community for a parade in Salt Lake City.

The branch members also helped connect Japanese Saints with other Latter-day Saints. Stake leaders invited branch members to form a choir for stake conference. In 1965 branch members provided a potluck between sessions of the stake conference and dressed in traditional attire at the stake leaders' request. Members of the stake and other members from Salt Lake attended the fundraising dinners and enjoyed Japanese cuisine. In 1970 branch members staffed the Salt Lake Temple so that 371 Saints from Japan could attend and participate in the ceremony in their native language.

The Dai-Ichi Branch met the needs of its members in many ways, including providing special programs and language classes. Another purpose, according to the branch's manuscript history, was to encourage courtship between young people of Japanese ancestry. In 1966 the history proudly recorded four temple marriages among its members:

> This is especially noteworthy as one of the basic purposes for the organization of our branch was that church members of Japanese heritage would thereby have [the] opportunity to meet and marry one of their own church and racial background. We feel very gratified that this purpose is also being realized.[32]

In Provo, however, there were not enough Japanese for a separate branch. During the 1970s, Church leaders organized a branch for all Asian international students at Brigham Young University. Since members spoke so many languages, sacrament meetings were in English with Sunday School classes in Mandarin, Cantonese, Korean, and Japanese. When southeast Asian refugees arrived, the branch added a Vietnamese Sunday School class.

The Asian branch activities were very similar to those of other wards. In 1973, when the ten BYU stakes held Gold and Green dances, many members from the Asian branch went to the "Asian Oriental" theme dance. Other branch activities included ice skating, spaghetti dinners, swimming parties, and canyon outings. Sometimes the branch met with the campus Chinese club. Since many members were international students, branch leaders served a traditional Thanksgiving turkey dinner to help them celebrate the American holiday.[33]

Unlike other BYU wards and branches, the Asian congregation combined married and single students. It also did not require members to be BYU students, so Asians from throughout Utah Valley attended. In 1994, Honam Rhee, a Korean professor at BYU, served as bishop. He believed Koreans moving to the United States needed to "get into the mainstream" of American life, and he felt that the ward provided an essential "bridge" in learning the American culture. It also helped some members who planned to return to their home country learn church procedures and accept leadership callings.[34]

In 1995, Church leaders divided the Asian congregation into married and single students. The singles' ward operated like other student wards on campus. Non-BYU students continued to attend the married student ward. The sacrament meetings were in English, and Sunday School was held in other languages. In 2002, Church leaders divided the Asian ward into a Chinese ward and an Asian branch that was mainly Japanese and Korean because there were so many Chinese members. The branch president of the Asian branch was a European American who spoke neither language, and thus could not be charged with favoritism of either culture. Translators allowed him to communicate in and out of church meetings, although most members were bilingual. Korean membership grew, and in 2004 Church leaders divided the branch again, creating the BYU 238th Korean-speaking and the BYU 239th Japanese-speaking branches. In 2005, Church leaders called Theodore H. Okawa, a Japanese American from Hawaii who served a mission to Japan and lived in Okinawa for a decade, to lead the Japanese-speaking branch.[35]

By having a separate branch for Asians, Japanese members studied the gospel in the "language of their heart." One ward member, Kurogi Minako, joined the Church as a young girl. She enjoyed the Asian ward in Provo because "we can learn the gospel in our own language. In English it is hard for me to concentrate. . . . I get tired. I feel the Spirit, of course, but I cannot gain the knowledge of gospel because of my poor English."[36]

Okawa recognized these concerns. As a native English speaker living in Japan, he felt spiritually "starved" as he attended church services and tried to understand the gospel in a foreign language. He was delighted when he returned to Provo and could worship in English. But he recognized that his Japanese-speaking wife had similar concerns about services in her native language. So he felt that attending the Japanese branch was now her chance to worship in her native language. He explained that a Japanese woman living in Orem, who had attended geographical wards for thirty years, was also attending the Japanese branch. She joined the Church in the United States and had never attended church services in her native language. She was surprised how much more she learned in Japanese.[37]

The Provo Asian singles' branch, like its Salt Lake City counterpart, also provided an opportunity to meet potential marriage partners. Okawa attended the Asian branch during the 1970s because he was attracted to young women who looked like him. While he was not sure that the Church needed to provide congregations as places to meet dating partners, he met, dated, and married a Japanese woman in the branch.[38]

Although the Asian ward combined cultures that had traditionally been enemies, some interviewees appreciated the opportunity to worship in their native languages and the chance to meet people from other Asian countries. Tsuchida Michiru, a Japanese immigrant and BYU student, agreed:

> I had a very different view before toward . . . people from other Asian countries because of the war. It is very embarrassing, but I had pre-judged Koreans, Chinese, Vietnamese, and people from other Asian countries. . . . I was thinking about going on a mission and I knew I needed to change at least before I go. I was afraid to stay that way and to be called to other Asian countries.

On her first visit to the Asian branch, "two Korean returned missionaries shared beautiful testimonies with us. I was touched. . . . I noticed how dumb I had been by prejudging [others] and avoiding to get to know these beautiful people." She continued, "I repented and changed a lot. Right now I have tons and tons of Asian friends. . . . The Asian branch is so spiritual and special. Everybody's so kind and loves everyone."[38]

A few Japanese interviewees attended the geographical wards. They explained that they were in the United States to learn English and to understand American culture. They felt they could not do that if they only associated with other Japanese. Ogasahara Hiroko, who joined the Church in Japan, did not want to attend a Japanese branch at BYU because the members "comfort each other, I think, just because they want to be with Asians. Maybe sometimes it's good but not all the time."[40] He wanted to branch out and have different experiences.

Yanagida Kaori, a Japanese BYU student, attended the Asian branch in Provo a few times but did not find it suitable to her particular needs. She explained, "If I go to the Asian ward, my friends are going to be Japanese.... Just hanging out with them all the time wouldn't help me improve my [English] language skills or become part of the society." She enjoyed going to a student ward, giving talks, and participating in a family home evening group where she was a leader. When she spoke in sacrament meeting, she said "a lot of people could understand where I was coming from and what I was going through."[41]

Watabe Masakazu never attended an Asian ward. If the Asians go to their own wards, he said, "American members can't appreciate them by having this diversity in the ward. They need to learn about the members from other cultures." He felt that by having separate branches, "we are really depriving some of the wonderful opportunities for American Saints to grow by associating with these Asian people or any other ethnic group."[42]

Conclusion

The Japanese Saints we interviewed have found life in Utah to be unique. They appreciated the opportunity to be with other Saints who shared their beliefs, yet they often struggled with the language and the culture. Many attended separate Japanese or Asian Church meetings, which offered opportunities to worship in their native language and to serve in teaching and leadership positions. As a result these young Saints gained invaluable experience and many became assets to the Church in their native countries.

This paper was presented at "A Centennial Celebration: The LDS Church in Japan, 1901–2001," October 13, 2001, Brigham Young University, Provo, Utah. An earlier version of this article appeared as Jessie L. Embry, "Japanese American Mormons in Utah: Bridging Cultures," The Bulletin of the International Research Group 3, no. 1 (1999): 125–36.

Notes

1. Feng Xi, "A History of Mormon-Chinese Relations, 1847–1993" (PhD diss., Brigham Young University, 1995), 202.

2. Tsuchida Michiru, Oral history, 4, interview by Matt Eyre, 1994, LDS Asian American Oral History Project, Charles Redd Center for Western Studies, L. Tom Perry Special Collections, Harold B. Lee Library, Brigham Young University, Provo, Utah.

3. Watanabe Masumi, Oral history, 3, interview by Matt Eyre, 1994, LDS Asian American Oral History Project.

4. Uchida Norikazu, Oral history, 2, interview by Matt Eyre, 1994, LDS Asian American Oral History Project.

5. Kawasaki Kinuyo, Oral history, 4, interview by Matt Eyre, 1994, LDS Asian American Oral History Project.

6. Kimura Kumiko, Oral history, 3, interview by Matt Eyre, 1994, LDS Asian American Oral History Project.

7. Watabe Masakazu, Oral history, 5–6, interview by Matt Eyre, 1994, LDS Asian American Oral History Project.

8. Watabe Masakazu, Oral history, 6.

9. Watabe Masakazu, Conversation, September 1, 1999, LDS Asian American Oral History Project.

10. Nishigaki Yukie, Oral history, 2–3, interview by Matt Eyre, 1994, LDS Asian American Oral History Project.

11. Miyagi Haruo, Oral history, 5–7, interview by Matt Eyre, 1994, LDS Asian American Oral History Project.

12. Nakanishi Yuko, Oral history, 3, interview by Matt Eyre, 1994, LDS Asian American Oral History Project.

13. Watabe Masao, Oral history, 6, interview by Matt Eyre, 1994, LDS Asian American Oral History Project.

14. Watabe Masakazu, Oral history, 17.

15. Spencer J. Palmer, *The Expanding Church* (Salt Lake City: Deseret Book, 1978), 191.

16. Ogasahara Hiroko, Oral history, 5, interview by Matt Eyre, 1994, LDS Asian American Oral History Project.

17. Yanagida Kaori, Oral history, 4, 8–9, interview by Matt Eyre, 1994, LDS Asian American Oral History Project.

18. Tsuchida, Oral history, 6.

19. Nishigaki, Oral history, 6.

20. Miyahira Akiko, Oral history, 3, interview by Matt Eyre, 1994, LDS Asian American Oral History Project.

21. Watabe Masakazu, Oral history, 10.

22. Seiko Higgins, Oral history, 9, interview by Matt Eyre, 1994, LDS Asian American Oral History Project.

23. Kurogi Minako, Oral history, 10, interview by Matt Eyre, 1995, LDS Asian American Oral History Project.

24. Nakanishi, Oral history, 6.

25. Kawasaki, Oral history, 7.

26. "Missionaries Baptize Six Japanese," *Church News*, published by *Deseret News*, July 17, 1954, 5. A cottage meeting is a group of missionaries and those of other faiths meeting to discuss gospel principles.

27. Dai-Ichi Branch, Minutes, 1952, Church Archives, The Church of Jesus Christ of Latter-day Saints, Salt Lake City.

28. "Pres. Smith Will Talk to Japanese," *Church News*, December 17, 1955, 2.

29. "S. L. Valley Regional Mission Shows Gains," *Church News*, January 7, 1956, 1, 8.

30. Dai-Ichi Branch, Manuscript History and Minutes, 1952–86, Church Archives.

31. Watabe Masakazu, Conversation.

32. Dai-Ichi Branch, Manuscript History and Minutes.

33. This information comes from the BYU Asian Branch Manuscript History, Church Archives. There is information for 1973, 1979, and 1983.

34. Rhee Honam, Oral history, interview by Steven Jenks, 1994, LDS Asian American Oral History Project, 15.

35. Theodore H. Okawa, Oral history, interview by Nacor Tortosa, 2005, LDS Asian American Oral History Project.

36. Kurogi Minako, Oral history, interview by Arien Hamblin, 1995, LDS Asian American Oral History Project, 10.

37. Okawa, Oral history.

38. Okawa, Oral history.

39. Tsuchida, Oral history, 7.

40. Ogasahara Hiroko, Oral history, 7, interview by Matt Eyre, 1994, LDS Asian American Oral History Project.

41. Yanagida, Oral history, 6.

42. Watabe Masakazu, Oral history, 11.

19

Mormonism and the Japanese:
A Guide to the Sources

Reid L. Neilson

By the time the First Presidency, led by Church President Lorenzo Snow, announced the opening of the Japan Mission in February 1901, Christian missionaries from Europe had already been proselytizing the Japanese off and on since the mid-1500s. In 1543, Portuguese sailors discovered Japan for the West. Within a decade, Francis Xavier, a Jesuit priest, established a thriving Catholic mission, which eventually numbered in the hundreds of thousands of Japanese converts. However, by the end of the sixteenth century, the Japanese government began to persecute Christian communicants, nearly wiping out the growing Catholic presence. Thereafter, the Japanese government closed its ports and severed foreign relations. Christianity suffered as a result.

Japan remained a closed country until 1854, when American Commodore Matthew C. Perry forced the shogunate to reopen its ports and reengage in international and economic affairs. In 1859, Protestant missionaries began proselytizing in Japan. Excellent overviews of these early Catholic and Protestant efforts among the Japanese include C. R. Boxer, *The Christian Century in Japan: 1549–1650* (Berkeley: University of California Press, 1951); George Elison (aka Jurgis Elisonas) and Richard H. Drummond, *A History of Christianity in Japan* (Grand Rapids, Mich.: William B. Eerdmans, 1971); Neil S. Fujita, *Japan's Encounter with Christianity: The Catholic Mission in Pre-Modern Japan* (New York: Paulist Press, 1991); George Elison, *Deus Destroyed: The Image of Christianity in Early Modern Japan* (Cambridge, Mass.: Harvard University Press, 1993); and Endō Shōsaku, *The Final Martyrs* [stories of early Japanese Christianity], trans. Van C. Gessel (Tokyo: Charles E. Tuttle, 1993).

In the years leading up to the reintroduction of Christianity in Japan, a number of Latter-day Saints were called by Church President Brigham Young to proselyte in the surrounding Asian nations of India, Burma, Siam, and China. Nevertheless, by mid-1850, only India remained a Mormon mission field due to discouraging results in the other areas and various issues in Utah that demanded immediate attention. Five decades would pass before Church leaders again sent missionaries to the Orient.

Efforts to chronicle early Latter-day Saint missionary work in Asia include Robert C. Patch, "An Historical Overview of the Missionary Activities of The Church of Jesus Christ of Latter-day Saints in Continental Asia" (master's thesis, Brigham Young University, 1949); and Spencer J. Palmer, *The Church Encounters Asia* (Salt Lake City: Deseret Book, 1970). The most comprehensive and updated source is R. Lanier Britsch, *From the East: The History of the Latter-day Saints in Asia, 1851–1996* (Salt Lake City: Deseret Book, 1998); five of the book's chapters are devoted to Japanese Latter-day Saint history and are listed in this bibliography. Britsch's companion volume, *Unto the Islands of the Sea: A History of the Latter-day Saints in the Pacific* (Salt Lake City: Deseret Book, 1986), offers researchers an overview of Latter-day Saint expansion in the Pacific, including Hawaii where a number of Japanese were eventually converted. For a general history of the Church in Japan, see Don W. Marsh, comp., *The Light of the Sun: Japan and the Saints* (Tokyo: The Church of Jesus Christ of Latter-day Saints Japan Mission, 1969); Eleanor Knowles, "The History of the Church in Japan," *Improvement Era* 73 (March 1970): 20–26; and Seiji Katanuma, "The Church in Japan," *BYU Studies* 14, no. 1 (1973): 16–28.

Despite being unable to send missionaries to Japan in the early 1850s, several Church leaders, such as George Q. Cannon, became strong advocates for the establishment of a Japan mission. As a result, Latter-day Saint periodicals featured a number of articles on Japanese history and culture as well as speculating on the prospects of Japan as a future mission field. These include "Editorial Thoughts," *Juvenile Instructor* 7 (February 17, 1872): 28; "A Japanese Idol," *Juvenile Instructor* 8 (May 10, 1873): 73–74; "A Country Scene in Japan," *Juvenile Instructor* 8 (October 25, 1873): 169–70; "Festival of the Idol Tengou in Japan,"

Juvenile Instructor 9 (February 28, 1874): 49; "Japanese Peasant in Winter Costume," *Juvenile Instructor* 9 (March 28, 1874): 81; "Japanese Houses," *Juvenile Instructor* 9 (August 29, 1874): 205; "Hari Kari," *Juvenile Instructor* 10 (May 15, 1875): 118–19; "Japanese Amusements," *Juvenile Instructor* 10 (August 21, 1875): 193–94; "Japanese Customs," *Juvenile Instructor* 11 (January 15, 1876): 18–20; "Japanese Temple," *Juvenile Instructor* 11 (June 1, 1876): 127–28; "A Japanese Shoe Store," *Juvenile Instructor* 13 (June 15, 1878): 133–34; "Japanese Children," *Juvenile Instructor* 13 (November 1, 1878): 245; "Japanese Soldiers," *Juvenile Instructor* 17 (May 1, 1882): 138–39; "Editorial Thoughts," *Juvenile Instructor* 18 (January 15, 1883): 24–25; "A Japanese Tea-House," *Juvenile Instructor* 18 (March 15, 1883): 81–82; "Editorial Thoughts," *Juvenile Instructor* 18 (June 1, 1883): 168; "A Japanese Meal," *Juvenile Instructor* 19 (March 15, 1884): 81–82; "A Japanese Execution," *Juvenile Instructor* 19 (April 15, 1884): 126–27; "Varieties. St. Peter's Toe. For the Girls. A Word for the Japanese. Dynamite," *Juvenile Instructor* 19 (May 15, 1884): 149–50; William Willes, "Tidings from Japan and China," *Juvenile Instructor* 19 (October 1, 1884): 291–92; "The City of Yokohama, Japan," *Juvenile Instructor* 20 (June 15, 1885): 177–78; "The Metropolis of Japan," *Juvenile Instructor* 22 (November 15, 1887): 337–38; "A Japanese Traveling Equipage," *Juvenile Instructor* 23 (April 15, 1888): 113; "Children's Sports and Occupations," *Juvenile Instructor* 26 (May 1, 1891): 265–68; Vidi (pseud.), "A Progressive People," *Juvenile Instructor* 28 (October 1, 1893): 595–97; George Q. Cannon, "Topics of the Times: The Parliament of Religions," *Juvenile Instructor* 28 (October 1, 1893): 605–8; "A Commercial City of Japan," *Juvenile Instructor* 30 (January 15, 1895): 41–42; George Q. Cannon, "Topics of the Times: Strength in Unity, Not in Numbers," *Juvenile Instructor* 30 (June 1, 1895): 341–43; "A Future Mission Field," *Contributor* 16 (October 1895): 764–65; R. A. C., "Japan," *Juvenile Instructor* 31 (January 1, 1896): 9–12; George Q. Cannon, "Topics of the Times: Filial Love and Its Effects," *Juvenile Instructor* 31 (November 15, 1896): 672–74; George Q. Cannon, "Topics of the Times: Japanese Progress," *Juvenile Instructor* 32 (June 1, 1897): 354–55; George Q. Cannon, "Editorial Thoughts: Word of Wisdom to Be Taught by Practice—Importance of Example as Well as Precept," *Juvenile Instructor* 33 (February 1, 1898): 124–26; "In the Land of the Mikado," *Juvenile Instructor* 33 (December 15, 1898): 809–11; and "Japan and Her People," *Juvenile Instructor* 36 (August 1, 1901): 473–78.

During the second half of the nineteenth century, the Mormons and the Japanese made a number of important contacts on both sides of the Pacific. For a history of some of the events leading up to the creation of the Japan Mission in 1901, see Sandra T. Caruthers, "Anodyne for Expansion: Meiji Japan, the Mormons, and Charles LeGendre," *Pacific Historical Review* 38 (May 1969): 129–39; William G. Hartley, "Adventures of a Young British Seaman, 1852–1862," *New Era* 10 (March 1980): 38–47; Shinji Takagi, "Tomizo and Tokujiro: The First Japanese Mormons," *BYU Studies* 39, no. 2 (2000): 73–106, reprinted herein; and Reid L. Neilson, "The Japan Mission: First Efforts," paper presented at "A Centennial Celebration: The Church of Jesus Christ of Latter-day Saints in Japan, 1901–2001," Provo, Utah, October 13, 2001, printed herein. To study the Iwakura Mission's 1872 Utah stopover, see Dean W. Collinwood, Ryoichi Yamamoto, Dazue Matsui-Haag, *Samurais in Salt Lake: Diary of the First Diplomatic Japanese Delegation to Visit Utah, 1872* (Salt Lake City: US-Japan Center, 1996); and Wendy Butler, "The Iwakura Mission and Its Stay in Salt Lake City," *Utah Historical Quarterly* 66 (Winter 1998): 26–47, reprinted herein.

In 1901 the First Presidency selected Elder Heber J. Grant to initiate missionary work among the Japanese. For sources on Elder Grant and the opening of the Japan Mission, see Joseph F. Smith, "Editorial Thoughts: The Last Days of President Snow," *Juvenile Instructor* 36 (November 15, 1901): 688–91; Heber J. Grant, "Address to the Great and Progressive Nation of Japan," *Millennial Star* 63 (September 26, 1901): 625–27; Murray L. Nichols, "History of the Japan Mission of The Church of Jesus Christ of Latter-day Saints, 1901–1924" (master's thesis, Brigham Young University, 1957); Ronald W. Walker, "Strangers in a Strange Land: Heber J. Grant and the Opening of the Japanese Mission," *Journal of Mormon History* 13 (1986–87): 20–43, reprinted herein; Heber J. Grant, *A Japanese Journal*, comp. Gordon A. Madsen (n.p., n.d.); R. Lanier Britsch, "Japan, 1901–1924: The Early Japanese Mission," in *From the East: The History of the Latter-day Saints in Asia, 1851–1996* (Salt Lake City: Deseret Book, 1998), 43–70; Reid L. Neilson, "The Japanese Missionary Journals of Elder Alma O. Taylor, 1901–10" (master's thesis, Brigham Young University, 2001; published by BYU Studies and Joseph Fielding Smith Institute for Latter-day Saint History,

2001); and Reid L. Neilson, "A Priceless Pearl: Alma O. Taylor's Mission to Japan," *Ensign* 32 (June 2002): 56–59.

Sources detailing the Japanese reaction to Mormonism in print and otherwise include "Mormon Missionary Activity," *Missionary Review of the World* 15 (July 1902): 540; Frederick R. Brady, "The Japanese Reaction to Mormonism and the Translation of Mormon Scripture into Japanese" (master's thesis, Sophia University, International College, Tokyo, 1979); Frederick R. Brady, "Two Meiji Scholars Introduce the Mormons to Japan," *BYU Studies* 23, no. 2 (1983): 167–78, reprinted herein; Shinji Takagi, "Mormons in the Press: Reactions to the 1901 Opening of the Japan Mission," *BYU Studies* 40, no. 1 (2001): 141–75, reprinted herein; and Sarah Cox Smith, "Translator or Translated? The Portrayal of the Church of Jesus Christ of Latter-day Saints in Meiji Japan," paper presented at "A Centennial Celebration: The Church of Jesus Christ of Latter-day Saints in Japan, 1901–2001," Provo, Utah, October 13, 2001, printed herein.

Several of the early Japan Mission (1901–24) elders recorded their missionary experiences in Japan and allowed them to be printed in Latter-day Saint periodicals. Their personal accounts include Alma O. Taylor, "Life in the Orient," *Improvement Era* 5 (February 1902): 288–90; Louis A. Kelsch, "The Japanese Mission," *Juvenile Instructor* 37 (February 15, 1902): 117–20; Alma O. Taylor, "Some Features of Japanese Life," *Improvement Era* 5 (April 1902): 449–55; (May 1902): 523–28; Alma O. Taylor, "How It Is Done in Japan," *Improvement Era* 5 (September 1902): 881–85; "Our First Sunday School in Japan," *Juvenile Instructor* 37 (October 15, 1902): 624–25; "To the Letter-box," *Juvenile Instructor* 37 (December 1, 1902): 734–36; Alma O. Taylor, "Funeral Rites of Japan," *Improvement Era* 6 (February 1903): 295, 369; "Introducing the Gospel in Japan," *Improvement Era* 6 (July 1903): 708–14; Sanford W. Hedges, "Scenery and Customs in Japan," *Improvement Era* 6 (September 1903): 817–22; Horace S. Ensign, "News from Japan," *Juvenile Instructor* 38 (December 1, 1903): 727–28; "Some of Our Sunday Schools. The Tokyo, Japan, Sunday School," *Juvenile Instructor* 39 (February 15, 1904): 119–21; Horace S. Ensign, "The 'Yellow Peril' as Seen in Japan," *Improvement Era* 8 (April 1905): 431–35; Alma O. Taylor, "About Japan and the Japan Mission," *Improvement Era* 10 (November 1906): 1–9; Daniel P. Woodland, "The Japanese Passover," *Improvement Era* 10 (October 1907):

979–80; Daniel P. Woodland, Japan Mission Journal, April 1908–February 1909, L. Tom Perry Special Collections, Harold B. Lee Library, Brigham Young University, Provo, Utah; Fred A. Caine, "Editor's Table," *Improvement Era* 10 (October 1907): 996–97; Justus B. Seely, "A Mormon Sunday School in Saphoro, Japan," *Juvenile Instructor* 43 (April 1908): 154–55; Alma O. Taylor, "A Few Words from Japan," *Improvement Era* 12 (August 1909): 782–88; Alma O. Taylor, "The Children of Japan," *Juvenile Instructor* 36 (December 1, 1909): 728–29; Alma O. Taylor, "Messages from the Mission," *Improvement Era* 13 (February 1910): 370; Elbert D. Thomas, "The Gospel Preached for the First to the Ainu," *Improvement Era* 14 (February 1911): 289–94; Elbert D. Thomas, "The Tokyo American Baseball Team," *Improvement Era* 15 (May 1912): 663–64; Alma O. Taylor, "In the Beginning," *Improvement Era* 17 (April 1914): 528; Alma O. Taylor, "The Light of the East," *Improvement Era* 17 (May 1914): 667–71; Amasa Clark, "Editor's Table," *Improvement Era* 18 (June 1915): 740–41; A. Ray Olpin, "The Art of Tracting in Japan," *Improvement Era* 21 (1917): 41–44; Kumagai Tamano, "Letter from a Japanese Convert," *Juvenile Instructor* 53 (April 1918): 180; Alma O. Taylor, "Japan, the Ideal Mission Field," *Improvement Era* 13 (June 1919): 779–85; E. Wesley Smith, "First Japanese Convert to the Church," *Improvement Era* 23 (December 1919): 177; David O. McKay, "Christmas in Tokyo," *Juvenile Instructor* 56 (March 1921): 113–15; Hugh J. Cannon, "The Land of China Dedicated," *Juvenile Instructor* 56 (March 1921): 115–17; Aldo Stephens, "Placing Books of Mormon in Japan," *Improvement Era* 25 (August 1922): 938–39; Ernest B. Woodward, "Thrilling Experience," *Improvement Era* 27 (December 1923): 127; "Passing Events," *Improvement Era* 28 (August 1924): 1013; and Alma O. Taylor, "Memories of Far-Off Japan, 1901–1903," *Improvement Era* 39 (November 1936): 690–91. See also Marlene Yeates Daly, "Cutler-San: A Mormon Missionary's Experience in Japan, 1912–1915" (bachelor's closure project, Brigham Young University, 1998); and Reid L. Neilson, "Alma O. Taylor's Fact-Finding Mission to China," *BYU Studies* 40, no. 1 (2001): 177–203.

In 1924, President Heber J. Grant instructed Hilton A. Robertson to temporarily close the early Japan Mission. For sources dealing with the mission closing, the subsequent "dark ages" of the Church in Japan and later efforts among the Japanese in Hawaii, see Hilton A. Robertson, in *Ninety-Fifth Semi-Annual Conference of The Church of Jesus Christ of Latter-day Saints* (Salt Lake City: The Church of Jesus Christ of

Latter-day Saints, 1924), 122–25; John A. Widtsoe, "The Japanese Mission in Action," *Improvement Era* 42 (February 1939): 88–89, 125, 127; R. Lanier Britsch, "The Closing of the Early Japan Mission," *BYU Studies* 15, no. 2 (1975): 171–90, reprinted herein; J. Christopher Conkling, "Members without a Church: Japanese Mormons in Japan from 1924 to 1948," *BYU Studies* 15, no. 2 (1975): 191–214, reprinted herein; Muriel Jenkins Heal, "'We Will Go': The Robertson Response," *Ensign* 12 (April 1982): 32–35; Yukiko Konno, "Fujiya Nara: Twice a Pioneer," *Ensign* 23 (April 1993): 31–33; R. Lanier Britsch, "Japan and Hawaii, 1924–1945: The Interim" in *From the East: The History of the Latter-day Saints in Asia, 1851–1996* (Salt Lake City: Deseret Book, 1998), 71–79; and Russell T. Clement and Sheng-Luen Tsai, "East Wind to Hawai'i: Contributions and History of Chinese and Japanese Mormons in Hawai'i," in *Voyages of Faith: Explorations in Mormon Pacific History*, ed. Grant Underwood (Provo, Utah: Brigham Young University Press, 2000), 89–106.

Following the surrender of Japan in 1945, American servicemen began the reestablishment of Mormonism in postwar Japan: see Hilton A. Robertson, in *One-Hundred Seventeenth Annual Conference of The Church of Jesus Christ of Latter-day Saints* (Salt Lake City: The Church of Jesus Christ of Latter-day Saints, 1947), 53–56; R. Lanier Britsch, "Japan, 1945–1962: The Reopening and Foundation Years," in *From the East: The History of the Latter-day Saints in Asia, 1851–1996* (Salt Lake City: Deseret Book, 1998), 80–113, reprinted herein; Shinji Takagi, "The Eagle and the Scattered Flock: Church Beginnings in Occupied Japan, 1945–48," *Journal of Mormon History* 28 (Fall 2002): 104–38; and Shinji Takagi, "Riding on the Eagle's Wings: The Japanese Mission under American Occupation, 1948–52," *Journal of Mormon History* 29 (2003): 200–232. Terry G. Nelson, "A History of The Church of Jesus Christ of Latter-day Saints in Japan from 1948 to 1980" (master's thesis, Brigham Young University, 1986), a summary reprinted herein; and R. Lanier Britsch, "Japan, 1962–1978: To the Building of the Tokyo Temple," in *From the East: The History of the Latter-day Saints in Asia, 1851–1996* (Salt Lake City: Deseret Book, 1998), 114–47. These last two sources describe the rapid growth of Mormonism in Japan leading up to the building and dedication of the Tokyo Temple.

The year 1970 was a watershed during these expansion years for the Church in Japan with the presentation of the Latter-day Saint pavilion at Expo '70 held in Osaka. Bernard P. Brockbank, *Conference Report* 140

(October 1970): 142–43; Bernard P. Brockbank, "The Mormon Pavilion at Expo '70," *Improvement Era* 73 (December 1970): 120–22; and Gerald Joseph Peterson, "History of Mormon Exhibits in World Expositions" (master's thesis, Brigham Young University, 1974), all detail this important event.

In his concluding chapter on the Church in Japan, "Japan, 1978–1996: From Temple Dedication Onward," in *From the East: The History of the Latter-day Saints in Asia, 1851–1996* (Salt Lake City: Deseret Book, 1998), 148–69, R. Lanier Britsch describes thirty years of Mormonism and the Japanese.

Latter-day Saint periodical articles covering the last five decades of the Mormon experience in Japan include Harold B. Lee, "Report on the Orient," *Improvement Era* 57 (December 1954): 926–30; Harrison T. Price, "'A Cup of Tea,'" *Improvement Era* 65 (March 1962): 160–61, 184, 186; Gordon B. Hinckley, "The Church in the Far East," *Improvement Era* 65 (June 1962): 440–43; Gordon B. Hinckley, "The Church in the Orient," *Improvement Era* 67 (March 1964): 166–93; Ezra Taft Benson, "The Future of the Church in Asia," *Improvement Era* 73 (March 1970): 14–15; Walter R. Bills, "Japan Mission," *Improvement Era* 73 (March 1970): 15–16; John W. Orton, "Genealogical Research in Asia," *Improvement Era* 73 (March 1970): 60–63; Caroline Eyring Miner, "Japan, Lovely Land of Contrasts," *Relief Society Magazine* 57 (June 1970): 428–36; Lorin F. Wheelwright, "The Rising Sun of the Gospel," *Ensign* 1 (March 1971): 68–72; Kan Watanabe, Kiyoshi Sakai, Suichi Yaginuma, Mildred E. Handy, and Grace Vlam, "Japan: Land of the Rising Sun," *Ensign* 5 (August 1975): 37–43; Cherie Campbell, "Temple to Be Built in Tokyo," *Ensign* 5 (October 1975): 86–87; "Elder Yoshihiko Kikuchi," *Ensign* 7 (November 1977): 101–2; Don A. Aslett, "My Souvenirs from World War II," *Ensign* 8 (July 1978): 24–26; Fujiya Nara, "The Tokyo Temple," *Tambuli* (October 1980): 18–19; Watabe Masakazu, "The Unspoken Words," *Ensign* 10 (December 1980): 22–23; "Japan Eighty Years Ago," *Ensign* 11 (August 1981): 76–77; Tim Nakamura, "Japanese Saints Celebrate Eightieth Anniversary," *Ensign* 11 (August 1981): 75–76; Richard M. Romney, "Hokkaido Holiday," *New Era* 13 (July 1983): 28–35; Richard M. Romney, "Home of Japanese Spirit," *New Era* 14 (January–February 1984): 32–37; Richard M. Romney, "City of the Temple and the Sun," *New Era* 14 (November 1984): 20–27; R. Lanier Britsch, "The Blossoming of the Church in Japan," *Ensign* 22 (October 1992): 32–38, and "'Strong and Firm' in Japan's Kumamoto District," *Ensign* 27 (April 1997): 79–80.

A number of Mormon scholars and leaders have written about the opportunities and challenges posed by Japan (and Asia) as a mission field. These studies include Hugh B. Brown, "Prophecies Regarding Japan," *BYU Studies* 10, no. 2 (1970): 159–60; R. Lanier Britsch, Paul S. Rose, H. Grant Heaton, Adney Y. Komatsu, and Spencer J. Palmer, "Problems and Opportunities of Missionary Work in Asia (A Symposium of Former Mission Presidents)," *BYU Studies* 12, no. 1 (1971): 85–106; Paul Hyer, "Revolution and Mormonism in Asia: What the Church Might Offer a Changing Society," *Dialogue: A Journal of Mormon Thought* 7 (Spring 1972): 88–93; Weldon Whipple, "The LDS Hymnal: Views on Foreign Editions: The Japanese Hymnal," *Dialogue: A Journal of Mormon Thought* 10 (Spring 1975): 53–54; Spencer J. Palmer, *The Expanding Church* (Salt Lake City: Deseret Book, 1978); Seiji Katanuma, "The Mormon Doctrine and Traditional Japanese Patterns: Suggestions from a Culture of Sight," in *Mormonism: A Faith for All Cultures*, ed. F. LaMond Tullis (Provo, Utah: Brigham Young University Press, 1978), 226–36; Jiro Numano, "How International Is the Church in Japan?" *Dialogue: A Journal of Mormon Thought* 13 (Spring 1980): 85–91; James R. Moss, R. Lanier Britsch, James R. Christianson, and Richard O. Cowan, *The International Church* (Provo, Utah: Brigham Young University Publications, 1982); Delbert H. Groberg, "Toward a Synoptic Model of Instructional Productivity" (PhD diss., Brigham Young University, 1986); Richard E. Durfee, "Modernity and Conversion: Mormonism in 20th Century Japan" (master's thesis, Arizona State University, 1988); Kary D. Smout, "Senkyoshigo: A Missionary English of Japan," *American Speech* 63 (Summer 1988): 137–49; S. B. C. L. Furuto, "Japanese Saints in Hawaii and Japan: Values and Implications for Baptism," in *Proceedings, Eleventh Annual Conference, Mormon Pacific Historical Society, June 10–16, 1990* (Laie, Hawaii: Brigham Young University-Hawaii, 1990); Tomoko Aizawa, "The LDS Church as a New Religious Movement in Japan" (master's thesis, Brigham Young University, 1995); Jiro Numano, "Mormonism in Modern Japan," *Dialogue: A Journal of Mormon Thought* 29 (Spring 1996): 223–35; Masakazu Watabe, "Japanese Pioneers: Masao and Hisako Watabe," in *Pioneers in Every Land*, ed. Bruce A. Van Orden, D. Brent Smith, and Everret Smith Jr. (Salt

Lake City: Bookcraft, 1997), 183–98; Jessie L. Embry, *Asian American Mormons: Bridging Cultures* (Provo, Utah: Charles Redd Center for Western Studies, Brigham Young University, 1999); Jessie L. Embry, "Japanese American Mormons in Utah: Bridging Cultures," *The Bulletin of the International Research Group* 3, no. 1 (1999): 125–36, reprinted herein; R. Lanier Britsch, "Historical and Cultural Challenges to Successful Missionary Work in Japan," paper presented at "A Centennial Celebration: The Church of Jesus Christ of Latter-day Saints in Japan, 1901–2001," Provo, Utah, October 13, 2001, printed herein; Van C. Gessel, "Languages of the Lord: Japanese Translations of the Book of Mormon," paper presented at "A Centennial Celebration: The Church of Jesus Christ of Latter-day Saints in Japan, 1901–2001," Provo, Utah, October 13, 2001, printed herein; Greg Gubler, "The Genealogical Society of Utah and Japan," paper presented at "A Centennial Celebration: The Church of Jesus Christ of Latter-day Saints in Japan, 1901–2001," Provo, Utah, October 13, 2001, printed herein; Takemura Kazuo, "A Geographical Study on the Acceptance of the Mission of the LDS Church in the Provincial Cities of Japan," paper presented at "A Centennial Celebration: The Church of Jesus Christ of Latter-day Saints in Japan, 1901–2001," Provo, Utah, October 13, 2001, printed herein; and John P. Hoffmann and Charlie V. Morgan, "Japanese Members' Experiences in the LDS Church: A Qualitative View," paper presented at "A Centennial Celebration: The Church of Jesus Christ of Latter-day Saints in Japan, 1901–2001," Provo, Utah, October 13, 2001, printed herein.

Finally, any serious scholar of Mormonism and the Japanese will want to review the manuscript collections at the Church Archives, The Church of Jesus Christ of Latter-day Saints, Salt Lake City (see Robert H. Slover II, "Resources in the Church Historian's Office Relating to Asia," *BYU Studies* 12, no. 1 [1971]: 107–18); the L. Tom Perry Special Collections, Harold B. Lee Library, Brigham Young University, Provo, Utah; Manuscripts Division, J. Willard Marriott Library, University of Utah, Salt Lake City; and Archives, Utah State Historical Society, Salt Lake City. These repositories hold the papers, personal histories, correspondence, talks, study manuals, scrapbooks, photo collections, and oral histories of many missionaries who labored in Japan in the twentieth century.

Contributors

Frederick R. Brady is a senior library specialist at the Marriott Library at the University of Utah and an employee at Sam Weller's bookstore in Salt Lake City.

R. Lanier Britsch is an emeritus professor of history and former director of the Kennedy Center for International Relations at Brigham Young University.

Wendy Butler earned her MA in history at Brigham Young University and teaches United States and world history at Springville High School in Springville, Utah.

J. Christopher Conkling teaches ancient literature, film history, and creative writing at the University of Judaism in Bel-Air, California.

Jessie L. Embry is the associate director for the Charles Redd Center for Western Studies and an instructor of history at Brigham Young University.

Van C. Gessel is a professor of Japanese and former dean of the College of Humanities at Brigham Young University.

Greg Gubler is an emeritus professor of history at Brigham Young University–Hawaii and a former archivist at the university's Joseph F. Smith Library.

John P. Hoffmann, a professor of sociology at Brigham Young University, specializes in the sociology of religion.

Takemura Kazuo is a lecturer of human geography at Rissho University in Tokyo, Japan.

Charlie V. Morgan is a doctorial student in sociology at the University of California–Irvine.

Reid L. Neilson is a PhD candidate in religious studies at the University of North Carolina at Chapel Hill.

Terry G. Nelson earned his MA in international studies at Brigham Young University and is a religious educator in Mantua, Utah.

Jiro Numano teaches English at Hiroshima Kokusai Gakuin University in Hiroshima, Japan.

Sarah Cox Smith is an assistant professor of Japanese at Brigham Young University.

Shinji Takagi, professor of economics at the University of Osaka (Japan), has been a visiting professor at Yale University. He co-authored a history of the Church in Japan in Japanese.

Yanagida Toshiko, a pioneer in The Church of Jesus Christ of Latter-day Saints during the post–World War II era, served as the first Relief Society president in Japan.

Ronald W. Walker is a professor of western American history at Brigham Young University.

Index

A

Adachi Yoshie, 336, *336*
Agricultural College of Utah, 87–88
airline, 328
Akimoto, Mr., 198
Akutagawa Ryūnosuke, 253
Amano Akira, 371, 372, 373
Amussen, Carl Christian, 88
Andersen, Dwayne N., 326–32, 337, 357, 368
Andersen, Peggy, 337, 338, 339
Anderson, Clarence LeRoy B., 325
Andrade, Philomena, 334
Andrus, Frances, 321
Andrus, Paul C., 312, 313, 321–26, 336, 351, 366
anshinritsumei, 15
Arnold, Mel, 312
Around the World in 80 Days by Jules Verne, 129
Articles of Faith, 184, 192, 222, 242
Ashton, Marvin J., 353
Aum Shinrikyō, 10

B

Bangerter, William Grant, 358
baptisms, 11, 88, 109–10, 157–158, 223, 229, 242, 276, 280, 286, 292, 294, 295, 298, 312, 316, 317, 322, 323, 328, 334, 346, 348, 351, 386, 387, 388, 389, 391, 426
Bennett, Archibald, 366
Benson, Ezra Taft, 347, 349, 350, 351, 353, 358, 370
Bernhisel, John M., 35
Bills, Walter R., 341, 346, 346–47, 351
Bird, Ralph, 324
Bodily, Myrl L., *266*, 267
Book of Mormon
    comparison of Japanese versions of, 245–58
    first Japanese translation of, 138–42, 230, 234–41
    original translation of, 134
    second Japanese translation of, 242–43, 322
    third Japanese translation of, 243–44
Book of Mormon placement program, 346
Booth, George, 42
Brady, Fred, 372
Brigham Young University–Hawaii, 349
Brinkley, F., 185
Brockbank, Bernard P., 350, 351
Brooke, J. H., 185
Brown, Hugh B., 345, 350
Browning, F. Wallace, 280
Buddhism, 4, 8, 15, 16–17, 192, 252, 253, 381, 383, 385, 386, 388, 389–92
Burton, Theodore M., 367, 370, 371

C

Caine, Frederick A., 138, 140, 158, *159*, 235–36, *236*, 241
Campbell, Cherie, 353
Cannon, Abraham H., 31, *44*, 44–47
Cannon, Angus M., 37–38, 39, 40, 196

Cannon, George Q., 39, 40, *40*, 41, 42, 44, 48, 94, 147–148
Cannon, Hugh J., 267
Central Branch, 326
Central Pacific Mission, 300, 308, 312, 345
Chiba Kikukō, 128
Chiba Yasubeie, 138, 140
Chicago Tribune, 76
Chinda Sutemi, 86
Chinese Exclusion Act of 1882, 86
Chinese Mission, 318
Chiseko Seda, 196
Chōkō Ikuta, 140
Christensen, Elwood L., 280
Christianity, 15
    compared to Buddhism, 390–91
    history of, in Japan, 2–7, 42–43, 127–28, 152–54, 182–83
    missionary statistics of, in Japan, 153–54, 270–71, 384
Christiansen, Henry, 367
Christian boom, 7, 308
Chukyo Shinpo, 200
Chuma Kauru, 349
Chuo Koron (Central Review), 180, 200
Chuo Shinbun, 200
The Church of Jesus Christ of Latter-day Saints
    area conference of, in Japan, 352–54
    descriptions of, by Japanese print, 128–37, 189–93
    descriptions of, by LDS missionaries, 137–38
    families' opposition to joining, 406–9, 417, 423
    finances of, 47
    Mutual Improvement Association, 274, 286, 286–87, 289, 314
    numbers of members of, in Japan, 276, 285, 300, 315, 322, 326, 359, 381, 383, 384
    property of, in Japan, 279, 310–12, *311*, 318, 321, 325–26, 327
    reasons for joining, 385, 386, 388, 389, 392–95, 406
    Relief Society, 336–43
        budget of, 337–38, 339
        teaching materials for, 339–40
    training of members of, in Japan, 328, 330, 347, 351
    and worldwide expansion, 48–49
City of New York, 42
City of Tokyo, 99
Clark, J. Reuben, Jr., 96, 297
Clissold, Edward L., 7, 84, 94, 96, 300, 308–15, *309*, 334, 336, 345, 355, 365, 367
Cole, William, 367
concubinage, 130, 195, 227
Confucianism, 17–18, 423
Contributor, 46
Cowley, Elva, 315
Cowley, Matthew, 242, 315
Crabb, Kelly, 354
culture, Japanese, 11–23
    effects of, on missionary work, 274

D

Dai-Ichi Branch, 427–28
Davies, Mitsuko, 377
Davies, William E., 280
DeLong, Charles E., 64, *65*, 73, 74, 75, 76
Deseret Evening News, 197
Deseret News, 66, 74, 75
Dokuritsu Shinbun, 200
Drummond, Richard H., 307

E

earthquake, in Tokyo, 277
Edo Castle, 103, 104
Eitaro Okano, 203–204
emperor, 3–4, 7–9
Emperor Heisei, 8
Emperor Hirohito (Showa), 7, 94, 307
Emperor Taisho, 93
Empress of India, 94, 154, 179, 193
Endo Mine, 86, 89, 112
Endō Shūsaku, 3, 233
English language classes, 273–74, 314, 427. *See also* language
Ensign, Horace S., 138, 150, *151*, 169, 179, 223, 235
Ensign, Mary, 158
Esplin, Rulon, 280
Evans, Preston D., 298
Expo '70, 341, 347, 348, 350–52, 370

F

Featherstone, Joseph, 158
Featherstone, Marie, 158
Featherstone, Vaughn J., 373
Fetzer, Emil B., 355
Fish, Hamilton, 76, 77
Fudge, George, 367
Fujiki Norio, 369
Fujin Shinpo, 197
Fujiwara Takeo, 287, 290, *290*, 291, 292–94, *293*, 295
Fukuzawa Yukichi, 131
Fuller, Frank, 72

G

Genealogical Service Center, 376
Genealogical Society, 363
    Oriental Committee, 366–67
genealogy, 363–78
Gibson, Walter Murray, 31, 34–37, *35*, 98, 105, 108
Glover, W. Lamont, 280
Grant, Augusta, 159–61, *160*, 169
Grant, Brigham F., 166
Grant, Heber J., 31, 45, 49, 83, 94, *151*, *160*, *163*, *169*, 179, 180, 222, 229, 271, 274, 291, 359
    applied for permit to preach, 199–200
    call to open Japan Mission, 147–48
    and closing of Japan Mission, 263, 264, 279–80
    and Japanese in Hawaii, 297–300
    and Japanese press, 154–55, 184–85, 188, 196, 197–98, 221–22
    organizing Japan Mission, 150–54
    preparations for mission, 148–50
    and proselyting in Japan, 155–70
Grant, Mary, 159, *160*, 169
Grant, Rachel, 152
Gubler, Greg, 373, *376*, 377

H

Hachimine Yoshiko, 338
Hanazawa Yo, 85
Hanks, Marion D., 358
Hanks, Ray, 312
Harlane, Wayne R., 334
Harris, Franklin S., 289–90
Harrison, Mr., 185
Harris Treaty, 3, 33
Hattatsu (The progress), 294, *294*
Hawaii, 36–37, 83, 84, 86, 89–91, 99, 101–2, 105–9
    Japanese in, 297–300
Hawaiian Mission, 94. *See also* Japanese Mission in Hawaii
Hawaii Temple, 329, 368
Hawaii Times, 92
Hayami Akira, 369, 370
Hedges, Sandford Wells, 158, *159*, 166
Heian period (800–1185), 364
Hicken, Irwin T., *266*, 267
Higgins, Seiko, 425
Hill, James J., 47
Hinckley, Gordon B., 325, 327, 329, 346, 350, 351, 353, 358
Hirai Hirogoro, 140
Hirai Kinza, 139
Hiranishi Tomoko, 368
Hirata Kin'itsu, 375
Hiroi Tatsutaro, 155, 163, 206
HMS *Retribution*, 34
Holley, Deloss W., *266*, 267
Home Ministry, 199
Honolulu Advertiser, 97
Horiuchi, Russell, 352
Hosaka, Brother, 373
Household Register Law, 106
Howard, Elizabeth A., 66
Hyer, Paul V., 312

I

Ichiki S., 157, 162
Ikuta Chōkō, 239–40
Imai Kazuo, 317
India, 42
Inoue Ryuichi, 354
Ishiye K., 42
Ishizaka Taizō, 349
Itō Hirobumi, 37–38, 58, 76, 77, 78, 196–98
Ivie, Lloyd O., 268, 286, 365, 368
Ivie, Nora, 268
Ivins, H. Grant, 273
Iwakura diplomatic mission, 3, 38–40, 57–78, 129, 197
    impressions of SLC residents by, 69–72
    lessons from, 77–78

Iwakura diplomatic mission, continued
   and national press, 72–76
   purpose of, 58–61
   Utahns' perceptions of, 67–69
Iwakura Tomomi, 57, 59, 61, 73, 77
Iwamoto Yoshiharu (Iwamoto Zenji), 132
Iwano Hōmei, 140

J

Japan Advertiser, 183–84, 187
Japan Central Mission, 352
Japan East Mission, 352
Japanese-Central Pacific Mission, 318
Japanese Dai-Ichi Sunday School, 426
Japanese Exclusion Act, 277–79
Japanese Language Training Mission, 349–50
Japanese Mission, 7, 298–300, 345
   reestablishment of, 308–15
Japanese Missionary Training Center, 354
Japanese Mission home, 310–12, *311*, 355
Japanese Mission in Hawaii, 96, 345
Japanese religious rituals, 412–16
Japan Evangelist, 131
Japan Herald, 184–85, 187, 193
Japan Mail, 185, 193, 198
Japan MIA. *See* The Church of Jesus Christ of Latter-day Saints: Mutual Improvement Association
Japan Mission (1901–24), 5–6, 345
   attendance patterns in, 269
   beginning of, 152–70
   closed, 229
   closing of, 263–81
      problems outside contributing to, 277–79
      problems within contributing to, 271–77
   events leading to establishment of, 31–50, 147–51
Japan Mission (1968–), 346, 346–47, 352, 365
Japan Mission headquarters, 161
Japan-Okinawa Mission, 341, 346, 347–49, 352
Japan Times, 185, 186
Japan West Mission, 352
Japan Women's Christian Temperance Union, 195
Jarvis, Erastus L., 158, *159*
Jensen, Elwin, 367
Jensen, Howard, *266*, 267
Jensen, Jay C., 300
Jiji Shimpō, 187, 188, 196, 197, 200, 221, 226
Jogaku Zasshi (The journal of women's education), 132–37, 194
Juvenile Instructor, 41, 43

K

Kajiko Yajima, 196
Kajima Construction Company, 342, 355
Kalihi (Honolulu) Branch, 96
Kamekona, Fukui, 109, 112
Kamekona, Kalala Keliihananui (Sato), 98, 107–8, 109, 110, 112
Kamekona, Kaniela (Daniel), 112
Kamomiya, Priest, 373
Kasuya Yoshizo, 86
Katanuma Seiji, 375
Katogi Naochika, 85
Katogi Shigenori, 86
Katogi Shutaro, 87, 95
Katsunuma Katsumi, 89, 112
Katsunuma Kiyomi, 90, 112
Katsunuma Takeo, 112
Katsunuma Tomizo, 83, 84–97, *85*, 110, 111, 112, 298
Katsunuma Woodrow, 112
Katsunuma Yasuko, 112
Katsunuma Yoshiko, 112
Katsura Tsuruichi, 289, 293, 298
Kawai Suimei, 140
Kawasaki Kinuyo, 423, 426
Kawashima, Sentaro, 108
Kei Hara, 203
Keio period (1865–68), 104
Kelsch, Louis A., 150, *151*, *169*, 179
Kido Takayoshi, 58, 66, 70, 72, 74, 78
Kikuchi Saburō, 158, 163
Kikuchi Yoshihiko, 327, 352, 353, 354, 358, 373, 375
Kimball, Camilla, 357
Kimball, Heber C., 35
Kimball, Spencer W., 353, 357, 363, 371, 427
Kimura Kumiko, 423
King Kalakaua, 108
Kitamura, Eugene M., 244
Kiyoyuki Higuchi, 373
Knapp, Arthur M., 183
Kobe Chronicle, 185–86
Koizumi Kotaro, 371

Koji Okauchi, 312
Komatsu, Adney Y., 330, 340, 346, 358
Korean War, 7, 316
Koshiishi, Mr., 158
Koya Saburo, 46
Kubota, Mr., 291
Kumagai Tamano, 286, 289, 297, 300
Kume Kunitake, 57, 66, 71
Kureha Branch, 383, 387, 388, 393
Kurogi Minako, 426, 429
Kyogaku Hochi, 192, 199
Kyoto Hinode Shinbun, 195
Kyushu Nippo, 200

L

language, 21–23, 155, 242–61, 271–74, 367–68, 375, 425–26. *See also* English language classes; translation
language-training centers, 349–50
Lee, Fern Lucinda Tanner, 320
Lee, Harold B., 319, 320
Lewis, Joseph E., 88
Lewis, R. M., 88
Logan, Utah, 87
London Daily News, 197
Lund, Anthon H., 166, 247
Lundberg, Don, 323
Lyman, Francis M., 147, 166

M

magazines, 129, 286–87, 289, 294, 325, 337, 366
Mainichi Shinbun, 194, 195
Makino Tomisaburo, 102, 105, 106
Mana Hale, Hawaii, 107–8
Manifesto, 132, 180, 185, 196
Man's Search for Happiness, 348
Matsukata Masayoshi, 86
Matsuoka Tatsusaburo, 89
Matsushita Shoko, 336
Mauss, Armand L., 316
Mauss, Vinal G., 280, 315–18, 334, 336
McCartney, Henry Maxwell, 47
McCune, Henry F., 42
McDaniel, Wayne, 312
McFee, Elder, 342
McGary, Owen, 266, 267
McKay, David O., 265, 267, 269–68, 276, 318, 346, 365
McKinley, William, 152

McPhie, Wallace G., 355
Meiji Constitution, 4, 198
Meiji period (1868–1912), 3–5, 37–39, 43–44, 85, 86, 100, 180–83, 194, 365
Meiroku Zasshi, 131
Mendelhall, Wendell B., 327
Metcalf, Wayne, 377
MIA. *See* The Church of Jesus Christ of Latter-day Saints: Mutual Improvement Association
missionaries
  arrival in Japan, press coverage of, 179–80, 183–94
  arrival of, in Japan, press coverage of, 154–55
  first efforts of, 34–37, 42–43
  local Japanese members as, 317, 354
  nisei members as, 312, 314
missionary training center, 354
missionary work
  arguments about allowing, in Japanese press, 184–87, 200–203, 204
missionary work, in Japan
  accomplishments in, leading to success of second Japan Mission, 229–30
  advantages for, 313–14
  challenges of, 1–24, 271–77, 279–80
  current methods of, 382–83, 385, 388
Miyagi Haruo, 424
Miyahira Akiko, 425
Miyara Toyoko, 336, 338
Miyazaki Toranosuke, 156
Mochizuki Reiko, 287, 294
Moore, Lewis H., 280
Moore, Ray A., 369
Mori Arinori, 131
Mori Hachirō, 138
Mori Ōgai, 130
Morita Yosaku, 280
Morumonkyō to Morumon kyōto (Mormonism and Mormons) by Takahashi Gorō, 165, 222, 224, 225
Morumon shū (The Mormon sect) by Uchida Yū, 224, 225
Moyle, Henry D., 325
Murphy, Castle H., 96

N

Nachie Tsuneko, 290, 298

Nagata Sado, 355
Naito Meisetsu, 92
Nakagawa Kōji, 300
Nakahigashi Mikio, 317
Nakamura Ayako, 324
Nakamura Nobu, 324
Nakanishi Yuko, 424, 426
Nakazawa Hajime, 83, 157, 163, 164, 223
Namekawa Hiroyuki, 140
Nampa, Idaho, 87
Nanjo Hiroko, 367
Napela, Harriet Panana, 108
Nara Fujiya, 286–87, 289, 291, 292, 309, 310
National Anti-Prostitution League, 194
Natsume Sōseki, 140, 239
Naumann, Edmund, 130
newspapers, 66, 67–69, 73–76, 92, 134–35, 154, 179–80, 183–207, 221–22, 264, 278, 309
New York Times, 76
New York World's Fair in 1965, 348
Nihonjinron, 21
Nippon Yusen Kaisha shipping line, 46, 47
Nippu Jiji, 92, 96
Niroku Shinpō, 188, 189–88, 189, 190–91, 203, 221, 226
Nishigaki Yukie, 424, 425
Niwa Motoji, 375
Noboru, Hiraga, 369
Noguchi Zenshirō, 139
Norio Fujiki, 373
Northern Far East Mission, 319, 336, 345

O

Ogasahara Hiroko, 425, 431
Ogasawara Hiroshi, 348
Ogden, Utah, 37, 38, 62, 83
Ogikubo Branch, 310
Okazaki, Chieko, 341
Okazaki, Edward Y., 341, 346, 348, 351, 370
Okubo Toshimichi, 58, 77
Okuma Shigenobu, 93
Oniki, Ben, 323
Ono, Brother, 297
Orton, John W., 367, 368, 369, 370, 371
Osaka, 202
Osaka Asahi, 199, 201, 202–3
Osaka Mainichi, 201–2, 202–3
Osaka World's Fair in 1970. *See* Expo '70

P

Packer, Boyd K., 312
Parker, John Palmer, 107
Parker, Samuel, 107, 108
Patriotic League, 86–87, 89
Payne, Joseph S., 266, 267
Penrose, Charles W., 354
Perry, Matthew C., 2, 32
Petersen, Mark E., 358, 427
polygamy, 129–30, 132–34, 137–38, 185, 194–96, 201, 225–29
Powell, Ted, 373
Pratt, Milson, 42
Pratt, Orson, 64
Price, Harrison Theodore "Ted," 312, 334
Price, Raymond C., 312, 313
Prince Takamatsu, 310
prostitution, 194–95

R

railroad, 44–45, 75–76, 83, 337, 338
Relief Society. *See* The Church of Jesus Christ of Latter-day Saints: Relief Society
Religious Bodies Law, 307
Religious Juridical Persons Law, 307
Religious Organizations Law, 6
Rescript on Education, 4–5, 43
Reynolds, George, 238
Ricci, Matteo, 252
Richards, C. Elliott, 312
Richards, Samuel Parker, 67
Ricks College, 349
Robertson, Hazel, 265
Robertson, Hilton A., 96, 263, 265, 269, 271, 277, 280, 285, 298, 318–21, 336, 345
Romney, Marion G., 353, 358
Russo-Japanese War, 6

S

Sacrament, prayer on, Japanese translations of, 256–58
Sada Saburō, 290
Sagara Kenichi, 352
Sakuma Komekichi, 105
Sakuraba Takeshirō, 138
Salt Lake Daily Herald, 66
Salt Lake Tribune, 66, 68, 73–75
Salvation Army, 195

San Francisco, 86
Satō Chiyo, 312
Sato, Emily, 109, 112
Satō Gisen, 349
Sato, Hana, 109, 112
Sato, Kalala. *See* Kamekona, Kalala Keliihananui (Sato)
Sato, Mary Melelaulani, 109, 110, 112
Sato, Ohumukini, 109, 110, 112
Sato, Pula, 109, 112
Satō Tatsui, 242–43, 312, 317, 319, 322, 329, *367*, 368–69, 370, 373
Sato Tokujiro, 83, 97–111, *98*, 112
Satō Tomoko, 376
Satō Yasuo, *367*
Scioto, 100–101, 102
Seito-No-Michi (Way of the Saints), 325, 337, 340, 374
servicemen, 308–9, 316–17, 319, 327
Shakai Shimpo, 95
Shimabukuro, Sam K., 325
Shino, Ralph Noboru, 427
Shintō, 4, 6, 7, 9–10, 15, 17, 43, 389
Shinyo Maru, 280
Shiraishi Genkichi, 313, 317
Shiraishi Makoto, 374, 376
Shizuoka Minyu Shinbun, 197, 200
Shuro (The palm), 286–87, *287*, 289, 291
Sino-Japanese War, 5, 44, 180
Smith, Elias Wesley, 97, 99, 111
Smith, Frank, *367*, 373
Smith, Joseph, 133, 134–35, 225–27, 228–29, 363
Smith, Joseph F., 363
Smith, Joseph Fielding, 242, 319
Smith, Walter, 45–46
Snow, Lorenzo, 39, 47–49, *48*, 64, 148–49, 225, 279
Soga, Yasutaro, 91, 92, 96, 97
Southern Far East Mission, 319, 345
Spear, Roy W., 298
SS *Aki Maru*, 169, 170
SS *President Cleveland*, 280
SS *President Pierce*, 280
Staniland, Mr., 193–94
Stanton, Robert Brewster, 45
Stapley, Delbert L., 323
Stimpson, Joseph H., 265, *266*, 267, 268, 273, 276, 286

Stimpson, Mary E., *266*, *267*, *268*
Stoker, John W., 158, *159*, 167, 252, 272
Sugawara Tsutau, 89
Suyenaga, Mr., 157
Suzuki Genta, 139
Suzuki Kenji, 371, *371*, 374, 375
Suzuki Nami, 298, 313
Suzuki Shozo, 337, 354
Suzuki Toshi, 336
Swenson, Fumie, 336

T

tairitsu, 20
Taiyo (Sun), 156, 180
Tai Fude, 300
Takagi Tomigoro, 313, 317, 323
Takahashi Gorō, 156–57, 164–65, 192, 206, 222–24, 225, 227–28
Takahashi Motoko, 340
Tamanaha Kuniko, 324
Tanaka Kenji, 341, *341*, 352
Tanaka Tadashichi, 87
Tange, Sister, 337
Taylor, Alma O., 94, 137, 151, *151*, 154, 158, *163*, 165, 179, 185, 193, 196, 198, 203, 223–24, 230, 234, 272, 273, 276, 278, 289, 291, 292, 294, 296
  and translation of Book of Mormon, 138–42, 234–41
Taylor, Milton B., 280
temple ordinances, 328–29
Thatcher, Guy W., 88
Thomas, Elbert D., 196, 230, 273, 291, 294, 300
tithing, 300
Tohma Misao, 338
Toko, John Sato, 109, 110, 112
Tokugawa, or Edo, period (1603–1867), 2–3, 37, 99, 102, 364
Tokyo Asahi Shinbun, 199, 202
Tokyo earthquake, 277
Tokyo First Branch, 317
Tokyo Nichinichi, 199, 200
Tokyo Second Branch, 317
Tokyo Service Center, 374, 376
Tokyo Stake, 351
Tokyo Temple, 341–42, 353–54, 354–58, *356*, 368
Tokyo Women's Temperance Union, 194

Tomigoro Takagi, 294
Tonga Mission, 279
Toshiyuki Yanase, 373
Toyama, 384, 386–88
Toyama Branch, 383, 387, 388, 393
train. *See* railroad
translation, into Japanese, 128, 192, 225, 245–58, 272–73, 322, 325, 347, 366. *See also* language
treaty negotiations, 32–34, 60, 76–77, 181
Tsubouchi Shōyō, 140, 239
Tsuchida Michiru, 423, 425, 430
Tsukayama Kiyoshi, 310
Tsukiyama Chomatsu, 97
Tsune Nachie, 290, 298, 365

U

Uchida Norikazu, 423
Uchida Yū, 224–25, 225–27
Uemura Masahira, 128
Ueno Kagenori, 102, 105, 106
Uenoyama Emiko, 337
Uozu, 384, 388–89
Uozu Branch, 383, 387, 388–89, 393
Utah Sugar Company, 149–50

V

Van Reed, Eugene M., 99, 101

W

Waipio Branch, 109
Wakamatsu Shizuko, 131–32
Watabe Masakazu, 421, 423, 424–25, 425, 427, 431
Watabe Masao, 366, 424
Watanabe Kan, 328, 352
Watanabe Masumi, 423
Watanabe Tazuko, 293, 295, 296, 300
Watanabe Yoshijirō, 293, 295, 298
Weenig, Melvyn A., 298, 300, 310
Whitaker, Lowring A., *266, 267*
Widtsoe, John A., 96
Willes, William, 42–43
Winder, John R., 247
women, 129–33, 194–97
Women's Christian Temperance Union, 131
Wood, William, 34
Woodruff, Abraham O., 167
Woodruff, Wilford, 34, 47, 67, 228, 363
Woodward, Ernest B., 280
Woolley, Samuel Edwin, 99
Word of Wisdom, 409–11, 417
World Conference on Records, 369–70
World Conference on Records, Second, 375
World War I, 6
World War II, 6, 297
Worthen, Joyce C., 366

X

Xavier, Francis, 2, 21, 251–52

Y

Yaginuma Setsuko, 337, 339, 340
Yamada Akiyoshi, 61
Yamada Goro, 328
Yamagata, 383–85
Yamagata Branch, 385, 393
Yamaguchi Masouka, 60
Yamaide Torao, 287, 288
Yamamoto, Willard Matsu (Kanuka), 109, 110, 112
Yamanaka Kenji, 328
Yamato Shinbun, 92, 187, 195
Yanagida Kaori, 425, 431
Yanagida Tohkichi, 334
Yanagida Toshiko, 333–43, *336, 343*
Yanase Toshiyuki, 369
Yang, Basil Pei-nai, 372
Yatabe Ryōkichi, 129
Yokohama, 100, 183
Yoneyama Kenji, 295
Yoneyama Morizō, 295, 300
Yoneyama Renji, 294–96
Yonezawa, 384, 385–86
Yonezawa Branch, 383, 386, 387, 393
Yonezawa Shinbun, 197
Yorozu Choho, 187
Yoshida Masao, 369
Yoshimizu Motoko, 286
Young, Brigham, 33, 35, 38, 73–75, 133
Young, Robert, 186